EXPERT RESUMES™ FOR BABY BOOMERS

Wendy S. Enelow and Louise M. Kursmark

jist Works

America's Career Publisher

Expert Resumes for Baby Boomers

© 2007 by Wendy S. Enelow and Louise M. Kursmark

Published by JIST Works, an imprint of JIST Publishing, Inc.
8902 Otis Avenue
Indianapolis, IN 46216-1033
Phone: 1-800-648-JIST   Fax: 1-800-JIST-FAX   E-mail: info@jist.com

Visit our Web site at **www.jist.com** for information on JIST, free job search tips, book chapters, and how to order our many products! For free information on 14,000 job titles, visit **www.careeroink.com**.

Quantity discounts are available for JIST books. Have future editions of JIST books automatically delivered to you on publication through our convenient standing order program. Please call our Sales Department at 1-800-648-5478 for a free catalog and more information.

Trade Product Manager: Lori Cates Hand
Cover Designer: designLab
Interior Designer: Trudy Coler
Proofreader: Jeanne Clark
Indexer: Kelly D. Henthorne

Printed in the United States of America
11 10 09 08 07 06   9 8 7 6 5 4 3 2 1

Library of Congress Cataloging-in-Publication Data

Enelow, Wendy S.
    Expert resumes for baby boomers / Wendy S. Enelow and Louise M. Kursmark.
        p. cm.
    Includes index.
    ISBN-13: 978-1-59357-363-8 (alk. paper)
    ISBN-10: 1-59357-363-4 (alk. paper)
 1. Résumés (Employment)--United States. 2. Baby boom generation--Employment--United
        States. I. Kursmark, Louise. II. Title.
    HF5383.E47873 2007
    650.14'2--dc22   2006026311

We have been careful to provide accurate information in this book, but it is possible that errors and omissions have been introduced. Please consider this in making any career plans or other important decisions. Trust your own judgment above all else and in all things.

Trademarks: All brand names and product names used in this book are trade names, service marks, trademarks, or registered trademarks of their respective owners.

ISBN-13: 978-1-59357-363-8
ISBN-10: 1-59357-363-4

TABLE OF CONTENTS

ABOUT THIS BOOK

If you were born between 1946 and 1964, you're one of more than 78.2 million baby boomers in the United States. In fact, according to the U.S. Census Bureau, the baby-boom generation makes up 47 percent of the total U.S. workforce.

Baby boomers are a diverse group of job seekers who tend to fall into one of three distinct categories: young baby boomers, under 45 years of age, who typically are at prime career performance levels and seeking increasing responsibilities; career-transition baby boomers, looking for more meaning and/or balance in their work life; and return-to-work baby boomers, who are rejoining the workforce after an absence to care for family, take a sabbatical, or another reason. Do you see yourself in one of those categories? If so, you're facing some unique resume-writing challenges that this book specifically addresses.

Learning to write a powerful "baby-boomer" resume that positions you as a competitive candidate for the new career path that you've chosen is what this book is all about. As you read through the early chapters, you'll learn that a resume is much more than just your job history, academic credentials, technical skills, and awards. A truly effective resume is a concise, yet comprehensive, document that focuses on your achievements, your contributions, and the value you bring to a company. Read this book and review the scores of samples, and you'll have the tools you need to create your own winning resume.

We'll also explore the changes in resume presentation that have arisen over the past decade. In years past, resumes were almost always printed on paper and mailed. Today, e-mail has become the chosen method for resume distribution in many industries and professions. In turn, many of the traditional methods for "typing" and presenting resumes have changed dramatically. This book introduces and explains the methods for preparing resumes for e-mail, scanning, and Web site posting, as well as the traditional printed resume.

By using *Expert Resumes for Baby Boomers* as your professional guide, you will succeed in developing a powerful and effective resume that opens doors, gets interviews, and helps you land a great opportunity!

INTRODUCTION

This book is unique because of its very specific focus on the baby boomer generation (individuals born between 1946 and 1964). According to the U.S. Census Bureau, as of July 2005, there were 78.2 million baby boomers living in the United States, of which more than 36 million were employed in either full-time or part-time positions.

Most fascinating, as we sat down to write this book in January 2006, the first of the baby boomers were turning 60 years of age. As such, there has been much recent research investigating everything about the baby-boom generation, from their purchasing patterns to their career goals and plans for retirement.

Despite the many homogenous behaviors and patterns of the baby-boom generation (individuals 42 to 60 years of age as of the writing of this book), when it comes to careers, there are three distinct populations of baby-boomer job seekers:

- **Young baby boomers** (under 45): People who are typically at prime career performance levels and seeking increasing responsibilities. Resumes for these individuals generally focus on the strength of their work history and accomplishments, positioning them for jobs with increased authority and responsibility.

- **Career-transition baby boomers:** People looking for more meaning in their work and better balance with their lives, and seeking a career transition exclusively for that purpose. This category includes individuals who are decelerating their careers, launching post-retirement careers, entering a completely new line of work or new industry, or volunteering. Resumes for these individuals often focus on experiences, skills, and activities that might not have been at the crux of their "professional career" but are extremely important in positioning them for new career-transition opportunities.

- **Return-to-work baby boomers:** Individuals returning to the workforce after extended absences due to parenting, caring for aging parents, taking a sabbatical, and so on. Resumes for these individuals generally showcase the strength of their previous careers and the skills they acquired as opposed to what they have done most recently outside of the workforce.

You'll read much more about these three distinct populations of baby boomers as you progress through this book. Identifying which category you fall into is critical in determining the resume writing strategy, wording, format, and design that will work best for you in your particular situation. Resume writing is not a "one-size-fits-all" activity. Rather, it is a customized writing process that allows you to showcase your skills, experiences, and achievements as they relate to your specific objectives. Always remember this: You're "writing to the future" and not about the past. You're simply using the past as your tool to reach the future.

The What, How, Which, and Where of Resume Writing

There are four key questions that you must ask yourself before you begin writing your resume:

- *What* **type of position/career track are you going to pursue?** Your current career goals dictate the entire resume writing and design process. If you're a vice president of sales looking to advance to a general management position, you'll approach your resume one way. If you're a retiring CEO whose goal is to lead a non-profit organization, you'll prepare your resume quite differently. And if you're returning to the workforce after five years of unemployment, you'll create an entirely different type of resume.

- *How* **are you going to paint a picture of your skills and qualifications that will make you an attractive candidate whether you're looking for a promotion, seeking a new "balanced" career, or ready to return to the workforce?** What types of information are you going to highlight about your past experiences (your work history, volunteer activities, association memberships, education, and other activities) that tie directly to your current objectives? What accomplishments, skills, and qualifications are you going to "sell" in your resume to support your new career goals?

- *Which* **resume format are you going to use?** Is a chronological, functional, or hybrid resume format going to work best for you? Which format will give you the greatest flexibility to highlight the skills, talents, and achievements you want to bring to the forefront to support your current career goals?

- *Where* **are you going to look for a job?** Once you have decided what type of position and industry you are interested in, how do you plan on identifying and approaching those companies?

When you can answer the what, how, which, and where, you'll be prepared to write your resume and launch your search campaign. Use chapters 1 through 3 to guide you in developing the content for your resume and selecting the appropriate design and layout. Your resume should focus on your skills, achievements, and qualifications, demonstrating the value and benefit you bring to a prospective employer as they relate to your current career goals. The focus should be on the "new" you and not necessarily what you have done in the past.

Review the sample resumes in chapters 4 through 6 to see what other people have done—people in similar situations to yours and facing similar challenges. You'll find interesting formats, unique skills presentations, achievement-focused resumes, project-focused resumes, and much more. Most importantly, you'll see samples written by the top resume writers in the U.S., Canada, and Australia (and even one from South Africa). These are real resumes that got interviews and generated job offers. They're the "best of the best" from us to you.

Identifying and Achieving Your Career Objectives

Before you proceed any further with writing your resume, you'll need to begin by defining your career or job objectives—specifically, the types of positions, companies, and industries in which you are interested. This is critical because a haphazard, unfocused job search will lead you nowhere.

KNOW THE EMPLOYMENT TRENDS

A good way to begin identifying your career objectives is to look at what opportunities are available today, in the immediate future, and in the longer-term future. And one of the most useful tools for this type of research and information collection is the U.S. Department of Labor's Bureau of Labor Statistics (www.bls.gov).

According to the Bureau, the employment outlook is optimistic, particularly for baby boomers. Consider these findings:

- There are an estimated 78.2 million baby boomers in the U.S. as of July 2005.

- Total employment in the U.S. is projected to increase 14.7% between 2004 and 2014, reaching 162.1 million by 2014. One of the major contributors to the projected labor force growth is the aging (and possible retirement) of the baby-boom generation.

- In 2014, baby boomers will be 50 to 68 years old. This group will grow significantly over the 2004–2014 period, with the number of workers in the 55-and-older group projected to grow 49.1% (nearly five times the growth projected for the overall labor force).

- It is projected that the 55-and-older age group will increase from 15.6% to 21.2% of the total labor force. (Note that average life expectancy is now at an all-time high of 77.4 years.)

- More than 60% of men ages 60 to 64 expect to be in the workforce in 2012 (up from 54% in 1992).

- Projections show that 7,918 Americans will turn 60 each day in 2006 (330 per hour).

- There will be roughly 57.8 million baby boomers living in the U.S. in 2030.

- A widely quoted estimate, based on Bureau of Labor Statistics data, is that the U.S. will experience a shortfall of 10 million workers by 2010.

- Perhaps even more significantly, there already exist skills and talent shortfalls in some areas (such as nursing, radiology, and some technical fields), and these shortfalls are predicted to become more severe.

Those statistics clearly demonstrate that there are and will continue to be tremendous employment opportunities for the baby-boom generation. Now, taking that information one step further, let's look at some general employment statistics from the Bureau that will help you identify where the opportunities are greatest for someone with your particular qualifications.

- Service-producing companies will continue to be the dominant employment generator, adding 20 million jobs by 2012, a gain of 19.2%.

- Goods-producing industries (manufacturing and construction) will also experience gains in employment, although not as significant as those in the service sector.

- Health services, business services, social services, engineering, and other services are projected to account for almost one of every two non-farm jobs added to the U.S. economy over the next 10 years.

- The 10 fastest-growing industries are in the service sector and include—from #1 in growth to #10—software publishing, computer systems design, management and technical consulting, employment, social assistance, child day care, professional and business services, motion picture and video, health services, and art/entertainment and recreation.

- Of all goods-producing industries, only four were projected to demonstrate growth. From #1 in growth to #4, they are pharmaceutical and medicine manufacturing, construction, food manufacturing, and motor vehicle and parts manufacturing.

- Transportation and material-moving occupations are projected to grow 15% (the average for most occupations).

- Office and administrative-support occupations are projected to grow more slowly than average, reflecting the need for fewer personnel as a result of the tremendous gains in office automation and technology.

- Production-related occupations are also projected to grow more slowly as manufacturing automation and technology reduce the need for specific types of employees.

- Offshoring is a concern for some workers, yet the number of U.S. jobs exported in any year represents less than 2% of total jobs; still, categories of jobs such as manufacturing and tech support might be affected.

- Occupations with the largest job growth are food preparation and service workers (#1), customer service representatives, registered nurses, retail salespersons, and computer-support specialists.

These facts and statistics clearly demonstrate that there are numerous employment opportunities across diverse sectors within our economy, from top management assignments in technology industries to opportunities in health care, services, and consulting. What's most impressive about these projections is the strength of the numbers as they relate to baby boomers. The tremendous opportunities available to you—in almost every employment sector—are virtually unlimited. Your challenge is to write a strong and focused resume that supports your current career objectives and positions you as a top candidate for those opportunities. (For more detailed information on the top opportunities, see *Best Jobs for Baby Boomers* [JIST Publishing].)

Another interesting trend that's specific to baby boomers is what we'll refer to as the "new retirement." A February 2005 survey by Merrill Lynch (conducted by

Harris Interactive in collaboration with Age Wave) reported that boomers are not interested in pursuing the traditional model of retirement. Rather, the majority of boomers say they plan to keep working and earning in retirement. Here are some interesting results of the survey:

- While 76% of boomers intend to keep working and earning in retirement, on average they expect to "retire" from their current job/career at approximately age 64 and then launch into an entirely new job or career.

- Of those who plan to keep working at least part time, 67% say they'll do so to stay mentally active and 57% said they will work to stay physically active.

- When probed about their ideal work situation in retirement, the most common choice was to "cycle" between periods of work and leisure (42%), followed by part-time work (16%), start their own business (13%), and full-time work (6%). Only 17% hope to never work for pay again.

A September 2005 article on Money.CCN.com reported that companies are scrambling to keep valued employees—those baby boomers who are getting ready for retirement. The potential for mass exodus of baby boomers out of the workforce is threatening to create a massive "brain drain" at major companies and government agencies. In turn, to encourage baby boomers to continue working after the traditional retirement age, companies are offering innovative models of employment that integrate telecommuting, flexible schedules, part-time opportunities, and more.

In summary, there is a huge demand within the employment market for baby boomers, those still in their mid-40s as well as those who are reaching the traditional age of retirement. To position yourself to take advantage of this trend and others that will arise, a powerful, achievement-focused resume is critical. It is an essential door-opener and positioning piece that you will need to launch your search and land your next position.

MANAGE YOUR JOB SEARCH AND YOUR CAREER

To take advantage of these opportunities, you must be an educated job seeker. That means you must know what you want in your career, where the hiring action is, what qualifications and credentials you need to attain your desired career goals, and how best to market your qualifications. It is no longer enough to have a specific talent or set of skills. You must also be a strategic marketer, able to package and promote your experience to pursue the opportunities most attractive to you at this point in your career. What you write in your resume and how you present it will depend entirely on your objective and which of the three baby-boomer job categories you fall into.

There's no doubt that the employment market has changed dramatically over the past few decades. If you are an older baby boomer, you might have grown up in an age when you believed that you would graduate from high school or college, accept a job or career opportunity, and then continue with that same company for most, if not all, of your career. That entire employment paradigm has changed during your working life, and stability is no longer the status quo. In fact, according to the U.S. Department of Labor, young adults should now expect to hold between 10 and 20 different jobs during their careers.

Today, the norm is movement, onward and upward, in a fast-paced and intense employment market where there are many opportunities for individuals building their careers. This includes many of the younger baby boomers (under age 45) as well as baby boomers returning to the workforce after extended absences. To take advantage of these opportunities, every job seeker—no matter the profession, no matter the industry, no matter the job goal—must proactively control and manage his or her career.

For the older baby boomers whose goals might not be to move forward in their careers, but rather to redirect their careers and seek a greater work/life balance, the same message holds true: You must proactively control your career. If you want to transition your skills from "corporate America" into a non-profit humanitarian organization, you will need to research and identify the organizations, opportunities, and decision-makers you'll need to reach. If your goal is to leverage your lifelong interest in antiques into working as an antiques buyer for an established company, then again, your challenge is to identify the opportunities, the organizations, and the people who would be interested in a candidate with your qualifications. Remember, job search is a job, regardless of your goals and aspirations.

And that is precisely why this book is so important to you. Rather than taking a "one-size-fits-all" approach to resume writing, we've focused on each of the three unique populations of baby-boomer job seekers and identified the strategies, techniques, and formats that are specific to each population. If you follow the recommendations in this book, you will be able to craft a powerful resume that positions you for just the right opportunities that you are pursuing at this point in your career.

Job Search Questions and Answers

Before we get to the core of this book—resume writing and design—we'd like to offer some practical job search advice that is valuable to virtually every job seeker who falls into the baby-boom generation.

WHAT IS THE MOST IMPORTANT CAREER CONSIDERATION FOR A BABY BOOMER?

As outlined previously, the single most important consideration for any baby-boomer candidate is how you're going to highlight your skills, qualifications, and achievements as they relate to and support your current career objectives. Remember, your resume is not a historical document that simply lists where you've worked and what you've done. Rather, a truly effective resume is one that takes all of the skills and experience you have that are relevant to your new career goal and brings them to the forefront in an attempt to create a picture of the "new" you.

Sometimes, this can be a relatively easy process, particularly for young baby boomers who are still working to move their careers forward. Let's consider a telecommunications equipment sales manager who is 43 years of age and now looking for opportunities in general management within the telecommunications industry. This candidate's resume should focus on all of the general management functions for which he has been responsible. This might include profit-and-loss management, sales recruitment and training, team building and leadership, new product development, merger and acquisition integration, and more. Of course, this candidate's success in building revenues, capturing new markets, launching new products, and selling key accounts is also essential to include. However, to "paint the picture" of a talented general manager, the general management skills are primary; the sales skills become secondary.

In other situations, the parallels between past experience and current objectives might not be so closely aligned. Consider the 62-year-old candidate who wants to transition out of her corporate career in human resources management and now devote her time to her personal interests in saving the environment. She has decided to apply for volunteer positions with the Sierra Club, Greenpeace, and several other similar organizations. In this situation, the resume becomes more of a challenge to write and will focus on her previous volunteer experience in environmental protection and advocacy, wildlife management, lobbying, and the like. This is the type of information that will come to the forefront of her resume rather than her years of experience managing corporate recruitment, benefits, and payroll. Remember, you always want to "paint the picture" that you want someone to see and the traditional resume structure and format is quite often *not* the right format for baby boomers seeking to find work/life balance.

Whatever your situation or objective, and whichever baby-boomer group of job seekers you fall into, when preparing your resume always keep one critical fact in mind:

> *Your resume is a marketing tool written to sell YOU for your next opportunity!*

How Do You Enter a New Career?

Entering a new career field calls for your careful attention to two important factors:

- Highlighting all relevant skills, qualifications, accomplishments, experiences, training/education, credentials, volunteer work, involvement with professional and/or civic associations, and more that tie directly into your current career objective.

- Using an integrated job search campaign that will get you in front of decision-makers at a wide array of organizations in your field of interest. You can read much more about job search strategy in the section titled "How Do You Get the Jobs?"

WHAT IS THE BEST RESUME STRATEGY FOR BABY BOOMERS?

The single most important factor for any baby boomer actively pursuing a new career opportunity is to remember that your resume must *sell* what you have to offer:

- **Young baby boomers:** If you're a teacher seeking to transition into a position in corporate training and development, *sell* the fact that you created new curricula, designed new instructional programs, acquired innovative teaching materials, and precepted new faculty.

- **Career-transition baby boomers:** If you're a corporate purchasing manager who has always enjoyed tinkering with computers on the side, and your goal is to transition into a part-time computer-repair position, *highlight* your hands-on skills in computer maintenance and repair, troubleshooting, diagnostics, fault analysis, and customer communication.

- **Return-to-work baby boomers:** Suppose you've been out of the workforce for 15 years while raising your children. Before becoming a stay-at-home mom, you were an accountant and want to continue in that line of work. Make sure that your resume focuses on the strength of your skills in journal entry, P&L statements, budgets, account reconciliation, and more.

When writing your resume, your challenge is to create a picture of knowledge, action, and results. In essence, you're stating "This is what I know, this is how I've used it, and this is how well I've performed." Success sells, so be sure to highlight yours. If you don't, no one else will.

WHERE ARE THE JOBS?

The jobs are everywhere—from multinational manufacturing conglomerates to the small retail sales companies in your neighborhood; from high-tech electronics firms in Silicon Valley to 100-year-old farming operations in rural communities; from banks and financial institutions to hospitals and health-care facilities in every city and town. The jobs are everywhere. Refer back to the U.S. Census Bureau statistics earlier in this chapter to identify specific industries and professions in which there is projected to be the greatest hiring activity and the most employment opportunities.

HOW DO YOU GET THE JOBS?

To answer this question, review the basic principle underlying job search:

Job search is marketing!

You have a product to sell—yourself—and the best way to sell it is to use all appropriate *marketing channels* just as you would for any other product.

Suppose you wanted to sell televisions. What would you do? You'd market your products using newspaper, magazine, and radio advertisements. You might develop a company Web site to build your e-business, and perhaps you'd hire a field sales representative to market to major retail chains. Each of these is a different *marketing channel* through which you're attempting to reach your audience.

The same approach applies to job search. You must use every marketing channel that's right for you. Unfortunately, there is no exact formula that works for everyone. What's right for you depends on your specific career objectives—the type of position you want, the industry you're targeting, your geographic restrictions (if you have any), your salary requirements, and other factors.

Following are the most valuable marketing channels for a successful job search for anyone who is part of the baby-boom generation. These are ordered from most effective to least effective.

1. **Referrals:** There is nothing better than a personal referral to a company, either in general or for a specific position. Referrals can open doors that, in most instances, would never be accessible any other way. If you know anyone who could possibly refer you to a specific organization, contact that person immediately and ask for their assistance. This is, by far, your single best marketing strategy to land a new position.

2. **Networking:** Networking is the backbone of every successful job search. Although you might consider it an unpleasant or difficult task, it is essential that you network effectively with your professional colleagues and associates, past employers, past co-workers, suppliers, neighbors, friends, and others who might know of opportunities that are right for you. Another good strategy is to attend meetings of trade or professional associations for your target profession. This is a wonderful strategy to make new contacts and start building your network in your new career field. And particularly in today's nomadic job market—where you're likely to change jobs every few years—the best strategy is to keep your network "alive" even when you're *not* searching for a new position.

3. **Responding to newspaper, magazine, and periodical advertisements:** Although, as you'll read later, the opportunity to post job opportunities online has reduced the overall number of print advertisements, they still abound. Do not forget about this "tried-and-true" marketing strategy. If they've got the job and you have the qualifications, it can be a perfect fit, even if you are a career changer.

4. **Responding to online job postings:** One of the greatest advantages of the technology revolution is an employer's ability to post job announcements online and a job seeker's ability to respond immediately via e-mail. In most (but not all) instances, these are bona fide opportunities, and it's well worth your while to spend time searching for and responding to appropriate postings. However, don't make the mistake of devoting too much time to searching the Internet. It can consume a huge amount of your time that you should spend on other job search efforts.

   To expedite your search, here are the largest and most widely used online resume-posting and job-posting sites—presented alphabetically, not necessarily in order of effectiveness or value:

http://careers.msn.com	http://hotjobs.yahoo.com
www.careerbuilder.com	www.careerjournal.com
www.careerweb.com	www.dice.com

www.employmax.com   www.employmentguide.com

www.execunet.com   www.hirediversity.com

www.hotjobs.com   www.hotresumes.com

www.job.com   www.monster.com

www.net-temps.com   www.netshare.com

www.sixfigurejobs.com

5. **Posting your resume online:** The 'Net is swarming with reasonably priced (if not free) Web sites where you can post your resume. It's quick, easy, and the only *passive* thing you can do in your search. All of the other marketing channels require action on your part. With online resume postings, once you've posted, you're done. You then just wait (and hope!) for some response.

6. **Targeted e-mail campaigns (resumes and cover letters) to recruiters:** Recruiters have jobs, and you want one. It's pretty straightforward. The only catch is to find the "right" recruiters who have the "right" jobs. Therefore, you must devote the time and effort to preparing the "right" list of recruiters. There are many resources on the Internet where you can access information about recruiters (for a fee), sort that information by industry (such as banking, sales, manufacturing, purchasing, transportation, finance, public relations, or telecommunications), and then cross-reference it with position specialization (such as management, technical, or administration). This allows you to identify the recruiters who would be interested in a candidate with your qualifications. What's more, because these campaigns are transmitted electronically, they are easy and inexpensive to produce.

   When working with recruiters, it's important to realize that they *do not* work for you! Their clients are the hiring companies that pay their fees. They are not in business to "find a job" for you, but rather to fill a specific position with a qualified candidate, either you or someone else. To maximize your chances of finding a position through a recruiter or agency, don't rely on just one or two, but distribute your resume to as many as meet your specific criteria.

   WARNING: Most recruiters are looking to fill specific positions with individuals with very specific qualifications. If you're attempting to make a career change, you may find that recruiters are not your best source of job opportunities because they are not known for "thinking outside the box." If their client (the hiring company) has said that they want a candidate with experience in x, y, and z, the recruiter will present only those job seekers with precisely that experience. Knowing that you're attempting to change careers and might not have precisely the background that the company is looking for, recruiters might simply pass you by. Don't be alarmed—it's their job!

7. **Targeted e-mail and print campaigns to employers:** Just as with campaigns to recruiters (see item 6), you must be extremely careful to select just the right employers that would be interested in a candidate with your qualifications. The closer you stick to "where you belong" in relation to your specific experience, the better your response rate will be. And like recruiters, human resource

professionals and hiring managers might have difficulty appreciating the unique set of skills and qualifications you bring to a position if you're attempting to change careers.

If you are targeting companies in a technology industry, we recommend that you use e-mail as your preferred method for resume submission. However, if the companies you are contacting are not in the technology industry, we believe that print campaigns (paper and envelopes mailed the old-fashioned way) are a more suitable and effective presentation—particularly if you are a management or executive candidate.

8. **In-person "cold calls" to companies and recruiters:** We consider this the least effective and most time-consuming marketing strategy. It is extremely difficult to just walk in the door and get in front of the right person, or any person who can take hiring action. You'll be much better off focusing your time and energy on other, more productive channels.

WHAT ABOUT OPPORTUNITIES IN CONSULTING?

Opportunities in consulting abound. According to the Bureau of Labor Statistics, the demand for consultants is strong and growing at an unprecedented rate. Its data project a 55% increase in the number of consulting opportunities between 2002 and 2012.

The reason for this growth is directly related to the manner in which companies are now hiring—or not hiring—their workforces. Companies can now hire on an "as-needed" or "per-project" basis and avoid the costs associated with full-time, permanent employees. Companies hire the staff they need just when they need them—and when those people are no longer needed, they're gone. This is great news for baby boomers who are interested in part-time positions, short-term assignments, and other nontraditional working situations—especially if you don't depend on an employer to provide your health insurance.

If you are a baby boomer with a particular expertise (for example, marketing communications, project management, new product development, business turn-around, or corporate relocation), you might want to give serious consideration to a consulting career where you will have options and flexibility for your work life and schedule.

If you are seriously considering a consulting career, pay close attention to the following recommendations:

• **Market yourself constantly.** Regardless of your area of consulting expertise, one of your most vital functions as an independent consultant will be to market yourself. Consider the talented financial executive who now wants to pursue a financial consulting career specializing in mergers and acquisitions. Her success as a consultant will not be tied only to her financial expertise, but just as significantly, to her ability to proactively market her consulting practice, establish her clientele, and build a strong revenue stream. If you're not an astute marketer and not willing to invest the time and resources essential to marketing your consulting practice, consider joining an established consulting company where the firm itself will capture the clients and you'll be responsible for product delivery.

- **Practice targeted networking.** As part of your ongoing efforts to market your consulting practice, you'll need to invest your time in targeted networking. In fact, initially, this might be where you devote an extraordinary amount of time—rekindling past business relationships and building new ones. It is essential that you commit yourself to a structured networking and relationship-development program to establish yourself within the consulting marketplace.

- **Manage your finances.** The income streams of consultants often vary widely from month to month. There will be good months when money will be flowing in; there will be slow months when money will only trickle in. Established consultants know that this is the norm and have learned to manage their money accordingly. This can be an extremely difficult lesson and might require some practice, but learning to manage your financial resources is critical to your long-term consulting success.

- **Live with the risk.** Learning to "live with the risk" and the volatility of a consulting career can also be an extreme challenge. Unpredictability is the status quo for most consultants and, as such, you must learn to live comfortably with that risk and not allow the stress associated with it to overtake your life and your mental health!

- **Check the Internet.** Before you proceed any further in evaluating your potential opportunities in consulting, be sure to take advantage of the thousands of online resources devoted to consulting. If you do an extensive Internet search, you'll find Web sites where you can search for consulting opportunities, sites where you can post your resume for review by companies seeking consultants, hundreds of sites with articles about consulting, other sites that offer the many tools you'll need to manage your practice, and much more. Many of these resources are free; others have a small fee associated with them.

Consulting can offer wonderful opportunities to baby boomers. If you do have a particular expertise and can commit yourself to marketing and building your practice, consulting might be just the right solution for you at this point in your career.

In Chapter 5 you will find a variety of resumes for baby boomers now seeking consulting careers. Be sure to take advantage of this resource if you are considering this option.

Conclusion

Career opportunities abound today and, in fact, are growing stronger and stronger for baby boomers. It has never been easier to learn about and apply for jobs than it is today with the vast resources that the Internet offers. Your challenge is to arm yourself with a powerful resume and cover letter, identify the best ways to get yourself and your resume into the market, and shine during every interview. If you're committed and focused, we can almost guarantee that you'll make a smooth transition into your new career field and find yourself happily employed in whatever capacity you choose.

PART I

Resume Writing, Strategy, and Formats

CHAPTER 1

Resume Writing Strategies for the Baby-Boom Generation

If you're reading this book, two things are true:

- You're a baby boomer, born between the years of 1946 and 1964 (in your early 40s to early 60s).

- You've decided to change your career direction; enter a new profession or industry; return to work after an extended absence; or pursue a new, more fulfilling opportunity.

Baby boomers represent the first wave of a new population of job seekers, raised in a generation during which the world of work as we once knew it changed phenomenally. The stability that past generations enjoyed, when they spent their entire working lives at one company, is now a mere memory. Today's job market is volatile and constantly changing. While older industries and professions are disappearing, newer industries, professions, and opportunities are exploding onto the scene every day. In fact, the U.S. Census Bureau projects a 14.7% increase in employment between the years 2004 and 2014—great news for all job seekers, particularly baby boomers!

What's more, the stigmas once associated with the "older" worker (individuals 50+ years of age) are rapidly fading away. People are living longer, healthier lives, and many are working well into their 70s, 80s, and beyond. Being a mere 52 years old is no longer considered a liability in most employment markets.

Today's new world of work demands talented individuals who are flexible and open to new ideas, new opportunities, and new challenges. Organizations need individuals who can deliver value—today and in the future. And, who better to fulfill that need than baby boomers, a generation that was raised to believe anything is possible and that their contributions will, indeed, lead us all into a better world. What's more, two vastly differing types of opportunities are available to you, depending on which of the categories you fall into: "regular" jobs and "work/life balance" jobs.

Regardless of the underlying reasons for your career change, you are faced with some unique challenges in your job search and, more specifically, in how you write your resume. What can you do to capture employers' attention, impress them with your qualifications and achievements, and position yourself for just the right opportunity?

If you're a young baby boomer seeking to further your career, writing your resume might be an easier and more straightforward task than it is for individuals who fall into the other two categories of baby boomers. Those individuals face the additional challenges of creating a resume that is powerful enough to not put them "out of the running" because they do not have experience in a particular industry or profession, because they've been out of the workforce for an extended period of time, or because they now want to pursue an entirely different opportunity that will offer more work/life balance and personal satisfaction.

Which Type of Baby Boomer Are You?

Before we address the specific issues and challenges of resume writing for baby boomers, let's talk about who this book was written for—a unique collection of people representing just about every profession and industry imaginable. The only thing that our readers have in common is that they are baby boomers seeking to make a career change or move. But before we proceed any further, it is essential that you identify the category of baby-boomer job seeker that best fits your unique circumstances.

YOUNG BABY BOOMERS (UNDER 45)

Young baby boomers typically are at prime career performance levels and seeking increasing responsibilities. Resumes for these individuals generally focus on the strength of their work history and accomplishments, positioning them for positions of increased authority and responsibility. Boomers who fall into this category of job seekers are often pursuing new career opportunities for one of the following reasons:

- Their original industry or profession was hard hit by the recession and volatility within the market over the past decade, and opportunities have virtually dried up.

- They've decided to pursue a career that will offer greater opportunities for upward career progression.

- They are driven to make more money, and the best strategy to do that is to pursue new opportunities.

- They fell into a position right out of college and worked in that career field for years, and then woke up one day and realized it was time to do what they really wanted to do professionally.

- They are relocating to a new area where opportunities for individuals with their experience are quite limited and they need to open themselves to new opportunities and career challenges to continue to advance their career.

CAREER-TRANSITION BABY BOOMERS

These boomers are looking for more meaning and/or balance in their work/life and seeking a career transition exclusively for that purpose. This includes individuals who are decelerating their careers, launching post-retirement careers, entering a completely new line of work or new industry, or volunteering. Resumes for these individuals often focus on experiences, skills, and activities that might not have been at the crux of their "professional career" but are extremely important in positioning them for new career-transition opportunities. Boomers who fall into this category of job seekers are often pursuing new career opportunities for one of the following reasons:

- They are now in a position to pursue their lifelong dream or hobby, which has been burning inside of them since their early days.

- They have always wanted to pursue a different career track but were unable to do so because of family, financial, or other personal obligations that have now been alleviated.

- Their volunteer work has become increasingly important and they want to pursue opportunities with an association or not-for-profit organization that will allow them to "contribute to the greater good."

- They retired from their original career and have now decided to return to work in a professional, yet more personally rewarding, position.

- They are tired of the tremendous responsibilities associated with their position and want to decelerate their career into a less-stressful job.

RETURN-TO-WORK BABY BOOMERS

These individuals are returning to the workforce after extended absences due to parenting, caring for aging parents, taking a sabbatical, and so on. Resumes for these individuals generally showcase the strength of their previous careers and the skills they acquired as opposed to what they have done most recently outside of the workforce. Boomers who fall into this category of job seekers are often pursuing new career opportunities for one of the following reasons:

- They've raised their children, cared for aging parents, or otherwise fulfilled their family obligations and are now ready to re-enter the workforce.

- They've been widowed or divorced and now, for financial reasons, must return to the workforce.

- They've completed recent training or education to refresh their skills, develop new skills, and make themselves more marketable in today's employment market.

- Their volunteer work has become increasingly important and they want to pursue a paid position in the field they care so deeply about.

For every job seeker—those currently employed and those not currently working—a powerful resume is an essential component of the job search campaign. In fact, it is virtually impossible to conduct a search without a resume. It is your calling card that briefly, yet powerfully, communicates the skills, qualifications, experience, and value you bring to a prospective employer. It is the document that will open doors and generate interviews. It is the first thing people will learn about you when you forward it in response to an advertisement, and it is the last thing they'll remember when they're reviewing your qualifications after an interview.

Your resume is a sales document, and you are the product! You must identify the *features (what you know* and *what you can do)* and *benefits (how you can help an employer)* of that product, and then communicate them in a concise and hard-hitting written presentation. Remind yourself over and over, as you work your way through the resume process, that you are writing marketing literature designed to sell a new product—YOU—into a new position.

Your resume can have tremendous power and a phenomenal impact on your job search, so don't take it lightly. Rather, devote the time, energy, and resources that are essential to developing a resume that is well-written, visually attractive, and effective in communicating *who* you are and *how* you want to be perceived.

Resume Strategies

Professional resume writers understand that resume writing—just like any other business function—has a process that is comprised of specific strategies and actions to achieve the desired result; namely, a job. Following are the nine core strategies that we utilize on a daily basis to write strong, effective, and well-targeted resumes.

RESUME STRATEGY #1: WHO ARE YOU AND HOW DO YOU WANT TO BE PERCEIVED?

Before you can even begin writing your resume, you must first identify your specific career goals, interests, and objectives. *This task is critical* because it is the underlying foundation for *what* you include in your resume, *how* you include it, and *where* you include it. Knowing that you want to make a career change, return to the workforce, or find a job that offers you the life balance you're striving for is not enough. You must know—with some degree of certainty—the type or types of position you will be seeking in order to write an effective and powerful resume.

There are two concepts to consider here:

- **Who you are:** This relates to what you have done professionally and/or academically. Are you a senior executive, sales director, financial professional, contract administrator, trainer, banker, engineer, technologist, or educator? What is it that you have done for a living all these years, or if you're not currently working, what did you do in the past? Who are you?

- **How you want to be perceived:** This is critical and relates directly to your current career objectives. Compare the following three scenarios for each type of baby-boomer job seeker:

Young baby boomers. Over the past 20 years, you've held a series of increasingly responsible sales and sales management positions with several major technology industry companies. You've been quite successful and are now ready to take the next step forward into a general management position where you will have greater responsibility and be better compensated. Rather than focus your resume on your sales management career, you want to highlight all of the skills and talents you've acquired that relate to general management. Specifically, you'll want to include information about profit-and-loss management, revenue and income growth (including your sales achievements), strategic planning, new market development, new product development, organizational design and leadership, human capital management, long-range business planning, and more. Write your resume—your summary, your job descriptions, everything— from the general manager perspective. You want to paint the picture of an individual who is already a qualified general manager and not *just* a sales manager.

Career-transition baby boomers. For 10 years now, you've been the CEO of a small financial advisory firm. In fact, your entire 30+-year career has been in financial services and investment banking. You've made enough money that you and your spouse can live comfortably, and now it's time to pursue your personal passion: aviation. Instead of writing a resume that highlights your professional career in finance, you want to take an entirely different approach and move to the forefront everything else in your life that supports your career objective. This might include associations you've belonged to, activities you've participated in, training you've completed, volunteer projects you've spearheaded, and more. This information will become the foundation for your resume; your work history will be briefly mentioned at the end. You want to paint the picture of an individual with a long history of interest and participation in the field of aviation, and *not* the picture of a talented financial services CEO.

Return-to-work baby boomers. After 15 years at home raising four children, you can't wait to go back to work! Before you had your first child, you graduated with a B.S. in Business Administration and worked for five years in health care administration. Those five years, and the skills you acquired during that time, will constitute the vast majority of your resume. Most likely you'll start your resume with a summary section that highlights your core competencies (for example, budgeting, cost control, patient relations, third-party insurance reimbursement, quality control, and regulatory reporting). You'll also want to include your specific work experience while downplaying the dates (see samples in subsequent chapters). Don't allow your resume to scream, "I've been unemployed for 15 years." Rather, paint the picture of a talented individual with strong skills that are valuable in today's employment market.

Bottom line, Resume Strategy #1 connects the *Who You Are* concept with the *How You Want to Be Perceived* concept to guide you in selecting what information to include in your resume, where to include it, and how to include it. By following this strategy, you're painting a picture that allows a prospective employer to see you as you want to be seen—as an individual with the qualifications for the type of position you are pursuing.

> **WARNING:** If you prepare a resume without first clearly identifying what your objectives are and how you want to be perceived, your resume will have no focus and no direction. Without the underlying knowledge of "This is what I want to be," you do not know what to highlight in your resume. As a result, the document becomes a historical overview of your career and not the sales document it should be in order to facilitate your successful job search.

RESUME STRATEGY #2: SELL IT TO ME...DON'T TELL IT TO ME

We've already established the fact that resume writing is sales. You are the product, and you must create a document that powerfully communicates the value of that product. One particularly effective strategy for accomplishing this is the "Sell It to Me...Don't Tell It to Me" strategy, which impacts virtually every word you write on your resume.

If you "tell it," you are simply stating facts. If you "sell it," you promote it, advertise it, and draw attention to it. Look at the difference in impact between these examples:

Tell It Strategy: Led turnaround of unprofitable 250-employee manufacturing plant.

Sell It Strategy: Led successful turnaround of unprofitable manufacturing operations, restaffed core management functions, upgraded technology, introduced best practices, and achieved double-digit profitability in just 24 months.

Tell It Strategy: Managed all administrative functions for the U.S. branch office of an international shipbuilding company.

Sell It Strategy: Implemented a series of process improvements that reduced operating costs 15%, expedited billing cycles, and increased bottom-line profits by 12% for U.S. branch of an international shipbuilding company.

Tell It Strategy: Implemented telecommunications network for major corporate account.

Sell It Strategy: Led implementation of $2.8 million project to upgrade telecommunications capabilities for all 412 employees of the North Shore Medical Center. Provided ongoing troubleshooting and technical support that reduced system downtime 54% over previous technology.

What's the difference between "telling it" and "selling it"? In a nutshell...

Telling It	Selling It
Describes features.	Describes benefits.
Tells what and how.	Sells why the "what" and "how" are important.
Details activities.	Includes results.
Focuses on what you did.	Details how what you did benefited your country, branch of service, unit, colleagues, and so on.

RESUME STRATEGY #3: USE KEYWORDS

No matter what you read or who you talk to about searching for jobs, the concept of keywords is sure to come up. Keywords (or, as they were previously known, buzz words) are words and phrases that are specific to a particular industry or profession. For example, keywords for the manufacturing industry include *production-line operations, production planning and scheduling, materials management, inventory control, quality, process engineering, robotics, systems automation, integrated logistics, product specifications, project management,* and many, many more.

When you use these words and phrases—in your resume, in your cover letter, or during an interview—you are communicating a very specific message. For example, when you include the word "merchandising" in your resume, your reader will most likely assume that you have experience in the retail industry—in product selection, vendor/manufacturing relations, in-store product display, inventory management, mark-downs, product promotions, and more. As you can see, people will make inferences about your skills based on the use of just one or two specific words.

Here are a few other examples:

- When you use the words **investment finance,** people will assume you have experience with risk management, mergers, acquisitions, initial public offerings, debt/equity management, asset allocation, portfolio management, and more.

- When you mention **sales,** readers and listeners will infer that you have experience in product presentations, pricing, contract negotiations, customer relationship management, new product introduction, competitive product positioning, and more.

- By referencing **Internet technology** in your resume, you convey that you most likely have experience with Web site design, Web site marketing, metatags, HTML, search-engine registration, e-learning, and more.

- When you use the words **human resources,** most people will assume that you are familiar with recruitment, hiring, placement, compensation, benefits, training and development, employee relations, human resources information system (HRIS), and more.

Keywords are also an integral component of the resume-scanning process, whereby employers and recruiters electronically search resumes for specific terms to find candidates with the skills, qualifications, and credentials for their particular hiring needs. Over the past several years, keyword scanning has dramatically increased in its popularity because of its ease of use and efficiency in identifying prime candidates. Every job seeker today must stay on top of the latest trends in technology-based hiring and employment to ensure that their resumes and other job search materials contain the "right" keywords to capture the interest of prospective employers. Refer to Chapter 3, "Printed, Scannable, Electronic, and Web Resumes," for more information about technology and its impact on resumes and job search in general.

In organizations where it has been implemented, electronic scanning has replaced the more traditional method of an actual person reading your resume (at least initially). Therefore, to some degree, the *only* thing that matters is that you have included the "right" keywords to match the company's or the recruiter's needs. Without them, you will most certainly be passed over.

Of course, in virtually every instance your resume will be read at some point by human eyes, so it's not enough to just throw together a list of keywords and leave it at that. In fact, it's not even necessary to include a separate "keyword summary" on your resume. A better strategy is to incorporate keywords naturally into the text within the appropriate sections of your resume.

For anyone changing jobs, changing professions, or changing industries, keywords are particularly relevant and require a good deal of thought, because you do not necessarily want to include keywords that are descriptive of your past experiences. Rather, you want to include keywords that reflect your current career goals so that those words are the ones that get your resume noticed and not passed over. There are basically two ways to accomplish this:

- Integrate keywords from your past experiences that directly relate to your current career goals. This can be accomplished in a number of sections throughout your resume. Referring back to the earlier example where a sales manager was seeking to transition into a general management position, that individual did have actual experience in many GM functions (for example, profit and loss management, human capital management, and new product development). And those skills (keywords) are what should be highlighted on his resume. Even though these functions were not his primary areas of responsibility, they are relevant to his current career goals and, therefore, should be prominently highlighted on his resume, in the summary and within his job descriptions.

- Include an objective section on your resume that states the type of position that you are seeking and the associated responsibilities. For example, "Seeking a position in global outreach where I can utilize my strong skills in organization, community advocacy, international affairs, and resource management." This is an excellent strategy for integrating keywords so that they are instantly noticeable at the beginning of your resume, particularly if you do not have a great deal of supporting work experience. This is particularly relevant for career-transition baby boomers.

Keep in mind, too, that keywords are arbitrary; there is no defined set of keywords for a secretary, production laborer, police officer, teacher, electrical engineer, construction superintendent, finance officer, sales manager, or chief executive officer. Employers searching to fill these positions develop a list of terms that reflect the specifics they desire in a qualified candidate. These might be a combination of professional qualifications, skills, education, length of experience, and other easily defined criteria, along with "soft skills," such as organization, time management, team building, leadership, problem-solving, and communication.

> **NOTE:** Because of the complex and arbitrary nature of keyword selection, we cannot overemphasize how vital it is to be certain that you include in your resume *all* of the keywords that summarize your skills *as they relate to your current objectives.*

How can you be sure that you are including all the keywords, and the *right* keywords? Just by describing your work experience, achievements, educational credentials, technical qualifications, objective, volunteer activities, professional and civic affiliations, and the like, you might naturally include most of the terms that are important to your new career field. To cross-check what you've written, you can review online or newspaper job postings and job descriptions for positions that are of interest to you. Look at the precise terms used in the ads and be sure you have included them in your resume (as appropriate to your skills and qualifications).

Another great benefit of today's technology revolution is our ability to find instant information, even information as specific as keywords for hundreds of different industries and professions. Refer to the appendix for a listing of Web sites that list thousands of keywords, complete with descriptions, along with many other valuable resources.

RESUME STRATEGY #4: USE THE "BIG" AND SAVE THE "LITTLE"

When deciding what you want to include in your resume, try to focus on the "big" things—new programs, special projects, cost savings, productivity and efficiency improvements, new products, technology implementations, and more. Give a good, broad-based picture of what you were responsible for and how well you did it. Here's an example:

> Directed daily sales, customer service, and fleet management operations for a $25 million transportation company in Manhattan. Recruited, trained, and led a staff of 24 and controlled a $4.8 million annual operating budget. Consistently achieved/surpassed all revenue, profit, cost control, and customer service objectives.

Then, save the "little" stuff—the details—for the interview. With this strategy, you will accomplish two things:

- You'll keep your resume readable and of a reasonable length (while still selling your achievements).

- You'll have new and interesting information to share during the interview, rather than merely repeating what is already on your resume.

Using the preceding example, when discussing this experience during an interview, you could elaborate on your specific achievements—namely, improving revenue and profit growth, managing key account relationships, improving employee training, reducing maintenance and repair costs, and directing special promotions.

This particular strategy is most relevant to individuals who fall into the young baby boomers or return-to-work baby boomers categories of job seekers. For career-transition baby boomers who are now decelerating their careers, resumes often do not focus on past work experiences and the "big" stuff, but rather on volunteerism, affiliations, personal interests and passion, hobbies, and other activities.

RESUME STRATEGY #5: MAKE YOUR RESUME "INTERVIEWABLE"

One of your greatest challenges is to make your resume a useful interview tool. Once the employer has determined that you meet the primary qualifications for a position (you've passed the keyword scanning test or initial review) and you are contacted for a telephone or in-person interview, your resume becomes all-important in leading and prompting your interviewer during your conversation.

Your job, then, is to make sure the resume leads the reader where you want to go and presents just the right organization, content, and appearance to stimulate a productive discussion. To improve the "interviewability" of your resume, consider these tactics:

- Make good use of Resume Strategy #4 (Use the "Big" and Save the "Little") to invite further discussion about your experiences.

- Be sure your greatest "selling points" as they relate to your current objectives are featured prominently, not buried within the resume.

- Conversely, don't devote lots of space and attention to areas of your background that are irrelevant or about which you feel less than positive; you'll only invite questions about things you really don't want to discuss. This is particularly true for career changers who want their resumes to focus on the skills that will be needed in their new profession and not necessarily on the activities of their past positions.

- Make sure your resume is highly readable—this means plenty of white space, an adequate font size, and a logical flow from start to finish.

RESUME STRATEGY #6: ELIMINATE CONFUSION WITH STRUCTURE AND CONTEXT

Keep in mind that hiring authorities will read your resume very quickly! You may agonize over every word and spend hours working on content and design, but the average reader will skim quickly through your masterpiece and expect to pick up important facts in just a few seconds. Try to make it as easy as possible for readers to grasp the essential facts:

- Be consistent. For example, put job titles, company names, and dates in the same place for each position.

- Make information easy to find by clearly defining different sections of your resume with large, highly visible headings.

- If relevant to your new career path, define the context in which you worked (for example, the organization, your department, and the specific challenges you faced) before you start describing your activities and accomplishments.

RESUME STRATEGY #7: USE FUNCTION TO DEMONSTRATE ACHIEVEMENT

When you write a resume that focuses only on your job functions, it can be dry and uninteresting and will say very little about your unique activities and contributions. Consider the following example:

> Responsible for daily sales training of all field sales associates in the organization.

Now, consider using that same function to demonstrate achievement and see what happens to the tone and energy of the sentence. It becomes alive and clearly communicates that you deliver results:

> Design and lead sales training programs for the entire Allstate field sales organization (2000+ individuals). Achieved 98%+ ratings for effectiveness of sales training and supported a 210% increase in annual sales revenues over the past two years.

Try to translate your functions into achievements and you'll create a more powerful resume presentation.

RESUME STRATEGY #8: REMAIN IN THE REALM OF REALITY

We've already established that resume writing is sales. And, as any good salesperson does, one feels somewhat inclined to stretch the truth, just a bit. However, be forewarned that you must stay within the realm of reality. Do not push your skills and qualifications outside the bounds of what is truthful. You never want to be in a position where you have to defend something that you've written on your resume. If that's the case, you'll lose the opportunity before you ever get started.

RESUME STRATEGY #9: BE CONFIDENT

You are unique. There is only one individual with the specific combination of employment experience, qualifications, achievements, education, and special skills that you have. In turn, this positions you as a unique commodity within the employment market. To succeed, you must prepare a resume that is written to sell *you* and highlight *your* qualifications and *your* success as they relate to your current career objectives. If you can accomplish this, you will have won the job search game by generating interest, interviews, and offers.

There Are No Resume Writing Rules

One of the greatest challenges in resume writing is that there are no rules to the game. There are certain expectations about information that you will include—principally, your primary skills, employment history, educational qualifications, and any other experiences that relate to your current objective. Beyond that, what you include is entirely up to you, what you have done in your career, and what type of opportunity you're currently pursuing. What's more, you have tremendous flexibility in determining how to include the information you have selected. In chapter 2, you'll find a wealth of information on each possible category you might include in your resume, the type of information to be placed in each category, preferred formats for presentation, and lots of other information and samples that will help you formulate your best resume.

Although there are no rules, there are a few standards to live by as you write your resume. The following sections discuss these standards in detail.

CONTENT STANDARDS

Content is, of course, the text that goes into your resume. Content standards cover the writing style you should use, items you should be sure to include, items you should avoid including, and the order and format in which you list your qualifications.

Writing Style

Always write in the first person, dropping the word "I" from the front of each sentence. This style gives your resume a more aggressive and more professional tone than the passive third-person voice. Here are some examples:

First Person

> Manage a team of 45 responsible for development and market introduction of a new line of health and beauty aids for Myers' $1.2 billion consumer-sales division.

Third Person

> Ms. Arnold manages a 45-person team responsible for the development and market introduction of a new line of health and beauty aids for Myers' $1.2 billion consumer-sales division.

By using the first-person voice, you are assuming "ownership" of that statement. You did such-and-such. When you use the third-person, "someone else" did it. Can you see the difference?

Phrases to Stay Away From

Try not to use phrases such as "responsible for" or "duties included." These words create a passive tone and style. Instead, use active verbs to describe what you did.

Compare these two ways of conveying the same information:

> Responsible for writing and designing newspaper advertisements and in-store circulars.

OR

> Orchestrate the design, copywriting, and production of newspaper advertisements, in-store circulars, and other promotional pieces for Nordstrom's flagship store in San Francisco.

Resume Style

The traditional **chronological** resume lists work experience in reverse-chronological order (starting with your current or most recent position and working backwards). The **functional** style de-emphasizes the "where" and "when" of your career and instead groups similar experiences, talents, and qualifications regardless of when they occurred.

Today, however, most resumes follow neither a strictly chronological nor strictly functional format; rather, they are an effective mixture of the two styles usually known as a "combination" or "hybrid" format.

Like the chronological format, the hybrid format includes specifics about where you worked, when you worked there, and what your job titles were. Like a functional resume, a hybrid emphasizes your most relevant qualifications—perhaps within chronological job descriptions, in an expanded summary section, in several "career highlights" bullet points at the top of your resume, or in project summaries.

We strongly recommend hybrid-format resumes for virtually all job seekers, baby boomers included. They allow individual job seekers to begin their resumes with an intense focus on skills, competencies, experiences, accomplishments, and more that are directly related to their new career objectives. Then, how the resume proceeds—experience, education, affiliations, volunteer activities, and more—depends entirely on each individual's objectives. Most of the examples in this book are hybrids and show a wide diversity of organizational formats that you can use as inspiration for designing your own resume.

Resume Formats

Resumes, principally career summaries and job descriptions, are most often written in a paragraph format, a bulleted format, or a combination of both. Following are three job descriptions, all very similar in content, yet presented in each of the three different writing formats. The advantages and disadvantages of each format are also addressed.

Paragraph Format

Vice President / General Manager
1996 to 2005

WAXMAN SYSTEMS OF AMERICA, Lansing, MI

Pioneered expansion of leading Australian manufacturer of high-end security access and control systems into North America and built venture from start-up into a well established and profitable player within a highly competitive industry. Led a team of 35 field sales representatives and manufacturer rep organizations throughout the U.S. and Canada.

Built sales from $500,000 to $18.5 million over 9 years. Personally negotiated and closed a $5 million contract with Appalachian Electric Power, positioning Waxman as the preferred provider of video/intercom door entry control systems at AEP locations throughout North and South America. Increased market share and brand recognition with delivery of top-down sales program for architects, engineers, and general contractors.

Structured end-user incentive program that halted competition and retained key distribution channels (accounted for 35% of all sales). Revolutionized Waxman's existing sales model to bring product sales and support closer to end-user.

Advantages

Requires the least amount of space on the page. Brief, succinct, and to the point.

Disadvantages

Achievements get lost in the text of the paragraphs. They are not visually distinctive, nor do they stand alone to draw attention to them.

Bulleted Format

Vice President / General Manager   1996 to 2005

WAXMAN SYSTEMS OF AMERICA, Lansing, MI

- Pioneered expansion of leading Australian manufacturer of high-end security access and control systems into North America and built venture from start-up into a well-established and profitable player within a highly competitive industry.

- Led a team of 35 field sales representatives and manufacturer rep organizations throughout the U.S. and Canada.

- Built sales from $500,000 to $18.5 million over 9 years.

- Personally negotiated and closed a $5 million contract with Appalachian Electric Power, positioning Waxman as the preferred provider of video/intercom door entry control systems at AEP locations throughout North and South America.

- Increased market share and brand recognition with delivery of top-down sales program for architects, engineers, and general contractors.

- Structured end-user incentive program that halted competition and retained key distribution channels (accounted for 35% of all sales).

- Revolutionized Waxman's existing sales model to bring product sales and support closer to end-user.

Advantages

Quick and easy to peruse.

Disadvantages

Responsibilities and achievements are lumped together, with everything given equal value. In turn, the achievements get lost and are not immediately recognizable.

Combination Format

Vice President / General Manager
1996 to 2005

WAXMAN SYSTEMS OF AMERICA, Lansing, MI

Pioneered expansion of leading Australian manufacturer of high-end security access and control systems into North America and built venture from start-up into a well-established and profitable player within a highly competitive industry. Led a team of 35 field sales representatives and manufacturer rep organizations throughout the U.S. and Canada.

- Built sales from $500,000 to $18.5 million over 9 years.

- Personally negotiated and closed a $5 million contract with Appalachian Electric Power, positioning Waxman as the preferred provider of video/intercom door entry control systems at AEP locations throughout North and South America.

- Increased market share and brand recognition with delivery of top-down sales program for architects, engineers, and general contractors.

- Structured end-user incentive program that halted competition and retained key distribution channels (accounted for 35% of all sales).

- Revolutionized Waxman's existing sales model to bring product sales and support closer to end-user.

Advantages

Our recommended format. Clearly presents overall responsibilities in the introductory paragraph and then accentuates each achievement as a separate bullet.

Disadvantages

If you don't have clearly identifiable accomplishments, this format is not effective. It also may shine a glaring light on the positions where your accomplishments were less notable. For career changers, past accomplishments may not be relevant to current career objectives; therefore, this format may be less appropriate.

You'll find numerous other examples of how to best present your employment experience in the resume samples in chapters 4 through 6. Remember, however, that your resume is more than *just* your work experience, particularly if you're a career-transition baby boomer. Be sure to pay special attention to chapter 2, where you'll find sample formats you can use to highlight your skills, achievements, volunteer activities, professional affiliations, and more if you choose to showcase them more prominently than your work history. This approach can be vital in getting you noticed and not passed over when you're in transition.

E-mail Address and URL

Be sure to include your e-mail address prominently at the top of your resume. E-mail has become one of the most preferred methods of communication between employers and job seekers. If you don't yet have an e-mail address, visit sites such as www.yahoo.com, www.hotmail.com, or www.mail.com, where you can get a free e-mail address that you can access through the Web.

In addition to your e-mail address, if you have a URL (Web site address) where you have posted your Web resume, be sure to also display that prominently at the top of your resume. For more information on Web resumes, refer to chapter 3.

PRESENTATION STANDARDS

Presentation focuses on the way your resume looks. It relates to the fonts you use, the paper you print it on, any graphics you might include, and how many pages your resume should be.

Typestyle

Use a typestyle (font) that is clean, conservative, and easy to read. Stay away from anything that is too fancy, glitzy, curly, and the like. Here are a few recommended typestyles:

Tahoma	Times New Roman
Arial	Bookman
Krone	Book Antiqua
Soutane	Garamond
CG Omega	Century Schoolbook
Century Gothic	Lucida Sans
Gill Sans	Verdana

Although it is extremely popular, Times New Roman is our least preferred type-style simply because it is overused. More than 90 percent of the resumes we see are typed in Times New Roman. Your goal is to create a competitive-distinctive document, and, to achieve that, we recommend an alternative typestyle.

Your choice of typestyle should be dictated by the content, format, and length of your resume. Some fonts look better than others at smaller or larger sizes; some have "bolder" boldface type; some require more white space to make them readable. Once you've written your resume, experiment with a few different typestyles to see which one best enhances your document.

Type Size

Readability is everything! If the type size is too small, your resume will be difficult to read and difficult to skim for essential information. Interestingly, a too-large type size, particularly for senior-level professionals, can also give a negative impression by conveying a juvenile or unprofessional image.

As a general rule, select type from 10 to 12 points in size. However, there's no hard-and-fast rule, and a lot depends on the typestyle you choose. Take a look at the following examples:

Very readable in 9-point Verdana:

Staff officer responsible for research, analysis, and presentation of Marine Corps critical long-range planning and policy development issues in support of the intelligence community.

Difficult to read in too-small 9-point Gill Sans:

Staff officer responsible for research, analysis, and presentation of Marine Corps critical long-range planning and policy development issues in support of the intelligence community.

Concise and readable in 12-point Times New Roman:

Developed and implemented a comprehensive training program that resulted in 60% increase in number of certified personnel.

A bit overwhelming in too-large 12-point Bookman Old Style:

Developed and implemented a comprehensive training program that resulted in 60% increase in number of certified personnel.

Type Enhancements

Bold, *italics*, <u>underlining</u>, and CAPITALIZATION are ideal to highlight certain words, phrases, achievements, projects, numbers, and other information to which you want to draw special attention. However, do not overuse these enhancements. If your resume becomes too cluttered with special formatting, nothing stands out.

> **NOTE:** Resumes intended for electronic transmission and computer scanning have specific restrictions on typestyle, type size, and type enhancements. These are discussed in detail in chapter 3.

Page Length

For most industries and professions, the "one- to two-page rule" for resume writing still holds true, whether you're a young baby boomer, a career-transition baby boomer, or a return-to-work baby boomer. Keep it short and succinct, giving just enough to entice your readers' interest. However, there are many instances when a resume might be longer than two pages, particularly for young baby boomers who are looking to move forward in their careers. For example:

- You have an extensive list of technical qualifications that are relevant to the position for which you are applying. (You might consider including these on a separate page as an addendum to your resume.)

- You have extensive educational training and numerous credentials/certifications, all of which are important to include. (You might consider including these on a separate page as an addendum to your resume.)

- You have an extensive list of special projects, task forces, and committees to include that are important to your current career objectives. (You might consider including these on a separate page as an addendum to your resume.)

- You have an extensive list of professional honors, awards, and commendations. This list is tremendously valuable in validating your credibility and distinguishing you from the competition.

If you create a resume that's longer than two pages, make it more reader-friendly by carefully segmenting the information into separate sections. Your sections might include a career summary, work experience, education, professional or industry credentials, honors and awards, technology and equipment skills, publications, public-speaking engagements, professional affiliations, civic affiliations, technology skills, volunteer experience, foreign-language skills, and other relevant information you want to include. Put each into a separate category so that your resume is easy to peruse and your reader can quickly see the highlights. You'll read more about each of these sections in chapter 2.

Paper Color

Be conservative. White, ivory, and light gray are ideal. Other "flashier" colors are inappropriate for most individuals unless you are in a highly creative industry and your paper choice is part of the overall design and presentation of a creative resume.

Graphics

An attractive, relevant graphic can really enhance your resume. When you look through the sample resumes in chapters 4 through 6, you'll see some excellent examples of the effective use of graphics to enhance the visual presentation of a resume. Just be sure not to get carried away…be tasteful and relatively conservative.

White Space

We'll say it again—readability is everything! If people have to struggle to read your resume, they simply won't make the effort. Therefore, be sure to leave plenty of white space. It really does make a difference.

ACCURACY AND PERFECTION

The very final step, and one of the most critical in resume writing, is the proofreading stage. It is essential that your resume be well-written; visually pleasing; and free of any errors, typographical mistakes, misspellings, and the like. We recommend that you carefully proofread your resume a minimum of three times, and then have two or three other people also proofread it. Consider your resume an example of the quality of work you will produce on a company's behalf. Is your work product going to have errors and inconsistencies? If your resume does, it communicates to a prospective employer that you are careless, and this is the "kiss of death" in job search.

Take the time to make sure that your resume is perfect in all the little details that do, in fact, make a big difference to those who read it.

CHAPTER 2

Writing Your Resume

For many job seekers, resume writing is *not* at the top of the list of fun and exciting activities. How can it compare to closing a major account, slashing costs, improving revenue, creating a new product, or expanding operations overseas? In your perception, we're sure that it cannot.

However, resume writing can be an enjoyable and rewarding task. When your resume is complete, you can look at it proudly, reminding yourself of all that you have achieved. It is a snapshot of your career and your success. When it's complete, we guarantee you'll look back with tremendous self-satisfaction as you launch and successfully manage your job search.

As the very first step in finding a new position or advancing your career, resume writing can be the most daunting of all tasks in your job search. If writing is not one of your innate skills or a past job function, it might have been years since you've actually sat down and written anything other than notes to yourself. Even for those of you who write on a regular basis, resume writing is unique. It has its own style, structure, and process, and a number of peculiarities, as with any specialty document.

Resume Strategies for Baby Boomers

Writing resumes for baby boomers offers many unique challenges largely because of the diversity of the baby-boom generation. As you'll recall from the previous chapter, there are three primary job seeker categories that most, if not all, baby boomers fall into:

- Young baby boomers
- Career-transition baby boomers
- Return-to-work baby boomers

We detailed the specific characteristics of each of these unique populations in chapter 1. If you want to refresh your memory about which category you belong to, refer to chapter 1.

Because the job search goals of baby boomers can transcend narrow classifications, their resumes also tend to be vastly different. Consider the following:

- Resumes for individuals who fall into the young baby boomer category are much more likely to follow the more "traditional" resume structure, with the emphasis on recent and progressive employment experience and the success of that experience.

- Resumes for individuals who fall into the career-transition baby boomer category often follow a more unique format, typical of many individuals who are making career changes. These resumes often downplay particular work experience while highlighting skills, core competencies, volunteer experiences, professional and civic affiliations, and other activities that are related to each individual's current career objectives.

- Resumes for individuals who fall into the return-to-work category often show-case skills and experiences from years past while downplaying the fact that the work history was many years ago.

KNOW YOUR CAREER OBJECTIVES

Regardless of which category you fall into, before you can even begin to start writing your resume, you must know the specific type(s) of position(s) you are going after. This will give your resume a "theme" around which you can build the entire document. Your "theme" (or objective) will dictate everything that you include in your resume, how you include it, and where. Writing a resume is all about creating a picture of how you want to be perceived by a prospective employer—a picture that closely mirrors the types of people who are hired in that career field or type of job.

Assuming that you have researched the type of career you want to pursue, you should have collected a great deal of information about the duties and responsibilities for positions in that field. You should then carefully review your past employment experience, educational background, volunteer work, professional affiliations, civic affiliations, and other activities to identify skills you've acquired that are relevant to your existing career (if you're a young baby boomer), transferable to your new career (if you're a career-transition baby boomer), or applicable to re-launching your career (if you're a return-to-work baby boomer). These skills are what become the foundation for your resume and the key themes that run throughout the entire document.

SPECIAL CONSIDERATIONS FOR CAREER-TRANSITION RESUMES

If you're planning to make a career transition, but you're not sure how to identify your transferable skills, here's an easy way. First, review advertisements for positions that are of interest. You can get this information from newspapers, professional journals, and hundreds of online resources. You can also talk to and network with people who are already working in your new career field and ask them about their specific responsibilities, the challenges they face, the opportunities that are available, how to get into the field, and so on.

Once you've collected this information, make a detailed list of the specific requirements for these jobs (for example, budgeting, staff training, staff supervision, project management, statistical analysis, or customer relationship management). Be as comprehensive as possible, even if the list goes on and on for pages. Then, go through the list and highlight each of the skills in which you have some experience, either from your work, your education, or outside activities. Finally, take some time to think of specific examples of how you've used those skills. Well-placed in your resume, these "success stories" are powerful proof that you already possess the very skills and competencies you want to use in your new job.

> **NOTE:** There is no need to describe these skills as "transferable" in your resume, cover letter, or conversations during your job search. Why highlight the fact that your skills are not directly related to the field you want to pursue? Quite simply, these are skills you possess, experiences you own, and activities you have accomplished. They are the foundation of your performance in past experiences and in your new role.

When you are writing a career-transition resume and focusing on your transferable skills, it is important to remember that your *entire* background counts—everything that you've ever done, from your 20-year management career to your six-year volunteer position coordinating the local Special Olympics. Just think of the great skills you acquired in event planning, logistics, volunteer training, fund-raising, media affairs, contract negotiations, and more from the Special Olympics experience. Those skills are just as important to include in your career-transition resume as any other skills you acquired in a paid position.

> **WARNING:** If you don't know what your objective is, we strongly urge that you spend some time investigating potential opportunities to determine your overall areas of interest. Without this knowledge, you cannot focus your resume in any one particular direction and, as a result, it simply becomes a recitation of your past work experience. This is especially fatal if you are attempting to change careers from what you have been doing in the past.

Your resume must have a theme and a focus to effectively position you for new career opportunities. If you're having difficulty determining your objective, consider hiring a career coach who can help you critically evaluate your skills and qualifications, help you investigate potential career opportunities, enable you to explore new professions, and guide you in setting your direction.

Resume Formats for Baby Boomers

Following are three excellent examples of baby-boomer resumes, one example for each of the three categories of job seekers. Think about which of these formats and styles is most appropriate for you, based on your particular situation and your specific career goals. It is unlikely that you will find an example that exactly "matches" your life, experiences, education, and other qualifications. Rather, use the following examples to understand the similarities and the differences in baby-boomer resumes, paying special attention to the category of resume most relevant to you.

YOUNG BABY BOOMERS

WILLIAM R. GILESON
wrg3@earthlink.net

122 Lunar Moon Drive
Preston, CA 99090

Home 909-555-3872
Cell 909-555-2763

SENIOR SALES, MARKETING & BUSINESS DEVELOPMENT EXECUTIVE
Advanced Telecommunications & Technology Products, Services & Solutions

<u>Value</u>: Building direct/channel partner sales teams, capturing key accounts, and delivering double-digit revenue and profit growth in volatile technology markets.

Strategic Planning & New Business Development	VAR/Channel Network Development & Leadership
New Market Development & Positioning	Customer Acquisition & Relationship Management
Merger Integration & Team Assimilation	Strategic Partnering, Alliances & Opportunities
Sales Training, Motivation & Leadership	Sales Budgeting, Forecasting & Reporting
Public Speaking & Presentations	One-on-One & Team Communications

---

PROFESSIONAL EXPERIENCE

CRISP COMMUNICATIONS, San Francisco, CA   2000 to Present
Leading provider of communication technologies and solutions enabling enhanced services and network connectivity for diverse application and service providers. $550 million annual revenues.

Vice President—North and South Americas Sales (2005 to Present)
Director—U.S. Enterprise Sales (2003 to 2005)
Director—U.S. Channel Sales (2001 to 2003)
Director—Emerging Accounts (2000 to 2001)
Senior Executive—Strategic Accounts—General Motors, Pfizer, Nabisco (2000)

Recruited by CEO and promoted rapidly through a series of increasingly responsible sales leadership positions. Key driver of several critical business/market development initiatives that have successfully positioned the company in new markets and helped sustain its profitability during the economic downturn of the telecommunications industry.

As the most senior sales executive in the business unit, provide strategic direction, sales leadership, and partner alliance management for the U.S., Canada, and South America. Sell advanced communication solutions to enterprise accounts, network equipment providers, independent software vendors, and OEM application developers. Lead a team of 12 regional sales executives and 10 channel partners.

- **Delivered 23% year-over-year growth** for 2005 and **$60 million in revenue.** Produced **25% of worldwide revenue** in 2003 and 2004. Increased 2000–2001 **year-on-year revenue by 32%.** On track to deliver **$76 million** in 2006.

- Revitalized focus on "out-of-favor" enterprise market, established new business development strategy, won corporate approval, and delivered a **32% increase in revenues within first year** ($22 million in sales).

- Created first-ever channel partner sales network and **built revenues to $28 million annually.** Effectively integrated channel network with direct sales team to accelerate market/account penetration.

- Retained by Crisp in 2001 (after only 16 months of employment) following a 50% reduction in sales force (including two "tenured" sales directors).

William R. Gileson: Young baby boomer, moving forward in his career (written and designed by Wendy Enelow, CCM, MRW, JCTC, CPRW, of Enelow Enterprises, Inc.)

WILLIAM R. GILESON
wrg3@earthlink.net

COSGROVE CORPORATION, Fresno, CA   1998 to 2000
Innovative provider of specialized digital projection technology and multimedia presentation systems for enterprise, government, education, and home use. $205 million annual revenues. Acquired by #1 competitor, BroadBand, in 2000.

National Sales Manager

Recruited by Director of Distribution Sales to professionalize U.S./Canadian sales organization and strategic channel partner network. Challenged to create a totally integrated sales organization with a clear market focus and strong sales leadership. Managed a team of 12 sales executives and a network of 40 VAR partners.

- Delivered **$130 million in sales** in 1999, a **38% increase** in year-on-year revenue growth and **120% of quota.**

- Joined Cosgrove one month after its acquisition by Austrian competitor. Given full responsibility for merging two sales teams and creating new coverage model. **Captured $18 million in new sales** in first six months.

- Recruited Country Manager and transitioned Canada into a separate sales and P&L organization. Resulted in **43% revenue growth** within first year.

- Restructured existing VAR program, developed formal infrastructure and accountability, and designed tiered service levels and compensation systems.

GLOBAL, INC., Bayview, CA   1997 to 1998
Developer of high-speed digital transmission products for enterprise, carrier, and Internet customers.

Business Development Manager

Recruited by Director of Business Development for newly created position focusing on development of strategic partnerships, Fortune 500 accounts, and OEM opportunities. Leadership interface between regional sales managers, VAR partners, and key accounts. Created program that provided **$1 million in incremental revenue** in first year.

WORLDWIDE COMMUNICATION NETWORKS, San Diego, CA   1995 to 1997
Developer of communication networking software and LAN/WAN products for enterprise customers and ISPs.

Director—U.S. Sales (1997)
Eastern Region Sales Manager (1995 to 1997)

Rebuilt regional sales organization, structured VAR agreements with 12 new partners, and increased revenues 18% over previous year (123% of quota). Promoted to design and execute national sales strategy for direct enterprise accounts, VAR partners, and large system integrators. **Projected $12 million in sales within first year.**

Previous Professional Experience:

District Sales Manager, Cross Communications—Voice, Data, Fax, and LAN/WAN Solutions (1989 to 1995)
Led direct/partner enterprise sales team. Delivered 20% revenue growth (138% of quota). #1 sales producer.

Sales Representative, NCR Networking Solutions (1984 to 1989)
Sold to Fortune 1000 accounts throughout the Western U.S. Twice achieved President's Club.

EDUCATION: B.S., Business Administration, UCLA, 1983

William is typical of many job seekers in the young baby boomer category. He's had a successful career thus far and is now interested in making a job change into a position of greater responsibility, increased decision-making authority, and improved compensation. His resume is typical of the style, structure, and format used by many job seekers interested in moving their careers onward and upward.

William's resume begins with a very strong summary section that clearly communicates the strength of his experience as it relates to his chosen career field. The headline format and wording ("SENIOR SALES, MARKETING & BUSINESS DEVELOPMENT EXECUTIVE … Advanced Telecommunications & Technology Products, Services & Solutions") clearly identify "who" William is and "what" he wants. The headline is followed by a "value statement" that briefly communicates his most notable areas of success and achievement. Finally, that information is supported with a double-column bulleted listing of his core competencies as they relate to sales and marketing.

After reading the summary section, it is clear that William is very qualified for the types of positions he is seeking; namely, senior-level sales and marketing opportunities. In fact, this format is one of our favorites because it allows the reader to quickly identify "who" William is and the value he brings to a new organization.

William's resume then proceeds with a strong presentation of his professional employment experience. Note that each job description on his resume begins with the name of the company and a one- or two-line description. Job titles follow with a short paragraph or two summarizing the overall responsibilities of the position. Then follows a bulleted listing of William's most notable achievements, with specific numbers and percentages in bold print to draw attention to them. The paragraphs tell what he was responsible for, and the bullets demonstrate how well he did it.

Looking at William's current job description, you'll note that the job titles are stacked one on top of the other. Because his jobs were cumulative and responsibilities carried over from one assignment to the next, this is an excellent way to summarize the overall success of William's career without having to repeat the same type of information under each specific position.

As you move on to page two of this resume, you'll note that a similar format was used for all of William's previous positions. To demonstrate that he's been a "producer" his entire career, his oldest positions are very briefly summarized with the most emphasis on his top one or two achievements.

The resume then closes with his education, which is "adequate" but not exceptional for the types of positions he is seeking. However, that truly doesn't matter. This resume is a powerful presentation of someone with outstanding qualifications and a long record of success. What he accomplished 20+ years ago in college is, to a large degree, incidental. If you're a baby boomer who is concerned about your lack of "Ivy League" academic qualifications, a bachelor's or MBA degree, or another educational credential that you feel is essential, let it go! At this point in your career, it is much more likely that someone will hire you based on the strength of your performance rather than a degree from decades past.

If you're a young baby boomer moving forward in your career, give serious consideration to using a format similar to this one. It communicates power, success, and achievement.

CAREER-TRANSITION BABY BOOMERS

ALAN RIFBACHER

13, rue du Môle, 75006 Paris, France
Cell: +33(0)1.55.65.25.50, Home: +33(0)1.55.23.55.66, E-mail: alan.rifbacher@aviatic.fr

ON-AIR BROADCASTER

Community Radio Host presents interviews and stories that have intrigued, informed, and influenced America and Europe for 25 years.

Skilled at identifying the right story, doing the research, reaching the targets, and setting up the interviews. Top-notch interviewer: immediately earn trust and build relationships; guests provide great interviews. Possess informed perspective on topics of the day, including health care, public media, and war coverage garnered from 20 years of living in Europe. Languages: English (primary), French (excellent). Citizenship: United States / French.

"Alan is a genius at ferreting out an eclectic mix of music and discussion." —Mark Johnson, Editor

Captured interviews of high-profile celebrities, authors, scientists, and politicians, including:

- Senator John McCain
- Prof. James Adrian, Harvard University
- Alan Garner, Counsel, NYC Comptroller
- Will Shortz, Puzzle Editor, *NY Times*
- Joan Tedesco, NPR Host
- Jon Stewart, Comedian / Political Satirist
- Greg Murtha, Editor, *Time Magazine*
- Johnny Depp, Actor / Playwright

Interviewed subjects on a broad range of topics, including:

- International Politics
- Discoveries in Physics
- Swiss Banks / Holocaust Money Restitution
- Puzzles & Culture
- National & Local Politics
- Political Satire / History
- Family Life Abroad / Travel
- Blues / Zydeco

EXPERIENCE

Marais Alternative Radio (Radio MarRa), Paris, France
Host: Blues Zeppelin: program features Blues and Zydeco Music
All segments online at http://www.marra.ch.
REGULAR PRESENTER 1989–Present
Interviews include

- October 2004—Joan Tedesco, National Public Radio host: discussed the expanding radio network and the upcoming Presidential election.

- September 2004—Jon Stewart, comedian, actor / author / political satirist: discussed his book, *America (The Book)* a tongue-in-cheek discussion of democracy in the United States.

- June 2003—Greg Murtha, contributing editor to *Time Magazine* / author: discussed his book, *Tales of an Expatriate American*.

- June 2002—Will Shortz, Puzzle Editor, *New York Times*: discussed puzzles and culture, and the 2002 World Puzzle Championship in Croatia in October 2002.

- November 1999—Alan Garner, associate general counsel to NYC Comptroller Anthony Deshan; discussed plans of NYC to boycott Swiss banks, Credit Suisse, UBS, re Holocaust money restitution.

National Public Radio, New York, NY
Segment for "What Can I Say?" with Arnold Shaw 2004
PRODUCER / INTERVIEWER

- September 19th: Senator John McCain, interviewed at Overseas Americans Registration in Paris, France: discussed the U.S. national election.

Radio Free America, Paris, France
Created proposal for a weekly show targeted at English-speaking expatriate community. 2002

Continued

Alan Rifbacher: Career-Transition Baby Boomer, from physicist to on-air broadcaster (Written and designed by Diana Holdsworth, CPRW, Action Communications Resumes)

ALAN RIFBACHER   Cell: +33(0)1.55.65.25.50

French National Radio (FRE 3), Paris, France
CORRESPONDENT   1996
- Correspondent at the New Orleans Jazz and Heritage Festival.

Radio Pays de Lyon, Lyon, France
Weekly English-speaking rock-and-roll show
PRESENTER   1984
- October 1984: Physics Professor James Adrian of Harvard University and Professor David Smith of the University of Michigan: discussed discovery that led to a Nobel Prize for Physics.

Radio Free Ann Arbor, **WCBN, "Free Your Mind,"** Ann Arbor, MI
Non-commercial, FM community radio station
CO-FOUNDER, PRESENTER   1980–1981
- Built and ran operation with core group from the University community.

PERSONAL TECHNICAL EQUIPMENT

Home Office Production Studio:	Digital Audio Editing Software
Remote Interviews:	Recorders / Microphones / Cables

CORPORATE BUSINESS EXPERIENCE

Live and Work in France   1988–Present
- Held executive-level positions for companies including Honeywell, ABB, and Johnson Controls.
- Work has included development and realization of software applications in a variety of domains: Logistics, Finance, Energy, and Telecommunications.

Science Magazine, Time, Inc., New York, NY
SCIENCE REPORTER   1984
- Researched / reported stories with emphasis on physics and technology for national science monthly.

European Foundation for Particle Physics, Paris, France
RESEARCHER, HIGH-ENERGY PHYSICS   1983–1989
- Connected with various experiments, including the collaboration responsible for discoveries that led to the Nobel Prize in Physics being awarded to two Foundation scientists in October 1984.

MEMBERSHIPS / ACTIVITIES

KPRW Radio, Santa Barbara, CA, Archangel [financial] Supporter	2004
Participant, American Crossword Puzzle Tournament	2001–2002
Captain, French team, World Puzzle Championships	2002, 2003
Annual [financial] Contributor, Mr. Holland's Opus Foundation	1997–2001
Board Member, French Folk Society	1990–2000
Master of Ceremonies, Paris Blues Festival Jam Sessions, Paris, France	2000

EDUCATION

MS—Physics, University of Michigan, Ann Arbor, MI	1985
BA—Physics, University of Michigan, Ann Arbor, MI	1982

Alan had a long and very successful career as a physicist working in the U.S. and Europe. Now, however, he was ready to leave his professional career behind to pursue his lifelong avocation of broadcasting. As we review this resume, it is important to note that *all* of Alan's broadcasting experience was unpaid. However, that does not make it any less important than his paid work history. In fact, in this situation where his goal is to transfer into the broadcasting industry, the strength of his volunteer experience is what qualifies him to make a successful career transition.

Alan's resume begins with a headline—"ON-AIR BROADCASTER"—to clearly identify "who" he is and what his objective is. That line is followed by a short summary of his overall experience and capabilities; namely, that he has "intrigued, informed, and influenced America and Europe for 25 years." A summary paragraph is included to highlight the depth of his experience, and the one-line testimonial from one of Alan's editors adds a nice touch to the resume.

The next two sections in the summary are critical. First is a double-column bulleted listing of some of the notable people he has interviewed. Second is a summary of the diversity of topics he has covered. By the time you have read the entire summary, you're certain that Alan is a well-qualified broadcaster.

Then, to substantiate what's written in the summary, a detailed listing of Alan's broadcast experience follows. This includes specific stations, shows, interviews, segments, and more. In fact, he has so much broadcast experience that it carries over to page 2 of the resume. Knowing how important technology has become to the industry, the next section of this resume briefly summarizes Alan's specific technical skills—a great addition!

The Corporate Business Experience section then, in less than half of a page, summarizes and tones down Alan's professional career as a physicist, science reporter, and researcher. The resume then returns to a focus on his memberships and activities as they relate to his current career transition goal. The resume ends with education, brief and to the point.

The writer of this resume did an outstanding job transitioning the perception of "who" Alan is. When we read this resume, we "see" a broadcaster, not a physicist; and, bottom line, that's the entire goal of a career-transition resume.

RETURN-TO-WORK BABY BOOMERS

MICHELLE PRESTON-SMITH
701 School Street • Saratoga Springs, NY 12866
518/555-4444 • preston-smith@myemail.com

Marketing/Public Relations/Business Professional with diverse background and proven ability to lead, manage, and achieve success with creativity and enthusiasm. Strengths span organization, planing, interpersonal skills, and communication. An insightful and dedicated individual and team member.

PROFILE

Marketing & Public Relations
- Created first marketing department and first ad campaign for manufacturing firm.
- Interviewed and selected outside advertising agency; collaborated on numerous projects.
- Performed marketing research; created and managed marketing databases.
- Authored press releases.
- Developed trade show exhibit.
- Developed, expanded, and promoted youth sports programs for two organizations.
- Created and implemented successful fund-raising initiatives.
- Created visual displays for retail sales.
- Designed and implemented sales promotions.

General Management
- Oversaw departments and stores with as many as 100 staff and $2M in sales.
- Hired, trained, and scheduled staff; handled discipline and performance review issues.
- Created, implemented, and managed budgets.
- Performed inventory control as well as purchasing/buying.
- Managed payroll for a $1M firm.

Industry background
- High-end, high-volume retail
- Education
- Electronics
- Manufacturing
- Non-profit and community organizations

ACCOMPLISHMENTS: MARKETING/PR/MANAGEMENT

Marketing Manager: Constellation Electronics, Inc. — New Haven, CT   4 years
- Promoted by owner of this $1M electronics manufacturer from Administrative Assistant.
- Worked closely with owner to select an outside advertising agency.
- Developed, managed, and performed all aspects an of in-house marketing program.
- Collaborated with ad agency in creation of print ad campaign and trade-show exhibit.
- Interfaced with the Sales department on lead generation and customer follow-up.

Michelle Preston-Smith: Return-To-Work Baby Boomer, from stay-at-home mom to marketing and public relations professional (written and designed by Salome A. Farraro, CPRW, Careers TOO)

Assistant Manager: Ann Taylor—Washington, DC   2 years
- Accountable for all facets of operation at this high-end women's clothing store, with $2M sales volume and as many as 20 employees.

Department Manager: JCPenney, Inc.—Albany, NY   3 years
- After completing management training program, appointed Assistant Buyer for the Jewelry Department for the 15 stores in central and eastern New York State.
- After six months, promoted to Manager of the accessories department in the downtown Albany store; first Department Manager in this store and under constant scrutiny of upper management with offices in the same building.
- Grew sales in accessories to $1M, third highest volume in the chain, managing 100+ employees during Christmas season.
- Promoted to manage $2M furniture department suffering reduced sales and low morale. Achieved/surpassed all turnaround objectives.
- Invigorated the sales staff by promoting and modeling a team approach, achieving increased and sustained sales that saw department move from 10th to 2nd in the chain.

ACCOMPLISHMENTS: NON-PROFIT/COMMUNITY/EDUCATION

Board Member/Secretary: Saratoga Springs Varsity Hockey Team—
Saratoga Springs, NY   Current
- Use creativity to identify and implement fund-raising events, including a skills clinic featuring two NHL players. Achieved notable financial success.

Aide: Saratoga Springs Central School District—Saratoga Springs, NY   Current
- Held several positions in the primary school, including kindergarten aide for three classrooms and 1:1 aide for a child with Cerebral Palsy; currently a substitute aide and volunteer.
- As 1:1 aide, assisted a severely disabled child in all curricula; managed ongoing communications among parents, teachers, and therapists; and coordinated all aspects of service delivery to allow student to achieve a wide range of goals.

Vice President/President: Varsity Girls Lacrosse Booster Club—Saratoga Springs, NY   5 years
- Created and developed program that generated opportunities for girls at all skill levels.
- Grew membership from 60 to 200+.
- Implemented and expanded fund-raiser that saw 1000% growth from first to fourth year.
- Led the organization through difficult transition due to death of its founding president.

EDUCATION

Bachelor of Science: Siena College—Albany, NY; major: Studio Art

PERSONAL PROFILE

Physically active: run, walk, swim, hike, ski, skate; climbed 14,000' mountain with family.
Enjoy cultural activities: cooking, art, painting, fine crafts, and travel across North America.

Michelle was a stay-at-home mom for 16 years. Although she put her career on hold to raise her family, she did *not* put her skills on hold. Rather, she put them to work in her community through participation in numerous organizations and activities. Although she might not have been thinking specifically about it at the time, the fact that she's kept her skills fresh is very important to her new career success.

Michelle's resume begins with a short three-line summary of "who" she is that combines both personal and professional attributes. The bulk of page 1 of this resume focuses on Michelle's core skills in marketing, public relations, and management. This format was chosen to summarize and showcase the strength of her qualifications and experience—from both her previous paid professional experience and her extensive volunteer work. At first glance, page 1 communicates the message of an individual with a good, strong set of skills in her target functional areas in a diversity of industries. This format is ideal for a return-to-work job seeker who wants to draw together diverse experiences into a cohesive presentation.

In an effort to draw further attention to her core skills, instead of titling the next section simply "PROFESSIONAL EXPERIENCE," a more descriptive headline has been used: "ACCOMPLISHMENTS: MARKETING / PR / MANAGEMENT," rather than "PROFESSIONAL EXPERIENCE." This is a professional writer's trick to further entrench within the reader's mind the fact that this candidate has a specific set of skills.

Note that Michelle's job descriptions are brief, focusing on what she has titled that section—her accomplishments. Also, pay special attention to how her jobs and her volunteer activities are "dated." Instead of using actual dates (which would immediately communicate the fact that she hasn't worked since 1990), she has used the number of years instead. The reality is that she's not fooling anyone; most people would assume she is currently unemployed. However, it also doesn't communicate the potentially negative message of "I've been unemployed for more than 16 years."

Note that a similar structure and format was used on page 2 to present the next section, "ACCOMPLISHMENTS: NON-PROFIT / COMMUNITY / EDUCATION." Again, job descriptions were used to highlight notable achievements and contributions.

The last two categories—Education and Personal Profile—finish off the resume on a very positive note. The writer of this resume has done an excellent job positioning Michelle as a well-qualified and well-rounded professional with a strong set of highly relevant and employable skills and experiences.

Step-by-Step: Writing the Perfect Resume

The remainder of this chapter might be the most important information in this entire book. What follows is a detailed discussion of each of the various sections that you might include in your resume, who should use each section, what each section should include, and where to include it. We'll explore the most common sections (for example, Career Summary, Professional Experience, Education, Professional Affiliations, Technology Skills, and Honors and Awards) along with some less common sections that might be the foundation for many baby boomers reading this book (for example, Volunteer Experience, Training Experience, Personal Profile, Publications, and Athletics).

CONTACT INFORMATION

Before we get into the major sections of the resume, let's briefly address the very top section: your name and contact information.

Name

You'd think writing your name would be the easiest part of writing your resume! But there are several factors to consider:

- Although most people choose to use their full, formal name at the top of a resume, it has become increasingly more acceptable to use the name by which you prefer to be called.

- Bear in mind that it's to your advantage when readers feel comfortable calling you for an interview. Their comfort level may decrease if your name is gender-neutral, difficult to pronounce, or very unusual; they don't know whether they're calling a man or a woman or how to ask for you. You can make it easier for them by following these examples:

Lynn T. Cowles (Mr.)

(Ms.) Michael Murray

Tzirina (Irene) Kahn

Ndege "Nick" Vernon

Address

You should always include your home address on your resume. If you use a post-office box for mail, include both your mailing address and your physical residence address if possible.

An exception to this guideline is when you are posting your resume on the Internet. For security purposes, it is a good idea to include just your phone and e-mail contact. You might choose to include your city and state (if you're looking for another position in the same geographic area); however, we recommend that you do not include your street address.

Telephone Number(s)

Your home telephone number must be included so that people can pick up the phone and call you immediately. In addition, you can also include a mobile phone number or a pager number (however, this is less desirable because you must call back to speak to the person who called you). You can include a private home fax number, if it can be accessed automatically.

E-mail Address

Without question, if you have an e-mail address, include it on your resume. E-mail is now often the preferred method of communication in job search, particularly in the early stages of each contact. If you do not have an e-mail account, you can obtain a free, accessible-anywhere address from a provider such as www.yahoo.com, www.hotmail.com, or www.netzero.com.

> **WARNING:** The e-mail address on your resume should always be a private, personal address, not your employer's. Using your work e-mail address gives the impression that you think it's acceptable to use the employer's resources as if they were your own—not a desirable trait in an employee.

As you look through the samples in this book, you'll see how resume writers have arranged the many bits of contact information at the top of each resume. You can use these as models for presenting your own information. The point is to make it as easy as possible for employers to contact you!

Page Two

We strongly recommend that you include your name, phone number, and e-mail address at the top of the second page of your resume and any additional pages. If, by chance, the pages get separated, you want to be sure that people can still contact you, even if they have only page two of your resume.

Now, let's get into the substance of the core content sections of your resume.

CAREER SUMMARY

The Career Summary is the section at the top of your resume that summarizes and highlights your skills, knowledge, and expertise as they relate to your current career objectives. This is a particularly important section because it "sets the tone" for your entire resume.

You might be thinking, "But shouldn't my resume start with an Objective?" Although many job seekers still use Objective statements, we believe that a Career Summary is a much more powerful introduction. The problem with Objectives is that they are either too specific (limiting you to an "Electrical Engineering position") or too vague (doesn't everyone want "a challenging opportunity with a progressive organization offering the opportunity for growth and advancement"?). In addition, Objective statements can be read as self-serving because they describe what *you* want instead of suggesting what you have to offer an employer.

In contrast, an effective Career Summary allows you to position yourself as you want to be perceived. A Career Summary allows you to immediately "paint a picture" of yourself that directly supports your current career objective, whether it be to continue in your existing career (young baby boomers), totally change directions or decelerate your career (career-transition baby boomers), or re-launch your career (return-to-work baby boomers).

It is critical that this section focus on your specific skills, qualifications, and achievements that are related to your current objectives. Your summary is *not* a historical overview of your career. Rather, it is a concise, well-written, and sharp presentation of information designed to *sell* you into your next position.

This section can have various titles, such as the following:

Career Summary	Management Profile
Career Achievements	Professional Qualifications
Career Highlights	Professional Summary
Career Synopsis	Profile
Skill Summary	Summary
Executive Profile	Summary of Achievement
Highlights of Experience	Summary of Qualifications

Or, as you will see in the Headline Format example shown later, your summary does not have to have any title at all.

Why Your Career Summary Is So Important

The Career Summary section of the resume can be the single most important section because of its content: the skills, qualifications, achievements, technical competencies, and other distinguishing characteristics that you offer that are in line with your current career objectives. Your goal is to capture your reader's attention and immediately communicate the value you bring to their organization. If you are able to do this—bring your relevant skills to the forefront—you will have favorably positioned yourself before a prospective employer; whether or not you have direct experience in your new career field becomes much less significant.

A Career Summary is a great thing because it allows you to include skills and competencies that you've acquired through volunteer work, training, internships, sabbaticals, association memberships, and other activities. The skills you include in your Summary *do not* have to be a direct result of paid work experience. This is wonderful news for boomers considering a career change! Remember, a summary is just that—a summary of the things that you do best, and it doesn't matter where you learned to do them.

The Career Summary is often the focal point of your resume. Be sure to package and sell all of your qualifications as they relate to your current career goals. Don't be concerned if your Career Summary is longer than normal. This section is the foundation for your entire resume, so be thorough and sell yourself into your next job.

Sample Career Summary Sections

Here are five sample Career Summaries, each followed by a specific recommendation for how each category of baby boomer might be able to use that particular format. Consider using one of these as the template for developing your Career Summary, or use them as the foundation to create your own presentation. You will also find some type of Career Summary in just about every resume included in chapters 4 through 6. Closely review them as well to find a format and style that's in line with your specific needs and career objectives.

Headline Format

MANUFACTURING INDUSTRY EXECUTIVE

Vice President / Executive Vice President / General Manager
Networking & Telecommunications Technologies & Solutions
Start-Up Ventures, Turnarounds & High-Growth Companies

- **Young baby boomers:** This is an excellent format for any boomer seeking to advance his or her current career. It is clear and concise and readily identifies "who" this job seeker is. Using just four lines of text, this boomer communicated (1) industry expertise; (2) level of position; (3) product expertise; and (4) diversity of company experiences.

- **Career-transition baby boomers:** This format can sometimes be used effectively by boomers seeking to transition their careers. However, it works only if you have powerful enough information to include in your headline that will allow you to communicate—very succinctly—the "new you."

- **Return-to-work baby boomers:** Just as with young baby boomers, this format can be particularly effective for individuals who are returning to work and planning to continue on in their previous career track. As you note in the sample, there is no mention of when these skills were acquired; it simply says that you possess them.

Paragraph Format

CAREER SUMMARY

CUSTOMER SERVICE PROFESSIONAL with 15+ years of experience delivering consistently high-quality services to key customer accounts nationwide. Outstanding skills in customer acquisition, customer service management, research and problem solving, customer relationship management, and customer retention. Competent communicator with strong interpersonal relations skills. Dedicated, conscientious, and always available to respond to customer needs.

- **Young baby boomers:** Considered to be a traditional format for your Career Summary, this presentation can be quite effective for any boomer seeking to advance within an established career field. As you'll note, the summary identifies "who" the job seeker is and then follows with a brief, yet comprehensive summary of all the core skills required for a successful customer service career.

- **Career-transition baby boomers:** For boomers in transition, this format allows you to move to the forefront of your resume the skills, experiences, and competencies that are most in line with your current objectives. Instantly, you've shaped the reader's perception as to "who" you are with the focus being on the "new you" and not necessarily your past career performance.

- **Return-to-work baby boomers:** For individuals returning to work after an extended absence, this format allows you to state, "This is who I am," with no mention of the fact that the experience was from many years past. However, use this format only if your goal is to return to a position similar to what you did years ago. If you're changing careers at this point, pay attention to the preceding bullet.

Core Competencies Summary Format

PROFESSIONAL QUALIFICATIONS SUMMARY
BUSINESS MANAGER
Manufacturing / Retail / Food Service

- Marketing & Business Development
- Human Resources Leadership
- Staff Training & Development
- Customer Relationship Management
- Contract Negotiations & Administration

- Budgeting & Cost Control
- Profit & Loss Management
- Policy & Procedure Development
- Product Control & Allocation
- Purchasing & Vendor Sourcing

- **Young baby boomers:** This format accomplishes two important things: (1) the headline clearly identifies "who" you are; and (2) the bulleted listing gives a quick overview of your specific skills and competencies. This is a great format for individuals looking to move their careers ahead.

- **Career-transition baby boomers:** This format can be effective for boomers in transition, regardless of whether you use the headline plus bullets or just the bullets. Again, this format allows you quickly to draw visual attention to the skills and talents you want to showcase in support of your new career objectives.

- **Return-to-work baby boomers:** Just as with young baby boomers, this format can work exceptionally well in identifying "who" you are and the value you bring to an organization. In essence, you're separating the strength of your skills from the fact that your work experience might have been years and years ago.

Bullet Format

CAREER HIGHLIGHTS

Sales & Business Development

➢ More than 10 years of successful experience in outside sales to businesses. Cold-called, prospected, and developed leads while expanding business with established accounts.

➢ Cultivated strategic relationships and maximized sales volume by identifying and seizing market opportunities and aggressively pursuing new business.

➢ Employed an entrepreneurial, customer-focused approach to build sales while ensuring customer retention by providing superior service.

Project Management & Event Planning

➢ Organized annual conventions to educate the public on how to start and operate block clubs in community neighborhoods. Secured locations, speakers, booths, and refreshments. Wrote educational materials and coordinated printing of literature. Managed publicity, convention operations, and post-convention follow-up.

➢ Played a key role in renovating and updating St. John School's library. Researched other libraries to generate ideas. Coordinated renovation plans, participated in fund-raising activities, and helped organize and execute the moving of books and fixtures.

➢ Volunteered in local and state-level political campaigns for candidates and issues. Helped organize and publicize fund-raisers, delivered literature door-to-door and at community events, made calls to arrange sign locations, wrote letters, and obtained signatures. Assisted with developing television, radio, and print ads. Worked the polls and answered voters' questions.

➢ Collaborated in organizing special events for St. John School. **Delivered record revenues and profits** through a combination of effective leadership, careful control of expenses, and successful advertising/publicity (obtained radio, TV, and newspaper coverage—all at no cost).

Communications

➢ Chaired Future Funding Committee, charged with soliciting major gifts ($10,000+) for St. John Church. Made presentations to individuals and corporate officers. Surpassed revenue goals by 23%.

➢ Maintained order in high school classrooms as a substitute teacher.

➢ Developed and taught creative-writing workshops.

➢ Published author of articles on topics ranging from travel and entertainment to issues and events of local interest. Writing samples furnished upon request.

- **Young baby boomers:** This format can be effective if you're attempting to highlight discrete yet related job functions, core competencies, and achievements from your past that are most relevant to your current career goals. We generally prefer a Career Summary that is shorter and more focused, but this can be effective if you're looking at several different types of positions while continuing to move your career forward.

- **Career-transition baby boomers:** This is one of our preferred formats for boomers in transition because it does allow you to highlight different areas of expertise. In turn, the resume then positions you for different types of opportunities with different types of organizations. This format puts a very heavy emphasis on skills and accomplishments while downplaying specific work experience; this can often be the best strategy for boomers in transition.

- **Return-to-work baby boomers:** Again, this is one of our recommended formats for individuals returning to the workforce because of its emphasis on skills and competencies and not on prior work experience. To use this format, however, you must have specific valuable information that you can include within each subsection of your Career Summary.

Project Format

PROFESSIONAL QUALIFICATIONS:

Programmer / Technologist with 15+ years of experience working with leading-edge technologies, including C/C++, Java (JDK 5.0), Visual Basic 2005, Oracle (SQL, SQL*Plus, PL/SQL), DataEase, Windows 2003, and UNIX. Major projects have included

- **Point-of-Sale (POS) System** for The Tech Corner, Inc. Created a normalized relational database (using DataEase on a Windows 2003 network) to provide complete invoicing, billing, accounts receivable, and accounts payable management for a $2 million company with 200 active accounts.

- **Client-Service Sales Module in Java** for Sounds Systems LLC. Using TCP/IP sockets, connected GUI front end to console application, allowing users to query server for price, availability, and credit status.

- **Sales Module in Visual Basic** for class project. Created GUI front end to Access database, allowing input of customer information, parts numbers, and quantities and automatically generating orders, invoices, and sales summaries.

- **Billing System in Oracle** for class project. Generated users, tables, views, sequences, and triggers using SQL, SQL*Plus, and PL/SQL to create Oracle database. Imported data and used Developer 2000 to create forms.

- **Young baby boomers:** If your career has focused on projects and if you're interested in continuing to pursue those types of opportunities, this is a recommended format. It allows you to showcase your most notable projects and achievements. If, however, you do not work on a project basis, this format is not appropriate for you.

- **Career-transition baby boomers:** If you're interested in transitioning into a career track that takes advantage of your past volunteer experience, community projects, educational research activities, and the like, this is an excellent format to present that information. Otherwise, consider using an alternative format for your Career Summary.

- **Return-to-work baby boomers:** This format works exceptionally well for individuals who want to highlight specific projects from their past work and/or volunteer experience. Again, the applicability of this format is limited to individuals who have worked on a project-by-project basis. If that's not you, consider an alternative format.

PROFESSIONAL EXPERIENCE

As a baby-boomer job seeker, how much information you include in your Professional Experience section depends entirely on how relevant that experience is to your current career objectives. If it's relevant (or if just parts of it are relevant), you'll want to be sure to highlight that information—in detail—on your resume. If it's irrelevant, you'll want to be very brief with your job descriptions, if you include them at all. As discussed previously, functional resumes are often the best strategy for baby boomers who are seeking to make a significant career transition. Read further and you'll understand.

The Most Time-Consuming Section to Write

Writing your Professional Experience section may perhaps take you the longest of any section of your resume. Suppose, for example, that you had the same position for 10 years. How can you consolidate all that you have done into one short section? If, on the opposite end of the spectrum, you've had several short-term jobs over the past several years, how can you make your experience seem substantial, noteworthy, and relevant? And, for all of you whose experience is in between, what do you include, how, where, and why?

These are not easy questions to answer. In fact, the most truthful response to each question is, "it depends." It depends on you, your experience, your achievements and successes, your current career objectives, and how closely your past experience ties into and supports those objectives.

Sample Professional Experience Sections

Here are five samples of Professional Experience sections. Review how each individual's unique background is organized and emphasized, and consider your own background when using one of these as the template or foundation for developing your Professional Experience section. Then be sure to review all the resume samples in this book to get even more ideas.

Achievement Format

Education Services Manager   2002 to Present
Simtech Corporation, Chicago, IL

Repositioned, upgraded, and transformed Education Services department from an underperforming training function to a profit-generating global organization. P&L management accountability for 12 global Customer Education Centers, team of 17 instructors, curriculum design, facilities management/leasing negotiations, and budget growth to $4M. Notable achievements:

- Introduced and educated team on concepts of adult learning theory to better serve students. Turned around team morale from a low of 2 to an average high of 4 as indicated by survey results.

- Determined core product offering, set revenue mix and gross profit margin, and developed knowledge-transfer process in collaboration with Product Management and Customer Support departments.

- Established a consistent learning environment for all students globally that eliminated revenue delays and led unit's revenue growth from $4M to $10M in billable customer education during 12-month tenure.

- Implemented ASP model for online registration and payment. Produced $600K in additional revenue in first 3 months; achieved double annual quota in first 6 months; doubled revenues in 6 months.

- Succeeded in creating additional revenue stream with multimillion-dollar potential where previous team failed after acquiring $250K of software that could not be implemented.

- Created multi-level certification programs with validation protocol for customers, partners, and employees using ASP model for less than $50K. The certification program revenue potential is millions of dollars annually.

- Took charge of and delivered new education class for applications product line in just 3 months despite failure of consulting team to produce program after 9 months of effort.

- **Young baby boomers:** The Achievement format is one of our favorites, particularly for young baby boomers who are seeking opportunities to move forward in their careers. With this format, you are communicating to your reader, "This is what I was responsible for and this is how well I did it." It's quick and easy to read and understand; achievements pop out; and a strong message of "I can deliver value" is readily apparent. If this format works for you, we would strongly urge you to consider it.

- **Career-transition baby boomers:** Although this is not generally the preferred format for boomers in transition, it can work well to highlight achievements and notable responsibilities from your "other" experience that is in line with your current objectives. Consider this format to strengthen the presentation of your professional affiliations, volunteer projects, and other activities as may be pertinent to your goals.

- **Return-to-work baby boomers:** Just as with young baby boomers, this format can be extremely effective in communicating your ability to produce and deliver results. If you choose to use this format, it might be to your advantage not to include dates of employment. If you're returning to work, your best strategy is to sell your success without drawing attention to the fact that you've been out of the workforce for an extended period of time.

Challenge, Action, and Results (CAR) Format

DIRECTOR OF SALES—NORTHEAST REGION   2003–Present
NETDOMINANT, Philadelphia, PA

Challenge: Re-energize the strategically critical Northeast territory, re-ignite sales, strengthen market position, and eliminate market barriers.

Action: Restructured the entire sales organization, redefined optimum market position, created new market-entry strategies, facilitated new product development, and built /stabilized a high-powered team. Restructured existing staff and hired/mentored 4 sales representatives, one of whom closed the two largest deals in the company's history.

Results:

Sales Team Performance	2005	2006
Sales Revenue	$21.23M	$28.77M
Quota Attainment	140%	130%
Profitability	#1 out of 7 Regions	#1 out of 7 regions
Proclub Attainment	Highest % in North America	Highest % in North America
Forecast Accuracy	#1	#1

- **Young baby boomers:** If you have strong numbers, percentages, and statistics to share, this is a great format for you. This example combines the CAR structure, which is always effective, with an easy-to-review table highlighting notable financial and performance results. By demonstrating that you were able to meet challenges and deliver results, you place yourself in an elite category of job seekers who really have made things happen.

- **Career-transition baby boomers:** The CAR format works well for boomers in transition only if you can use your job descriptions to highlight challenges (or opportunities), action (skills), and achievements that support your current objectives.

- **Return-to-work baby boomers:** If your past experience, regardless of how long ago it was, fits comfortably into this format, we strongly recommend you use it. The obstacle you're faced with—returning to the workforce—will be substantially minimized if you can immediately communicate results and success in your past career.

Functional Format

CHASE, Portland, OR   2002 to 2006

Vice President/Branch Sales Manager charged with managing $70M branch with 10 employees. Consistently ranked in top 10% in multiple sales categories.

Business Development

- Top producer in region for referrals with twice as many referrals as branch in #2 spot.

- Ranked #1 in investment and multiple service household growth out of 25 branches.

- One of top three producers for check-card usage, with increase from 59% to 67%.

- Accelerated consumer lending volume 400% during tenure.

- Bolstered online banking usage from 31% to 47%.

- Grew non-interest income categories by 38.5%.

Process Improvement

- Designed and launched company's first automated branch sales tracking system that was implemented nationally in 342 branches. Standardized methods for tracking sales, referrals, and account activity; rewarded successful sales; and identified growth opportunities.

- Spearheaded and facilitated 30-hour consumer loan program training for branch that was expanded to 25 locations.

Relationship Management

- Boosted customer service scores by 15 points and maintained service ratings of 95% or higher over six quarters.

- Received consistent 100% client servicing scores in 2005.

Staff Development

- Mentored new assistant manager, now a top producer.

- Recruited and trained five tellers and customer service representatives with virtually no turnover.

- Created and led weekly customer service role-plays for staff focusing on specific area of relationship management.

- Organized morning and afternoon "huddles" to discuss daily focus and accomplishments.

Company Awards

- Recognized with *Score Award* for referrals to various business lines.

- Received first-place award for multiple service household growth and service excellence.

- Presented with *Community Service Award* for various community activities, including teaching economics-based curriculum to K–7 graders with Junior Achievement.

- **Young baby boomers:** The strength of this format is that it allows you to showcase a combination of skills and competencies across different business disciplines; it also arranges relevant information in easy-to-scan groupings to make your resume more readable. Be forewarned, however, that if there are too many functional headings, or headings are unrelated, this format might leave your reader wondering, "Who is this candidate and what does he/she want to do?" As such, it might not be the best approach for young baby boomers moving onward and upward in their careers.

- **Career-transition baby boomers:** For baby boomers in career transition, this can be an extremely effective format because it allows you to highlight several key areas of knowledge without pigeonholing yourself into one particular field. If you're one of the tens of thousands of boomers in transition, strongly consider using this format to position yourself for a broad range of opportunities.

- **Return-to-work baby boomers:** This format is recommended for only the return-to-work boomers who are uncertain as to their specific career direction. The plus is that it allows you to show your strengths in several related disciplines; the negative is that it does not communicate that you're an expert in any one particular field.

Project Highlights Format

Director of Research & Development (Software)   1998 to 2005

AUDITECH, USA, Des Plaines, MN

Specialists in enterprise and desktop software development for financial auditors and tax consultants.

Assumed control of major project to develop a standardized format and application for the German government that would allow publicly listed companies to transfer mandatory financial data electronically. Delivered the project on time and on budget—from concept and quality control through training, documentation, key deliverables, end-user testing, defect tracking, and customization for local and international markets. Project highlights:

Project: TTR Banking Solutions. Three-tier enterprise solution, tracking financial details of publicly traded corporations.

- Led 4-person development team to create software. Written in C++, exploited DCOM to communicate with middle-layer components connecting to MS SQL Server or Oracle.

Project: Countermarks. Internet-available, benchmark data warehouse and successor to TTR Banking Solutions.

- Java-based development. Used Oracle TopLink, STRUTS for the architecture, and Oracle 9i for the back end. Managed 10 internal and external software developers, and personally conducted extensive software development research for the production of solution prototypes.

Project: Data Warehouse: 2.2 Terabyte, MS SQL Server, Oracle 8i. Distributed data warehouse excelled in reporting payroll information and real-time sales results from thousands of call-center employees.

- Managed, optimized, developed, and upgraded $U.S. 2+ million distributed data warehouse—traveling to 20 call centers to upgrade systems and monitor operations.

Project: Visual Basic client/server program, handling project requirements. SQL Server 6.5 backend database.

- Implemented the consultant-produced design and plan, and later managed the entire project—transitioning to become the sole project developer.

- **Young baby boomers:** This format works only for individuals who work on a project-by-project basis. If you fall into this category, give serious consideration to this format. If you do not fall into this category, select another, more appropriate format to showcase your skills and performance.

- **Career-transition baby boomers:** For boomers in transition who want to highlight their professional affiliations, civic affiliations, volunteer activities, or other non–work-related efforts, this can be an excellent format. Most advantageous is the fact that it allows you to highlight specific projects, activities, and achievements associated with those roles and clearly communicate to your reader that you have the "right stuff" for the positions you are applying for.

- **Return-to-work baby boomers:** If you're returning to work, want to continue in your past career field, and worked on a project-by-project basis, strongly consider this format (although you might exclude dates). Conversely, if you're returning to work and seeking new career opportunities that will leverage the skills you've developed through volunteerism, parenting, home health care, and more, again, this format can be very effective.

Experience Summary Format

District Manager, National Bank, Hamlet, Washington

- Supervised operations of 9–23 branches and up to 900 people—continually negotiated goals and mediated personnel issues. Consistently ranked within top 5 districts of the state for outstanding overall performance.

VP / Regional Operations Manager, Community Bank, Eastern Washington

- Established an audit program in the branches that helped all branches receive high levels of audits from independent and in-house auditors.

CFO, Rivers Bank, Tri-Cities, Washington

- Developed and implemented operational policies and procedures subsequently adopted by other banks.

Administrative Assistant, West Henderson Bank, Joliet, Illinois

- Assisted with launch of new bank—profitable the first year.

- **Young baby boomers:** Generally, unless yours is a particularly unusual circumstance, this is not our recommended format for individuals seeking to move forward in their careers. This format is very brief and does not give a great deal of information (other than the basics of your work history). If your goal is to advance your career, consider one of the other formats presented in this section.

- **Career-transition baby boomers:** If you're a career-transition boomer whose resume is going to focus on non–work-related activities that support your current career objectives, this format can be quite effective for a brief listing of your paid, professional experience. It's succinct and does not take up much space, yet it gives all of the factual information that a prospective employer will expect, along with a handful of your most notable achievements. Whether or not you choose to include dates depends entirely on your age and your current goals. See "Include Dates or Not?" later in this chapter for more about when to use dates and when to omit them.

- **Return-to-work baby boomers:** We often use this format when working with boomers seeking to re-enter the workforce. As you'll note, no dates are included, thus eliminating the potential for someone to look at your resume and immediately exclude you from consideration because of the length of time you've been unemployed. On the other hand, it does give a comprehensive, yet brief, listing of your work experience and notable achievements. Consider this format if you think it will work best for you.

EDUCATION, CREDENTIALS, AND CERTIFICATIONS

Your Education section should include college, certifications, credentials, licenses, registrations, and continuing education. It might also include high school diploma if that is the highest level of education you've completed.

For most baby boomers reading this book, it's likely that you earned your degree(s) or diploma quite a while ago. As such, be sure to position this information near the end of your resume because it's not your #1 selling point. Conversely, if you're in career change and you've just completed a degree, specialized training, or another educational program that supports your current objective, be sure to prominently display that information immediately after your Career Summary.

Here are five sample Education sections that illustrate a variety of ways to organize and format this information. These formats are applicable to all baby-boomer job seekers, regardless of which category you fall into.

Academic Credentials Format

EDUCATION

M.S., Information Technology, University of Minnesota, 1978

B.S., Computer Programming, University of Toledo, 1976

Microsoft Certified Systems Engineer (MCSE), 1997

Highlights of Continuing Professional Education:

- Networking Technologies on the Horizon, Information Technology Executives, 2005
- Optimizing IT Solutions, Harvard University, 2005
- Y2K Program Management, Institute for Technology Advancement, 1998

Executive Education Format

EDUCATION

Executive Leadership Program	NORTHEASTERN UNIVERSITY
Executive Development Program	HARVARD UNIVERSITY
Master of Business Administration (MBA) Degree	UNIVERSITY OF PENNSYLVANIA/ WHARTON
Bachelor of Science Degree	UNIVERSITY OF DELAWARE

Certifications Format

TECHNICAL CERTIFICATIONS & DEGREES:

Registered Phlebotomist, State of Arizona, 2005

Certified Nursing Assistant, University of Arizona, 1982

Certified Nursing Aide, State of Arizona, 1978

Associate of Arts Degree, Smithville College, Lewiston, Maine, 1974

Non-Degree Format

TRAINING & EDUCATION:

UNIVERSITY OF HAWAII, Honolulu, Hawaii

BS Candidate—Marketing (senior class status)

UNIVERSITY OF CALIFORNIA, Los Angeles, California

Dual Majors in Marketing & Economics (2 years)

Completed 100+ hours of continuing professional education through the University of California, University of Phoenix, and Oregon State University. Topics included marketing, sales administration, team building and leadership, customer relationship management, and forecasting/budgeting.

Detailed Academic Training Format

ACADEMIC CREDENTIALS

B.S., Recreational Therapy, Texas A&M University, 2006

Highlights of Coursework:

- Recreational Therapy
- Special Client Populations
- Case Management
- Inter-Agency Relations
- Planning & Administration
- Resource Management
- Budgeting & Forecasting
- Crisis Intervention

B.S., Management, University of Houston, 1970

NOTE: This format, including coursework details, is the exception to the rule and should be used only by baby boomers who are seeking to make a career transition. In this example, this individual had a successful corporate management career but is now changing directions and moving into a position that is less stressful, more personally rewarding, and more fun. If you're this type of job seeker—who has returned to earn additional academic credentials to support your career transition—be sure to be as detailed as possible when listing your education to substantiate your qualifications.

THE "EXTRAS"

The primary focus of your resume is on information that is directly related to your career goals, whether from your paid work experience, volunteer experience, education and training, affiliations, or other areas of your professional life. However, you also should include things that will distinguish you from other candidates and clearly demonstrate your value to a prospective employer. And, not too surprisingly, it is often the "extras" that get the interviews.

Following is a discussion of the other categories you might or might not include in your resume depending on your particular experience and your current career objectives. Review the information. If it's pertinent to you, use the samples for formatting your own data. Remember, however, that if something is truly impressive or directly related to your current career goals, you might want to include that information in your Career Summary or move that particular section to the top of your resume.

Immediately following your Career Summary should be whatever information is most supportive of that summary (and your objective). For most job seekers, that will be either their employment experience or their education. However, for baby boomers in transition, it might very well be that your professional affiliations, volunteer activities, or the like are what is most relevant to your current search. If so, be sure to move that information to the beginning of your resume for the strongest impact.

Technology Skills and Qualifications

Many technology professionals will have a separate section on their resumes for technology skills and qualifications. It is here that you will summarize all the hardware, software, operating systems, applications, networks, and more that you know that are relevant to your current career objectives.

You'll also have to consider placement of this section in your resume. If the positions for which you are applying require strong technical skills, we recommend you insert this section immediately after your Career Summary (or as a part thereof). If, on the other hand, your technical skills are more of a plus than a specific requirement, the preferred placement is further down in your resume.

Either way, these skills are vital in virtually any technology-related position. As such, this is extremely important information to a prospective employer, so be sure to display it prominently.

Here are two different ways to format and present your technical qualifications.

TECHNOLOGY PROFILE

Operating Systems:	Windows 2000/XP/98/Server 2003; Novell Netware 6.x;
Protocols/ Networks:	TCP/IP, NetBeui, IPX/SPX, Ethernet 10/100Base-T
Hardware:	Hard drives, printers, scanners, fax/modems, CD-ROMs, Zip drives, Cat5 cables, hubs, NIC cards
Software:	Microsoft Office Modules, FileMaker Pro, PC Anywhere, MS Exchange, ARCserve, Project Manager

TECHNOLOGY SKILLS SUMMARY

Windows 2000/XP/98	SAP	TCP/IP
Novell 6.x	MRP	Ethernet 10
Windows Server 2003	DRP	IPX/SPX
Microsoft Office	MS Exchange	ARCserve
Project Manager	PC Anywhere	Filemaker Pro

If your goal is simply to mention the fact that you are proficient with specific PC software, a quick line at the end of your Career Summary should cover this information. For example:

PC proficient with Word, Excel, Access, and WordPerfect. Internet savvy.

Equipment Skills and Qualifications

Many of you employed in the manufacturing, construction, engineering, and related industries have a unique portfolio of equipment skills and knowledge. If these skills are relevant to your current career goals, it is critical that you communicate this information in your resume, highlighting all the equipment with which you are proficient and/or familiar. Consider this format for an individual with extensive experience in pharmaceutical product packaging:

Trained in and worked on a diversity of packaging equipment and technology, including R.A. Jones, Hoppmann, Syntron, Lakso, Scandia, Westbrook, Wexxar, and Edson:

Leaflet Inserters	Cappers	Bottle Cleaners & Elevators
Fillers	Desiccants	Neckbanders
Heat Tunnels	Labelers	Cartoners
Case Packers & Sealers	Hoppers	Bundlers
Sorters	Carousels	Cottoners

Honors and Awards

If you have won honors and awards, you can include them in a separate section near the end of your resume; or you can integrate them into the Education or Professional Experience section if they are particularly noteworthy and/or related to your current career objectives. If you choose to include them in a separate section, consider this format:

- Winner, 2006 **"Sales Performance Award"** from the Miller-Motte Technology College

- Winner, 2004 **"Sales Achievement Award"** for outstanding contributions to sales and market share for IBM

- Winner, **"Sales Producer of the Quarter"** for double-digit revenue growth for IBM (6 awards, 2001–2003)

- **Cum Laude Graduate,** University of Alaska, 1974

Public Speaking

Experts are the ones who are invited to give public presentations at conferences, seminars, workshops, training programs, symposia, and other events. So if you have public-speaking experience, others must consider you an expert. Be sure to include this very complimentary information in your resume. Here's one way to present it:

- Keynote Speaker, "Emerging Investment Strategies for Corporate America," RISK International, Miami, FL, 2006

- Seminar Presenter, "Finance for Non-Finance Executives," Miami-Dade International Business Conference, Miami, FL, 2005

- Session Leader, "Non-Cash Financing Alternatives," METLIFE Associates, New York, NY, 2004

Publications

If you're published, you must be an expert (or at least most people will think so). Just as with your public-speaking engagements, be sure to include your publications. They validate your knowledge, qualifications, and credibility. Publications can include books, articles, Web site content, manuals, and other written documents. Here's an example:

- Author, "Strategic Planning for the *NEW* Venture Capitalist," *Fortune* magazine, November 2005.

- Author, "Optimizing New Markets & New Opportunities," *Executive Edge* magazine, April 2004.

- Co-author, "Currency Hedging in Emerging Markets," Venture Capital Conference, June 2004.

Teaching and Training Experience

Many professionals, regardless of their industry or profession, also teach or train at colleges, universities, technical schools, and other organizations, in addition to training that they may offer "on the job." If this is applicable to you and your current objectives, you might decide to include that experience on your resume. If someone hires you (paid or unpaid) to speak to an audience, it communicates a strong message about your skills, qualifications, knowledge, and expertise. Here's a format you might use to present that information:

- **Adjunct Faculty,** Department of Environmental Engineering, Rhode Island University, 2001 to 2006. Taught Introductory and Advanced Environmental Engineering.

- **Guest Lecturer,** Department of Environmental Affairs, Lancaster Community College, 1998 to 2001. Provided semi-annual, day-long lecture series of emerging trends in environmental protection and conservation.

- **Trainer,** Environmental Engineering Institute, 1980 to 1990. Taught courses in environmental engineering, sample collection/analysis, laboratory procedures, and writing to professional engineers.

Committees and Task Forces

Many professionals serve on committees, task forces, and other special project teams either as part of, or in addition to, their full-time job responsibilities. Again, this type of information further strengthens your credibility, qualifications, and perceived value to a prospective employer when it is related to your current objectives. Consider a format such as this:

- Member, 2004–05 Corporate Governance Task Force
- Member, 2002 Study Team on "Maximizing Employee Productivity Through Technology Innovation"
- Chairperson, 1997–98 Committee on "Safety & Regulatory Compliance in the Workplace"

Professional Affiliations

If you are a member of any educational, professional, or leadership associations, be sure to include that information on your resume. It communicates a message of professionalism, a desire to stay current with the industry, and a strong professional network. What's more, if you have held leadership positions within these organizations, be sure to include them. Here's an example:

AMERICAN COUNSELING ASSOCIATION (ACA)

Professional Member (1978–Present)

Fund-raising Committee Member (2001–2002)

Curriculum Committee Member (1997–1998)

AMERICAN SOCIETY FOR TRAINING & DEVELOPMENT (ASTD)

Professional Member (1989–Present)

Conference Committee Member (2002–2005)

Technology Task Force Member (1996–1998)

LEWISTON COUNSELING ASSOCIATION (LCA)

President (2004–Present)

Vice President (2002–2004)

Treasurer (1997–1998)

If these affiliations are more in line with your current objectives than your past employment experience, you'll want to move them to the forefront of your resume and include much more information about each of your positions, responsibilities, accountabilities, achievements, and more.

Civic Affiliations

Civic affiliations are fine to include if they

- are with a notable organization,
- demonstrate leadership experience, or
- may be of interest to a prospective employer.

However, things such as treasurer of your local condo association and singer with your church choir are not generally of value in marketing your qualifications—unless, of course, that experience is directly relevant to your current career objectives. Here's an example of what to include and how:

- Volunteer Chairperson, Habitat for Humanity, Memphis, TN, 2002
- President, Coleman Falls Historic District, 1999 to 2002
- Treasurer, United Way of Iowa, 1996 to 1997

For boomers in transition, it is important to remember that if this experience is particularly relevant to your current career goals, you will want to move it closer to the beginning of your resume and further expand on your experiences and contributions to these organizations.

Personal Information

We do not recommend that you include such personal information as birth date, marital status, number of children, and related data. However, there may be instances when personal information is appropriate. If this information will give you a competitive advantage or answer unspoken questions about your background, by all means include it. Here's an example:

- Born in Portugal. U.S. Permanent Residency Status since 1997.
- Fluent in English, Portuguese, and Spanish. Conversational French.
- Competitive Triathlete. Top-5 finish, 2006 Midwest Triathlon and 2004 Ohio State Triathlon.

Note in the preceding example that the job seeker is multilingual. This is a particularly critical selling point and, although it might be listed under Personal Information in this example, we recommend that it also be mentioned in your Career Summary.

Consolidating the Extras

Sometimes you have so many extra categories at the end of your resume, each with only a handful of lines, that spacing becomes a problem. You certainly don't want to have to make your resume a page longer to accommodate five lines, nor do you want the "extras" to overwhelm the primary sections of your resume. Yet you believe the information is important and should be included. Or perhaps you have a few small bits of information that you think are important but don't merit an entire section. In these situations, consider consolidating the information using one of the following formats. You'll save space, avoid overemphasizing individual items, and present a professional, distinguished appearance. Here are two examples of how to consolidate and format your "extras":

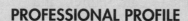

PROFESSIONAL PROFILE

Technology Qualifications	Microsoft Office Suite, SAP R/3, ProjectPlanner, MRP, DRP, LAN, WAN, KPM, Lotus Notes, Novell NetWare
Affiliations	Data Processing Management Association (DPMA)
	Networking Association of America (NAA)
	Technology Consortium of North America (TCNA)
Public Speaking	Speaker, DPAM Conference, Detroit, 2004
	Presenter, NAA National Conference, San Francisco, 2002
	Presenter, TCNA Global Conference, Washington, DC, 1998
Languages	Fluent in English, German, and Japanese

ADDITIONAL INFORMATION

- Co-Chair, Outreach Committee, San Francisco School of the Mentally Challenged.
- Member, Pittsburgh Professional Women's Association.
- PC literate with the entire suite of Microsoft Office.
- Available for relocation worldwide.
- Eagle Scout ... Boy Scout Troop Leader.

Writing Tips, Techniques, and Important Lessons

At this point, you've done a lot of reading, probably taken some notes, highlighted samples that appeal to you, and are ready to plunge into writing your resume. To make this task as easy as possible, we've compiled some "insider" techniques that we've used in our professional resume writing practices. We learned these techniques the hard way through years of experience! We know they work; they will make the writing process easier, faster, and more enjoyable for you.

GET IT DOWN—THEN POLISH AND PERFECT IT

Don't be too concerned with making your resume "perfect" the first time around. It's far better to move fairly swiftly through the process, getting the basic information organized and on paper (or on screen), instead of agonizing about the perfect phrase or ideal formatting. When you've completed a draft, we think you'll be surprised at how close to "final" it is, and you'll be able to edit, tighten, and improve formatting fairly quickly.

WRITE YOUR RESUME FROM THE BOTTOM UP

Here's the system to use to write most efficiently and productively:

1. **Start with the easy things**—Education, Technology, Professional Affiliations, Public Speaking, Publications, and any other extras you want to include. These items require little thought and can be completed in just a few minutes. The only exception is if any of this information is important to showcase to position you for a career transition. If so, you'll need to spend a bit more time writing any text associated with this information to be sure that it communicates the skills and experiences you want to showcase.

2. **Write short job descriptions for your older positions, the ones you held years ago.** Be very brief and focus on highlights such as rapid promotion, achievements, innovations, professional honors, or employment with well-respected, well-known companies.

   NOTE: Even if you plan to create a functional resume that combines job achievements in one "front-and-center" location, we recommend that you first draft these descriptions in a chronological format. It will be easier to remember what you did if you take each of your jobs in turn. Later you can regroup your statements to emphasize related skills and abilities, and leave your employment history as a simple list or brief description to support your career-change objectives.

   Once you've completed this, look at how much you've written in a short period of time! Then move on to the next step.

3. **Write the job descriptions for your most recent positions.** This will take a bit longer than the other sections you have written if you're writing a chronological or combination resume. Remember to focus on the overall scope of your responsibility, major projects and initiatives, and significant achievements as they relate directly to your current objectives. Tell your reader what you did and how well you did it. You can use any of the formats recommended earlier in this chapter, or you can create something that is unique to you and your career.

   Now, see how far along you are? Your resume is 90 percent complete with only one section left to do.

4. **Write your career summary.** Before you start writing, remember your objective for this section. The summary should not simply rehash your previous experience. Rather, it is designed to highlight the skills and qualifications you have that are most closely related to your current career objective(s). The summary is intended to capture the reader's attention and "sell" your expertise. It is *the* most important section for virtually any baby-boomer resume.

That's it. You're done. We guarantee that the process of writing your resume will be much, much easier if you follow the "bottom-up" strategy. Now, on to the next tip.

INCLUDE NOTABLE OR PROMINENT "EXTRA" STUFF IN YOUR CAREER SUMMARY

Remember the "extra-credit sections" that are normally at the bottom of your resume? If this information is particularly significant or prominent—you won a notable award, spoke at an international conference, developed a new teaching methodology, designed a new product that generated tens of millions of dollars in new revenues, or slashed 60% from operating costs—you might want to include it at the top in your Career Summary. Remember, the summary section is written to distinguish you from the crowd of other qualified candidates. As such, if you've accomplished anything that clearly demonstrates your knowledge, expertise, and credibility, consider moving it to your Career Summary for added attention. Refer to the sample career summaries earlier in the chapter for examples.

USE RESUME SAMPLES TO GET IDEAS FOR CONTENT, FORMAT, AND ORGANIZATION

This book is just one of many resources where you can review sample resumes to help you formulate your strategy, write the text, and format your resume. These books are published precisely for that reason. You don't have to struggle alone. Rather, use all the available resources at your disposal.

Be forewarned, however, that it's unlikely you will find a resume that fits your life and career to a "t." It's more likely that you will use "some of this sample" and "some of that sample" to create a resume that is uniquely "you."

INCLUDE DATES OR NOT?

If you are 50 years old or younger, we recommend that you date your work experience and your education. Without dates, your resume becomes vague and difficult for the typical hiring manager or recruiter to interpret. What's more, it often communicates the message that you are trying to hide something. By including the dates of your education and your experience, you create a clean and concise picture that one can easily follow to track your career progression.

If you want your dates to be prominent, consider putting them at the right margin. Conversely, if you want to downplay your dates, put them in small type immediately after the name of your company or the title of your position, or even at the end of the descriptive paragraph for each position.

One exception to our "include the dates" recommendation is return-to-work baby boomers who do *not* want to publicize and draw visual attention to the fact that they have not worked in 10, 15, or more years. If you fall into this category of job seeker, consider eliminating dates from your resume or using the "number-of-years" approach (for example, four years in this position, six years in that position, and so on).

An Individual Decision

If you are a baby boomer who is 50+ years of age, you'll need to give special consideration to including dates on your resume. It might very well be that you do want to include dates with your most recent positions (if you're currently employed or out of the workforce for only a short period of time). However, dating your "older" positions can be more questionable. On the one hand, you do not want to "date" yourself out of consideration by including dates from the 1960s and early 1970s. On the other hand, those positions might be worth including for any one of a number of reasons. Further, if you omit those early dates, you might feel as though you are misrepresenting yourself (or lying) to a prospective employer.

Here is a strategy to overcome those concerns while still including your early experience: Create a separate category titled "Previous Professional Experience" in which you summarize your earliest employment. You can tailor this statement to emphasize just what is most important about that experience.

If you want to capitalize on the good reputation of your past employers, include a statement such as this:

> • Previous experience includes supervisory positions with IBM, Dell, and Xerox.

If you want to focus on the rapid progression of your career, consider this example:

> • Promoted rapidly through a series of increasingly responsible sales and marketing management positions with Hilton Hotels.

If you want to focus on your early career achievements, include a statement such as this:

> • Member of 6-person task force credited with the design and rollout of Davidson's first-generation videoconferencing technology.

By including any one of the preceding paragraphs, under the heading "Previous Professional Experience," you are clearly communicating to your reader that your employment history dates further back than the dates you have indicated on your resume. In turn, you are being 100 percent above-board and not misrepresenting yourself or your career. You're focusing on the success, achievement, and prominence of your earliest assignments.

Include Dates in the Education Section?

If you are over age 50, we generally do not recommend that you date your education or college degrees. Simply include the degree and the university with no date. Why eliminate yourself from consideration by immediately presenting the fact that you earned your college degree in 1968, 1972, or 1976—about the time the hiring manager was probably being born? Remember, the goal of your resume is to share the highlights of your career and open doors for interviews. It is *not* to give your entire life story. As such, it is not mandatory to date your college degree.

However, if you use this strategy, be aware that the reader is likely to assume there is *some* gap between when your education ended and your work experience started. Therefore, if you choose to begin your chronological work history with your first job out of college, omitting your graduation date could actually backfire, because the reader might assume that you have experience that predates your first job. In this case, it's best either to *include your graduation date* or *omit dates of earliest experience*, using the summary strategy discussed earlier.

ALWAYS SEND A COVER LETTER WHEN YOU FORWARD YOUR RESUME

Sending a cover letter every time you send a resume is expected and is appropriate job search etiquette. Your cover letter is *vital* to the success of your job search campaign.

Consider the following: When you write a resume, you are writing a document that you can use for each and every position you apply for, assuming that the requirements for all of those positions will be similar. You invest a great deal of time and effort in crafting just the "right" resume for you, but once it's done, it's done.

Your cover letter, however, is a document that is constantly changing to address the needs of each individual position for which you apply. In essence, it is the tool that allows you to customize your presentation to each company or recruiter, addressing their specific hiring requirements. Use your cover letter to highlight the most important qualifications, experiences, and achievements you bring to that specific organization so that a prospective employer doesn't have to search through your resume to find what is most important. Your cover letter is also the appropriate place to include any specific information that has been requested, such as salary history or salary requirements (see the following section for more on including salaries).

Your cover letter will allow you to briefly address why you're making a career transition or returning to the workforce. Some examples might include the following:

> After a strong and successful career in the development of educational technologies, I have decided to transition my skills into an educational outreach position. My goal is to relocate to a third-world country where I can become an active participant in the design, development, and delivery of educational programs critical to the needs of emerging nations. I do realize that such a career change will also significantly lower my salary, but I am ready, able, and willing to make that accommodation.
>
> Although my career with Merrill Lynch has been exceptional and presented me with opportunities I never imagined possible, my real passion has

always been a career in nursing home administration. As such, to prepare myself, I enrolled in Madison University's nursing home administration program several years ago and have just graduated. I have now resigned my position with Merrill Lynch and am ready to move forward in my new career.

When I graduated from college, I was immediately recruited by UPS and held a number of mid-level management positions in its Communications Division. I resigned from the company six years later to raise my family. During that time, I have chaired the Communications Committee for several public schools, been an active leader in numerous community-outreach programs where my focus was on education and communications, and participated in several Habitat for Humanity projects. Now I'm ready to return to the workforce where I can continue to provide strategic and tactical leadership to a communications organization.

My eight-year career with Digital Electronics was wonderful. Initially recruited as a Sales Representative, I earned four promotions and left the company as its Midwest Regional Sales Manager. Over the next 10 years, I cared for aging parents and a special-needs child who is now living independently. As such, I am most anxious to return to my professional sales career and am looking to DePortTech for such opportunities.

NEVER INCLUDE SALARY HISTORY OR SALARY REQUIREMENTS ON YOUR RESUME

Your resume is *not* the correct forum for a salary discussion. First of all, you should never provide salary information unless a company has requested that information and you choose to comply. (Studies show that employers will look at your resume anyway, so you might choose not to respond to this request, thereby avoiding pricing yourself out of the job or locking yourself into a lower salary than the job is worth.)

When contacting recruiters, however, we recommend that you do provide salary information, but again, only in your cover letter. With recruiters you want to "put all of your cards on the table" and help them make an appropriate placement by providing information about your current salary and salary objectives. For example, "Be advised that my most recent compensation was $110,000 annually and that I am interested in a position starting at a minimum of $125,000 per year." Or, if you would prefer to be a little less specific, you might write, "My annual compensation over the past three years has averaged $100,000+."

ALWAYS REMEMBER THAT YOU ARE SELLING

As we have discussed over and over throughout chapters 1 and 2, resume writing is sales. Understand and appreciate the value you bring to a prospective employer, and then communicate that value by focusing on your achievements. Companies don't want to hire just anyone; they want to hire "the" someone who will make a difference. Show them that you are that candidate.

CHAPTER 3

Printed, Scannable, Electronic, and Web Resumes

After you've worked so tirelessly to write a winning resume, your next challenge is the resume's design, layout, and presentation. It's not enough for your resume to simply read well and highlight your core skills, experiences, and accomplishments; your resume must also have just the *right* look for the *right* audience.

Resume design and presentation have become somewhat more complicated over the past five years. As the Internet has penetrated every aspect of our lives, so has it impacted the manner in which we look for new jobs and new career opportunities.

For every baby boomer reading this book, you remember when resumes were *only* transmitted on paper and then forwarded via mail. Well, those days are long since gone. There will certainly be many opportunities for you to use your printed resume, but now you also need to concern yourself with the newest resume versions in use today.

The Four Types of Resumes

In today's employment market, job seekers use four types of resume presentations:

- Printed
- Scannable
- Electronic (e-mail attachments and ASCII text files)
- Web

This chapter explores the various types of resumes in use today, how to prepare them, and when to use them.

THE PRINTED RESUME

You know the printed resume as the "traditional resume," the one that you mail to a recruiter, take to an interview, and forward by mail or fax in response to an advertisement. When preparing a printed resume, you want to create a sharp, professional, and visually attractive presentation. Remember, that piece of paper conveys the very first impression of you to a potential employer, and that first impression goes a long, long way. Never be fooled into thinking that just because you have the best qualifications in your industry, the visual presentation of your resume does not matter. It does, a great deal.

THE SCANNABLE RESUME

The scannable resume can be referred to as the "plain-Jane" or "plain-vanilla" resume. All of the things that you would normally do to make your printed resume look attractive—bold print, italics, multiple columns, sharp-looking typestyle, and more—are stripped away in a scannable resume. You want to present a document that can be easily read and interpreted by scanning technology.

Although the technology continues to improve, and many scanning systems in fact can read a wide variety of type enhancements, it's sensible to appeal to the "lowest common denominator" when creating your scannable resume. Follow these formatting guidelines:

- Choose a commonly used, easily read font such as Arial or Times New Roman.
- Don't use **bold,** *italic,* or <u>underlined</u> type.
- Use a minimum of 11-point type size.
- Position your name, and nothing else, on the top line of the resume.
- Keep text left-justified, with a "ragged" right margin.
- It's okay to use common abbreviations (for instance, scanning software will recognize "B.S." as a Bachelor of Science degree). But, when in doubt, spell it out.
- Eliminate graphics, borders, and horizontal lines.
- Use plain, round bullets or asterisks.
- Avoid columns and tables, although a simple two-column listing can be read without difficulty.
- Spell out symbols such as % and &.
- If you divide words with slashes, add a space before and after the slash to be certain the scanner doesn't misread the letters.
- Print on smooth white paper using a high-quality inkjet or laser printer.
- If your resume is longer than one page, be sure to print on only one side of the paper; put your name, telephone number, and e-mail address on the top of page 2; and don't staple the pages together.
- For best possible results, mail your resume (don't fax it), and send it flat in a 9 × 12 envelope so that you won't have to fold it.

Of course, you can avoid scannability issues completely by sending your resume electronically, so that it will not have to pass through a scanner to enter the company's databank. Read the next section for guidelines on how to prepare electronic resumes.

THE ELECTRONIC RESUME

Your electronic resume can take two forms: an e-mail attachment and an ASCII text file.

E-mail Attachments

When sending your resume with an e-mail message, simply attach the word-processing file of your printed resume. It's that easy! We strongly recommend that you prepare your word-processed resume using Microsoft Word. The vast majority of businesses use Word and, therefore, it is the most acceptable format and should transmit easily.

However, given the tremendous variety in versions of software and operating systems, not to mention printer drivers, it's quite possible that your beautifully formatted resume will look quite different when viewed and printed at the other end. To minimize these glitches, use generous margins (at least 0.75 inch all around). Don't use unusual typefaces and minimize fancy formatting effects.

Test your resume by e-mailing it to several friends or colleagues and having them view and print it on their systems. If you use WordPerfect, the text editor that comes with Microsoft Works, or another word-processing program, consider saving your resume in a more universally accepted format such as RTF or PDF. Again, try sending it out to a few friends to make sure that it transmits well before you send it to a prospective employer.

ASCII Text Files

You'll find many uses for an ASCII text version of your resume:

- To avoid formatting problems, you can paste the text into the body of an e-mail message instead of sending an attachment. Many employers actually prefer this method.

- You can readily copy and paste the text version of your resume into online job application and resume bank forms with no worries that formatting glitches will cause confusion.

- Although it's unattractive, the text version is 100 percent scannable.

To create a text version of your resume, follow these simple steps:

1. Create a new version of your resume using the Save As feature of your word-processing program. Select "text only" or "ASCII" in the Save As option box.

2. Close the new file.

3. Reopen the file, and you'll find that your word processor has automatically reformatted your resume into Courier font, removed all formatting, and left-justified the text.

4. To promote maximum readability when sending your resume electronically, reset the margins to 2 inches left and right, so that you have a narrow column of text rather than a full-page width. This margin setting will not be retained when you close the file, but in the meantime you can adjust the text formatting for best screen appearance. For instance, if you choose to include a

horizontal line (perhaps something like this: +++++++++++++++++++++++++++)
to separate sections of the resume, by working with the narrow margins you
won't make the mistake of creating a line that extends past the normal screen
width. Plus, you won't add hard line breaks that create odd-length lines when
seen at normal screen width.

5. Review the resume and fix any "glitches" such as odd characters that might
   have been inserted to take the place of "curly" quotes, dashes, accents, or
   other nonstandard symbols.

6. If necessary, add extra blank lines to improve readability.

7. Consider adding horizontal dividers to break the resume into sections for
   improved skimmability. You can use any standard typewriter symbols, such as
   *, -, (,), =, +, ^, or #.

To illustrate what you can expect when creating these versions of your resume,
here are some examples of the same resume in traditional printed format,
scannable format, and electronic (text) format.

This outstanding baby boomer resume was written by Norine Dagliano of ekm
Inspirations.

THE WEB RESUME

This newest evolution in resumes combines the visually pleasing quality of the
printed resume with the technological ease of the electronic resume. You host
your Web resume on your own Web site (with your own URL), to which you
refer prospective employers and recruiters. Now, instead of seeing just a "plain-
Jane" version of your e-mailed resume, with just one click a viewer can access,
download, and print your Web resume—an attractive, nicely formatted presentation of your qualifications.

Because the Web resume is such an efficient and easy-to-manage tool, you can
choose to include more information than you would in a printed, scannable, or
electronic resume. Consider separate pages for achievements, technology qualifications, equipment skills, honors and awards, management skills, volunteer contributions, professional membership, civic memberships, publications, public speaking,
international travel and foreign languages, and more, if you believe they will
improve your market position. Remember, you're working to sell yourself into
your next job!

For those of you in creative and technology-related professions, you can take
it one step further and create a virtual multimedia presentation that not only
tells someone how talented you are, but also visually and technologically demonstrates it.

Web resumes and complete Web-based portfolios are emerging as powerful tools
for lifetime career management. You might want to consider developing such a
portfolio and adding to it as your career advances. You can view several outstanding examples on these Web sites: http://brandego.com and http://
blueskyportfolios.com.

RICHARD J. BARONE

924 Market Street ▪ Lancaster, PA 17603
(717) 662.8712 ▪ rbar1@yahoo.com

PROJECT MANAGER: HOME DÉCOR INDUSTRY

Professional Goal: To employ 25+ years of business experience and recent technical training to support a retail or customer-service operation, while positively impacting profits and customer satisfaction.

Career Profile: Ambitious self-starter with more than 20 years of manufacturing management experience. Computer literate. College graduate, committed to lifelong learning. Possess proven skills and experience in the following areas:

- Production Scheduling
- Project & People Management
- Independent Decision Making
- Budgeting & Financial Management
- Mathematical Calculations

- Analytical Problem Solving
- Time Management & Priority Setting
- Customer Service & Vendor Relations
- Quality Monitoring
- Precision Work & Attention to Detail

CERTIFIED SOFT TREATMENT INSTALLER

- Completed 50-hour apprenticeship training through **Lafayette Training Center,** West Lafayette, IN. Core competencies include precision measuring, numerical calculations and conversions, mechanical aptitude, operation of hand tools, and familiarity with basic construction substructures.
- Secured part-time employment and subcontracted with independent interior decorators, establishing a strong residential and commercial customer base while fine-tuning skills and custom installation techniques.

Custom Drapery Installation by Richard, Lancaster, PA   2004–Present

- Launched sole proprietorship following completion of apprenticeship. Established strong networking contacts that led to numerous subcontracting assignments with local interior decorators.
- Demonstrate an ability to "think outside the box" in completing custom installation and repair projects, while earning a reputation as a talented and conscientious craftsman.
- Key Projects
  - Ephrata Public Library: Completed major repair and replacement of nonfunctioning draperies and related hardware.
  - Lancaster County Parade of Homes: Independently completed all window treatment installation for an 18-room, $2M home.
  - Millersville University: Installed 80 blinds in a newly constructed medical building.
  - Elizabethtown College: Installed window treatments in first floor of classroom building.
  - Lititz Country Club: Completed all dining room window treatments.

ADDITIONAL EMPLOYMENT EXPERIENCE

Custom Coating Specialist / Front Line Supervisor, Red Lion   1979–2003

A manufacturer of blast cleaning machines and after-market repair parts supplying automobile manufacturers and foundries worldwide.

- Completed a successful 20-year career in management, leading to early retirement. Demonstrated outstanding performance and contributions in several key areas.
- Directly supervised up to 30 hourly employees in a union shop.
- Coordinated manufacturing activities in a multi-step process, from order receipt through completion.
- Prioritized as many as 1,000 daily orders and expedited work orders in response to customer requirements. Scheduled manpower and work schedules to meet demanding deadlines, while remaining immediately responsive to daily changes in production needs.
- Maintained more than $50K daily inventory from department inventory of more than 35,000 parts.
- Developed and manipulated Excel spreadsheets to track production scheduling and generated planning data from company electronic inventory management system.

EDUCATION: Bachelor of Science, English, Millersville University, Lancaster, PA

The print version of the resume.

RICHARD J. BARONE
924 Market Street, Lancaster, PA 17603
(717) 662.8712 • rbar1@yahoo.com

PROJECT MANAGER: HOME DECOR INDUSTRY

Professional Goal: To employ 25+ years of business experience and recent technical training to support a retail or customer-service operation, while positively impacting profits and customer satisfaction.

Career Profile: Ambitious self-starter with more than 20 years of manufacturing management experience. Computer literate. College graduate, committed to lifelong learning. Possess proven skills and experience in the following areas:

- Production Scheduling
- Project and People Management
- Independent Decision Making
- Budgeting and Financial Management
- Mathematical Calculations
- Analytical Problem Solving
- Time Management and Priority Setting
- Customer Service and Vendor Relations
- Quality Monitoring
- Precision Work and Attention to Detail

CERTIFIED SOFT TREATMENT INSTALLER

- Completed 50-hour apprenticeship training through Lafayette Training Center, West Lafayette, IN. Core competencies include precision measuring, numerical calculations and conversions, mechanical aptitude, operation of hand tools, and familiarity with basic construction substructures.

- Secured part-time employment and subcontracted with independent interior decorators, establishing a strong residential and commercial customer base while fine-tuning skills and custom installation techniques.

Custom Drapery Installation by Richard, Lancaster, PA, 2004–Present

- Launched sole proprietorship following completion of apprenticeship. Established strong networking contacts that led to numerous subcontracting assignments with local interior decorators.

- Demonstrate an ability to "think outside the box" in completing custom installation and repair projects, while earning a reputation as a talented and conscientious craftsman.

- Key Projects
— Ephrata Public Library: Completed major repair and replacement of nonfunctioning draperies and related hardware.
— Lancaster County Parade of Homes: Independently completed all window treatment installation for an 18-room, $2M home.
— Millersville University: Installed 80 blinds in a newly constructed medical building.
— Elizabethtown College: Installed window treatments in first floor of classroom building.
— Lititz Country Club: Completed all dining room window treatments.

ADDITIONAL EMPLOYMENT EXPERIENCE

Custom Coating Specialist / Front Line Supervisor, Red Lion, 1979–2003
A manufacturer of blast cleaning machines and after-market repair parts supplying automobile manufacturers and foundries worldwide.

- Completed a successful 20-year career in management, leading to early retirement. Demonstrated outstanding performance and contributions in several key areas.

- Directly supervised up to 30 hourly employees in a union shop.

- Coordinated manufacturing activities in a multi-step process, from order receipt through completion.

- Prioritized as many as 1,000 daily orders and expedited work orders in response to customer requirements. Scheduled manpower and work schedules to meet demanding deadlines, while remaining immediately responsive to daily changes in production needs.

- Maintained more than $50K daily inventory from department inventory of more than 35,000 parts.

- Developed and manipulated Excel spreadsheets to track production scheduling and generated planning data from company electronic inventory management system.

EDUCATION

Bachelor of Science, English, Millersville University, Lancaster, PA

The scannable version of the resume.

```
RICHARD J. BARONE
924 Market Street, Lancaster, PA 17603
(717) 662.8712 * rbar1@yahoo.com

=====================================================
PROJECT MANAGER: HOME DECOR INDUSTRY
PROFESSIONAL GOAL: To employ 25+ years of business experience and recent technical
training to support a retail or customer-service operation, while positively impacting
profits and customer satisfaction.

CAREER PROFILE: Ambitious self-starter with more than 20 years of manufacturing management
experience. Computer literate. College graduate, committed to lifelong learning. Possess
proven skills and experience in the following areas:

* Production Scheduling
* Analytical Problem Solving
* Project and People Management
* Time Management and Priority Setting
* Independent Decision Making
* Customer Service and Vendor Relations
* Budgeting and Financial Management
* Quality Monitoring
* Mathematical Calculations
* Precision Work and Attention to Detail

=====================================================
CERTIFIED SOFT TREATMENT INSTALLER
* Completed 50-hour apprenticeship training through Lafayette Training Center, West
Lafayette, IN. Core competencies include precision measuring, numerical calculations and
conversions, mechanical aptitude, operation of hand tools, and familiarity with basic
construction substructures.
* Secured part-time employment and subcontracted with independent interior decorators,
establishing a strong residential and commercial customer base while fine-tuning skills
and custom installation techniques.

Custom Drapery Installation by Richard, Lancaster, PA, 2004-Present
* Launched sole proprietorship following completion of apprenticeship. Established strong
networking contacts that led to numerous sub-contracting assignments with local interior
decorators.
* Demonstrate an ability to "think outside the box" in completing custom installation and
repair projects, while earning a reputation as a talented and conscientious craftsman.
* Key Projects
= Ephrata Public Library: Completed major repair and replacement of nonfunctioning
draperies and related hardware.
= Lancaster County Parade of Homes: Independently completed all window treatment
installation for an 18-room, $2M home.
= Millersville University: Installed 80 blinds in a newly constructed medical building.
= Elizabethtown College: Installed window treatments in first floor of classroom building.
= Lititz Country Club: Completed all dining room window treatments.

=====================================================
ADDITIONAL EMPLOYMENT EXPERIENCE
Custom Coating Specialist / Front Line Supervisor, Red Lion, 1979-2003
A manufacturer of blast cleaning machines and after-market repair parts supplying
automobile manufacturers and foundries worldwide.
* Completed a successful 20-year career in management, leading to early retirement.
Demonstrated outstanding performance and contributions in several key areas.
* Directly supervised up to 30 hourly employees in a union shop.
Coordinated manufacturing activities in a multi-step process, from order receipt through
completion.
* Prioritized as many as 1,000 daily orders and expedited work orders in response to
customer requirements. Scheduled manpower and work schedules to meet demanding deadlines,
while remaining immediately responsive to daily changes in production needs.
* Maintained more than $50K daily inventory from department inventory of more than 35,000
parts.
* Developed and manipulated Excel spreadsheets to track production scheduling and
generated planning data from company electronic inventory management system.

=====================================================
EDUCATION
Bachelor of Science, English, Millersville University, Lancaster, PA
```

The electronic/text version of the resume.

The Four Resume Types Compared

This chart quickly compares the similarities and differences between the four types of resumes we've discussed in this chapter. Use it to help determine which resume versions you need in your job search and how to prepare them.

	PRINTED RESUMES	SCANNABLE RESUMES
TYPESTYLE/ FONT	Sharp, conservative, and distinctive (see our recommendations in chapter 1).	Clean, concise, and machine-readable: Times New Roman, Arial, Helvetica.
TYPESTYLE ENHANCEMENTS	**Bold,** *italic,* and <u>underlining</u> for emphasis.	CAPITALIZATION is the only type enhancement you can be certain will transmit.
TYPE SIZE	10-, 11-, or 12-point preferred... larger type sizes (14, 18, 20, 22, and even larger, depending on typestyle) will effectively enhance your name and section headers.	11- or 12-point, or larger.
TEXT FORMAT	Use centering and indentations to optimize the visual presentation.	Type all information flush left.
PREFERRED LENGTH	1 to 2 pages; 3 if essential.	1 to 2 pages preferred, although length is not as much of a concern as with printed resumes.
PREFERRED PAPER COLOR	White, Ivory, Light Gray, Light Blue, or other conservative background.	White or very light with no prints, flecks, or other shading that might affect scannability.
WHITE SPACE	Use appropriately for best readability.	Use generously to maximize scannability.

ELECTRONIC RESUMES	WEB RESUMES
Courier.	Sharp, conservative, and distinctive... attractive onscreen and when printed from an online document.
CAPITALIZATION is the only enhancement available to you.	**Bold,** *italic,* and <u>underlining</u>, and color for emphasis.
12-point.	10-, 11-, or 12-point preferred... larger type sizes (14, 18, 20, 22, and even larger, depending on typestyle) will effectively enhance your name and section headers.
Type all information flush left.	Use centering and indentations to optimize the visual presentation.
Length is immaterial; almost definitely, converting your resume to text will make it longer.	Length is immaterial; just be sure your site is well organized so viewers can quickly find the material of greatest interest to them.
N/A.	Paper is not used, but do select your background carefully to maximize readability.
Use white space to break up dense text sections.	Use appropriately for best readability both onscreen and when printed.

Are You Ready to Write Your Resume?

To be sure that you're ready to write your resume, go through the following checklist. Each item is a critical step that you must take to ensure that you are writing and designing your very *best* resume—a resume that will open doors, generate interviews, and help you land a great new opportunity.

- ❑ Clearly define "who you are" and how you want to be perceived.

- ❑ Document your key skills, qualifications, and knowledge.

- ❑ Document your notable career achievements and successes.

- ❑ Identify one or more specific job targets or positions.

- ❑ Identify one or more industries that you are targeting.

- ❑ Research and compile keywords for your profession, industry, and specific job targets.

- ❑ Determine which resume format suits you and your career best.

- ❑ Select an attractive and appropriate font.

- ❑ Determine whether you need a print resume, a scannable resume, an electronic resume, a Web resume, or all four.

- ❑ Secure a private e-mail address (not your employer's).

- ❑ Review resume samples for up-to-date ideas on resume styles, formats, organization, and language.

PART II

Sample Resumes for Baby Boomers

Resumes for Young Baby Boomers

In this chapter you'll find resumes for people who fit our definition of "young baby boomer"—people born toward the end of the baby boom, typically under 45 years of age, who are seeking to advance their careers.

As you peruse these resumes, you'll observe that, for the most part, they follow a traditional chronological format, with the emphasis on recent and progressive career experience and the activities and accomplishments related to that experience.

Professions included in this chapter:

MEGAN REYBOURNE

2197 Bonnie Brook Drive, #32
Grosse Point, Michigan 48236
(313) 333-0101
reybourne@comcast.net

GOLF PROFESSIONAL

- **17 YEARS OF EXPERIENCE IN MANAGEMENT OF CLUB OPERATIONS**
- **8 YEARS OF EXPERIENCE IN PROFESSIONAL TOURNAMENT PLAY**

AFFILIATION

• **Member, LPGA (Ladies' Professional Golf Association)**	1994–Present

PROFESSIONAL GOLF ACHIEVEMENTS

• *Local Qualifier (2nd of 42)*, **LPGA U.S. Open**	2002
• *Finalist*, **LPGA Great Lakes Finals**	2000
• *Player of the Year*, **LPGA North Shore Tour**	1998
• *Round 1 Qualifier (83rd Place Finish)*, **LPGA Jamie Farr Classic**	1997
• *Round 1 Qualifier (99th Place Finish)*, **LPGA Atlantic City Classic**	1994

EXPERIENCE

- <u>GOLF PROFESSIONAL</u>, *Bentbrook Shores Golf Club*, Grosse Point Park, Michigan   1997–Present
- **Golf Manager:** Direct all aspects of $12 million golf operations, ensuring profitable business performance and positive experiences for upper-echelon clientele / membership.
- **Supervisor** of 23 employees: Recruiting, hiring, training programs, mentoring, and evaluation.
- **Innovations / Contributions** for revenue production, growth, and improvements:
  - Increased annual sales more than 100% within 4 years, from $950,000 in 2000 to $2 million 2005.
  - Spearheaded golf clinics; increased enrollment in lessons by 50% in first 2 years.
  - Secured annual Ford Motor Company outing, Greektown Tournament, and Windsor Gold event.

- <u>GOLF ASSISTANT</u>, *Worth Estates Club*, West Palm Beach, Florida   1989–1997
- **Coordinator, Upscale Golf Services:** Acted as liaison in balancing internal operations and exceptional service delivery. Supervised 130 caddies; organized 12 clinics weekly; planned and executed 255+ corporate golf outings and 45–50 tournaments annually.

EDUCATION

• **Bachelor of Arts, Commercial Recreation,** *The University of Toledo*, Toledo, Ohio	1989

AMATEUR / COLLEGIATE GOLF

• *Qualifier*, **Futures Golf Tour**	1992
• *2-Time Member*, **All-Mid-American Conference Team**	1988, 1989
• *Captain*, **Women's Golf Team, The University of Toledo**	1988–1989
• *Individual Champion*, **Mid-American Conference (MAC), Women's Golf**	1988–1989

Strategy: *Equally emphasized professional golf accomplishments and golf management experience because both are key qualifiers.*

STEPHEN M. FRANKLIN, L.M.T.
1234 Seneca Ave. • Baldwinsville, New York 13027
(H) 315.423.1234 • (C) 315.415.4321 • smflmt@juno.com

LICENSED MASSAGE THERAPIST

Talented and highly requested New York State Licensed Massage Therapist with more than 4 years of full-time experience at a Mobil four-star resort.

CREDENTIALS

1,000-hour Training Program—Manlius School of Therapeutic Massage, Manlius, NY, 5/2000
Massage Therapist License # 013555-0—The University of the State of New York, NYS Exam, 9/2000
Insured through ABMP—Professional Member Level

PROFESSIONAL EXPERIENCE

GLIMMERGLASS INN & SPA—Sherrill Springs, NY   11/2001–Present
Licensed Massage Therapist
Perform various forms of massage and body treatments on an average of 20 clients per week at Mobil 4-star resort. Serve in-house guests, transient guests, and local clients.

- Assess and evaluate clients, many with different medical conditions, prior to treatment to determine massage technique to be used.
- Conduct ongoing diagnostics during treatment to determine effectiveness of bodywork technique and appropriateness of altering method to accommodate client's condition or situation.
- Keep record of client evaluation and treatment.

Selected Highlights and Contributions

❑ Distinguished as one of the most requested therapists out of more than 20 working at the Glimmerglass.

❑ Consistently given high marks from customers as a "very caring" and "genuine" individual who is "proficiently skilled" in bodywork techniques.

❑ Adept in making each client's experience unique, comfortable, and relaxing.

❑ Able to maintain comfort level working with a wide range of individuals and with clients who are not healthy or who may have a medical condition.

EDUCATION

Bachelor of Arts Degree—Hobart College, Geneva, NY
Major: Psychology

PROFESSIONAL DEVELOPMENT
Cranio Sacral Therapy Level I Workshop, 10/2004
The Scala Institute, Inc.

Thai Yoga Massage, 6/2003 & 1/2004
Glimmerglass Inn & Spa, Sherrill Springs, NY
Franz Lieder, Instructor

Pain Management and Sports Injury Seminar, 11/2000
Jonathan Trueblood—Program Director, Instructor
20 hours of orthopedic medical massage and continuing education
in the treatment of chronic pain and common athletic injuries.

Reiki 1st Degree, 1/2001
Usui Shiki Ryoko

Strategy: *Omitted early 15-year career in another field and focused on just the most recent five years of related experience and strong educational credentials.*

Cynthia Bergman

727 Forest Drive
Westbrook, NJ 07424

Home Phone: (201) 569-0407
Cellular Phone: (973) 600-7392
E-mail: cindybergman22@optonline.net

Certified Dietary Manager

Seeking increasing responsibilities in managing all aspects of food services and nutrition at a hospital or long-term-care facility in order to enhance the quality of life for its patients.

Relevant Experience

OAK MANOR NURSING HOME, Bellaire, NJ 2000–Present
Director of Food Services/Quality Control Coordinator (2003–Present)
Cook/Dietetic Assistant (2000–2003)
Currently accountable for meeting the specialized dietary needs of the geriatric population at this 98-bed private facility. Also ensure that total quality standards are maintained in the areas of nursing, housekeeping, laundry, building maintenance, social services, and recreational therapy.

➢ Manage dietary staff of 17 in the planning, coordination, preparation, and service of appetizing, balanced meals, meeting all nutritional requirements. Ensure that proper food restrictions/substitutions are considered with regard to individuals' medical conditions such as diabetes, heart disease, gastrointestinal disorders, anemia, etc.

➢ Purchase all food and ingredients, keeping well within the budgetary framework. Reduced food costs 20% by implementing portion and waste controls.

➢ Enforce department policies to conform with established government regulations and procedures for food storage, preparation, equipment and department sanitation, employee safety, and other personnel matters. For the past three years, dietary department has been rated deficiency-free in all state inspections.

➢ Educate staff through monthly in-service meetings to support patients' bill of rights in all aspects of care and feeding. Encourage discussions on regulations, procedures, grievances, and recommendations for improving food service. Promote loyalty and harmonious working relationships by resolving conflicts in their early stages.

Other Employment

Home Health Care Aide, Montclair, NJ 1994–2000
➢ Concurrent with education, held private-duty assignment for elderly gentleman until his death.

Co-Owner/Operator, Gold Star Cafe, Hackensack, NJ 1980–1994
➢ Exposed to the various management processes associated with running a successful restaurant.

➢ Developed an interest in food service, which carried over to career decision.

Education

Montclair State University, Upper Montclair, NJ
B.S. Home Economics with concentration in Foodservice Management 2002

Certified Dietary Manager credentialed by State of New Jersey 2003
Continuing education thereafter through attendance at seminars (45 hours annually)

Professional Associations

New Jersey Dietary Managers' Association
2004–2005 Vice President

➢ Held seminars at resident care facilities throughout the state to educate administrators and employees of dietary departments on ways to improve the quality of care for their clients.

➢ Represented the State of New Jersey in rallies for federal intervention to mandate certification for all directors of food service at long-term-care facilities.

Educational Testing Services
Certified as an on-site test examiner for the Food Protection Certification program.

Strategy: *Presented "other employment" as a separate category, to keep the chronology consistent while drawing attention to the fact that the experience is less relevant to current goals.*

Kaylor Tamburman

4425 Columbia Drive
Sugarloaf, NY 12405

(845) 729-5515
coolbeans@yahoo.com

EXPERIENCED FOOD TECHNOLOGIST
Proactive and forward-thinking individual with a record of success for developing breakthrough products
Offering a strong chemistry background and the technical creativity necessary to drive forward new products and improve existing products

PROFESSIONAL PROFILE	AREAS OF KNOWLEDGE & EXPERIENCE
◆ Experienced project manager with proven industry networking skills, effective partnering skills, and sharp presentation abilities	◆ Idea Generation / Trend Identification / Prototype & Process Development / Product Introductions
◆ Maintain an advanced understanding of the commercial effects of product development as well as the process to get to market	◆ Novel Ingredient Utilization / Sensory Evaluation Ingredient Functionality / Formulation Development
◆ Highly skilled at identifying market opportunities/gaps and leveraging competencies to convert ideas into prototypes	◆ Applications & Technology Assessment / Shelf-Life Testing / FDA & TTB Guidelines / Production Issues
◆ Expert in formulating flavor combinations and taking new products/line extensions from bench to launch	◆ Focus Groups / Risk Assessment / Consumer Testing Marketing / Supplier Relations / Records Management

EMPLOYMENT EXPERIENCE

Scar Beverages International
2004 to Present
(World's leading premium drinks business with product leaders)

Liquid Innovation Manager
Collaborate with marketing and innovation teams to create development plans and deliver new products for highly specialized niche markets. Provide strategic input to ensure that each project matches up with brand objectives. Confer on the design of sensory and consumer tests, recommend testing methodologies, and analyze consumer data. Function as an active member of the marketing, innovation, and launch teams to provide product guidance on ingredients, specifications, process requirements, and cost of goods. Work closely with ingredient suppliers to ensure regulatory compliance, quality, and availability.

- Led the creative development of a new-age flavored malt beverage.
- Consistently called upon to help determine testing methodologies, interpret data, and identify emerging markets.
- Completed specialized training on industry standards for beer, whiskey, and rum.

Worldwide Beverages & Foods (WBF)
1999 to 2004
Senior Scientist—Innovation Group *(2/02 to 2/04)*
Research Scientist—Innovation Group *(7/99 to 2/02)*
Worked with marketing, operations, and focus groups to identify potential product opportunities and develop differentiated concept liquids from idea generation to launch. Partnered with internal business groups to ensure flawless commercialization and adherence to consumer-defined specifications. Instrumental in developing value-added products and responsible for new product ideation, prototyping, and projects in R&D. Worked with suppliers to develop new applications and new technologies to support reapplication, flavor extensions, and region-initiated projects. Also served as a mentor and trainer for new scientists.

- Honored with the "Chairman's Award" in 2000 (WBF's highest award) for the development of a new drink.
- Received an initiative recognition award for spearheading efforts to improve overall safety in R&D facility.
- Received the very first award for "best laboratory notebook," which became the standard format used throughout R&D.
- Led the development of an orange-juice drink by reformulating a fledgling WBF product and fine-tuning the technology at the plant level. Leveraged the orange name, which reinvigorated the product and was well received by bottlers.
- Member of the R&D Safety Committee, selected to serve on the Documentation Improvement Committee and appointed to the Technical Operations Improvement Committee.
- Restructured documentation procedures, established criteria regarding raw materials, and developed processing manuals. Worked closely with suppliers and plants to standardize procedures and ensure continuity on plant production runs.

Strategy: *Emphasized exceptional achievements and extensive experience in the niche food/beverage industry.*

Kaylor Tamburman   Page Two

EMPLOYMENT EXPERIENCE continued...

Flavorade, Inc., *Mohawk, NY*   1996 to 1999

R&D Manager

Led the complete R&D function for this family-owned company. Custom-created flavor systems, developed new beverages, prepared manufacturer's formulations, provided per-unit pricing, and formulated nutritional fact panels to regional, national, and Fortune 500 companies. Supervised lab personnel. Served as a liaison and resource person from initial sales presentation through feasibility and development to first-run supervision.

- Maintained a high prototype approval rating and fast, accurate turnaround time through extensive technical knowledge, broad experience, and complete understanding of ingredient compatibility.

- Increased client base and profits by enhancing services (i.e.: providing nutritional fact panels).

- Invited to collaborate on critical business decisions due to unique insight into client goals and objectives, understanding of market trends, and knowledge of government regulations.

- Consistently enhanced existing products and identified/developed value-added products.

ADDITIONAL EXPERIENCE

Common Foods, Inc., *Mohawk, NY*   1996
Product & Process Specialist

Worldwide Food Network, *Mohawk, NY*   1992 to 1996
Lab Technician

Cornell University Food Science Department, *Ithaca, NY*   1991 to 1992
Dairy Microbiology Technician

PROFESSIONAL DEVELOPMENT

Education: **Specialized Training**

A.A.S. in Dairy & Food Sciences   Basic Food Science—Rutgers University
Cornell University, Ithaca, NY   Food Science—Cornell University
                                                             Food Microbiology—Cornell University

Computer Skills: **Professional Association**:

MS Word, Excel, PowerPoint, Project   Institute of Food Technologists

Dan Waterfield
CADC III, SAP

584 N. Commercial Drive
Grand Junction, CO 81505
(970) 265-8888 ▪ d.waterfield@gmail.com

Drug & Alcohol Counselor

Certified Alcohol & Drug Counselor III / Employee Assistance Program Counselor
Certified Substance Abuse Professional

Dedicated Substance Abuse Counselor with 20+ years of experience counseling individuals and groups (adolescent through geriatric populations) in inpatient, outpatient, and private-practice environments, including Residential Treatment Facility (RTF). Expertise includes EAP, SAP, and CADC III.

Additional background in collateral counseling. In-depth experience with issues including addiction, substance abuse, denial, grief, spirituality, abuse, anger management, and aging. Use multidisciplined approach, including 12-step program, Gestalt, role-playing, intervention, and conflict-resolution techniques. Leverage persistence, listening, and interpersonal skills, empathy, sense of humor, and broad education encompassing mental-health issues to guide and support clients toward recovery. Rapidly establish rapport with clients from highly diverse backgrounds. Recognized for contributions in implementation of and participation in new programs and methodologies related to AODA treatment.

Core Competencies

- AODA Training
- Drug & Alcohol Abuse Counseling
- Client Needs Assessment
- Crisis Intervention
- Employee Assistance Program
- Discharge Plan Preparation

- SAP Assessments
- Coaching & Motivation
- Diagnostic Assessment & Evaluation
- Individualized Treatment Plans
- Community Education
- Case Management Planning

Career Highlights

Pinecrest Associates, Grand Junction, CO   1989–Present
Private mental-health clinic with 15-member team headed by experienced psychiatrist.
ALCOHOL & DRUG ABUSE COUNSELOR

Provide individual and family counseling for patients of all ages with chemical dependency. Engage in all phases of treatment, including assessment, counseling, collateral support, and referral. Organize and lead treatment groups and play active role in forwarding community-based AODA-intervention programs. Perform all hard-copy charting and data entry throughout patients' entire treatment plan.

Key Achievements:

- Introduced AODA treatment model to entire staff of mental-health and psychiatric practitioners. Developed addiction-focused programs from scratch, with addictions being the primary mental diagnosis or mental-health concern.
- Initiated and established teen group in addition to running adult addiction group with 75% recovery rate, compared to average of 50%. Initiated follow-up on all group members.
- Successfully expanded client base by developing and instituting new programs and by stimulating client/patient referrals—leveraged outstanding community rapport to generate word of mouth.

Strategy: *Introduced the candidate with a strong profile and comprehensive list of core competencies, followed by a traditional chronological format emphasizing achievements.*

Dan Waterfield
CADC III, SAP
Résumé ▪ Page 2

- Facilitated center's state certification by thoroughly researching federal guidelines and conceptualizing policy and procedures manual.
- Introduced relaxation and art as treatment modalities in center's chemical-abuse counseling program.
- Spearheaded development of successful assessment and intensive inpatient program for alcohol detoxification and short-term treatment at St. John's Hospital.
- Selected to lead new EAP-program based on breadth of experience. Received Award of Excellence in recognition of 10 years of work with EAP-program—sold EAP contracts, performed initial assessments, and conducted brief counseling for new program.
- Played key role in $15,000 increase in revenue (from $70,000 to $85,000) within 18 months by adding SAP evaluations and increasing caseload.
- Increased efficiency and productivity by providing more group-based therapy sessions and by assuming retiring colleague's caseload.

Good Shepherd Inpatient Drug & Alcohol Unit, Denver, CO　　　　　　　　　　1980–1989
Multidisciplinary, 22-bed residential facility serving patients statewide.

LEAD COUNSELOR

Served as key staff member of 21-day inpatient program, with involvement in all aspects of treatment. Counseled both individuals and groups. Trained and provided field supervision to students in nursing, counseling, and social work with regard to AODA patients. Interfaced with family members, employers, attorneys, and social workers—provided continued support, collateral counseling, and education. Collaborated with AA and similar organizations, and provided community education.

Key Achievements:

- Developed team-oriented approach to effectively manage highly diverse client population.
- Helped transition clients through detoxification by working closely with nursing and physician staff.
- Improved patients' mental, physical, emotional, and spiritual health by promoting passage through denial to breakthrough by using various modalities.

Education, Certification & Professional Affiliation

- **Substance Abuse Professional (SAP) Certification**
- **CADCIII Certification**—State of Colorado (member # 518)
- **Drug & Alcohol Counselor Certification,** Cardinal Hill Rehabilitation Hospital, Denver, CO
- Internship at Spaulding Treatment Center, Boulder, CO

Continuing Education
- Receive 24 hours of continuing education annually in AODA and related fields.
- Suicide Prevention.
- Advanced Issues in Ethics.

Professional Affiliation

- NAADAC (Association for Addiction Professionals), since 1982

Registered Nurse

MICHELLE ETIENNE, R.N.
1397 Seawind Crescent
Brampton, ON L6C 3P4
Telephone: (905) 298-5678
Email: etiennem97@yahoo.ca

PROFESSIONAL PROFILE

Caring ▪ People-Oriented ▪ Innovative in Problem Solving
Self-Reliant ▪ Optimistic ▪ Enthusiastic
Won the **2005 Patients' Award** for *"Excellent Patient
Care and Professional Expertise"*

MEDICAL AREAS OF SPECIALIZATION
Medical-Surgical ▪ Gastroenterology ▪ Holistic Wellness
Occupational Therapy ▪ Prostheses & Orthotics ▪ Vascular Technology

An enthusiastic, caring, and people-oriented nursing professional skilled in managing overall patient care and support, providing pre- and post-operative care and assessment, handling wound care monitoring & management, coordinating patient transfers, handling traumas and cardiac arrest patients, and educating patients in their rehabilitation. Adept in establishing priorities and making swift decisions. Function effectively in multidisciplinary teams and work collaboratively with doctors, nurses, and other healthcare professionals to enhance service delivery.

PROFESSIONAL EXPERIENCE

Ingleside Memorial Hospital, Ingleside, England   2000–2005
(A 500-bed healthcare facility recognized as one of England's top hospitals for patient care)
Senior Staff Nurse (August 2002–May 2005)
Pain Link Nurse (July 2002–May 2005)
Staff Nurse (March 2000–July 2002)

Recruited to the hospital as **Staff Nurse;** promoted to **Senior Staff Nurse** within 2 years based solely on performance, not seniority, and concurrently carried out the responsibilities of **Pain Link Nurse** for 2 units. Offered ideas and insights to improve patient care, and participated in fund-raising activities that raised **£72,000** for cancer research. In absence of Line Manager, directed operations of a 36-bed medical/surgical unit:

- Supervised 20 team members consisting of staff and student nurses, care assistants, and dietary aides, and ensured all staff were aware of their roles; involved in decision-making processes and well prepared to respond to emergencies.
- Maximized quality of patient care through needs assessment and resource optimization.
- Ordered all drug supplies for the ward and monitored supply to ensure adequate quantities were available at all times.
- Made the rounds with doctors, updating them on status and medical changes in patients and being available to answer questions or concerns.

Strategy: Presented a clear picture of nursing skills and experience to help this individual transition to a new job in a new country.

Résumé for MICHELLE ETIENNE   Page 2

As **Staff & Pain Link Nurse**

- Chaired meetings of Pain Control Nursing team.
- Developed Teaching Boards and confidently explained the nature of pain: how it is assessed, how it is managed, and what patients can do to control it.
- Updated pain-management literature for patients.
- Trained, mentored, supervised, and assessed student nurses, junior staff nurses, and care assistants.
- Performed physical, emotional, and psychological assessments of patients.
- Managed documentation for all patients and ensured confidentiality was never breached.
- Developed strong rapport with patients and family and cultivated a relaxed atmosphere to put them at ease.
- Provided emotional support to patients and their families during recovery and crisis situations.

Bushwick Community & Home Care Centre, Bushwick, England   1995–1999
Health Care Assistant

- Provided care and support for adults with learning disabilities.
- Assisted day-care officers with social sessions and therapies.
- Coordinated activities of daily living for the elderly—hygiene, food preparation, and feeding.
- Offered encouragement and support to aid in patients' independence.

EDUCATION, TRAINING & CERTIFICATIONS

- **Registered Nurse Certification,** College of Nurses of Ontario   2005
- **Bachelor of Arts, Healthcare,** University of London, England   2003
- **Diploma of Nursing,** University of London, England   1999

Intensive Continuing Education Courses
- **Tracheotomy Care,** Ingleside Memorial   2004
- **Basic Counselling Skills,** Ingleside Memorial   2003
- **Mentor/Assessor Update Session,** University of London   2003
- **Fire Training Certification,** The Edward & Cowan Hospital   2003
- **Blood Transfusion Session,** Ingleside Memorial   2002
- **Blood Glucose Monitoring Session,** Ingleside Memorial   2002
- **Stoma Care,** Ingleside Memorial   2001
- **Adult Basic Life Support,** Bushwick Centre   2001

RESUME 7: BY DON ORLANDO, MBA, CPRW, JCTC, CCM, CCMC

Curriculum Vitæ   *Available for relocation to the Livingston area*

Travis Martindale, Ed.D.
4112 Comstock Drive   303.285.5632 (cellular)
Harland Heights, Colorado 36111   travis.martindale@gmail.com

WHAT I CAN OFFER COLLIER COUNTY SCHOOL BOARD AS YOUR SUPERINTENDENT:

❑ A documented record of success building and maintaining mutually successful partnerships between schools and their constituencies—from administrators to teachers to children to parents to the community.

❑ The vision to describe the right end state… and the skill to guide others to see that same vision as the natural outcome of their own good ideas.

❑ The leadership skills to help people strive for opportunity when others see only frustrating challenges.

❑ A passion for building trust in teachers, administrators, and students by proving my willingness to get them the resources they must have.

> *"I want to commend you…(on) the academic achievement of your students…*
> *much of the credit must go to you and your faculty.*
> *Our state is blessed to have school leaders who are encouragers. You set an example of that…."*
> —Lucy Baxley, Lieutenant Governor, State of Colorado
> December 15, 2004

EDUCATION AND CONTINUING PROFESSIONAL DEVELOPMENT:

❑ **Doctor of Educational Leadership,** Nova Southwestern University, Greeley, Colorado, 2002
   Education Specialist, Mountain University at Montgomery, Sumpter, Colorado, 1998
   (Degree ranks above the master's level)
❑ **Master's in Educational Administration,** University of Colorado, Denver, Colorado, 1996
❑ **Master of Education,** University of Colorado, Denver, Colorado, 1994
❑ **Bachelor of Science** in Broadcast Journalism, Miner State University, Miner, Colorado, 1991

❑ **Governor's Congress on School Leadership,** 2004–Present: Invited by Governor of Colorado to join Congress; selected to serve on task force of 15 superintendents, business leaders, and community leaders that will focus on recruiting and retaining principals.
❑ **Superintendents' Academy:** Selected by Colorado State Department of Education as one of 25 chosen from 41 educators to attend the Academy. Expect completion in August 2005.
❑ **Principals' Academy,** 2001–2002: Selected by Collier County School District to attend Academy administered by Colorado University.
❑ **Blue Ribbon Schools' Conference,** 2000 and 2002: Sole representative from my district.
❑ **Collier County School District's Strategic Planning Training,** 2002–2003.
❑ **How to Deal with Disruptive Students,** Colorado University, 1997.
❑ **Stephen Covey's First Things First Seminar,** Colorado University, 1996.
❑ **Mastering the Maze,** Colorado State Department of Education, 1994 (three-day workshop focused on legal compliance for special-education teachers).

Strategy: *Shared short "performance stories" that communicate the ability to get results in the sometimes difficult-to-measure field of education. The four-page length is not unusual for this field.*

CONFIDENTIAL

Travis Martindale   **Superintendent**   303.285.5632

RELEVANT EMPLOYMENT HISTORY WITH EXAMPLES OF QUALIFICATIONS IN ACTION:

❑ **Assistant Principal** *promoted over eight competitors with years' more experience to serve as* **Principal,** Zebulon Pike High School, Denver, Colorado   2000–Present

Pike's 1,400 students are served by 94 teachers, counselors, and administrators. More than half of the faculty holds master's degrees. This 100% Title I school is the second largest in the city. It was built 56 years ago.

LAYING THE GROUNDWORK FOR OUR NEWEST STUDENTS' SUCCESS

Reduced a chronic problem quickly: 9th graders' behavior problems and truancy were growing as fast as teachers' complaints. Drew on my experience to reach out to other principals with the same problems. Worked with my teachers and administrators to design and implement a new, three-week orientation program in just eight weeks. *Outcomes:* Recruited 134 students for our first program during the summer months when making contact was difficult. Brought this Title I program element in **17% below budget.**

TRANSFORMING A POTENTIAL PUBLIC RELATIONS SETBACK INTO BROAD-BASED SUPPORT

Moved quickly and decisively to step up parental involvement and counter the effects of a recent unflattering news story. My "town hall" meeting brought together all our stakeholders to counter rumors and build commitment to the right solutions. *Outcomes:* More than 300 supportive parents exchanged ideas with representatives from the mayor's office, the job corps, local churches, our school board, the state board of education, the chief of police, teachers, administrators, and business leaders. **Every constituent group signed up for specific actions.**

TURNING AN ADMINISTRATIVE CHALLENGE INTO A TEAM-BUILDING ACCOMPLISHMENT

Helped teachers and staff see a new administrative requirement from our regional accrediting authority as a tool for school-wide improvement. Most thought the re-accreditation self-study a bureaucratic exercise of no value. I reeducated our team to take on the challenge of building a mission statement of which we could be proud. Got everyone—right down to the janitorial staff—involved in shaping our new mission and setting the goals to help us measure progress. *Outcomes:* For the first time, **everyone began living our mission statement.** Whenever they had more tasks than time, they **consistently chose the course that moved us forward fastest.**

FOLDING IN CONSTANT IMPROVEMENT WITH TAILORED INSTRUCTION

Overhauled our in-service training program so that it really worked for my teachers and students. Organized curriculum specialist teams to observe almost every class. Then shared the results with each teacher, making sure to emphasize strengths to build trust. Finally, drew out the teachers' concerns to help them tailor their teaching to individual student needs. *Outcomes:* **95% of teachers show up** for our in-service. Students now striving for subject-matter mastery. **Academic failure rate continues to drop.**

HELPING FREE TEACHERS AND FACULTY FROM IMPACT OF STUDENT DISCIPLINE PROBLEMS

Reacted quickly to a situation I inherited: too many suspensions, too many students sent to my office for behavior problems. Made "leadership by being present" a top priority. Soon I knew my teachers, staff, and students as well as they knew me. Worked in small groups to help teachers find strategies that worked for them. Guided students to understand what

Page 2

CONFIDENTIAL

Travis Martindale · · · · · · · · · · · **Superintendent** · · · · · · · · · · · 303.285.5632

frustrated them in school and how to deal with those factors. Developed many alternatives to suspension. *Outcomes:* **Discipline cases fell 30% in two years. Test scores rising 10% a year.** A professional organization invited me to speak to their members about our success. Our **model is now used in other schools.**

GOING BEYOND SOLVING PROBLEMS TO DEMONSTRATE EXCELLENCE

Saw both an obstacle and an opportunity as I walked through my school: Students were lingering in the halls after the starting bell. We were losing instructional time and stressing our teachers unnecessarily. I proposed a new, simple way to encourage students to be in their seats, ready to learn, on time. We locked the classroom doors at the bell. Any students left in the hall had to attend Saturday school—with at least one parent. Introduced the program slowly, after full coordination with staff, faculty, and parents. After our local Gannett paper ran a positive story about our success, a Fox News affiliate picked it up on the Associated Press wire. Soon a TV crew drove 180 miles roundtrip to see our system for themselves. *Outcomes:* **Tardiness cut in half. Positive media coverage singled out Pike as a model for solving a tough problem well.**

❑ *Sought out by the District Superintendent from a field of eight to be* **Principal,** Charles Norton High School, Bessemer, Colorado · · · · · · · · · · · 1999–2000

Built in 1958, this school had 1,340 students and a faculty and staff of 78.

LEADING OUR SCHOOL OUT OF DEBT

Scrutinized every support cost. Didn't replace people we lost through attrition. Led our teachers to see their success as tied to our school's success. Offered lots of support and resources to help team building. Successfully introduced cooperative learning to lessen teaching loads. *Outcomes:* **Debt fell from $61,000 to $0. Discipline problems declined,** even though class size increased.

❑ *Sought by name by the district's Assistant Superintendent and Superintendent to serve as* **Assistant Principal,** Central High School, Silver City, Colorado · · · · · · · · · · · 1998–1999

❑ *Requested by the Principal to be her* **Assistant Principal,** Jack Martin High School, Alexander City, Colorado · · · · · · · · · · · 1996–1998

TAILORING EDUCATION PLANS TO A MULTITUDE OF NEEDS

Reinvigorated our advisor/advisee program to match our teachers' excellence to the long-term career needs of our students. Made certain every student, from those who saw college in their futures to those focused on the trades, knew which courses would suit them best every year. Then ensured parents not only knew of our program, but got detailed course outlines as well. *Outcomes:* **Students and parents began to see our classes** not as pass-fail exercises, but **as career building blocks. Parent participation grew to 90%. Graduation rate rose; attrition fell.**

CONFIDENTIAL

Travis Martindale   **Superintendent**   303.285.5632

- ❑ *Asked by the Director of Human Resources for the Greeley Public Schools to serve as a* **Special Education Teacher,** Woodlawn High School, Greeley, Colorado   1994–1996

- ❑ *Requested by the Director of the Greeley School District to be a* **Special Education Teacher,** Huffman High School, Greeley, Colorado   1993–1994

PROFESSIONAL AFFILATIONS:
- ❑ Member, Council of Exceptional Children   Since 2001
- ❑ Member, Council for Leadership in Colorado Schools (CLCS)   Since 1996
- ❑ Member, Colorado Education Association   Since 1991
- ❑ Member, National Education Association   Since 1991

RECOGNITION IN MY FIELD:
- ❑ Finalist, Man of the Year   2000
  Nominated by my students for this honor during my first year at Charles Norton High School.

RECENT PROFESSIONAL CERTIFICATION:
- ❑ Certified by the State of Colorado Department of Education to be a K–12 Special Education Teacher and a K–12 Administrator

SERVICE TO MY COMMUNITY:
- ❑ Service as a commissioned officer in the Colorado Army National Guard   1999–Present
  Assignments included deployment to Iraq.
- ❑ Assignments as a commissioned officer in the Air Force Reserves   1990–1998

TECHNOLOGY SKILLS:
- ❑ Completely comfortable with STI educational software suite, Word, Excel, and advanced Internet search protocols.

Page 4

RESUME 8: BY LOUISE GARVER, MCDP, CEIP, CMP, CPRW, JCTC

Nancy A. Monroe

670 E. Higgins Road • Naperville, IL 60563

630.983.7544
namonroe@hotmail.com

VALUE OFFERED AS DIRECTOR OF EDUCATION DELIVERY

Demonstrated track record of improving and directing global education services programs that maximize instructor contributions, curriculum quality, revenue growth, and profitability at technology organizations.

- **Provide the vision, innovation and leadership to improve internal processes in Education Services** with a talent for identifying and resolving operational challenges to enhance revenues/profits.
- **Effective in assessing and driving instructor skill set development, budget and resource management,** as well as partnering with internal departments to meet education needs for a diverse customer base.
- **Experienced in the design and delivery of curriculum programs** that support and achieve business objectives.
- **Repeatedly built and empowered cohesive teams that achieved high standards** of quality and productivity in competitive markets.
- **M.B.A. and B.S. in Education,** Springfield College, Springfield, MA.

PROFESSIONAL EXPERIENCE

SIMTECH CORPORATION, CHICAGO, IL   1996 to present

Promoted through series of high-profile management positions in global Education Services and Customer Support: Global Support Programs Manager (2003 to 2005), Best Practices Manager (2000 to 2003), and Education Services Manager (1996 to 2000).

► **As Education Services Manager, repositioned, upgraded, and transformed Education Services department from an underperforming training function to a profit-generating global organization. P&L management accountability for 12 global Customer Education Centers, team of 17 instructors, curriculum design, facilities management/leasing negotiations, and revenue growth to $10MM.**

- Introduced and educated team on concepts of adult learning theory to better serve students. Turned around team morale from a low of 2 to an average high of 4 as indicated by survey results.
- Determined core product offering, set revenue mix and gross profit margin, and developed knowledge transfer process in collaboration with Product Management and Customer Support departments.
- Established a consistent learning environment for all students globally that eliminated revenue delays and led unit's revenue growth from $4MM to $10MM in billable customer education during 12-month tenure.
- Implemented ASP model for online registration and payment. Produced $600K in additional revenue in first 3 months; achieved double annual quota in first 6 months; doubled revenues in 6 months.
- Succeeded in creating additional revenue stream with multimillion-dollar potential where previous team failed after acquiring $250K of software that could not be implemented.
- Created multi-level certification programs with validation protocol for customers, partners, and employees using ASP model for less than $50K. The certification program revenue potential is millions of dollars annually.
- Took charge of and delivered new education class for applications product line in just 3 months despite failure of consulting team to produce program after 9 months of effort.
- Enhanced company's ability to launch new product lines by designing and ensuring curriculum availability on all product lines by the rollout date. Created incremental education product updates for existing customers.

WORLDWIDE SOLUTIONS, NEW YORK, NY   1995 to 1996

► **As Operations Manager of Education Services, provided strategic planning and leadership effectiveness that drove Education Services revenue growth by 150% ($5MM to $7MM). Directed 12 instructors globally. Supervised curriculum development with team in Germany.**

- Managed the training channel, created certification program, conducted Partner Certification programs, and ensured accreditation of internal resources and third-party delivery resources (partners and subcontractors).
- Automated Education Services function and enrollment process using Access database, turning around employee morale and reducing customer calls from 500 a week down to just 25 while improving customer satisfaction.

Strategy: Created a tightly focused one-page resume that communicates just the relevant experience to match her current goals. Unrelated roles and responsibilities have been omitted.

ANITA ALLEN, SPHR
45 Parsons Way
Medford, New York 11763
(631) 231-1598 Home; (631) 853-2318 Cell
E-mail: anitaallen62@yahoo.com

EXECUTIVE SUMMARY

Diversified and progressive Human Resources (HR) Manager with more than 15 years of experience focusing on generalist responsibilities. Track record of excellence in supervising daily human resources activities while being bottom-line oriented. Demonstrated capabilities include employee/labor relations, staffing, performance management, employee retention, and organizational development. Additional strengths include wage and salary policies/procedures implementation and the creation and execution of workplace programs.

A creative, resourceful, and results-oriented team contributor and builder who promotes a collegial relationship to address business and employee needs.

PROFESSIONAL EXPERIENCE

ABBOTT LABORATORIES, Syosset, N.Y.   1991–2006
Began as an **Employment Interviewer** and advanced through successive promotions to the level of **Division Human Resources Supervisor.**

Provided HR leadership, direction, and support to an eight-member division management team covering multiple sites. Dual reporting relationship to Vice President of Human Resources and VP/General Manager. Acted as advisor to division and senior management in meeting organization's strategic HR goals. Led a Human Resources staff of 9 supporting an employee population totaling 275.

- Assumed a key player role in organization's cultural transformation from a domestic institution to a global organization within a three-year period. Adapted and implemented new HR systems and programs, achieving both budgetary and time frame mandates.

- Partnered with business units to reorganize human resources staff functions, leading to more effective problem solving and turnaround time in resolution of employee issues and concerns.

- Revamped and implemented performance management program from annual to quarterly basis, improving goal achievement for both supervisors and employees.

- Reduced HR staff by 40% without curtailing any support services to operations. Motivated and strengthened HR team through coaching and supportive leadership.

- Managed and resolved complex employee-relations situations utilizing a thorough understanding of Federal and New York State employment laws. Efforts averted potential legal liabilities.

- Pioneered and initiated a 360-degree feedback program for 76 management and supervisory staff. Improved leadership skills and created a model for broader corporate implementation.

Strategy: *Described a wide range of accomplishments to illustrate diversity and upward career movement throughout 15 years with the same company.*

ANITA ALLEN, SPHR   (631) 689-3022   Page 2

PROFESSIONAL EXPERIENCE (Continued)

- Spearheaded and instituted workplace and work/life effectiveness programs that enhanced employee morale, as evidenced by an employee satisfaction survey score of 84%. Company won annual Long Island Family Friendly Employer Award in addition to New York State's Psychologically Healthy Workplace Award for initiatives. Attained corporate recognition for these achievements.

- Designed and implemented innovative staffing strategies to successfully recruit highly qualified employees at minimal or no cost while reducing turnover from 11% to 6%.

- Instituted mentorship and intern programs with local educational institutions, earning community recognition as "an outstanding example of school/business partnerships."

- Selected consistently by senior management to serve on global cross-functional teams to improve organizational effectiveness.

- Chaired and served on business advisory boards for community agencies working on furthering employment opportunities for people with disabilities.

PRIOR EXPERIENCE includes **HR Associate** at EED Manufacturing Company and **Human Resource Assistant** at Timber Operators Council.

EDUCATION

Long Island University, C.W. Post Campus, Brookville, N.Y.
Master's Degree, Human Resources Management and Labor Relations
John Thorne Award for Outstanding Scholarship

LEHMAN COLLEGE, Bronx, N.Y.
Bachelor of Arts Degree

PROFESSIONAL CERTIFICATIONS

Senior Professional in Human Resource Management (SPHR)
Certified Toastmaster (CTM)

PROFESSIONAL ASSOCIATIONS

Society for Human Resource Management
WorldatWork Society (formerly American Compensation Association)
Industry Liaison Group for Affirmative Action
Adults and Children with Learning and Developmental Disabilities

RESUME 10: BY BARBARA SAFANI, MA, CPRW, NCRW, CERW, CCM

JAMES C. SLAVIN
jslavin@nyc.rr.com

51-01 88th Street
Middle Village, NY 11379

Home: 718-455-3335
Cell: 917-952-1522

BROADCAST JOURNALIST

Producer ▪ Writer ▪ Correspondent ▪ Co-Anchor ▪ Assignment Manager ▪ Narrator

CBS Evening News ▪ The Early Show ▪ WCBS ▪ Learning Channel ▪ Money News ▪ Financial Forum

- Over 20 years of experience ensuring the creative execution, content focus, and journalistic integrity of national and syndicated news television programming.

- Innovative storyteller with excellent news judgment and ability to write compelling, clear, and imaginative copy for breaking news, enterprise stories, and documentaries under tight deadlines in environments where priorities change quickly.

- Poised television and voice-over talent with exceptional story delivery and on-air presence.

- Proven leader with notable success overseeing pre- and post-production requirements and logistics, including crew assignment, production scheduling, pre-interview coaching, and linear/non-linear tape editing.

PROFESSIONAL EXPERIENCE

MONEY NEWS BUSINESS MAGAZINE, New York, NY   **2000 to Present**
Producer/Correspondent for syndicated half-hour financial news program aired in ten American markets including CNBC and all of Canada.

Creative Influence/Interview Highlights
- Conceptualized, wrote, reported, and produced *Post 9/11 Spending,* exploring the effects of the WTC disaster on consumer spending habits.
- Researched and produced *Fitness Frenzy,* a look inside New York City's elite "boot camp" physical fitness programs and the price consumers will pay to participate.
- Investigated, scripted, and produced *Corporate Sky,* a piece exploring the business air-travel industry and measures corporations are taking to reduce expenditures.
- Interviewed Henry Kissinger for segment on economic and geopolitical impacts of 9/11.

Production Enhancements
- Revamped opening graphics/audio to better communicate show brand and improve consistency.
- Streamlined narrative content to complement video and graphics and reduce redundancies.

JCS PRODUCTIONS, New York, NY   **2000 to Present**
Owner and Proprietor of production company specializing in all aspects of video, audio, and Web-based production for news coverage, documentary, radio advertising, and corporate communications.

Corporate Branding Initiatives
- Managed all pre- and post-production work for ten-minute promotional video for *CHC Systems,* a global leader in chemical risk-management software.
- Produced eight-minute video for *Electrotech* to introduce breakthrough chemical vapor analysis technology with strong applications in homeland security market.
- Generated original multimedia Web content for above-mentioned companies.
- On-air talent for fifteen 30-second consumer products radio spots.

FINANCIAL FORUM, New York, NY   **1996 to 2000**
Senior Correspondent, Writer, Producer, and Co-Anchor for syndicated half-hour weekly business magazine TV show seen in more than 70 markets throughout the U.S. and Canada. Produced over 130 episodes in studio and on location, domestically and overseas. Oversaw staff of 15 writers, editors, and production assistants.

Innovative Programming
- Developed three-part miniseries uncovering the economic influence of NASA on local communities in Florida and Texas.
- Explored the changing face of higher education in piece that looked at new options for attaining a degree and the corresponding effects on the economy.

Strategy: *Included former big-name employers in the headline to create "clout"; and, in the rest of the resume, painted the picture of a well-rounded professional who fits in at both large and small organizations.*

JAMES C. SLAVIN, Page Two

FINANCIAL FORUM (continued)
- Secured unprecedented glimpse inside the world of telemarketing to uncover how sales are solicited and the Internet's impact on the future of the business.

Reporting Highlights
- Interviewed U.S. Senator Ted Kennedy on controversial 1966 immigration law and its influence on today's economy.
- Questioned Malcolm Forbes on economic trends and investment strategy.
- Met with Aikio Morita to discuss Sony's humble beginnings and current position in the market.

Production Improvements
- Pioneered leading-edge show format and transitioned from simple studio show to three-segment show that included field pieces, live remotes, video, and guest panels.
- Slashed camera crew costs by $150,000+ annually by recommending automated cameras.
- Cut post-production expenses more than half a million dollars annually by suggesting use of more adaptable digital beta camera.
- Trimmed studio expenses significantly by negotiating alternative shooting schedules and sharing studio space whenever possible.

CBS NEWS, New York, NY   **1992 to 1996**
Assignment Manager, Writer, and Producer, WCBC-TV, Channel 2 NY, the #1 CBS news affiliate.
Coordinated daily news story coverage and story progress with news management and affiliates. Efficiently and expeditiously assigned crews for breaking news and features. Generated story ideas and made editing decisions.
- Troubleshot transmission issues related to 1993 WTC attack to minimize station downtime.
- Selected to deliver live phone report to CBS LA affiliate following NW Airlines plane crash.
- First network to air news of Gold Venture Chinese refugee boat off Rockaway Beach (6/92).

WNBC TV, New York, NY   **1994 to 1996**
Freelance Reporter, Writer, and Producer, American Business Journal
- Created 25 pieces for weekly business digest show.

THE LEARNING CHANNEL, New York, NY   **1991 to 1992**
Writer, Producer, and Narrator
- Blended stunning visuals, rare archival material, and dramatic interviews for *Fighters in the Sky,* 15-part documentary hosted by William Hurt chronicling the realities of WWII fighter pilots.
- Developed 26 shows for *I-Spy* series focusing on this secretive world of intrigue and espionage.

CBS NEWS, New York, NY   **1983 to 1991**

Writer, Producer, and Assistant Bureau Chief, Northeast Bureau	**1989 to 1991**
Foreign and Domestic Assignments Manager	**1987 to 1989**
Writer, The Early Show	**1986 to 1987**
Overnight Assignment Manager, Domestic/Foreign Desk	**1985 to 1986**
News and Feature Assistant	**1984 to 1985**
Desk Assistant	**1983 to 1984**

Distinguished career highlighted by rapid promotion through series of increasingly responsible positions.
- Turned around at-risk 12-person Northeast News Bureau by systematizing procedures, implementing accountability standards, and rebuilding relationships with affiliates.
- Made story decisions, wrote, and field-produced numerous high-profile pieces including the death of Leonid Brezhnev, Cicippio hostage crisis, and PanAm Flight 103 crash.
- Interviewed Elizabeth Taylor for first annual "Day Without Art" commemorating victims of AIDS.

EDUCATION
B.A., COMMUNICATIONS, SYRACUSE UNIVERSITY, Syracuse, NY   **1984**

TECHNOLOGY
Familiar with all technical aspects of broadcasting, including Media 100, Final Cut Pro, Macromedia Player, QuickTime Pro, jpeg and mpeg technology and web development, and Microsoft Office suite.

Patricia K. Hewitt

500 North Blvd. • Raleigh, NC 27616

e-mail: patriciak@hewitt.net
h. 919-876-5555 • m. 919-876-1111

ACCOMPLISHED MARKETING AND PUBLIC RELATIONS EXECUTIVE with 15 years of executive management experience. Results-oriented leader possessing solid program-management and program-development skills.

AREAS OF PROFICIENCY

BUSINESS DEVELOPMENT	BUDGET MANAGEMENT	STAFF DEVELOPMENT
OPERATIONS MANAGEMENT	COMMUNICATION	STRATEGIC PLANNING
PROJECT MANAGEMENT	MARKETING	PUBLIC RELATIONS

Honored among North Carolina's Top 100 Women by *The Daily Record*.

KEY STRENGTHS

➤ Well-established business networking connections throughout the region.

➤ Expertise in building solid collaborative partnerships between for-profit and nonprofit sectors resulting in "win-win" marketing initiatives with public/community appeal.

➤ Ability to garner support among diverse personnel and implement guidelines and operational standards that result in a unified and cohesive team-oriented environment.

➤ Talent for intuitively assessing organizations' strengths/weaknesses and restructuring organizational alignment to improve efficiency, increase morale, and achieve new goals.

➤ Skill in recruiting and maintaining diversity and unity among nonprofit executive boards.

PROFESSIONAL HISTORY

Executive Director   Student's Friend Organization, Raleigh, NC   *2003–present*
Collectively recruited by two partnering corporations to promote, direct, and build student-focused philanthropic partnerships between Raleigh businesses and Raleigh public high schools.

Selected Accomplishments

➤ Incorporated a collective vision and built and directed a tangible nonprofit organization that functions as a philanthropic venue for corporations to participate with high schools in workplace mentoring, leadership training, and skill-building programs.

➤ Initiated strategic development plans and recruited corporate sponsors to invest, promote, and encourage the student mentoring concept within their organizations.

➤ Met with public officials, school administrators, and key stakeholders to generate interest, recruit students for the program, and establish parameters to ensure optimal opportunities for students' long-term success. Current graduation rate among participants exceeds 90%.

➤ Recruited, trained, and advised internal program coordinators and mentors to create accountability and continuity among volunteers and increase employee retention.

Strategy: *In addition to professional experience and accomplishments, emphasized connections with the surrounding community as added value in her target role of nonprofit leadership.*

Patricia K. Hewitt   h. 919-876-5555 • m. 919-876-1111 • patriciak@hewitt.net • page 2 of 2

Executive Director   Citizens for Change, Inc., Raleigh, NC   *1992–2003*
Selected for this leadership position from an executive board—charged with revitalizing a struggling organization, enforcing staff accountability, and broadening its mission.

Selected Accomplishments

➢ Expanded programs and established community partnerships that enhanced the organizational structure, increased visibility, and restored employee accountability, making the organization a more viable and attractive resource for employers.

➢ Designed and implemented operational plans to earn national licensing and accreditation.

➢ Spearheaded aggressive marketing and public relations campaign incorporating a new name, logo, and brand that more accurately depicted the organization's mission and purpose—significantly improved public perception within two years.

➢ Quadrupled revenues following the development and implementation of a strategic growth plan targeting niche educational/training services for young adults.

➢ Strategically aligned organization for a successful merger with a human services partner agency; guided and directed the process to ensure positive long-term results.

ADDITIONAL EXPERIENCE
Extensive Human Services background in nonprofit organizations with versatile experience in case management, grant management, and program development/management for diverse populations with social, physical, mental, developmental, and emotional challenges.

EDUCATION & PROFESSIONAL DEVELOPMENT
M.S. Counseling Psychology—Loyola College, Baltimore, MD
B.S. Social Work—Slippery Rock University, Slippery Rock, PA
Leadership—North Carolina Leadership Training Program

COMMUNITY LEADERSHIP/EXECUTIVE BOARD AFFILIATIONS
2005–present	Board Member, The Greater Metro Committee (GMC) LEADERship Program
2004–present	Member, Network 2000
2002–2004	Mentor, Enterprise Women's Network Mentoring Program (in James K. Polk Middle School)
2000–2004	Mentor, University of North Carolina Business Policy Course
1999	Member, Allocations Committee, United Way of North Carolina
1999–2001	Member, Board of Directors, Citizens New Directions
1998–present	Class Rep., Current President GMC Alumni LEADERship Association
1997–1999	Member, Board of Trustees, St. Elizabeth School
1995–1996	Member, Board of Directors, Metro Association of Community Services (MACS)
1993–2001	Immediate Past Chair, Chairperson, and Secretary, Board of Directors, Citizens for Change, Inc.

RESUME 12: BY LISA CHAPMAN, CPRW

BRIAN G. HOBART

2720 U.S. 16 • Petoskey, MI 49770 • 231.576.7865 • bghobart1962@netzero.com

SALES PROFESSIONAL
Territory Manager... Regional Manager / Director... Sales Manager

Motivated, dedicated, and productive sales leader offering more than 13 years of practical sales expertise within diversified industry categories. Rich career background encompasses thorough knowledge of new business development, account management, sales closing, multi-channel sales penetration, and sales team leadership. Recognized for possessing excellent negotiation capabilities, needs assessment talents, and sales presentation proficiencies. Proven track record of success includes revenue growth, solutions selling, team building, customer retention, sales forecasting, and customer satisfaction. Thrive on opportunities to drive bottom-line profitability. **Additional competencies include**

• New Market Development	• Direct Account Sales	• Sales Cycle Management
• Profit & Loss Management	• Customer Service	• New Product Introduction
• Competitor Analysis	• Employee Supervision	• Key Account Management

CAREER PATH

NORTHERN MICHIGAN SANITARY SUPPLY—Petoskey, MI...**2003–Present**

SALES TEAM LEADER

Recruited to company to lead $500,000 regional branch. Embraced challenge to increase profitability and secure new business opportunities. Key activities include supervising branch staff comprising one Sales Coordinator and one Sales Representative, managing inventory, generating new business, retaining established accounts, facilitating sales training, and more.

- Recognized for achieving 90%+ client retention rate.
- Rejuvenated failing relationship with Michigan State University to acquire $25,000+ in annual sales during 2004.
- Reduced branch loss 50% while accelerating in-branch sales 400% in just one year.
- Secured key account with Traverse City Schools, generating $80,000+ in annual sales.
- Negotiated long-term contracted agreements with clients such as Petoskey Public Schools, Christian Church and School, Boyne Falls Public Schools, and Traverse City Schools.
- Boosted year-over-year sales 15% from 2003 to 2004.
- Retained and expanded $80,000+ business at North Central Michigan College.

THE HOME IMPROVEMENT CENTER—Traverse City, MI... **2000–2003**

COMMERCIAL OUTSIDE SALES SPECIALIST (2002–2003)

Promoted to produce new business opportunities while accelerating annual revenues within the residential and commercial building sales channel. Tasked with monitoring sales and market share, identifying and securing new sales, retaining established customer base, and collaborating with Store Manager to establish sales forecast.

- Repositioned worst-performing department in district as number-one rated Commercial Sales Department in less than one year by conceptualizing and implementing new sales methodologies.
- Secured 45%+ of department's $2.7 million annual sales revenue during fiscal year 2001.
- Strengthened pricing structure by conducting thorough competitor analyses.

... Résumé Continues ...

Strategy: *Emphasized sales strengths while downplaying lack of formal education—note that the traditional Education section on page 2 is titled "Professional Development."*

Brian G. Hobart   231.576.7865 · bghobart1962@netzero.com   Page 2 of 2

- Diversified customer base and secured additional market penetration by cultivating relationships within various industries, including recreational vehicle and manufactured housing, residential and commercial construction, apartment complex sector, and municipally owned low-cost housing.

ASSISTANT STORE MANAGER—LUMBER/MILLWORKS—COMMERCIAL SALES (2000–2001)

Accepted position with one of the region's largest home-improvement retailers to address need to heighten departmental success through leadership and reorganization. Directed department by fostering a customer-centric work environment where merchandising and sales performance were vital. Led all operational efforts, resolved customer complaints, monitored and identified sales opportunities, managed payroll hours, supervised 20+ employees, served as "Manager on Duty," and more.

- Increased sales by securing new commercial business accounts, establishing relationships with individual customers, and expanding enrollment in company-sponsored credit program.
- Boosted departmental sales by facilitating employee sales training focused on sales closing, relationship building, and company credit program knowledge.

MCCOY'S CREEK TRADING COMPANY—Denver, CO 1992–2000

SALES MANAGER

Challenged with growing sales for start-up company specializing in the sale, marketing, and distribution of gourmet foods and novelty candies. Designed packaging prototypes, managed customer service function, assisted with product development efforts, oversaw company's financials, and established diversified sales channels with the gift basket, retail, grocery, and national park industries.

- Grew start-up business to 300 nationwide accounts within 6-month time frame.
- Strengthened annual sales by instituting integrated marketing methodology.
- Led trade-show coordination and staffing efforts.

PROFESSIONAL DEVELOPMENT

Professional Sales Training
NORTHERN MICHIGAN SANITARY SUPPLY

Vendor Sales Training
RUBBERMAID... WAUSAU PAPER... RENARD PAPER

COMPUTER SKILLS INVENTORY

QuickBooks Pro... Microsoft Windows, Word

RESUME 13: BY LOUISE GARVER, MCDP, CEIP, CMP, CPRW, JCTC

Stephen Reynolds

E-mail: sreynolds@aol.com

732.575.8113
177 Washington Avenue • Edison, NJ 08818

Sales Management

Delivering consistent and sustainable revenue gains, profit growth, and market-share increases through strategic sales leadership of multi-site branch locations. Valued offered:

✓ Driver of innovative programs that provide a competitive edge and establish company as a full-service market leader.
✓ Proactive, creative problem solver who develops solutions that save time, cut costs, and ensure consistent product quality.
✓ Empowering leader who recruits, develops, coaches, motivates, and inspires sales teams to top performance.
✓ Innovator in developing and implementing win-win solutions to maximize account expansion, retention, and satisfaction.

Selected Career Achievements

RANFORD COMPANY • Edison, NJ   1990 to 2004

As Branch Manager, reinvigorated the sales organization, growing company revenues from $9MM to $11MM, expanding account base from 450 to 680, and increasing market share 15%. Established new performance benchmark and trained sales team on implementing sales-building customer inventory rationalization programs.

- **Revitalized and restored profitability of 2 underperforming territories** by coaching and developing territory reps.
- **Penetrated 2 new markets** and secured a lucrative market niche in abrasive products. Staffed, opened, and managed the 2 branch locations in New Jersey—one of which alone produced $3MM+ over 3 years.
- **Initiated and advanced the skills of sales force to effectively promote and sell increasingly technical product lines** in response to changing market demands.

Increased profit margins and dollar volume through product-mix diversification and expansion. Created product catalogs and marketing literature.

- **Ensured that the company maintained its competitive edge in the marketplace** by adding several cross-functional product lines.
- **Led highly profitable new product introduction with a 40% profit margin** that produced $100K annually in new business.

BERLIN COMPANY • Trenton, NJ   1985 to 1990

As Account Executive, rejuvenated sales performance of a stagnant territory. Turned around customer perception by cultivating exceptional relationships through solutions-based selling and delivering value-added service. Recognized as a peak performer company-wide who consistently ranked #1 in sales and #1 in profits.

- **Positioned and established company as a full-service supplier** to drive sales revenues by translating customer needs to product solutions.
- **More than doubled territory sales from $700K to $1.6MM** during tenure and grew account base from 80 to 125 through new market penetration. **Landed and managed 3 of company's 6 largest accounts** and grew remaining 3.
- **Captured a lucrative account and drove annual sales from $100K in the first year to $400K in 3 years**—outperforming the competition without any price-cutting.
- **Mentored new and existing territory reps** on customer relationship management, solutions-selling strategies, advanced product knowledge, and customer programs.

Education

B.S. in Business Management—University of Rhode Island, Kingston, RI

Strategy: *Positioned this individual for a significant step up by boldly stating strong sales and management achievements.*

RESUME 14: BY JEAN CUMMINGS, MAT, CPRW, CEIP, CPBS

ROBERT COSTELLO

☑ **DRIVING EARLY- TO MID-STAGE SOFTWARE COMPANIES TO MARKET DOMINANCE**

55 Lansing Street
Philadelphia, PA 19120
267-218-3409
TopSales@gmail.com

SALES EXECUTIVE—SOFTWARE INDUSTRY

☑ **SALES & SALES MANAGEMENT**
☑ **ALLIANCE-BUILDING**
☑ **CALL-CENTER IMPLEMENTATION**
☑ **NEW PRODUCT LAUNCH**
☑ **STRATEGIC PLANNING**

TOP PRODUCING SALES MANAGER AND MULTIMILLION-DOLLAR INDIVIDUAL CONTRIBUTOR with 12 years of experience selling innovative products and professional services into the enterprise software space. Fast-track career (6 promotions in 6 years). Proven leader who played key role in growing company from startup to $189 million in annual sales. Inspirational manager with a record of building loyal, high-performance teams. Effective communicator up and down the organization. Passionate, competitive, and driven to succeed. MBA degree.

Regional Director MVP Award	Q3—2003, Q4—2003, Q2—2004, Q3—2004
Proclub	1999–2003 (all years measured)
#1 Sales Rep; #1 Sales Manager; #1 Sales Director	1998–2004

PROFESSIONAL EXPERIENCE

NETDOMINANT, Philadelphia, PA   1997–Present
Played key strategic sales role in growing company from 1 customer to 825 corporate accounts and achieving #2 position in emerging market of identity and access-management solutions—out of 20 rivals (IBM, Sun, Novell, etc.).

Director of Sales—Northeast Region (2003–Present)
Promoted to reenergize the strategically critical Northeast territory. Direct 8 sales reps and 6 sales engineers.

- Built and stabilized a high-powered team. Restructured existing staff and hired/mentored 4 sales representatives, one of whom closed the 2 largest deals in the company's history.
- Achieved impressive metrics for both contribution margin and overall revenue attainment.

Sales Metrics for Team	2003	2004
Sales Revenue	$21.23M	$28.77M
Quota Attainment	140%	130%
Profitability	#1 out of 7 Regions	#1 out of 7 regions
Proclub Attainment	Highest % in North America	Highest % in North America
Forecast Accuracy	#1	#1

Director of Sales—Firewall Sales/Corporate Sales (2002–2003)
Tapped to lead development of inside sales/corporate sales model. Full P&L accountability for $2 million product line.

- Re-envisioned and rebuilt the call center. Developed/implemented a call-center automation system. Devised creative online tools and strategies that enabled the company to sell technical products over the phone.
- Built team of 8. Established call metrics and targets. Doubled productivity per sales rep in one quarter alone.
- Grew call center business to one of company's top revenue generators at $1.4 million in Q2 2004 sales.
- Ramped up to $1.2 million per quarter within 2 quarters. Slashed sales cycle by 78% (compared to outside sales).
- Revamped firewall sales business, increasing profits by $110,000. Improved forecasting accuracy.
- Dramatically increased lead generation and sales of maintenance agreements.

Strategy: Established this individual's "professional brand" as a top-performing sales professional in his specific industry. Table format makes sales achievements jump out.

ROBERT COSTELLO

NETDOMINANT (Continued)
Director of Alliances and Channel Sales (2001–2002)
Promoted to accomplish a three-fold mission: design and execute a comprehensive OEM channel strategy; develop a CRM/ERP Solutions Program; and eventually develop the System Integrator Alliances Program. Managed team of 5.

- Managed OEM program to a sustainable $600,000 per quarter.
- Developed a groundbreaking CRM/ERP Solutions Program to provide integration of access-management software with ERP systems.
- Accelerated quarterly revenue achievement in the CRM/ERP Solutions Program from $100,000 to $1,000,000.
- Built alliances with system integrators that yielded $7+ million in indirect or influenced revenue.
- Implemented a training program, delivering more than 1,000 trained system integration consultants.

Director of Sales—Strategic Global Accounts (2000–2001)
Challenged to develop a global accounts region across North America. Managed 30 Fortune 500 accounts. Hired and managed team of 3 sales reps and 3 sales engineers.

- Earned top ranking out of 8 regions as measured by percentage of goal achieved through first half of 2001.
- Drove $11 million in 2000 revenue with 11 assigned accounts.
- Contributed 20% of total corporate revenue (including maintenance renewals).
- Played integral role in producing 400% corporate growth in 2000.

Sales Executive/Manager—Northeast Region (1997–2000)
Launched the Major Accounts Program. Evangelized innovative software solutions to major corporations.

- Signed many of the company's first and largest customers—FAA, Tokai, GE, The Hartford, Liberty Mutual, Electronic Payment Services, Cigna, Akamai, CVS, State of NY, Xerox, Paychex, United Technology.
- Closed company's first $500,000 and $1 million deals.
- Delivered watershed account, valued at $2 million with follow-on revenue of $25 million.
- Exceeded quota in all 13 quarters.
- Achieved 200% of goal in 2000 and 30% in 1999.
- Leveraged partner relationships to accelerate growth into new accounts and grow size of deals.
- Established the company's most profitable territory based on resource-to-revenue ratio.

TITAN SOFTWARE, INC., Philadelphia, PA   1995–1997
Global provider of enterprise fax and forms solutions for AS/400 systems.

Corporate Sales Manager
Built strategic relationships with major software firms to leverage the business model.

- Ranked #1 or #2 out of a field of 8 reps for 10 straight quarters. Responsible for 30% of all new business.
- Generated more than $450,000 in gross margin in 1996.

Education and Professional Development

UNIVERSITY OF PENNSYLVANIA, Philadelphia, PA
Master of Business Administration   1997

Bachelor of Science: Business Management   1993

TYLER R. PRESTON

302 Indian Way, Mahwah, NJ 07430
Phone (201) 359-3328 • Cell (201) 423-2129
trpreston@hotmail.com

SENIOR SALES & BUSINESS EXECUTIVE
Highly Skilled across All Points of the Sales Cycle from Prospecting to Closing

More than 15 years of experience with a track record of building measurable value •
Management ability enhanced by marketing savvy and a strong technology orientation •
Versatile across large, small, and start-up organizations • Effective cold-caller • Creative thinker
Ability to find new niche markets • Identify and capture new business opportunities
Dynamic professional • Driven by the opportunity to create value • Motivated by creative energy

QUALIFICATIONS

- Business development
- Contract negotiations
- Client-relationship management
- Competitive market analysis
- Product positioning
- Multi-site operation management
- New product/service design & launch

- Key-account development
- P&L management
- ROI optimization
- Internet technologies
- Product & service distribution
- Revenue driver
- Business operational streamlining

Extensive Knowledge of Retail, Manufacturing, Construction Trades, & Real Estate

---

PROFESSIONAL HISTORY

Elite Building Services, Inc., Newark, NJ   August 1988–March 2004
President

Challenged to create a new industry niche by marketing a unique store-renovation solution to household-name national retailers. Organized and supervised the store-repair process. Guaranteed insurance, rates, and qualified workers. Centralized repair, maintenance, and renovation work orders across all construction trades throughout the U.S., Puerto Rico, and Canada. Competitively bid against local contractors, eliminating the need for individual store managers to call out jobs locally.

Developed a strategy to market services to retail executives. Secured business with high-end, mid-market, and discount retailers. Negotiated contracts with local construction trades to develop a national network of preferred vendors. Annual contracts ranged from $20,000 to $800,000; annual service agreements were as large as $1 million.

Selected accomplishments include
- Driving force in growing the company to more than $9 million in revenues over seven years.
- Managed 50 employees in two offices (Reno, de novo growth, and Chicago, by acquisition).
- Initiated vendor-discount prepayment program, which generated $100,000 in annual revenues.

Continued...

Strategy: *Presented 15 years of entrepreneurial work with as much of a corporate "look and feel" as possible.*

TYLER R. PRESTON   PAGE TWO

- Trained employees in sales techniques to successfully identify and close new accounts, manage assigned accounts, and cross-sell new business to existing accounts.
- Arranged a network of more than 10,000 independent contractors nationwide.
- Worked with as many as 500 corporate clients, including Cartier, Gap, and Payless Shoes. Client contacts ranged from project managers up to senior executives. Client companies ranged from multinational corporations to two-person startups.
- Booked more than 50,000 jobs a year at the height of the company's growth.

Facilitated company's revenue growth through the development of a computer tracking system for client work orders. Innovative and a frontrunner for its time in the early 1990s, the system was used by such clients as Barnes & Noble and J.Crew.

Strategically diversified revenue base into related business lines. *Divisions included*
- **Retail store fixtures**—Leveraged existing client relationships to diversify into the installation and repair of store fixtures, i.e., changing out signage on bank buildings and ATMs post-merger.
  - Developed this segment into $2 million in revenues.

- **Kiosks**—Installed, repaired, and maintained kiosks offering free Internet access at airports and malls.
  - Personally built this business line up from zero to $500,000 in revenues.

- **Teddy Bear Care**—Only U.S. distributor to provide national sales and installation of Teddy Bear Care baby changing stations. Sold to malls, airports, churches, doctors' offices, and public parks.
  - Grew business segment to $250,000 in revenues within one year.

- **Real Estate**—Drove the acquisition, development, and management of commercial and multi-family real estate. Considered shopping centers, office buildings, industrial parks, multifamily homes, and student housing nationwide.
  - Identified properties through a network of brokers, local newspapers, and word of mouth.

Closed down less-profitable divisions and spun off both the real estate and Teddy Bear Care business lines in early 2004.

CompleteArtSupply.com, Mahwah, NJ   November 2003–January 2005
President
Online art-supply company that sold to both wholesale and consumer markets.
- Established a new retail presence in several markets, including schools, artists, and consumers.

ChangingStations.com, Mahwah, NJ   April 2004–Present
President
Online sales platform for Teddy Bear Care products. Earned up to $300,000 in annual revenues.
- Refined business model to eliminate installation service, with only a minor reduction in profit margin.

EDUCATION

University of Maryland, College Park, MD   April 1985
Bachelor of Arts in English

SUSAN G. CLIFTON

2944 Steeplechase Drive, Cincinnati, OH 45242
513-791-6843 (h) • 513-200-6974 (c) • sueclifton@cinci.rr.com

DISTRIBUTION / WAREHOUSING EXECUTIVE

Results-oriented, forward-thinking leader with extensive experience in all facets of logistics management, with special attention to efficiency while maintaining the highest levels of customer support. Skills include training and mentoring personnel of varying work skills, ages, and ethnic backgrounds.

Areas of Expertise

Excellent Organizational Skills	High Level of Team Participation/Leadership	Project Management in Line with Corporate Policies & Procedures
Comprehensive Written and Verbal Communications	Adeptness in Adjusting to Changing Business Priorities	Maximum Results from Available Resources
Effectiveness as Interdepartmental Liaison and In-House Business Advisor	Problem Identification & Resolution within Budgets and Timelines	Budget/Asset Controls through Annual Operating Plans and Forecasts

KEY ACHIEVEMENTS

System Development/Implementation:
- ▶ Effectively monitored inventory placement/packing, shipping, receiving, delivery, and controls to consistently meet/exceed financial targets.
- ▶ Competed in 2005 AAAWorld Finals in category of warehouse merging.
- ▶ Developed/implemented new and more cost-saving company returns process.
- ▶ Negotiated contract with new scrap vendor, saving average $8K annually.
- ▶ Leased and organized warehouse space (60K sq.ft.), increased revenue, and met performance metrics through negotiated contracts with Baxter Specialized Content, AMO Metal Brokers, and other trading and manufacturing companies.
- ▶ Managed all DC document processing and inventory transactions and significantly increased inventory accuracy.

Personnel Management:
- ▶ Supervise direct/indirect/perm/temp employees/reports. Developed effective programs to reduce costs by eliminating overtime and rewarding performance.
- ▶ Implemented third-shift receiving and increased service level from 92.5% to 95%.
- ▶ Provided training on software/hardware data-entry systems updates and upgrades.
- ▶ Assisted in facility ballast operations standards development in compliance with high-level corporate policies and procedures.

Page 1 of 2

Strategy: *Used functional format to group a broad range of experience and achievements from more than 20 years with the same firm.*

SUSAN G. CLIFTON

KEY ACHIEVEMENTS, continued

Customer Relations:
- ▶ As Western Region Customer Care Manager, support West Coast Customer Connection Team.
- ▶ Respond to and resolve customer issues as they relate to warehouse operations with in-house personnel.
- ▶ Provide on-site warehouse and customer support.
- ▶ Receive all trucks/cross docks on a daily basis to meet customer's satisfaction.
- ▶ Commended for immediately addressing and resolving customer service issues.

EMPLOYMENT HISTORY

Calhoun Electronics North America—1980–Present

Regional Distribution Director / Corporate Liaison Manager, 2004–Present

Regional Distribution Manager, 2001–2004

RDC System Specialist, 1998–2001

Regional Office Supervisor, 1994–1998

Regional Office Manager, 1988–1994

Senior Sales Coordinator, 1980–1988

EDUCATION

B.S., Business Management: Xavier University, Cincinnati, OH, 2002
(GPA: 3.75)

COMPUTER SKILLS

P.C. literacy includes Microsoft Office (Word, Excel, PowerPoint);
Minitab; Lotus; Internet.

Page 2 of 2

RICHARD R. McCARTHY

265 Charlotte Street ▪ Asheville, NC 28801 ▪ (828) 254-7893 *home* ▪ (828) 230-2114 *cell* ▪ rrmccar@aol.com

Bindery/Finishing Manager & Maintenance Manager

Growth-driven, proactive, with 25-year finishing and maintenance career in printing industry

Innovative, quality-oriented leader and team builder on a relentless quest for profitability and efficiency. Expert technical/mechanical ability and knowledge. Rapport builder with vendors and manufacturers. Hands-on manager willing to work with all team members side by side. Expertise with folders (Stahl, MBO, Baum), stitchers (Muller-Martini, Stahl), cutters (Polar, Itoh), perforators (Rollem), punches (Punchmaster), and press repair. One of the best folder operators in the country. Quick and able student; honest; loyal. Willing to travel and relocate.

Transformed shop from worst to first, with 35% margin of gross, within 3 years.
Drove 200% increase in productivity.

AREAS OF EXPERTISE

- Quality & Performance Improvement
- Cost Reduction & Revenue Gain
- Process & Productivity Improvement
- Turnaround & Change Management

- Team Building & Staff Training
- Vendor Relations & Negotiations
- Purchasing Strategies
- Customer Satisfaction

PROFESSIONAL EXPERIENCE

SUNRISE PACKAGING / ACME GROUP
Sheet-fed printer with full finishing capabilities—multimedia and commercial printing of graphics for CD/DVD/computer games/Playstation, etc. $40M division, with 3 plants and 175 employees at Aracne facilities; $35M in sales, 150 employees in Asheville facility. Sunrise purchased Acme Group in 1999.

Finishing/Maintenance Manager, Asheville, NC   1999–Present
Gained additional maintenance accountability in transition environment, leading a maintenance team of 5. Control $250,000 maintenance budget.
- Captured almost $20,000 in cost savings by moving 2 stitchers in-house. Vendor cost was $11,000 each with 2-week downtime—we moved both in 3 days for $2,500.
- Boosted productivity 75% by converting roller perforator from pile feed to continuous, in-house.
- Converted all maintenance work through MP2 application.
- More than doubled finishing equipment run from 2 pieces at a time to 4–5 at a time.
- Drove unit to #1 in customer satisfaction and profitability with a fully cross-trained staff (during busy times, even office staff can run the equipment). Current turn times are 24 to 48 hours from order to delivery.

Finishing Manager, Asheville, NC   1998–1999
Managed finishing department with $750,000 budget and 60 full-time and temporary employees. Scheduled coverage (including vacations). Worked one-on-one with employees on machinery to achieve their highest level of competence, evaluating and reviewing progress at monthly and half-year meetings.
- Ignited turnaround and growth of failing department, driving facility to #1 in company. Initiated new goals at or above manufacturing standards, new layouts, quality checks, and PM program generated through MP2 program. Personally rebuilt hand-me-down equipment and trained inexperienced operators on lube points, wear points, and state-of-the-art technology.
- Accelerated productivity 200% by introducing new production-line method for cassettes, completing both die-cutting and folding on the same machine. Within a year, was only plant running cassettes profitably.
- Led maintenance and tech operators to highest efficiency and best practices.
- Slashed costs by meeting directly with vendors, putting those selling equivalent materials into a bidding war.

Strategy: *Emphasized problem-solving and profit-building record to put this individual in the forefront for a limited number of positions within an industry that has shrunk significantly due to global out-sourcing (commercial printing).*

RESUME *17*, CONTINUED

(828) 254-7893 *home* • (828) 230-2114 *cell* • rrmccar@aol.com　　　　**RICHARD R. McCARTHY**

Operator, Aracne, NJ　　　　　　　　　　　　　　　　　　　　　　　　　　1992–1998
2nd-shift Bindery Lead over 15 people. Set goals and scheduling for all finishing equipment, approved jobs, operated and troubleshot equipment, and coordinated work among pressroom, bindery, shipping, and QA.
- Sourced and negotiated with vendors for best-price cost reductions.
- Worked with manufacturers on the limits and expectations of their equipment, enabling me to design the proper PM service for each piece of equipment and expect more productive numbers. Eliminated all excuses.
- Increased profit margins by training existing operators on new, more productive operating methods.

ALL-AROUND COLOR BOOKS, Aracne, NJ
Machine Operator / Truck Driver / Maintenance　　　　　　　　　　　　　1980–1992
Privately owned book bindery for commercial print shops specializing in giant coloring books.
Instrumental in growth of small coloring-book manufacturer to a full commercial bindery with confident, efficient staff. Supervised 8 of 25 employees in the company. Set up and ran 4 folding/cutting/stitching operations. Maintained building and equipment for on-time delivery of product. Assisted in creating effective layouts for customers and sales group.
- Boosted productivity and cut costs. Learned manuals of all the equipment; then worked with manufacturers to achieve the maximum speeds while applying appropriate PMs. Worked with vendors to lower consumables costs. Trained staff on proper functions and PMs for equipment; set goals on run speeds.

STANLEY MAGIC DOORS, Aracne, NJ
Apprentice Door Installer　　　　　　　　　　　　　　　　　　　　　　1978–1980
After-school position, loading and installing automatic doors for supermarkets and hospitals.

PROFESSIONAL TRAINING

WEI Supervisor Training
Front Line Team Leader Training (IP)
Problem Solving (IP)
Marshal Institute's World Class Maintenance Course Work System
(3-day, tested course on planning/scheduling of preventive and predictive maintenance
and storeroom management)

Technical skills include Excel, Word, PowerPoint, Oracle, MP2

Theodore C. Smith

5415 N. Clark Street	(773) 249-1641
Chicago, Illinois 60640	tcsmith@yahoo.com

OBJECTIVE: To obtain a position as a **Senior Manager.**

PROFILE:

EXPERIENCE: Versatile **Engineer** who can impact strategic management, international markets, and industry trends.

LEADERSHIP: Articulate team builder who listens to internal partners, clients, and vendors; finds areas of common ground; and motivates people with conflicting interests to work together.

TECHNICAL SKILLS: Results-oriented professional who has led projects to design customized products, open/close facilities, and migrate knowledge so that quality and production are not compromised.

EDUCATION:

Northwestern University, Evanston, Illinois
M.B.A.   2005
Relevant courses: Strategic Planning; Executive Decision Making

Purdue University, West Lafayette, Indiana
B.S., Mechanical Engineering   1984

EXPERIENCE:

Acme Industries, Chicago, Illinois   2001–Present

PROJECT LEAD ENGINEER
Design products and manage projects in the production of retractors and tool balancers for industrial use (automotive, food processing). Communicate daily with design and manufacturing engineers at Mexican, European, and domestic units to resolve issues related to design, performance, and operation. Oversee special projects involving prototypes and custom orders, working closely with marketing and business development. Maintain product quality through site visits and training. Evaluate and recommend potential manufacturing and sourcing partners. Source materials, including die cast and plastic parts. Resolve logistic and pricing questions related to manufacturing.

- Assigned to lead an extensive migration of engineering and design intelligence from a central location to new operations, including subcontractors, in the U.S., U.K., Mexico, and China.
- Selected to design a new product for a world leader in power tools. Created a 3D prototype using SLA method. Collaborated with marketing, business development, and patent attorneys to prepare bids and research patent issues.
- Inspected units throughout Illinois to replace faulty parts that could malfunction and expose the company to liability. Reported directly to senior management and attorneys.
- Implemented sourcing and subassembly operations in China that will result in cost savings of $480,000.

John Jones Manufacturing, Niles, Illinois   2000–2001

PROJECT ENGINEER
Performed a wide range of duties in design, project management, and sourcing. Directed internal and vendor teams that installed equipment for line production of electromechanical and galvanized tubing. Designed parts for machines and components that can accommodate speeds up to 1,000 feet per minute, including

(continued)

Strategy: *Positioned this new MBA for a leadership role by emphasizing his leadership skills as well as his technical background.*

Theodore C. Smith

Page Two

slide mechanisms, driver track systems, drive shafts, timing pulleys, and gear-driven lift systems for height adjustment. Assessed needs and determined materials for each project, paying special attention to stress of each line. Created project plans (MS Project), layout (AutoCAD), and design components (Autodesk Inventor).

- Selected to close a plant, evaluate equipment for reuse, and arrange transportation and reinstallation at the new site.
- Played a key role in sourcing management for a $26 million plant expansion that required evaluation of domestic and international vendors.

EBM Electrical Group/Simon Electric, Skokie, Illinois   1996–2000

PROJECT ENGINEER
Designed and developed multi-branded lighting fixtures for general and hazardous uses. Tested products to comply with all UL and NEC standards. Used advanced software to design and reengineer metal and plastic products. Inspected new products and partnered with manufacturing engineers to maximize production and quality in domestic and international locations.

- Served on product management team that forecast competition and costs.

Masterseal Company, Chicago, Illinois   1992–1996

MECHANICAL ENGINEER
Led projects to research, design, prototype, and test new product lines. Monitored on-site production, examining parts to ensure quality. Provided client sales training and technical support. Collaborate with marketing team to answer questions and develop catalogs. Sourced and purchased materials, including o-rings, gaskets, and springs.

- Played key role in 33% worldwide gain for Pin-Tech relief valve by contributing to marketing efforts, pricing, and EPA compliance.

American Materials LP, Elk Grove Village, Illinois   1984–1992

PROJECT ENGINEER
Conducted engineering analysis, identified problems, and set priorities to improve line efficiency and coating consistency at a steel processing plant. Maintained quality by following ASTM standards.

COMPUTER SKILLS: Algor-FEA, AutoCAD 2004, Mechanical Desktop 6, Autodesk Inventor 9, SolidWorks 2000, Pro-E Wildfire 2.0, ERP/J.D. Edwards, MS Project 2003, Logia Product Configurator, Access, Excel, PowerPoint, and Word

STANDARDS: UL, CSA, NEC, NFPA, API, ASTM, EPA, OSHA, ISO 9001, ISO 9002

AFFILIATION: American Society of Mechanical Engineers (ASME)

References Available upon Request

STEPHEN KANE

stepkane@verizon.com

275 Riverview Road • Tionesta, PA 16353 • 814-851-1277 • cell: 814-863-8676

INFORMATION SYSTEMS • INFORMATION TECHNOLOGY
Systems Administration • Networks • Security • Installation • Troubleshooting

▶ Notable 19+ years as Information Systems and Technology administrator and instructor. Expertise in strategic and tactical actions that deliver revenue gains and cost savings through analytical and complex problem-solving abilities. Solid supervisory/management skills and excellent interpersonal, written, and oral communication skills (network, collaborate, negotiate).

▶ Deliver technical and programmatic consultation skills related to soundness of approach, compliance to technical standards, reflection of industry best practices, satisfaction of functional requirements, and ability to integrate with existing technical and system architecture.

▶ Plan, organize, and lead complex projects. Develop status reports and formal guidelines. Apply information engineering principles as they relate to application life cycle, operating systems, web development, directories, databases, network, and wireless technologies.

▶ Possess exceptional organizational skills. Motivate teams and create team-based atmosphere to meet goals within deadlines: identify common objectives, establish and communicate specific expectations, stress attention to detail, and recognize individual personnel on attainment of goals.

▶ Direct IS/IT policies, standards and procedures to support consistent solutions delivery and effective implementation. Evaluate emerging technology risks and potential infrastructure impact, and provide solutions that meet business requirements.

COMPUTER SKILLS SUMMARY

- Windows 3.x, 95, 98 (SE), 2000, NT, XP, ME
- Solaris 2.5, 8.0, 9.0
- IT 21
- LAN Administrator
- SCI ADNS; ADNS
- DOS

- Networks Set Up
- Network Security
- Routers, Hubs, Switches
- Firewalls
- Servers
- Microsoft Office 98, 2000

AREAS OF EXPERTISE

- Data Center Management
- Systems Installation/Configuration
- Information Protection
- Field Service Administration
- Repair of Peripherals
- Systems Administration

- Network Operations
- IS/IT Security
- Computer Security
- Troubleshooting
- Diagnostics/Testing
- Project Management

- Fiber-optics
- Microwave
- Wireless Technology
- Satellite Technology
- CAT 5
- Land Lines

PROFESSIONAL EXPERIENCE

U.S. Navy   1986–2005
NETWORK SECURITY AND VULNERABILITIES TECHNICIAN INSTRUCTOR *(2001–2005)*
NETWORK SECURITY AND VULNERABILITIES ADMINISTRATOR *(1991–2001)*
CRYPTOLOGIC COMMUNICATIONS SYSTEMS *(1986–1991)*

- Managed internal information technologies (IT) operations to maintain integrity of fleet-wide communications and worldwide networks. Improved system functionality through upgrades and implementation of new software. Facilitated introduction of new technologies (e.g., ADNS, SCI ADNS). Operated from bases in various U.S. locations, the Orient, and the Middle East.

- Recognized as Network Security and Vulnerabilities Technician (NSVT) subject matter expert.

Strategy: *Translated Navy experience to the corporate world, covering a wide array of technical skills, projects, and accomplishments.*

STEPHEN KANE • 814-851-1277 • *Page 2*

U.S. Navy, *continued*

- As 1 of 3 administrators for Fleet Network Operations Center, was sought out personally by an outside civilian computer company, developer of the new computer communication systems for the Naval Fleet, to personally install all computer systems on shore and on all ships for the Navy. Originated Standard Operating Procedures (SOPs) that streamlined processes and boosted accuracy. Managed technical documentation, including classified materials and databases.

- Created updated network system that optimized worldwide communications. Installed computer-based satellite network communications for Navy ships; administered shore-based network centers.

- Provided hands-on support for computer-related hardware and software problems. Always produced exceptional work. Wrote documentation to assist in training and as reference for users.

- Served as lead instructor in training centers for NSVT course; sought out by, and provided training to, other instructors. Taught 332 students within 2½ years. Wrote learning objectives, prepared test items, and evaluated instructional materials and results of instruction. Counseled students on academic learning problems.

- Performed in-flight functions as cryptologic operator/analyst. Knowledgeable in airborne data collection systems, and emergency and flight procedures.

- Proficient in shipboard system operations. Planned and conducted operations in sending and receiving communications; maintained circuit quality. Prepared operations and technical reports. Inspected, cleaned, and made operational adjustments to equipment. Supervised and evaluated 21 subordinates providing network administration.

MILITARY

Top Secret Clearance *(Most recent clearance update completed May 2005)*

United States Navy, 1985–2005, Honorable Discharge

United States Marine Corps, 1983–1985, Honorable Discharge

EDUCATION / COMPUTER TRAINING

Certificate, **Interconnecting Cisco Network Devices,** 2003
Certificate, **Router and Switching CCNA Course,** 2003
New Horizons Computer Learning Center – Orlando, Florida

Certificate, **Information Systems Administration, Navy Course,** 2002

Certificate, **Windows 2000 Security** (graduated top of class), 2002
Global Knowledge—Atlanta, Georgia

Network Security Vulnerability Technician Training, 2002

Fleet Integrated **Cryptologic Communications Systems** Training, 1998

Credit recommendation from American Council on Education in baccalaureate/associate degree category:
    Computer Systems and Organizations, 2 semester hours
    Records and Information Management, 3 semester hours
    Personnel Supervision, 3 semester hours
    Computer Applications, 3 semester hours
    Technical Writing, 3 semester hours
    Security Operations, 2 semester hours

Appliance Servicing Certificate, 1983, Crawford County Vo-Tech—Atlantic, Pennsylvania

Graduate, 1982, Sheffield High School—Sheffield, Pennsylvania

Linda C. Van Kirk

3624 Edgewood Drive · Winston-Salem, NC 27106 · (336) 758-9999 · lvankirk@triad.rr.com

IT Project Manager

Professional Project Manager who sets the strategic direction, articulates the benefits, and delivers bottom-line results. Possess the ultimate combination of technical depth, methodology and process knowledge, and strong interpersonal skills. Project management experience includes delivery of projects to distributed and centralized systems; UNIX/ORACLE and Windows/SQL platforms; multi-lingual systems; and web-based applications. Accomplishments and experience in the areas of

- Multi-Project Management
- Performance Optimization
- Staff Training & Development

- Risk Projection/Minimization
- Pre- & Post-Deployment Support
- Documentation & Presentations

Professional Experience

S&P Technology, Winston-Salem, NC   2001–present
Senior IT Project Manager
Selected to implement and enforce a standard project management discipline. Oversaw the company's project portfolio of more than 25 simultaneous projects including scope, status, resource allocation, impact, and risk projections. Managed a $5 million budget with full P&L responsibility and 12 direct reports.
- Surpassed expectations and received the **President's Excellence Award** for an application that revolutionized operations and drove the company to #1 in its field.
- Developed project budget and change-order processes that **doubled efficiency** and reduced head count while increasing number of projects in the pipeline by 65%.
- Created a fully integrated project-management discipline that improved philosophy and environment of the department and substantially increased performance and results.
- Advised and mentored employees and developed accelerated career paths based on each employee's increased knowledge, goal attainment, and finely honed technical skills.

Superior Cellular Systems, Inc., Greensboro, NC   1995–2001
Project Manager
Managed multiple simultaneous projects with full responsibility for design, development, training, testing, documentation, deployment, and post-deployment support for a premier provider of wireless services. Moved to client-side support from application side.
- Delivered final project after announcement of merger with AT&T; reduced headcount and **saved the company $2 million.**
- Performed feasibility analysis and recommended policy changes to upper management; when implemented, **reduced cycle time by 25%.**
- Brought standardization to processes and utilized extensive knowledge of systems to transition outsourced financial reporting to an in-house billing and rating system.
- Established and promoted professional development of project managers and staff. Collaborated with other project managers to build effective cross-functional teams.

Strategy: *Focused on management experience; key accomplishments; and strong blend of technical knowledge, certifications, and people-management skills.*

Linda C. Van Kirk   lvankirk@triad.rr.com

Ace Electronic Marketing, Winston-Salem, NC   1990–1994
Project Manager, Software Development
Managed the e-business infrastructure for an international electronic marketing company. Directed and supported teams in the United States and Asia for the development and support of transaction-based tracking software.

- Led a talented team of culturally diverse software project engineers in a multi-currency, multi-lingual environment.
- Collaborated with team members to develop and deliver software releases with sophisticated automated update capability on time and within tight budget constraints.
- Created pertinent documentation, conducted training, and provided support on new tools and procedures.
- Played a crucial role in the development of next-generation software for enhanced performance and customer satisfaction.

Education

B.S., Information Systems, Wake Forest University, Winston-Salem, NC

Certification/Professional Development

Project Management Professional (PMP)
Certified Associate in Project Management (CAPM)
Center for Creative Leadership, Management Workshop
Topical Training: Diversity, Sexual Harassment, Time Management, and Change Leadership

RESUME 21: BY SUSAN GUARNERI, NCC, NCCC, CPRW, CPBS, CCMC, CEIP, IJCTC, DCC, MCC

MARK K. MINADEO
773 Jefferson Street, Madison, WI 55715
(608) 663-5555 Home ▪ markminadeo@gmail.com

Director, Software Development
Client/Server and Mainframe Applications Development Management

Business-savvy IT manager with track record of goal-surpassing performance delivering large-scale product development projects on time. Team builder and "big picture" thinker who maximizes productivity and team spirit. Pragmatic leader with M&A implementation and IPO experience. Hands-on software development experience with DBMS applications. Proven skills in

☑ Product Lifecycle Management   ☑ Vendor Partnerships   ☑ Matrix Management
☑ Team Leadership / Motivation   ☑ Software Engineering   ☑ Technical Team Building
☑ Software Lifecycle Management   ☑ Project Management   ☑ Budget Forecasts / Savings

---

PROFESSIONAL EXPERIENCE

MADISON SOFTWARE SOLUTIONS, Madison, WI   1995–present
Market leader in enterprise database archiving and test data management software for information lifecycle management. More than 2,100 customers (many Fortune 500) in 30 countries, 250 employees in 5 countries (US, Europe, Canada, and Asia) with revenues in excess of $40 million.

Director of Development—function as **VP of Development,** report to CEO (2002–present)
Matrix-manage client/server and mainframe development projects (full lifecycle management), coordinating product lifecycle (PLC) with Product Management, Documentation, and Quality Assurance (QA). Supervise 60 technical staff. Manage $6.6 million budget and budget forecasting.

ACCOMPLISHMENTS

- **Turnaround Management.** Turned around department struggling with bug-laden products and failure to meet release-to-manufacture (RTM) dates. Unified and rallied staffs from 4 departments around PLC timelines, meeting RTM dates 100% of time, on budget, and with no bugs.

- **Product Lifecycle Management.** Review enhancements for 15–20 products representing 80% of company's revenues. Oversee new product releases (3–4 Client/Server and 1 Mainframe each year) that support 6 DBMS and 4 platforms. Core product: DBMS Archive/Restore application that speeds DBMS response time while conserving system resources.

- **Vendor Management and Alliances.** Built 40 third-party vendor partnerships with companies such as IBM, EMC, and Oracle, integrating vendor apps for seamless customer experience. Diplomatically negotiated and resolved issues involving vendors, internal customers, and clients.

- **Human Resources and Talent Management.** Established and maintain 0% turnover in department (far below industry norms) through team building, vision "buy-in," improved cross-team communications, mentoring, and coaching. Oversee training and certification. Recruit, hire, and supervise 7–10 developers and staff annually for development of offshore operations in India.

- **Quality and Best Practices.** Implemented and monitor best practice metrics, and streamlined QA to increase efficiency and maximize resources. These initiatives, combined with a customer-first mentality, resulted in 100% client loyalty in competitive tech industry, as well as cost savings.

Strategy: *Highlighted relatively brief management experience on page 1, using functional keywords to introduce key accomplishments.*

MARK K. MINADEO   Page 2
(608) 663-5555 Home ▪ markminadeo@gmail.com

Senior Developer (1995–2001)

- **Applications Development.** Created Windows-based Database Management System (DBMS) Archive/Restore application, supporting top 7 most popular DBMS, as team lead within 9 months. Became core product and established groundwork for additional software products.

- **Project Management.** Led team development of ancillary products that interface with third-party ERP/CRM applications, such as J.D. Edwards and PeopleSoft. Created new product allowing users to relationally edit, browse, and join DBMS tables across databases and database systems.

- **Productivity Improvements.** Created and programmed in-house automated source management system, standardizing source change process and product packaging for RTM. This utility increased productivity by removing duplication of work and eliminating potential errors.

- **Advanced Programming.** Designed and implemented high-volume, fast-performance DBMS load facility with ability to interface with top 7 DBMS (PC platform). Created algorithms to improve processing of data terabytes (reduced 10 million-row run to 45 seconds).

Developer, COMPUTER RENAISSANCE, INC., New York, NY   1990–1995
Fortune 500 software development company (systems applications for mainframe).

- **Mainframe Development Project.** Teamed with 11 developers in partnered development effort with SBM to create and develop SBM CICS Plex Management system. Played key team role in designing main product features (message routing, monitoring, and workload management).

Developer, DATA PARTNERS, INC. (fka Applied Data Systems), New York, NY   1986–1990
Fortune 100 company—third-largest computer software company.

- **Advanced Development Programming.** Enhanced and maintained CA-ROSCOE (TSO-like facility permitting multi-user applications in single address space). Created and programmed ESTAE exits and Functional Recovery routines, facilitating synchronous task termination and coordination with main task. Wrote IPCS verb exits to analyze diagnostic materials obtained.

EDUCATION & TRAINING

MS Project Training Seminar, New York, NY—September 2005
Best Practices Conference, Philadelphia, PA—September 2005
SBM Share Conferences—2000 through 2005
UDB and Oracle DBMS Conferences—2000 through 2005
Associate's Degree, Computer Science, Suffolk County College, Suffolk, NY

TECHNOLOGY SUMMARY

Languages:	C, C++, COM, VB, VBA, z/OS ASM, Java, z/OS JCL, HTML, JavaScript
DBMS:	Sybase, Oracle, UDB, DB2, Informix, SQL Server
Platforms:	UNIX (Sun, HP, AIX), Windows (2K, XP), z/OS, Linux
Software:	MS Word, MS Project, MS Visio, MS Developer Studio, MS Excel, MS Access, CSI, MS SourceSafe, PVCS, Subversion, MS PowerPoint, MS Office, XML, Middleware

NICK CURTIS

22355 South Milford ▪ Cincinnati, OH 45209 ▪ 513-525.7495 ▪ curtis678@hotmail.com

—TAX APPRAISER/CONSULTANT—

QUALIFICATIONS

- Substantial knowledge of advanced appraisal methods and techniques using income, sales comparison, stock and debt, and cost approaches emphasizing unitary concept evaluation and economic principles.
- Experience researching, analyzing, and interpreting economic and financial data for use in appraisals, and documenting with written appraisal reports.
- Exceptional ability to work with customers and taxpayers to negotiate and mediate problems.
- Outstanding customer service—pride in exceeding customer expectations.
- Experience applying computer software including Gentax for appraisals; income, sales, travel, convention, and withholding taxes.
- Successful collection skills utilizing a variety of resourceful and alternative methods to find and collect from individuals who owe taxes.
- Assertive, effective decision–making and problem–solving skills.
- Excellent communication skills—negotiating, writing, listening, and verbalizing.

EMPLOYMENT

COMPLIANCE TECHNICIAN. Tax Commission, Cincinnati, Ohio. January 2003–Present.
- Provide taxpayer assistance and collection services via telephone and for walk-in customers.
- Advise taxpayers and co-workers about tax laws and rules and how to complete and file tax returns.
- Make decisions on audits and explain taxpayer rights and limitations.
- Collect delinquent taxes via telephone, create and distribute collection letters, and use locator methods.
- Enforce state tax laws and rules through administrative procedures.
- Use state skip-tracing resources, including automated system databases and alternative methods, to collect on delinquent accounts.
- Train and support employees on successful collection procedures and equipment issues.

OFFICE SPECIALIST/TECHNICIAN. Tax Commission, Columbus, Ohio. March 2001–January 2003.
- Explained legal ramifications of non-compliance, prepared written documentation, and initiated legal action when necessary.
- Executed levies, wage assignments, electronic funds transfers, and payment agreements with taxpayers.
- Maintained a caseload of collection accounts while completing bank deposits.
- Calculated interest and penalties on taxes due; secured and monitored payment agreements with taxpayers.
- Researched and reviewed various records for potential sources of income.
- Provided computer support to the Toledo Field Office.
- Presented ideas to improve work environment, productivity, and efficiency.

Strategy: *Presented a strong slate of qualifications, followed by chronological work history that supports his advancement goal.*

NICK CURTIS

22355 South Milford ▪ Cincinnati, OH 45209 ▪ 513-525.7495▪ curtis678@hotmail.com

EMPLOYMENT, CONTINUED

CUSTOMER SERVICE RESOURCE. Center Partners—AT&T, Columbus, Ohio. August 1987–April 2001.
- Provided support to agents giving service to AT&T customers.
- Received supervisor–level calls, explaining policies and procedures to agents.
- Mentored new agents to instill confidence and provide guidance.
- Troubleshot connectivity issues.
- Assisted with credit problems on billing issues.
- Worked as a team player to assist in solving technical questions.
- Presented ideas to improve work environment and efficiency.

CUSTOMER SERVICE AGENT. Center Partners, Columbus, Ohio. March 1983–August 1987.
- Provided telephone technical support to Acer customers.
- Troubleshot issues with monitors, keyboards, CD writers, scanners, and CD/DVD-ROMs.
- Solved technical questions and presented ideas to improve work environment and efficiency.
- Maintained assigned computer equipment.

EDUCATION

Center Partners/AT&T, Columbus, Ohio. Extensive training in Acer Peripherals, AT&T Procedures, Lucent
Telephone Training, Advanced Customer Service Representative Systems, and Vantive. 1999–2001.
CC Computer Services & Training. Windows, Word, Visio, Excel, Outlook, Visual Basic, Project, HTML, Web
Site Design, WordPerfect, and Internet. 1998–2005.
The Ohio State University, Columbus, Ohio. **BSBA in Computer Information Systems.** December 1983.

TECHNICAL SKILLS

- Proficient knowledge of Gentax, Word, Excel, Access, PowerPoint, Project, Visual Basic 6 and .NET,
Visio, Minitab, WordPerfect, Macromedia Suite, Internet, Macintosh Operating Systems, and Windows
Operating Systems, including 95, 98, NT, XP, and 2000.
- Strong technical background in information technology, systems analysis design, advanced business
programming, database administration, and information security.
- Outstanding analytical skills in diagnosing and correcting problems involving software and hardware
as well as excellent ability to use resources successfully to determine solutions.

RESUME 23: BY BILL MURDOCK, CPRW

JACKSON KUNOFSKY, C.I.C.P.

5712 Federal Way, Seattle, Washington 98911
Home: 425-468-9961 • Mobile: 425-556-6666
E-mail: debtguy@aol.com

DIRECTOR OF CREDIT AND COLLECTIONS
**Global Credit Operations ~ National Credit Association Leadership ~ Advisor to D & B
Departmental Growth and Development ~ Utilities and Public Companies**

A nationally recognized and respected credit executive with an impeccable array of professional leadership accomplishments and contributions to corporate profits and revenue. Experienced in pre- and post-IPO environments, troubled consolidations, and stressed remote operations. Empowering, proactive, and innovative. Major areas of expertise include

Credit Analysis	Policies and Procedures	Standards and Benchmarks
Letters of Credit	Redemptions	Automated Systems
PUC / SOX Stipulations	Fraud Detection	Staff Development / Incentives
Process Analysis	Risk Management	Portfolio Credit Insurance
Delinquency Reductions	TQM–Texas A & M	Outsourcing

MS Office (All) ~ Lotus Notes ~ AS400 ~ JD Edwards ~ PeopleSoft ~ SAP ~ Lawson

Credit Executive of the Year
Reimer Reporting–1996

Certified International Credit Professional
University of Michigan / FCIB / NACM–2004

PROFESSIONAL HIGHLIGHTS

Consolidated Communications Company—Seattle, Washington • 2002–2006
Formerly Texas Communications. Revenues of $350 million. Divested in 2005.

Director of Credit and Collections

Recruited to guide the consolidation of three independent phone companies (ILEC and CLEC), establish uniform operating and collection procedures, and forestall imminent and substantial out-of-compliance fines by the PUC. Inherited 210,000 residential and business customers, $35 million in receivables, and a combination union / non-union workforce using six separate billing systems. Staff of 15; three direct reports.

- Created and chaired a cross-functional team (Customer Care, Sales, Billing, Accounting, and Regulatory) to improve efficiencies and ensure compliance in all areas of operations. Performed CFO-mandated monthly audits to verify collection was in compliance with PUC and SOX regulations.
- Consulted with the Human Resources department to establish standardized job descriptions, recruit management, and move collections away from union administration.
- Implemented a four-step collection strategy that reduced DSO by 10 days within the first seven months, then led the way for decreasing bad-debt write-offs from $5.5 million in 2002 to $1.7 million in FY 2004; added a 40% reduction of overall 90+-day aging from January 2003 through October 2003.
- Produced a 65% sell-off and recovery of WorldCom's $2.5-million Chapter 11 write down.
- Managed the end-to-end transition and shut-down of all credit and collection activities from Seattle to the corporate offices in Illinois. Praised by the acquiring CEO for the quality of the hand-over.

Winstar Telecom—New York, New York • 1998–2002
Local and long-distance telecommunications provider. $700M in annual revenue.

Director of Credit and Collections (2001–2002)

Guided the efforts of a 44-person collection staff, including two direct-report managers and one supervisor, servicing more than 200,000 business accounts and $100 million in accounts receivable. Developed annual departmental budgets, created in-house incentive programs, and oversaw hiring and policy administration.

Strategy: *Created a high-impact "first impression" that includes not only highlights on the job, but also contributions to professional associations and his specialized certifications.*

JACKSON KUNOFSKY, C.I.C.P.

Winstar Telecom—continued

- Oversaw departmental reorganization for the credit teams, implementing the Aspect ACD system that increased collection call volumes by more than 300% within 90 days.
- Outsourced routine print communications to the outside print vendor, reducing overall processing costs by 20% within 60 days. Shed responsibility for 25,000 dun letters and 5,000 suspension notices monthly.
- Implemented monthly production and performance incentives for the collection staff, increasing cash by 15% in the first month and ultimately providing up to a 30% increase in cash availability. Held staff turnover to less than 15%.
- Added responsibility for Internet collections, and created new monthly reporting matrices for aging, disputed dollars, high-risk exposure, DSO, bad debts, and credit approval activities.

Senior Manager of Credit and Collections (1998–2001)

Recruited to guide the initial pre-IPO start-up with operational reliance on temporary collection staffers; then advised the Director of Credit and Collections in a post-IPO environment with responsibility for implementing new policy and procedures to address rapidly expanding sales and revenues.

- Project Lead for the selection and deployment of Equifax's APPLY automated credit-scoring and decision-making system. Designed acceptance / rejection thresholds.
- Chosen by the CFO to develop requirements and identify functionalities in the customization of InterTech Systems billing and collection module. Later performed a similar role with Savile Systems.
- Interviewed, evaluated, and hired the first 20 employees within the department. Created training programs in new applicant credit approval, collection treatment process, change in ownership, return check, credit refund, suspension and permanent disconnect, fraud collection agency placement, and bad debt write-offs.
- Successfully intercepted and prevented distribution of cut-off notices and dunning letters destined for the World Trade Towers on the morning of 9/11, avoiding substantial negativity and bad press.

Chip-tastic Corporation—Spokane, Washington • 1996–1998

Manufacturer of microprocessors. $250M in annual revenue. Sold to National Semiconductor in 1998.

Manager of World Wide Credit and Collections

Managed credit and collections and also devised risk-management strategies for currency fluctuations, prepared documentary letters of credit, and managed exotic transactions including forfeiting and collections. Accountable for $70 million in receivables and 3,000 accounts, of which 2/3 were in the Pacific Rim.

- Slashed DSO by 30 days by outsourcing the Letter of Credit collection process, eliminating in-house handling, and establishing new guidelines for documentation and presentation. Ultimately reduced average letter of credit redemption time to under a week.
- Implemented forfeiting strategies that freed nearly $10 million in working capital and reduced A/R by nearly $20 million.
- Streamlined credit analysis and approval strategies for end-of-quarter purchasing traffic jams as sales discounted pricing.
- Outsourced the retail-based collection effort to third-party collection agencies, ultimately recovering 60% of the A/R due from small retailers and retail-based manufacturers.
- Established new international collection and payment procedures, global credit applications, underwriting and analysis, documentation, pre-export and term financing, and shortage and rebate issues. Generated cash forecasts, and oversaw wire transfers, budgetary matters, and bad debts.
- Partnered with National Semiconductor's management team to create, then manage, a transition plan to relocate and merge all credit and collection activities to its corporate collections organization.

JACKSON KUNOFSKY, C.I.C.P.

Page 3 of 3

Chip-tastic Corporation—continued

Contributions to Professionalism

- Elected Chairperson of Dun & Bradstreet's Northwest Advisory Council, assisting in continuous improvement campaigns and championing new products and services to Credit Managers in the Northwest.
- Member (1996 to 1998), National Computers High-Profile Credit Group serviced by NACM.

TRW—Yakima, Washington
Wholesale distributor of passive electronic components ~ $600M in Annual Revenue
1992–1996

Corporate Credit and Collections Manager

Directed the daily credit and collections function for the nation's 10th-largest electronic component distributor and coordinated the oftentimes conflicting decision-making process for eight remote regions / operations. Oversaw a 16-person staff with responsibility for $60 million in receivables and more than 7,000 domestic / international accounts.

- Achieved the lowest bad-debt expense percentage (among the nation's ten largest distributors) within three years; reduced DSO from 54 to 42 days within 24 months.
- Implemented a partnering strategy with regional vice presidents, addressing the misuse of VP-based collection overrides and adding "ownership" of the collection process to the sale matrix.
- Outsourced the Inside Sales division's collection process at the 45-day delinquent point, providing additional and substantial impact to decreased DSO.
- Instituted four-day annual training workshops for the Regional Credit and Collections Managers and their support staff, covering areas including bankruptcy, security, and phone skills to improve professionalism and customer service. Results included an increased willingness of VPs to release important accounts to the credit department.
- Recruited, evaluated, hired, and trained six new Regional Credit Managers during the four-year period.

Contributions to Professionalism

- Named Credit Executive of the Year by Reimer Reporting—1996.
- Elected President of the National Electronic Distributors Credit Association—1996. Orchestrated the national agenda for 1996 / 1997, including the merger of the regional electronic credit groups with Dun and Bradstreet. Guided the pricing of services with member companies and D & B.
- Achieved TQM Certification at Texas A & M.

RESUME 24: BY BARBARA SAFANI, MA, CPRW, NCRW, CERW, CCM

DANIEL LINDEN
linden23@yahoo.com

15 Spring Drive
Portland, OR 97219

Home: 503-743-4691
Cell: 503-307-6586

BANK MANAGER

Business Development ▪ Sales Training ▪ Operations

- ✓ Over 15 years of experience managing $50M to $2.5B branch operations and staffs of up to 45.
- ✓ Consistent top performance and recognition for superior sales, operations, and customer service.
- ✓ Expertise creating systems to track bank-wide performance and optimize growth opportunities.
- ✓ Proven success developing and facilitating regional sales/customer service training programs.
- ✓ Seasoned leadership skills and a knack for mentoring staff and building strong teams.

PROFESSIONAL EXPERIENCE

BANK ONE, Portland, OR   **2003 to Present**
Vice President/Branch Sales Manager charged with managing $70M branch with ten employees.
Consistently ranked in top 10% in multiple sales categories.

Business Development
- Top producer in region for referrals, with twice as many referrals as branch in #2 spot.
- Ranked #1 in investment and multiple service household growth out of 25 branches.
- One of top three producers for check-card usage with increase from 59% to 67%.
- Accelerated consumer lending volume 400% during tenure.
- Bolstered online banking usage from 31% to 47%.
- Grew non-interest income categories by 38.5%.

Process Improvement
- Designed and launched company's first automated branch sales tracking system that was implemented nationally in 342 branches. Standardized methods for tracking sales, referrals, and account activity; rewarded successful sales; and identified growth opportunities.
- Spearheaded and facilitated 30-hour consumer loan program training for branch that was expanded to 25 locations.

Relationship Management
- Boosted customer-service scores by 15 points and maintained service ratings of 95% or higher over six quarters.
- Received consistent 100% client servicing scores in 2005.

Staff Development
- Mentored new assistant manager, now a top producer.
- Recruited and trained five tellers and customer service representatives with virtually no turnover.
- Created and led weekly customer service role-plays for staff focusing on specific area of relationship management.
- Organized morning and afternoon "huddles" to discuss daily focus and accomplishments.

Company Awards
- Recognized with *Score Award* for referrals to various business lines.
- Received first place award for multiple-service household growth and service excellence.
- Presented with *Community Service Award* for various community activities, including teaching economics-based curriculum to K–7 graders in conjunction with Junior Achievement.

BEST BANK, Portland, OR   **2000 to 2003**
Vice President/Branch Manager and Regional Sales Manager challenged with managing $90M branch
with 12 employees.

Sales and Operations
- Named *Branch Leader* for ranking in top 10% of branch managers bank-wide.
- Top producer in Portland area for three consecutive years.

Strategy: *To help this individual transition to a smaller market, revenue numbers were deemphasized while his record of performance in multiple areas was highlighted using subheadings.*

DANIEL LINDEN, page two

BEST BANK (continued)
- Consistently ranked #1 in area in every category including consumer and business banking, investments, referrals, and new accounts.
- Captured 23% increase in customer base during tenure.
- Selected to act as interim manager of another branch office for nine months; managed two offices simultaneously for two quarters.

Training and Development
- One of five managers out of pool of 52 selected to facilitate the *Extraordinary Sales Leadership* and *Proactive Relationship Banking Program.*
- Trained team of 52 managers in successful sales meeting strategies.
- Groomed seven employees and promoted four to officer positions.
- Facilitated weekly sales meeting with area branch managers.

PORTLAND SAVINGS BANK, Portland, OR   **1997 to 2000**
Assistant Vice President/Branch Manager tasked with managing $80M branch and nine employees.
- Inaugural member of *Portland Team One for* achievement of all five goal categories in a six-month period.
- Increased branch *ServQual* scores as much as 25 points over nine-month period; achieved highest service level since program inception.
- Opened 1,000 new accounts in five months by promoting special rates and creating aggressive marketing campaign.
- Significantly improved compliance procedures over predecessor, as evidenced by exceptional performance on branch audits.

MANHATTAN BANK, New York, NY   **1994 to 1997**
Branch Service Manager/Regional Compliance Officer for $190M branch with 14 employees. Ensured branch and regional compliance to all federal regulations and bank policies and recommended service improvements.
- Pioneered *Super Teller* referral recognition program, resulting in 400% increase in referrals and #1 ranking in the region.
- Initiated referral training program.
- Recognized for only perfect audit record in the region.

NEW YORK BANK, New York, NY   **1989 to 1994**
Operations Manager with responsibility for $2.5B branch and staff of 50. Started career as teller and was promoted consistently over four years. Performed audits, updated and troubleshot general ledger accounts, and opened individual and business accounts.
- Developed customer-centered teller training that significantly increased customer-service scores.
- Winner of numerous *Big Apple Pride* awards for sales and service.
- Recognized on several occasions with annual *Stellar Seller* sales awards.

EDUCATION

M.B.A., Fordham University, New York, NY   **1993**

B.S., Computer Science, Queens College, Flushing, NY   **1989**

TECHNOLOGY

Advanced user of Microsoft Office programs, including Word, Excel, Outlook, and PowerPoint

COMMUNITY SERVICE

Executive Board Member, Business Consultant, and recipient of *2004 Worldwide Bronze Leadership Award,* Junior Achievement

Chairman, John Smith Elementary School Advisory Council

RESUME 25: BY JILL GRINDLE, CPRW

WILLIAM M. STEVENSON

12345 Fairway Drive / Longmeadow, MA 01106 / Home: (413) 567-2002 / Cell: (413) 567-1100

Areas of Expertise

- Client-focused Team Building
- Sales & Strategic Planning
- Home Office & Field Relationships
- New Business Development
- Asset Retention Initiatives
- Cross-selling Techniques
- Account Management

Professional Licenses & Certifications

- NASD Series 3, 7, 63, 66 Licenses
- Life, Variable Life, Annuity, Accident and Health Licenses
- Certified Long-Term Care Consultant (CLTC)
- Certified Senior Advisor (CSA)

VICE PRESIDENT—FINANCIAL SERVICES

13 + years of experience in sales of investment and insurance products

"Bill is one of the finest producers I have ever had on board…his energy, commitment, and passion are unmatched. He and his team have been major contributors in growing our annuity business to where it is today." Senior Vice President of Sales, MetLife

Top-producing sales professional and leader who has personally generated millions in premiums at record-breaking levels. Recognized as having a natural talent for developing and leading high-performance sales teams. Track record of cementing strategic alliances with influential agencies and wire houses that keep financial products ahead of the competition.

HIGHLIGHTS OF ACHIEVEMENTS

MetLife

> **Shattered all company and agency records with a scorecard of $90 million** in new premium—a 45% increase over 2004—as a team leader who piloted a product awareness program with a focus on aggressive sales strategies.

> **Cultivated over $40 million** in prospective trust, qualified, non-qualified, foundation, and endowment assets in fee-based accounts within first year of company operations.

> **Recruited to head up a new asset-retention program**—achieved a 70% retention rate within 12 months and protected retirement assets of $550 million.

Merrill Lynch

> **Led a team of sales professionals who were best-in-class**, amassing more than $60 million in new premium in 3 years.

> **Selected as 1 of 85 brokers out of 5,000** to help launch a retirement funds retention program; recognized for expertise in asset-allocation options from qualified plans.

> **Three-time Global World Class Director designee** for the highest rate of mutual fund and annuity production.

PROFESSIONAL EXPERIENCE

METLIFE, Hartford, CT 1999–Present
Vice President, Annuity Sales (2003–Present)

Serve as agency subject-matter expert on all annuity-related matters; develop business plans and set sales strategies. Train agents and affiliated brokers on products, commission structures, and retention initiatives. Leverage home office relationships and network with key resources to achieve production goals.

- Groomed a team to become top sellers nationally—100 agents received GAMA awards in 2003 and 2004. Team raked in over $90 million in new premiums.
- Led agents to surpass production goals by over 150% every year by crafting business plans that capitalized on emerging retirement-plan changes.
- Developed a premium training program that emphasized proven, practical selling skills and prospecting systems.
- Introduced recruiting and retention initiatives that were adopted in 3 other divisions.

Strategy: *This resume presents compelling information up front—a tag line, endorsement, Areas of Expertise, and Highlights of Achievements all paint the picture of an eminently qualified executive. Chronological work history supports this picture.*

WILLIAM M. STEVENSON • Page Two

METLIFE (Continued)

Regional Sales Vice President, Northeast & Midwest Territories (2000–2002)

Oversaw regional sales operations, territory, and division management that covered 8 states and 19 agencies. Spearheaded innovative strategies to increase sales of life insurance and other financial asset management products in the development of estate plans. Coached and managed sales representatives in the integration of traditional life insurance business into managed trust accounts.

- Generated $6 million in new revenues in one year by collaborating with independent agents to develop fee-based sales opportunities.
- Cultivated new business channels by joining forces with company's Blue Chip Group that grew renewal premiums by over 50% in a year.
- Introduced round-table sessions across the region to foster exchange of competitive intelligence.

Associate Vice President/Sales Manager—Retirement Funds Retention Program (1999–2000)

Selected to implement a multimillion-dollar asset-retention program for over 4,400 corporate qualified plans that covered more than 500,000 participants. Managed all functions, including training, compliance, and marketing. Supervised 12 registered representatives and conducted performance evaluations.

- Championed creative strategies that retained pension funds and educated participants on retirement planning. Shielded 70% of program assets, surpassing industry norm of 50%.

MERRILL LYNCH, Springfield, MA   1992–1999
Associate Vice President (1995–1999)/**Financial Consultant** (1992–1995)

As financial consultant, marketed and sold full array of financial products. Upon promotion, managed agency and broker networks for an enterprise with $300 million in assets serving 300 retail accounts. Directed activities of 25 sales representatives and led all recruitment efforts. Developed business plans and marketing programs. Marketed and sold all aspects of financial products.

- Conceived of and implemented innovative selling and prospecting techniques that resulted in 20 out of 25 representatives earning highest sales in new business for 3 consecutive years.
- Hooked top talent from major competitors by introducing a lucrative rewards and bonus program.
- Recognized for expertise in retirement planning and investing. Asked to present a financial commentary on local radio station, WXYZ, that reached a listening audience of 7,000.
- Won several awards for ushering in over $150 million in mutual fund and annuity business.

EDUCATION & TRAINING

UNIVERSITY OF MASSACHUSETTS, Amherst, MA ~ **MBA,** 1998

WESTERN NEW ENGLAND COLLEGE, Springfield, MA ~ **BS in Finance,** 1991

~ Corporate Financial Training Workshops ~ Dale Carnegie – Sales and Public Speaking ~ NASD Continuing Education Courses ~ MetLife Insurance Training

RESUME 26: BY SUSAN GUARNERI, NCC, NCCC, CPRW, CPBS, CCMC, CEIP, IJCTC, DCC, MCC

Peter M. Dube, CPA, CMA, CFM

9391 Birch Avenue
Caldwell, NJ 07006

Home: 975-618-5598
Mobile: 975-930-2123
petedube@verizon.net

CORPORATE FINANCE EXECUTIVE
CFO / Controller / Audit Director—High-Growth & Multinational Corporations

- **Versatile finance professional with 23-year track record** of top-notch corporate finance and Sarbanes-Oxley Section 404 Project Management expertise. Achieved billions of dollars in financial gains through cost reductions, strategic business development, and efficient business redesign.

- **Experienced cross-cultural communicator, international liaison, and customer relationship manager.** Well-honed presentation and negotiation skills (English and German). Recognized consultative business partner to clients, integrating technical, financial, project management, human resource, transaction structuring, and sales and marketing know-how to achieve business objectives.

AREAS OF EXPERTISE

- Sarbanes-Oxley Section 404
- Financial Planning & Analysis
- Strategic Business Development
- Client Relationship Management

- Internal Audit Assurance
- Finance & Cost Controls
- Risk Management
- Audit Compliance

- Executive Negotiations
- Acquisition Due Diligence
- Team Building & Motivation
- Budgeting & Forecasting

PROFESSIONAL EXPERIENCE

COMPUTER CONTROLS, INC. (CCI), New York, NY (corporate headquarters)   2005–present
Global provider of internal audit assurance services for 300 publicly traded Fortune 500 companies with international subsidiaries. 800 consultants worldwide. Annual revenues of $50 million.

Senior Manager, Mid-Atlantic Region, New York, NY (Jan. 2006–present)
Promoted to full-time position overseeing SOX 404 engagements for 250 small to mid-size Fortune 500 companies, with primary focus on risk management and compliance advisory services.
- **SOX 404 Project Management.** Develop and direct project planning and supervise SOX engagements, ensuring client retention by assuring high quality and meeting all project deliverables on time.

Manager (Consultant Contractor), SOX 404 Project Engagements (Sept. 2005–Dec. 2005)
Project 1—American Graphics, Inc., New York, NY (corporate headquarters)
- **Internal Audit Control.** Evaluated internal control structure (SOX 404) for publicly traded company with 3,500 employees and annual revenues of $116 million. Revised and updated Narratives and Risk Control Matrix for Revenue Cycle (Revenue Recognition, Accounts Receivable, Collections, and Bad Debt).

Project 2—U.S. Computers (premier software company), New York, NY (corporate headquarters)
- **Project Leadership.** Headed SOX 404 testing in Germany. Served as test lead, project manager, and primary local interface with client. Completed testing one week ahead of schedule, despite 2-week delay in preparation by client. Motivated team to work weekends without monetary incentives or swap-outs.

- **SOX Testing.** Reviewed test scripts, selected and validated samples, and performed Phase 1 testing for 9 cycles (327 Key Control Activities). Field work, including first level of review, completed within 4 weeks.

SARBANES-OXLEY, SECTION 404 CONSULTING—Internal Controls   2004–2005
- **European subsidiary of PharmaInternational, Inc.,** Munich, Germany (October 2004, January 2005)— Verified narratives of accounting processes and tested controls for design suitability and effectiveness.
- **Edison Computers, Inc.,** Edison, NJ (March 2004)—Wrote test procedures for internal controls.

KELLERMAN AG (multi-national conglomerate), Berlin, Germany   1982–2003
Controller, Enterprise Division—Sales RSA, Kellerman AG, Germany (2002–2003)
Appointed to turn around ailing Regional Unit of South Africa (RSA), with $50 million in business volume.
- **Turnaround Financial Analysis.** Instrumental in identifying root cause of dysfunctional income-reporting system. Recommended financial systems improvements centered on replacing inadequate accounting systems and procedures with computerized systems.

Strategy: *A chronological format is enhanced by a strong introduction and Areas of Expertise. In the Professional Experience section, highlighted phrases or functional descriptions lead each bulleted accomplishment.*

Peter M. Dube, CPA, CMA, CFM · petedube@verizon.net · Page 2

CFO Network Division—Kellerman Communications Ltd., UK (1998–2002)
Tasked with establishing Network as major contender in UK. Business volume $95 million, 8 direct reports.

- **Strategic Business Development.** Propelled Network to top-three supplier status in highly competitive market. Captured business from Euro-Telecommunications (ET), top-10 carrier worldwide. Negotiated multimillion-dollar contracts and created profitable business relationships in expanding market.

- **Cost Management and Revenue Generation.** Managed resource adjustments during economic downturn. While competition struggled, won $15 million systems contract from ET by creating atmosphere of trust and dependability. Result: $50 million annual sales. (Network now viewed as strategic ET supplier.)

- **Debt Collection.** Spearheaded collection of $15 million in doubtful receivables from financially troubled OLO customers. Negotiated settlements and created payment schedules satisfying all stakeholders.

BA Dept. Head—Sales International Network, Kellerman AG, Germany (January–June 1998)
Short-term assignment to gain knowledge of ET in preparation for CFO assignment in new Network Division.

- **Financial Operations.** Managed 4 BA Executives in delivering sales budgets and forecasting for $220 million in business volume. Generated monthly variance analyses and oversaw risk management.

- **Contract and Pricing Leadership.** Created terms and conditions (T&Cs) for $500 million in long-term RFPs and sales contracts. Researched and prepared international competitive pricing for bids and offers.

Program Controller—Kellerman AG, Germany (1994–1997)
Appointed to oversee Restructuring Program for $6 billion Telecom Networking Division (predecessor of Communications Networking Division). Reported directly to Group President and CEO.

- **Financial Control.** Devised and launched financial-control system to capture restructuring program results. Implemented control tools to measure program-induced cost savings of $300 million.

- **Revenue Oversight.** Closely monitored impact of sales-stimulation projects. Group sales increased to $8.5 billion during program restructuring period.

- **Cost Reductions.** Saved $2 million in consulting fees by initiating rigorous consultant bidding procedure as well as crafting tight consultancy agreement (adopted by all German subsidiaries).

Audit Director / Manager—Kellerman Corporation, New York, NY (1989–1994)

- **Audit Performance.** Appointed to senior-level audit team as Audit Team Leader (10 Audit staff). Resolved major fraud incidence involving senior sales managers at second-largest U.S. operation.

- **Cost Savings.** Initiated cost-savings proposals of between $20 million and $50 million for each audit project. Achieved average adoption rate exceeding 80% for audit proposals to company boards.

- **Acquisition Due Diligence.** Participated on Due Diligence Team in proposed $500 million acquisition. Team identified $100 million tax-risk exposure that led to abandonment of acquisition initiative.

BA Executive—Domestic Network Sales, Kellerman AG, Germany (1982–1989)

- **Business Development.** Fast-tracked to Team Leader, supervising 4 BA Executives and 1 Team Assistant. Oversaw $150 million in business volume with partnering agreement T&Cs up to $50 million. Key role in introduction of inter-working technology to German Network, with initial order of $1 million.

─────────── **EDUCATION & CERTIFICATIONS** ───────────

Bachelor & Master of Economics, Diplom Volkswirt, Berlin University, Berlin, Germany
Certified Public Accountant (CPA), University of Chicago Graduate School of Management—2005
- Passed on first attempt. Audit & Attestation—perfect score (99%), Overall Average Score—93%.
Certified Management Accountant (CMA), Institute of Management Accountants (IMA)—since 1990
Certified in Financial Management (CFM), Institute of Management Accountants (IMA)—since 2000
Technology Summary: Windows 2000/XP, MS Office 2000/XP (Word, Excel, PowerPoint), MS Outlook
Prof. Associations: Illinois CPA Society, American Institute of Certified Public Accountants (AICPA), IMA

KAREN JAMES

1234 Los Angeles Canyon Road • Los Angeles, California 90049
Residence (310) 875-1234 • Mobile (310) 209-9873 • karenjames@email.com

ATTORNEY AT LAW

Practice Areas Include Commercial, Transactional, and Employment Law

Attorney with 20 years of experience and excellent track record of structuring, negotiating, and litigating successful outcomes. Strengths in research, investigation, communications, problem resolution, team building, and leadership. Skilled communicator and consensus builder who works well with diverse populations, opposing counsel, and all stakeholders. Expertise includes

General Contracts / Third-Party Agreements / Real Estate / General Litigation / Contracts
Claims / Company Policy / Trademarks / Patents / Intellectual Property / Trade Secrets / Regulatory Matters

PROFESSIONAL EXPERIENCE

Partner • 1990 to Present
KRAMER & JAMES, LLC, Los Angeles, CA
Joined boutique practice in 1990 and, upon becoming partner in 1993, was solely responsible for doubling size of clients and revenues. Provide legal counsel, including drafting sophisticated transactional documents, and represent clients in all aspects of litigation—from filing initial pleadings through trials and settlements. Additionally, co-manage daily operations of law practice including hiring, training, and coaching staff members.

Illustrative Experience

- Represented technology client from start-up through multimillion-dollar operations in forming corporation, ensuring regulatory compliance, and drafting personnel policies to avert potential future litigation. Handled trademark, patent, and other intellectual property issues.
- Defended leading international architectural firm in alleged sexual harassment case. Advised company against out-of-court settlement, subsequently prevailing in court proceeding and averting substantial award.
- Reviewed and evaluated sophisticated leases on behalf of both tenants and commercial property owners.
- Defended real estate developer against $5 million construction claims; resolved case for under $50,000.
- Tried trademark violation case on behalf of small manufacturing company; prevailed and received jury award of $10 million.
- Negotiated sophisticated acquisition of leading competitor on behalf of restaurant client.
- Represented entertainment client in copyright infringement case, receiving substantial award for damages.
- Retained by national restaurant company to draft and update internal employment policies and advise on areas of potential liability. Represented company over a ten-year period in matters requiring outside counsel.

Previous Experience—Attorney with Los Angeles District Attorney's Office

EDUCATION

J.D.—University of California at Los Angeles (UCLA); 1984
B.A. in Economics—University of California, Berkeley; 1980

LICENSES / BAR MEMBERSHIPS / PROFESSIONAL AFFILIATIONS

California State Bar / U.S. District Court of the Central District / US Court of Appeals, 9th Circuit
Member—California Bar Association, Beverly Hills Bar Association, Los Angeles County Bar Association
Computer Skills—Windows, Word, Excel, Lexis, Westlaw

Strategy: *Used a straightforward, concise format to present diverse legal experience to support this person's goal of moving from private practice to corporate law.*

ROBERT DAWSON

2410 Hunter Drive, #75 • Davenport, IA 52806
(516) 225-8769 • rdawson@aol.com

MULTI-UNIT RESTAURANT MANAGEMENT

Annual Business & Strategic Planning. . . P & L Management. . . Training & Team Building
New Establishment Start-up. . . Food & Labor Cost Controls. . . Sales & Marketing
New Program & Product Launch. . . Contract Negotiations & Administration

PROFILE

Hospitality industry executive with more than 12 years of restaurant management experience and a proven record of success in building profitable businesses by achieving the highest standards in service, employee development, marketing, expense control, and asset management. Hands-on administrator and expert troubleshooter who is able to identify key market trends and profitable opportunities, plan and direct business openings, and bring together diverse individuals to form cohesive teams.

PROFESSIONAL EXPERIENCE

Regional Manager, 2000–Present
GOOD FOOD TRAVEL PLAZAS, Moline, IL

Senior operations executive with full management responsibility for seven 24-hour restaurants comprising three concepts (two fast-food and one family-dining) located in Midwest region travel centers. Build and develop highly effective teams of seven General Managers and 250 employees by recruiting, hiring, and training quality individuals. Drive all related sales/marketing, vendor negotiations, financial analysis, pricing, reporting, quality, and property management operations.

Challenge: Inherited four operations with stagnant sales as well as three with declining profit performance and patronage.

Solution: Introduced new beverage and hot deli programs. Updated equipment and restaurant decor. Re-staffed management team and empowered managers to lead in the development of company objectives. Introduced regional menu specials and began to advertise locally in radio and print.

Results: Boosted sales from $10.5 million to $12.2 million in just one year and increased market penetration and profitability by 12.5%. Increased overall beverage sales by 3% and deli sales by 15% the first month. Deli program was adopted company-wide.

Regional Manager, 1997–2000
GRANTS AMERICAN RESTAURANTS, Memphis, TN

Directed all aspects of fourteen 24-hour, full-service restaurants and six fast-food concepts. Managed all P&L, budgets, financial analysis, human resources, and menu planning and development for Southeast region.

Challenge: Lead start-up operations including capital equipment purchases, floor layout design, and construction project management. Increase profit margins in retail and food categories of existing locations.

Solution: Recruited and trained several high-caliber General Managers and initiated new operational and training guidelines. Introduced buffet-style dining, thus reducing food costs and increasing customer satisfaction.

Results: Successfully opened 24 profitable locations. Increased retail and food profit margins by 12%.

continued. . .

Strategy: *A Challenge-Solution-Results format showcases this executive's ability to solve problems and deliver results.*

ROBERT DAWSON

Page Two

Restaurant General Manager, 1993–1998
CIRCLE B TRAVEL CENTERS, Franklin, KY

Full management responsibility for multi-unit, 3-concept restaurants and deli shop, consisting of 24-hour family-dining restaurant with all-you-can-eat buffet, Chinese restaurant, and pizzeria. Directed overall daily operations in areas of fiscal/revenue responsibilities, employee development, process improvement, and customer development/satisfaction.

Challenge: Build sales and profitability in service-driven business that caters to a diverse clientele.

Solution: Restructured low-performing deli program. Revamped buffet menu selection, portions, and pricing. Implemented employee incentive programs and contests to build morale and team concept. Closely monitored food costs by negotiating contracts and sourcing for new vendors.

Results: Deli shop sales skyrocketed from $57,000 to $79,000 in one year. Ranked #1 in food costs for five years out of 119 locations. Obtained a 27% food cost for buffets, well below the 35% industry standard. Organized and opened the largest-volume restaurant in company history; exceeded $3.79 million the first year. Selected to be one of two corporate training facilities and successfully trained eight General Managers. Slashed expenses $500,000 annually by successfully negotiating rebates with vendors.

Executive Associate, 1990–1993
WILSONCO OIL AND GAS INC., Cincinnati, OH

Challenge: Successfully market and sell oil and natural gas securities.

Solution: Implemented strategic marketing and business plans. Cultivated new accounts through cold calling, lead prospecting, networking, and referrals.

Results: Recognized as company's top producer for two consecutive years, selling $2.5 million in securities annually.

General Manager, 1985–1990
ORANGE PARK RAINBOW, Cherry Glen, CO

Challenge: Charged with managing and positioning Rex Air Vacuum retail franchise for success.

Solution: Structured and implemented company's business plan, coordinated daily activities, monitored inventory and purchasing, and ensured quality service and strong customer relations. Supervised and trained top-performing staff of 17 employees.

Results: Increased sales from $175,000 to $375,000 in one year. Franchise was sold for a considerable profit.

EDUCATION

UNIVERSITY OF IOWA, Iowa City, IA

B.A., Business Marketing; 1985

ANTHONY BATTISTA

SENIOR-LEVEL OPERATIONS MANAGER

Well-regarded manager whose accomplishments reflect exceptional team-building skills, a process-oriented approach, and a passion for achievement

SUMMARY OF QUALIFICATIONS

Performance-driven executive with a wealth of management and operations experience. Demonstrated expertise in driving performance improvement. Respected, hands-on leader known for open, upfront communication style and ability to motivate teams to achieve exceptional results. Solution-oriented and flexible in approach. Valued for ability to plan for and achieve long-term business success. Stellar record of accomplishment includes

- Maximizing profitability through effective leadership and team-building.
- Re-engineering processes to improve service and reduce costs.
- Orchestrating performance turnarounds in floundering locations.
- Maintaining top-level team performance, motivating staff through effective coaching and mentoring.
- Developing customer-driven operational solutions to win new business and build volume.

PROFESSIONAL EXPERIENCE

WORLDWIDE DELIVERY SERVICES, New York, NY   1982 to present
Division Manager, Operations (1999 to present)
Direct team of nearly 500 service providers through 6-member management team in one of the company's largest regional facilities. Manage $3 million monthly expense budget for unit that averages 2.2 million packages picked up and delivered per month. From 1999 to 2001, simultaneously led 4 facilities, overseeing operations that totaled 1.7 million packages handled per month. Initially hired as driver; successfully rose through ranks to key management positions.

Leadership & Performance Excellence

- Established record of success in meeting and exceeding performance goals across multiple locations. Improved operations in every facility managed, raising volume and revenue by an average of 30% while reducing costs as much as 20%. At the same time, cut injuries and accidents by 50%.

- Tapped to take over leadership of neglected regional center, revamped operations, and re-energized staff to turn around performance, elevating facility to premier status.

- Took over operation of troubled New York facility, leading team to first-place ranking in district in first year at helm. Tackled tough issues, including growing sense of mistrust between management and union employees, to build cohesive team committed to achieving shared goals.

- Won Operations Manager of the Year 4 years running, achieving the highest employee relations index in the district each year from 1996 to 1999.

- Led cross-functional team that evaluated closing of facility to reduce costs. Successfully designed and implemented plan to disband operation and disperse routes and resources between two other facilities to achieve savings of $1 million per month.

- Featured in "Making of a Champion," a newsletter piece that highlighted the leadership and team-building skills that helped bring company sports team to local championship.

(Continued)

35 YORKSHIRE WAY ▪ TUCKAHOE, NY 10707 ▪ (914) 961-0001 ▪ abattista@aol.com

Strategy: *Highlighted business achievements that resulted from exceptional team-building and leadership skills.*

WORLDWIDE DELIVERY SERVICES   Continued

Business Growth

- Developed and executed operating plans to meet market challenges and exploit new opportunities. Among successes, implemented new operating plan that allowed regional facility to meet the demands of new mall, the second largest in the country, effectively providing cost-effective service.
- Brought on $4.5 million account with well-known financial services group, winning business from key competitor through effective pricing and customized service.
- Saved $3 million contract with national sports association by changing pick-up procedure to accommodate customer needs.

Safety and Regulatory Compliance

- Taking on role as OSHA Compliance Administrator, successfully brought 2 facilities that failed OSHA audits into full compliance through the implementation of new training/educational programs.
- Served as RCR Compliance Officer to ensure that hazardous materials were shipped according to regulatory requirements.

Team-Building Initiatives

- Established programs designed to enhance team performance. Initiated Stretch and Flex exercises, nutritional programs, and healthy lifestyle informational bulletin boards that have been credited with helping to maintain service providers at peak performance levels.
- Implemented unmatched recognition program that built on early successes to become an extremely effective motivational tool.

Charity & Community Service

- Raised $1.5 million during 3-year tenure as district United Way Coordinator, exceeding goals by creating and implementing 12-month operating plan that made charitable giving a year-round priority. Doubled district contributions in two years. Won President's Award for outstanding achievements.
- Led highly successful golf tournament that raised as much as $30,000 for charity. Brought on several prominent sponsors to bring recognition to event.
- Serve as local coordinator for grass-roots, district-level program aimed at building relationships with lawmakers to promote company interests. Led team of 8 managers involved in program while maintaining relationships with influential congressmen and senators.
- Took over leadership of internal fund-raising campaign to support company interests. Substantially improved participation rate and contributions during 3-year tenure.

PROFESSIONAL DEVELOPMENT

Completed extensive training that includes workshops in leadership, management, team-building, coaching, quality improvement, compliance, and labor relations.

COMMUNITY LEADERSHIP & SERVICE

Coach, Tuckahoe Pioneers (football), Recreation Basketball, Travel Basketball, 2000 to present.

35 YORKSHIRE WAY ▪ TUCKAHOE, NY 10707 ▪ (914) 961-0001 ▪ abattista@aol.com

RACHEL DAVIDSON
Operations/Business Manager

334 East Main Street • Glenside, PA 19038

215.764.1254 • r-davidson@myemail.com

More than a dozen years of experience managing retail, wholesale, manufacturing, distribution, and export businesses. Creative, entrepreneurial spirit. Ability to quickly identify and resolve problems, effectively analyzing and troubleshooting to avoid recurrence. Solid communication skills. Passion for customer service and quality products. Enthusiasm, energy, and exceptional work ethic.

Expertise includes

- Marketing
- Sales & Account Management
- Customer Service
- Human Resources Management
- Accounting
- Payroll
- Regulatory Compliance
- Event Management
- Purchasing & Inventory Management

HIGHLIGHTS OF RECENT PROFESSIONAL EXPERIENCE

GEPETTO'S INC. – Philadelphia, PA   2002–present; 1990–1996

Manufacturer and international wholesaler of high-quality, custom imprinted specialty wood toys begun in the 1970s; most well known for line of tops. Major clients among 2,000+ active customers include Nobel Museum, Smithsonian, Australian Geographic, Museum of Modern Art, Pacific Science, Wall Street Journal, and Science for Kids.

Business/Operations Manager

Member of management team with CEO/owner and operations manager from 1990 to 1996. Handled all human resources management, accounting, MIS, and payroll duties in addition to marketing, trade show planning and attendance, sales, customer relations, exporting, regulatory compliance, purchasing, and oversight of shipping operations. To spend more time with family, gave a four-month notice; hired and trained replacements.

Operations manager purchased the business in 2001 and extended invitation to rejoin the company, currently with 7 employees and $425K in annual sales.

Accomplishments:

- Identified and attended strategic trade shows (attendance had lagged during hiatus); re-established Gepetto's visibility and gained return business as well as new clients.

- Built relationships with potential customers and distributors that have led to fruitful partnerships, including Neiman Marcus, Science for Kids, XToys and Shining Gifts (Japanese distributors), and Mountain Ridge Gifts (Canadian distributor).

- Researched target markets and initiated direct mailings; one such effort netted a 10% return in first-time business.

- Achieved increased sales consistently since 2002; 2005 sales are up 15% compared to FY2002 despite a less-than-perfect economic climate and fierce competition from overseas.

- Shared in the creation and manage the business side of Gepetto's website, which has successfully generated retail sales of existing, test-marketed, and closeout products.

- Identified opportunity via Federal Trade Program and authored application for grant that assisted in the development, design, and implementation of a marketing program; application was accepted and the subsequent marketing plan garnered new clients.

- Recommended, sourced, and selected payroll service; cut weekly payroll processing time in half.

- Collaborated with CEO and operations manager on policy making and project planning; the company's annual catalog and website are prime examples.

Strategy: *Emphasized accomplishments to overcome lack of formal education. Note explanation for leaving and returning to her present company.*

OTHER NOTABLE EXPERIENCE

Rachel Davidson Handweaver (since 1996)

- Design and create hand-woven fiber art, both for display and practical use. Participate in approximately six art shows per year. Significant experience in leatherwork.

Co-Owner & Managing Partner of Freedom's Bounty (1996–1999), a mail-order food and gift business featuring products by area artisans

- Launched this local business, handling all operations functions from marketing to accounting to shipping. Produced hand-woven fiber products as one of the participating artisans. Dissolved partnership in 1999 so that both owners could pursue other interests.

Manager of Fanny Farmer Candy Shop (1989–1990), a specialty retail business

- Tapped to join district merchandising team after one month with the company; trained new managers and redesigned existing and new stores.
- Led new store opening (Gallery at Market East) that set company-wide sales records.

Manager of Visitor Services & Retail Operations at Franklin Vineyards (1986–1988), whose winery/retail sales and visitor services center income exceeded $400K annually

- Oversaw direct sales, tours, and the scheduling of outside tastings and promotions. Full accountability for staff, regulated recordkeeping related to sales/tasting of alcohol, inventory management, purchasing, restaurant sales, and buildings and grounds maintenance.
- Organized and promoted a shipping program that dramatically improved wine sales during typically low-volume winter months.

EDUCATION & PROFESSIONAL DEVELOPMENT

Human Services & Child Development coursework: Delaware County Community College—Havertown, PA

Weaving I & II: Philadelphia Museum and Science Center—Philadelphia, PA

CPR & First Aid certified

COMMUNITY INVOLVEMENT

Girl Scout Troop Leader & Registered Girl Scout; since 1998

Past board member, Delaware River Valley Fiber Arts Guild

OTHER

PC proficient: Microsoft Works ... Microsoft Word ... Peachtree Complete Accounting ... Prosper Manufacturing and Accounting Software

Other interests: acting/performance art ... gardening ... other fiber arts

Rachel Davidson—Page 2   215.764.1254   r-davidson@myemail.com

CLARE YOUNG

GENERAL MANAGER
STRATEGIC PLANNING ◆ OPERATIONS LEADERSHIP ◆ PERFORMANCE IMPROVEMENT
"Recognized go-to person for flawless execution of strategic corporate initiatives"

WELL-REGARDED BUSINESS MANAGER with a proven record of accomplishment in leading key revenue-driving projects and programs in marketing, sales, customer care, and call-center organizations. Respected team leader and valued business partner with collaborative approach that engages teams and individuals across organizational functions to achieve shared goals. Customer-focused leader able to pinpoint business needs and deliver innovative solutions. Persuasive and influential communicator with strong presentation skills. Change driver known for ability to step in and get results.

Core Expertise:

◆ *Strategic Planning*	◆ *Process & Performance Optimization*	◆ *Team-Building/Leadership*
◆ *Operations Management*	◆ *Executive Negotiations & Presentations*	◆ *Program/Project Leadership*
◆ *Budget Management*	◆ *Problem-Solving/Decision-Making*	◆ *Facilities Management*

CAREER HIGHLIGHTS

BLUE SKY COMMUNICATIONS, New York, NY   1997 to present
Senior Manager, National Sales Operations (2001 to present)
Provide high-level support for product marketing activities in all national markets. Plan and execute rollout of new products and promotions through distribution channels. Partner with cross-functional groups to develop and deliver processes, procedures, and tools to ensure business goals are met.

- Hand-picked by management to plan and execute projects and programs identified as key revenue drivers; won Team Circle of Excellence Award in 2003 and earned Quality Achiever Award finalist status in recognition of outstanding performance and substantial contributions to bottom-line profitability.

- Flawlessly launched new pay-as-you-go technology. Established systems, policies, and procedures for customer-care organization and sales channels to ensure successful rollout. Product delivered $570,000 in revenue, exceeding forecasts by 20%.

- Implemented roll-out plans for key company initiative based on entirely new platform, positioning company to enter and successfully compete in new market. Developed robust training program designed to build understanding, excitement, and the desire to sell among sales partners.

- Rolled out new compensation plan based on complex model that better met channel needs. Planned and managed all phases of launch from concept to impact. Developed and delivered new processes, staffing support plans, and collateral materials, including the development of mitigation plans.

- Stepped in to take over failing effort to develop new B2B extranet website at request of senior management. Implemented aggressive plan to successfully launch website in compressed time frame. Website reduced sales transaction processing time by 50% and was adopted as best practice across company.

- Manage product line content in corporate website, providing compelling, up-to-date information for channel distributors and effectively delivering tools to help partners sustain and grow business.

- Developed creative recruitment strategy based on maintaining ready pipeline of suitable candidates. With strategy in place, exceeded recruitment goals for 30-, 60-, and 90-day placements by 30%.

6 MANNERS ROAD ◆ WHITE PLAINS, NY 10610 ◆ (914) 287-0001 ◆ clareyoung@yahoo.com

Strategy: *Presented a big-picture perspective and impressive bottom-line results to position this individual for a step up to a General Manager role.*

CLARE YOUNG   PAGE 2

BLUE SKY COMMUNICATIONS, New York, NY   Continued
Manager, Sales Operations (1997 to 2001)
Led sales operations in third-largest U.S. market while directing four-member team responsible for training, operational efficiency improvement, and compensation and recognition programs. Managed departmental IT, recognition, and facility budgets.

- Aggressively recruited to position based on reputation for cross-functional leadership and ability to get the job done. Made key contributions and succeeded in driving operations where others failed previously.
- Among successes, helped reduce cost of acquiring accounts by 35% while posting record-breaking revenue gains. Won seven Quality Achievement Awards during tenure. Named as Service Legend finalist in 1999.
- Successfully rolled out products and programs that consistently exceeded targets, helping unit achieve banner years that saw substantial, record-breaking subscriber growth and revenue generation.
- Implemented multi-pronged sales career management program that built employee satisfaction and improved employee retention rates by 11%.
- Spearheaded initiatives that were effective in reducing manual processes and improving overall departmental efficiency.

PROVIDENCE BANK, New York, NY   1994 to 1997
Product Manager (1995 to 1997)
Created and launched new products for nation's sixth-largest bankcard provider and recognized pioneer in secured credit-card market. Earned quick promotion to product manager position after one year as call center manager.

- Conceived and successfully launched company's first fee-based products, achieving unheard-of 78% sign-up rate in initial offerings.
- Initiated list-management process for program that delivered 5% incremental lift in response rate. Based on its success, list-management method was adopted across products.
- Established audit and control procedures for programs that ensured 100% compliance with internal and external regulatory guidelines.

Senior Manager, Call Center Operations (1994 to 1995)
Recruited to manage day-to-day operations and development needs of several call centers throughout the U.S.; effectively managed department that enjoyed ten-fold growth during tenure.

- Benchmarked and implemented strategies that were highly successful in building sales. At the same time, managed exponential departmental growth to effectively support new business.
- Created and implemented comprehensive training program for fee-based products that increased sales productivity by 50%. Led teams to achieve all quality and productivity goals while maintaining top 25% performance rankings among all units.

Additional Experience

Sales and Operations Manager, New World Trading Company, New York, NY
Marketing Manager, East Coast Financial Investments, Inc., New York, NY

EDUCATION

Bachelor of Arts, *cum laude,* University of Pennsylvania, 1986

6 MANNERS ROAD ◆ WHITE PLAINS, NY 10610 ◆ (914) 287-0001 ◆ clareyoung@yahoo.com

MARY KELLERMAN

3160 Main Boulevard/2A • Los Angeles, CA 90005 • 213.733.4422 • e-mail: kellermanm@yahoo.com

Founder and **former Director** of **Los Angeles CIS (Cities in Schools),** uniquely qualified to advance CIS' mission and initiatives through background with CIS, lifelong commitment to youth services, and availability for extensive travel.

Expert in educational development, implementation, and administration, with proven success in leadership, fund-raising, and program innovation roles. Proven leader combining passion for education services with pragmatism and results-oriented business skills. A "doer" with a reputation for dependability, energy, perseverance, and ability to bring structure to chaotic situations. Team player successful at motivating, coordinating, and leading teams, consistently achieving high buy-in ratios for initiatives. Effective communicator in cross-level, cross-cultural, and cross-functional environments, fluently interfacing with people from high-level government officials to support staff.

Proven achievements in

• Federal Grant Administration	• Persuasion & Negotiation	• Fund-raising
• Prioritization & Coordination	• Community Outreach	• Problem Solving
• Grass-roots Initiatives	• Public Relations	• Budget Analyses
• Project Management	• Program Development	• Multitasking
• Conflict Management	• Project Implementation	• Crisis Intervention

PROFESSIONAL EXPERIENCE

SAC FOUNDATION—San Diego, CA   4/2002 to Present

Acting Executive Director, Program Development (5/2003 to Present)
Consultant, Foundation Development (4/2002 to 5/2003)

Recruited, based on extensive record of success in non-profit leadership, to assist in launch of private, non-profit foundation serving minority and low-income youths through athletic and academic activities, with ultimate goal of guiding youth toward scholarships.

Started without budget (other than $1 million construction funds) and lack of guidelines. Rapidly structured position and processes. Liaised with building contractor, designed program activities model, hired and supervised initial start-up staff, and contributed to development of Board of Directors.

Key achievements:

- Raised $20,000+ in private contributions through mailings (personally designed materials) and in-person visits, simultaneously developing 500+ contact list of individual and business sponsors.
- Handled PR, research, and community awareness at more than 100 key public forums attended by Fortune 500 executives, including Starbucks, Verizon, Salomon Smith Barney, and Coca-Cola, Inc.
- Managed successful construction of 12,000 sq. ft. facility, passing inspections, securing Certificate of Occupancy, and completing construction within 6 months through effective coordination, problem solving, and monitoring of progress.
- Generated front-page press coverage in metro area's largest newspaper—*San Diego Herald Leader.*
- Offset utility costs for at least 1 year and generated $4,000 in yearly income for SAC facility by securing several space rental contracts with private institutions.
- Initiated, coordinated, launched, and monitored 20+ program groups and activities, sports camps, team sports, and individual instruction during start-up. Programs remain active to date.
- Handled design, layout, and production of logo, informational/fund-raising materials, and SAC Foundation apparel. Distributed handouts and mailings to population of 5,000+.

Continued...

Strategy: *In addition to more recent experience, emphasized extensive prior experience with the organization (Cities in Schools) that she is currently applying to return to as its senior executive.*

MARY KELLERMAN

CONSULTING PROJECTS—Los Angeles, CA   1987 to Present

Expediter

Provide project management services to small business owners in collaboration with government and business departments, focusing on license and permit application renewal and compliance.

LOS ANGELES COMMUNITIES IN SCHOOLS, INC., Los Angeles, CA   1976 to 1987

Founder & Director (1983 to 1987)

Appointed founder and leader of non-profit Los Angeles Cities in Schools, Inc., to facilitate local institutionalization of previously federally funded project, formerly part of (now) Communities in Schools (CIS), Inc.—operating 194 programs in 31 states, serving 2 million students as the nation's leading community-based organization incorporating social services into schools to increase attendance and grades, and decrease juvenile criminality. Twice selected by Worth *Magazine as 1 of 100 charities most likely to save the world.*

Orchestrated successful establishment of Los Angeles CIS and its transition from federal to local funding through careful planning and negotiations. Operated under Community Development Agency and LA Human Resources Administration.

Key achievements:

- Generated $100,000+ in local funding and resources within 1 year. Additionally, raised $22,000 in private funding and resources within 12 months.
- Led successful negotiations for project and program sites and office space, staffing 100+ city agencies participants. (Listing available.)
- Facilitated 80% increase in student attendance, academic improvement of at least 1 grade point, and more than 50% increase in service delivery to student and family populations through effective program development, implementation, and coordination.
- Featured at Los Angeles Museum of the Arts (capturing Los Angeles pride and importance of community cooperation in stabilizing Los Angeles neighborhoods).
- Featured in *LA Times* front-page article (community section) in addition to receiving other press coverage.
- Received recognition and numerous awards for effective project leadership leading to measurable results in schools and communities. (See last page for listing.)

City Director for Cities in Schools/Los Angeles Project, Washington, D.C. (1980 to 1983)

Operating under umbrella of U.S. Department of Education, Urban Initiatives Office, Washington, D.C. with $1+ million in private and public-sector funds.

Chief Administrator of nationally funded project. Accountable for identifying and negotiating grantee agencies, authoring proposals, developing budgets, implementing projects, and negotiating public and private involvement in supporting model's institutionalization in Los Angeles. Acted as liaison, directing ongoing administrative and management relationships with city and government agencies, including White House Federal Coordinating Office, Office of the Mayor, mayoral agencies, Office of the Chancellor, and Los Angeles Board of Education. (Partial list.)

Key achievements:

- Achieved CIS-school reported attendance increase of 15%–41%, resulting in 80%–91% attendance levels.
- Authorized by U.S. Department of Health, Education, and Welfare to identify grantees for receivership of U.S. Department of Education funds.
- Spearheaded first *Cities In Schools/LA Newsletter:* managed development, production, and layout design, and grew circulation to 5,000+ nationally within 3 years. Successfully negotiated printing/publication sponsorship with major corporations.
- Member of and contributor to CIS LA Policy Board; liaised between CIS and public/private sector.
- Established audit process (with Mitchell/Titus & Co.) and evaluation design (with AIR—American Institutes for Research).

MARY KELLERMAN

Page 3 of 3   213.733.4422

Associate City Director for Los Angeles In Schools and **Project Operations Director** (1977 to 1980)

Held responsibility for total program budget of $2.5+ million. Additionally, functioned as Fiscal Administrator of federal and private funds, overseeing $1.5+ million in funds.

Designed, created, and implemented initial administrative office, including fiscal and personnel departments, computerized budget analysis, and payroll system. Coordinated fiscal relationship with agencies, including Office of the Mayor, Community Board Assistance Unit, acting as liaison and primary contact for federal grant administration.

Key achievements:

- Secured $60,000 grant from Community Services Administration Region II.
- Frequently attended and participated in White House meetings.
- Served as CIS liaison with Congressman Charles B. Rangel.
- Developed office management system from scratch, including comprehensive personnel manual.
- CIS-program site winner of LA Board of Education Award for attendance rise of 10% (resulting in 86.7% attendance rate), up 4½ % from previous year.
- Personally invited by First Lady Rosalyn Carter to attend educational forum.

Project Manager for Los Angeles Cities In Schools Projects (1976 to 1977)

Managed project implementation and program development.

EDUCATION & LICENSING

MASTER OF EDUCATION DEGREE (M.ED.) IN SECONDARY EDUCATION—Full Scholarship Award
University of Louisville, Louisville, KY

BACHELOR OF SCIENCE DEGREE (B.S.) IN ART EDUCATION—Kappa Pi Art Fraternity Scholarship
Murray State University, Murray, KY

Notary Public: Los Angeles and California State (current).

AWARDS & AFFILIATION
(past and present, partial list)

Presidential Citation for Excellence—LA City Board of Education Community School District 11
Certificate of Merit, Distinguished Volunteer Service—CA State 46th Assembly District
Outstanding Contributions—People's Development Corporation Summer Youth Employment
Certificate of Appreciation Award for Volunteer Services—YM-YWHA
White House (Federal Coordinator) recommendation

American Cancer Society, Fund-Raising Committee
John Keller Classics and JK Classic Student Scholarship Awards, founder and fund-raiser (raised $7,000+)
US Department of Agriculture/Gramercy Boys Club Association—Childcare Feeding Program
Montefiore Comprehensive Health Center, member Board of Directors

CHAPTER 5

Resumes for Career-Transition Baby Boomers

As we've discussed, most career-change resumes do not focus simply on past work history. Because you are making a significant career change—perhaps voluntarily decreasing your level of responsibility, beginning a post-retirement career, or entering a completely new line of work or new industry—you will want to include all of your relevant activities and accomplishments, whether they occurred during employment, volunteer, or other experiences. The resumes in this chapter show you how professional resume writers addressed this kind of challenge.

We have organized the chapter into three sections:

- **Career Deceleration Resumes:** Resumes for people seeking "less"—less challenge, less stress, fewer hours on the job, or perhaps part-time work—a position with significantly less responsibility than the one held most recently.

- **Career-Change Resumes:** Resumes for people making a significant shift in career function and/or industry.

- **Consulting Resumes:** Resumes for baby boomers who have had a rich career in one profession and now want to apply all of their wisdom, skills, and experience as a consultant to other organizations.

These resumes reflect a wide variety of professions.

Career Deceleration Resumes

Career-Transition Resumes

Consultant Resumes

MARILYN GREENE

1489 RIDDLE STREET • KALAMAZOO, MICHIGAN 49008 • 269.456.9239 • iloveplants@yahoo.com

HORTICULTURE / NURSERY PROFESSIONAL

Greenhouse Operations • Landscape Design • Landscape Management

▶ Professional horticulturist with 30+ years of experience in producing and cultivating top-quality plants, including bedding plants, perennials, shrubs, topiary, and fruit trees.

▶ Extensive experience in overseeing the daily operation of a family nursery and completely knowledgeable in all aspects of nursery operations. Familiar with the identification and culture of a broad range of ornamental plants. Maintain current nursery plant inventory, procure plants based on plant requests, and ensure the quality of purchased and home-grown plant materials. Engage in nursery planning to optimize both future and long-term use of the nursery resources. Knowledgeable of proper planting, transplanting, harvesting, and transporting a variety of trees and shrubs from liner stage to mature specimen size.

▶ Specialty in landscape design and estimating for residential and commercial clients. Dedicated to creating, building, and maintaining sustainable landscapes using solid plant knowledge and innovative approach. Engage in site master planning and budget management. Coordinate all aspects of project flow, oversee proper installation methods, and train subordinates.

▶ For clients, oversee landscape/garden collection care; manage all aspects of cultivation and renovation, including new landscape designs and changes; maintain plant records systems; and manage natural areas.

▶ Comfortable multitasking. Able to assess client needs and provide products and services to meet those needs. Interface effectively with diverse populations of clients and all levels of company personnel. Resolve client problems in a timely manner to ensure satisfaction and maintain customer loyalty.

Areas of Expertise

Greenhouse Production	Workflow Planning/Prioritization	Commercial Landscape Design
Plant Nutrition/Insect/Disease Control	Landscape Architecture/Design	Customer Service Management
Tree Fruits Production	Ornamental Horticulture	Staff Training/Supervision
Organic/Sustainable Plants	Soils	Multitask Management
Flower/Vegetable Gardening	Scheduling/Logistics/Detail Coordination	Inventory Management

PROFESSIONAL EXPERIENCE

GREENE HORTICULTURAL SERVICES, INC., Kalamazoo, Michigan   **October 2004–Present**
(Professional gardening/landscaping contractor offering full line of horticultural services to clients in Southwest Michigan.)

MASTER HORTICULTURIST

Offering an array of design-build and consultation services to help clients maintain an attractive home or business environment. Services include expert advice on planting and pruning ornamental, flowering, and fruit-producing trees and shrubs, providing guidance on master-planning or managing clients' property, and creating imaginative design for specialty gardens.

Highlights of Qualifications

▶ Involved in all aspects of serving diverse clientele, including high-end, high-quality residential/commercial design and construction projects.

▶ Demonstrated ability to communicate effectively with homeowner and commercial clients to design breathtaking landscape designs.

▶ Outstanding estimating abilities. Familiarity with construction plans, including a solid foundation of irrigation and lighting systems, plant knowledge, landscape layout, patio and walk construction, grading and drainage, retaining wall construction, and water garden installation. Ability to read and implement blueprints and landscape schematics.

▶ Up to date with all local codes and requirements.

Strategy: To help client transition from business owner to less-demanding role as a nursery worker, demonstrated a wide range of hands-on experience within the specialized field of horticulture.

 MARILYN GREENE   PAGE 2

PROFESSIONAL EXPERIENCE (CONT.)

Highlights of Qualifications (cont.)

▸ Able to identify opportunities to enhance and/or value-engineer landscapes of residential and commercial clients. Detect potential pitfalls that are evident in proposed plans that could arise in the course of installation; consult with clients; and make appropriate changes as required.

▸ Capable of multi-tasking in a fast-paced, deadline-driven setting. Very flexible and creative in scheduling and producing quality work under time-sensitive circumstances.

▸ Plan and schedule contractors, directing daily work and conducting quality assurance and control. Maintain good client relationships and perform other tasks in support of quality work and satisfied clients.

▸ Conduct complete disease and insect analysis and initiate proper controls.

GREENE JEANS NURSERIES, Kalamazoo, Michigan
(Seventy-year-old family-owned nursery specializing in gardening and landscape services and supplies through retail, wholesale, and catalog/mail-order sales.)

GREENHOUSE/NURSERY MANAGER   May 1972–October 2004

Professional horticultural diagnostician holding full responsibility, accountability, and decision-making authority for core business-development functions. Recruited, staffed, and trained a team of 30+ employees in the fulfillment of revenue and service objectives.

Highlights of Qualifications

▸ Demonstrated outstanding skills in building relationships and ensuring customer loyalty in a highly competitive nursery market.

▸ Trained and advised nursery sales staff on effective sales presentations, success strategies, and closing methods, concentrating on customer needs.

▸ Developed and implemented innovative marketing initiatives that included community gardening and plant clinics, "Garden Pharmacy," new plant and product research programs, gardening presentations on public television, creative seasonal store displays, and trade shows.

▸ Coordinated production of mail-order catalog—content planning, layout, editing, proofreading, and mailing.

▸ Expanded sales program through print advertising, generating an increase in cash-and-carry customers of 80%.

EDUCATION & PROFESSIONAL DEVELOPMENT

WESTERN MICHIGAN UNIVERSITY, Kalamazoo, Michigan
Bachelor of Science, Horticulture Management, 1972

SEMINARS & ADDITIONAL TRAINING
Albion University Horticulture Workshops
Western Michigan University Horticulture Workshops
Central Michigan University Botanical Management Seminars

PROFESSIONAL AFFILIATIONS

Michigan Council of Nurserymen
Mail Order Gardening Association of Southwest Michigan

VOLUNTEER/COMMUNITY SERVICE

Habitat for Humanity • Kalamazoo Valley Memorial Gardens Landscaper
Wilson House Historic Site Landscaper • Tree Committee, City of Portage

Sean Arnold

Mobile: 0417 800 366
Telephone: (08) 8278 0404

9 Currawong Grove
Glenalta, South Australia 5052

WORK SOUGHT

Property Maintenance / Renovation
• Domestic • Rural • Commercial

BACKGROUND

Continuous employment in the automotive industry and completion of a number of courses in vehicle-related technology and occupational health and safety. Casual practical experience in farm and property improvement and maintenance. Confident in the use of a wide range of hand and power tools and machinery. Demonstrated ability to learn new skills quickly and apply knowledge in practical situations. Keen to transfer skills, interest, and experience to working in general maintenance, preferably with a combination of outdoor and indoor work.

DEMONSTRATED COMPETENCIES

- use of hand and power tools, including heavy-duty brush-cutters, chainsaws, drills
- experienced and competent with a range of farm and commercial machinery including ride-on mower, slasher, heavy-duty powered mower, dingo-digger (trencher), forklift
- practical ability and experience with motor vehicle maintenance and repairs
- ability to prioritise workloads and work within strict time constraints and job quotes
- good understanding of occupational health & safety requirements
- experience in home maintenance and on rural properties
- confident with all rural stock / building animal shelters and yards
- rubbish removed / firewood cut, split, and stacked
- on-site welding or oxy-cutting

RECENT JOBS

- rural property brush and fence-line clearance • paddock slashing
- tree lopping and removal • water tank removal • patio paving • horse shelter construction
- installation of heavy-duty irrigation (fire-fighting), including over a kilometer of trenching

RECENT WORK HISTORY

Farm Work (casual)	Nately and Moss Roses: Echunga	1999–current
Property Renovations (casual)	Bellevue Heights: Glenalta	2003–2004
Vehicle Dismantler	U-Strip It Auto Dismantlers	2002–2005
Workshop Assistant	Rippota Restorations: Torrensville	1999–2002
Production Assistant	Mitsubishi Motors	1996–1999
Assistant Manager	Beaurepaires: Warradale	1988–1996

Strategy: *Created a simple one-page resume highlighting "demonstrated competencies" for target positions in property maintenance.*

◆◆◆ Johnny Dexter ◆◆◆

721 Third Street, Topeka, KS 66603
(785) 630-7411
jdexter@aol.com

◆◆◆

OBJECTIVE

Position as custodian in a school or institutional building

QUALIFICATIONS

Solid work history of 30 years with the same employer. Experience has included sanitation duties and various maintenance tasks for quality assurance of consumer products. Earned reputation for reliability and doing more than expected.

WORK EXPERIENCE

ROCK CREEK MILLS, TOPEKA, KS
Packing Machine Operator
1976–2006

◆ Ran machine that packed processed flour and wheat by-products for shipment to various food industries.

◆ Had complete responsibility for monitoring the quality of the product and recording data.

◆ Maintained 100% record for clean work area in an environment frequently inspected by FDA officials.

◆ After normal work shift, willingly performed sanitation procedures that were not part of the job. These included:
  - ◆ general cleaning
  - ◆ mopping floors
  - ◆ scraping excess paint
  - ◆ painting in production area
  - ◆ cleaning of cafeteria and restroom facilities
  - ◆ dusting surfaces covered with flour
  - ◆ wiping machinery with sterilizing solutions

Was the only production worker ever to receive "Employee of the Month" award, for discovering contaminants in product and bringing this to the attention of supervisor. As a result, prevented product recall and saved substantial money for the company.

CHEM-BRIGHT CARPET CLEANING, INC., SHAWNEE, KS
Rug Cleaner
2004–Present, Part-Time

Strategy: *Paved the way for a post-retirement career by demonstrating reliability, work ethic, and the skills that are called for in a position as a school custodian.*

KARL GREGG

727 Sequoia Circle • Rochester, New York 14612 • 585-227-5939 • E-mail: kgregg13@resumesos.com

- **Excellent team-building and leadership skills.**
- **Delivery and order picking/packing experience.**
- **Superb interpersonal and customer relations skills.**
- **Mature, dependable, and flexible, with ability to adapt to variety of settings.**
- **NYS Class B CDL with Passenger Endorsement.**

EMPLOYMENT HISTORY

Delivery Driver / Warehouse, NATIONAL JANITORIAL SUPPLY, Rochester, NY
2005–Present (Part time)

Make deliveries to businesses throughout Monroe and surrounding counties. Pick and pull orders, plan delivery routes, and respond to customer-service inquiries.

Director of Human Resources, SAINT ELIZABETH'S NURSING HOME, Rochester, New York
1979–2005

Directed human resource functions for multi-level geriatric care facility with 900 employees. Accountable for recruitment and hiring, wage/salary policies, pension and benefits administration, and employee training.

- Administered health insurance, pension, 403B, life and disability insurance, and workers'
- compensation programs.
- Developed selection standards for new hires; interviewed and hired professional staff.
- Established and regularly reviewed personnel policy and wage/salary guidelines.
- Designed and implemented employee orientation and ongoing training programs.
- Instituted uniform performance appraisal process.
- Represented corporation in hearings on unemployment, discrimination, and other labor-related issues.

EDUCATION

Bachelor of Arts: Sociology—Case Western Reserve University; Cleveland, Ohio
Diploma: Office Management & Supervision—University of Rochester; Rochester, New York
United States Air Force Command & General Staff College

MILITARY SERVICE

Colonel, United States Air Force Reserve
Instructor, United States Air Force Reserve Forces School
Executive Officer, Civil Affairs Unit
Military Police Officer (Active Duty)

COMPUTER SKILLS

Windows, MS Office, and Lotus Notes skills

Strategy: *Positioned this individual for a post-retirement job as a delivery driver and warehouse assistant by grouping highly relevant qualifications at the top of the resume.*

Jon Maxfield

Erzbergerstr.123
21221 Monhench
Germany

Tel: +49 123 498 4323
Tel/Fax: +49 173 463 3397
Email: Jon.Maxfield@gernet.net

Solutions & Enterprise Architect

Software R&D ■ Enterprise, Distributed Computing ■ Data Warehousing ■ SDLC ■ CM ■ SQA ■ CMM

Technological know-how and an intense quality commitment have characterized performances on commercially successful enterprise software development projects for more than 20 years. Cited throughout career for inherent capacity to design, develop, and implement stable and innovative solutions that cement business reputations and deliver growth.

Key Credentials

- Project Management
- Application Programming
- Software Development
- Solutions Architecture
- Team Supervision/Training

- Defect Tracking
- User Acceptance Testing
- Distributed Computing
- Enterprise Software Development

- Software Development Lifecycles
- Use Cases
- Configuration Management
- Data Warehousing

Technology Summary

Development, Programming, Methodologies, Tools	C++, STL, MSVC, MFC, ATL, C#, .NET, XML, SAX, DOM, COM, COM+, DCOM, SCRUM, Sockets, Win32, Cryptography, Java, JavaBeans, LDAP, Visual Basic, PERL, SQL, OLTP, UML, Erwin, OLAP, DTS, WSDL
Databases	Microsoft SQL Server, Oracle, VLDB, OLE DB
Platforms	J2EE, Linux, Windows

Project Highlights

Project: CleverT, SmartV, GDPdU.

- Created a national technical standard that met recently passed laws governing the transfer of tax information during audits of publicly traded companies in Germany. CleverT became the solution—a desktop application now used by 20,000 people including 13,000 government auditors to import data into a target database. Application imports data 20 times faster than other company products and is on par with leading Microsoft technologies.
- Produced index in XML describing the data format stored in variable or fixed-length formats.
- Steered the development of CleverU, a syntax-grammar checker to analyze and validate data. The project, with 250,000 lines of code, incorporated use of C#, .Net, C++, LDAP, COM+, XML, XSLT, CryptoAPI, and Microsoft SQL Server.

Project: TTR Banking Solutions. Three-tier enterprise solution, tracking financial details of publicly traded corporations.
- Led four-person development team to create software. Written in C++, exploited DCOM to communicate with middle-layer components connecting to MS SQL Server or Oracle.

Project: Countermarks. Internet-available, benchmark data warehouse and successor to TTR Banking · Solutions.
- Java-based development. Used Oracle TopLink, STRUTS for the architecture, and Oracle 9i for the back end. Managed ten internal and external software developers and personally conducted extensive software development research for the production of solution prototypes.

Project: Data Warehouse: 2.2 Terabyte, MS SQL Server, Oracle 8i. Distributed data warehouse excelled in reporting payroll information and real-time sales results from thousands of call-center employees.
- Managed, optimized, developed, and upgraded $US 2+ million distributed data warehouse—traveling to 20 call centers to upgrade systems and monitor operations.

■ ■ ■ Continued ■ ■ ■

Strategy: *Helped this individual decelerate to a hands-on technology job by downplaying executive skills and experiences while highlighting technical skills from his lengthy career in IT.*

Jon Maxfield

Jon.Maxfield@gernet.net
■ ■ ■ Page 2 ■ ■ ■

Project Highlights ■ Continued

Project: Visual Basic client/server program, handling project requirements. SQL Server 6.5 backend database.
- Implemented the consultant-produced design and plan and later managed the entire project—transitioning to become the sole project developer.
- Extracted best performances from the ODBC to drive swift response times from the SQL Server.

Project: SLIM. Desktop application written in Visual Basic with custom controls developed in C.
- Lead creation of POS software that priced, specified, and ordered fleet vehicles via satellite.
- Conquered issue connecting minicomputer to serial port, facilitating satellite transmissions.

Experience Overview

AUDITECH, USA   4/2001–Present
Specialists in enterprise and desktop software development for financial auditors and tax consultants.
Director of Research and Development (Software)

REVAMP TECHNOLOGIES, USA   4/2000–3/2001
Dot-com start-up—creating software for financial institutions.
Chief Technology Officer

TELCO-INC, USA   3/1999–4/2000
Lead Developer

NBI WORLDLINK, USA   6/1997–1/1999
Senior Systems Analyst II

SWIFTON CARTONS, USA   6/1988–12/1997
Systems Analyst

Education

Oracle: Developing Applications Using Database Procedures | Advanced SQL and SQL Plus

RESUME 38: BY BETH WOODWORTH, MS IN HR COUNSELING, CPC, CPCC

EVELYN DAVIDSON

617-527-2201		P.O. Box 1011
617-966-1302	ebd1122@yahoo.com	Boston, MA 02134

OBJECTIVE: ACCOUNTING CLERK

- Strong background in accounting with emphasis on public relations and customer service
- Dedication to the job and strong drive for excellence and success
- Highly effective verbal and written communications skills
- Ability to work in a multi-task environment, performing with completeness all work duties and assignments

PROFESSIONAL EXPERIENCE

Account Technician/ Building Information Clerk   *1976–2004*
Suffolk County, Department of Building and Safety   *Boston, MA*

ACCOUNTING/BOOKKEEPING
- Performed complex accounting tasks quickly and accurately.
- Prepared department's budget for each fiscal year.
- Maintained personnel files and forms needed for various county departments.
- Processed daily deposits for all monies collected.
- Reconciled accounts daily and monthly with County Auditor and outside independent auditors.
- Assembled and analyzed information and prepared written reports and records in a clear, concise manner for governmental agencies and the general public.

CUSTOMER SERVICE
- Remained calm, focused, and highly productive in a fast-paced environment, balancing multiple customer requests.
- Streamlined construction projects for general public and private companies.
- Resolved difficult problems and inquiries from the public.
- Interpreted and applied pertinent laws, rules, and principles in the building industry and other areas; dealt with many different government agencies at federal, state, and local levels.

COMPUTER USAGE
- Implemented computer software program designed for the department, as part of a team.
- Maintained computers and program backups on weekly basis.
- Proficient in MS Windows, Word, Excel, Internet Explorer, and Quicken.
- Maintained department's wireless network system for each workstation and network server.
- Accurately maintained knowledge and concise data in word-processing programs.

EDUCATION

B.A. in Business/Accounting, Boston College
Continuing education through community college to keep updated on accounting practices

Strategy: *Used functional headings to group and emphasize accounting, customer service, and computer skills that will be valuable in a lower-level accounting clerk position.*

RESUME 39: BY DAYNA FEIST, CPRW, CEIP, JCTC

Martha L. Brown

265 Charlotte Street, Asheville, NC 28801 ■ (828) 254-7893 ■ martha@yahoo.com

Administration ■ *Customer Relations* ■ *Efficient Operations* ■ *Team Leadership*

PEAK-PERFORMING, COLLABORATIVE Administrative Professional—with 20+-year career facilitating high productivity, friendly customer service, and strong business growth—seeks part-time administrative or customer-service position.

- Characterized by former managers and staff as a fair, empowering **team builder,** able to mold a diverse group into a high-achieving team by encouraging participation and input . . . lead by example to make and meet goals.
- 14 years of **administrative** experience in the banking industry, driving branch to top position in 6-branch organization in highly competitive market—"*...always thinking of ways to make our jobs in the branches faster, easier, and more efficient."*
- Recognized for extensive knowledge of banking **operations;** go-to person for problems and questions.
- Expert in **customer relationship management,** with a knack for giving customer full attention; committed to improving the customer's situation by providing the best service possible.
- Astute at **cross-selling** products and services. Trained staff to recognize and act on selling opportunities.
- **Technically proficient,** contributing to implementation of numerous software packages (e.g., lending, tellering, customer service programs).

> *Branch Contributions:*
> ❖ *Almost 100% successful in closing $100K in loans every week.*
> ❖ *Lowest rate of employee turnover in company.*
> ❖ *Lowest error rate involving back-office departments.*
> ❖ *Fewest customer complaints and many compliments.*

CHRONOLOGY OF EXPERIENCE

ACME FEDERAL CREDIT UNION, Gary, IN
Progressive promotion to increasingly responsible positions in credit union serving employees of Cellular and Bell in Chicago metropolitan area. During my tenure, credit union grew from 3 branches and $43 million in assets to 100 employees in 6 branch offices and $260 million in assets.

SENIOR BRANCH MANAGER 1999–2003
BRANCH MANAGER 1989–1999
ASSISTANT BRANCH MANAGER 1987–1989
ASSISTANT LOAN MANAGER 1986–1987
LOAN OFFICER 1984–1986
TELLER 1982–1984

Accountable for all branch operations. Challenged to make company a primary financial institution in a highly competitive banking environment, despite a market limited to Cellular and Bell employees. Consultant to executive management on all branch operation matters (programs, policies, procedures) directly impacting branch-level staff.

Led and trained industrious, goal-driven team of 6–8 banking professionals (tellers, head teller, loan processors, customer service reps), with ability to perform and troubleshoot every job in the branch. Completed annual written evaluations for each team member; maintained complete performance records; conducted weekly staff/training meetings.

Strategy: *Emphasized knowledge of the banking industry to help this post-retiree find a new, part-time job in a customer-service or administrative position, a step down in responsibility from her management career in the same industry.*

Processed, reviewed, and disbursed loan applications to a limit of $100K lending authority for consumer loans, $25K for personal/unsecured loans, $50K for auto loans, and $100K for second mortgages. Approved 80%–100% of loans in office.

- Top-rated branch in company.
- Member of task forces charged with evaluating and selecting new credit-union systems such as loan processing and teller programs, working with data processing and other departments involved (e.g., collaborated with ATM Service Manager to write branch procedures when credit union ATMs began accepting deposits for the first time). Improved work life for branch staff while meeting goals and priorities of executive management.
- Teller auditor, at site, in cases of large teller differences (more than $200) at any branch.
- Generated loyal, repeat clientele with fast turnaround (often 24-hour) and attentive loan service.
- Consistently met quota of $100K in consumer loans per week, much of it generated by studying applications/credit reports and making customer-friendly refinancing/consolidation suggestions.

MANSION FEDERAL CREDIT UNION, Chicago, IL
Teller 1980–1982
- Earned Top Secret FBI Security Clearance.

BANK OF ILLINOIS, Chicago, IL
Teller 1980

EDUCATION

A.A., Merchandising, 1980—Illinois College, Chicago, IL

Hundreds of hours of professional training on such topics as Principles of Lending, Financial Management, and Cross-Selling & Marketing for Credit Unions

265 Charlotte Street, Asheville, NC 28801 ▪ (828) 254-7893 ▪ martha@yahoo.com   *Martha L. Brown*

Donald L. Stevens

2525 Fourth Street NE, Renton, WA 98058
(425) 795-9958 ● dlstevens@hotmail.com

SALES and MANAGEMENT PROFESSIONAL

Key Account Management / Solution Selling / New Business Development
Customer Service / Team Building / Organization Leadership / Turnarounds

Focused sales professional recognized for overachieving goals. Record of leadership in strategic business planning that drives profitability. Proven ability to build business relationships through performance, credibility, and customer service.

PROFESSIONAL EXPERIENCE

Owner
Stevens Business Products, Inc., Renton, WA, 1994–Present
Business Forms and Printed Products Distributorship.

- Started successful Business Forms & Printing distributorship. Authored marketing plan featuring product-line brochure that aided prospecting, cold calling, selling, and closing accounts. Grew business from zero to $679,000 in annual sales in five years.

General Manager
English Office Products, Seattle, WA, 1990–1994
Office Products and Office Furniture Company with 5,000-sq.-ft showroom and 25,000-sq.-ft. warehouse.

- Led turnaround of under-achieving office products company by personally selling major accounts and recruiting, hiring, training, and managing a cross-functional team of customer service representatives, sales representatives, and warehouse staff that grew monthly sales from $30K to $120K in less than four years.

Expert Computer Services, Tacoma, WA, 1984–1990
Branch office selling computer hardware, software, supplies, and full line of business forms and labels.

District Sales Manager, 1987–1990

- Directed all business activities for Tacoma office. Recruited and motivated high-performance sales team and authored long-range plan for mature branch office that increased annual sales from $2.11 million to $2.55 million over three years.

Account Representative, 1984–1987

- Built sales territory with motivated, organized selling and closing skills, achieving $420K in second year and $380K in first 9 months of third year before promotion to Sales Manager.

EDUCATION and TRAINING

Bachelor of Arts (BA), *Political Science,* UNIVERSITY OF WASHINGTON, Seattle, WA

Strategy: *Focused on sales activities and accomplishments to pave the way for a transition from business owner to account representative.*

GREGORY FOSTER

847-476-0874
gregfoster@gmail.com

1306 Piper Lane
Prospect Heights, IL 60070

SALES / MANAGEMENT PROFESSIONAL

A highly experienced, profit-oriented professional with an impressive record of accomplishments in both sales and management. Highly creative, detail oriented, capable, and motivated; readily inspire confidence of clients. Exemplify leadership qualities and professionalism backed by a consistent, verifiable record of achievement. Broad skill-set encompasses

- Sales—Exceptional Customer Service
- Creative Design / Merchandise Display
- Employee Development

- Problem Solving / Human Relations
- Inventory & Pricing Controls
- Product Research & Analysis

PROFESSIONAL EXPERIENCE

MANZO'S, Redding, CA   1994–2006
Owner/Operator
STRONG LEADERSHIP AND EFFECTIVE MANAGEMENT
SALES / CUSTOMER SERVICE / QUALITY CONTROL

- Demonstrated mastery of food selections and styles. Skilled at menu development, recipe creation, culinary arts, image, and concept.
- Designed monthly special promotions, organized sales training programs, and worked on special incentives for employees
- Determined all components of interiors: color schemes, furnishings, lighting, accessories, window treatments, etc.
- Budgeted and managed all aspects of purchasing, inventory planning, stock replenishment, expense control, menu planning/pricing, and facilities management.
- Recruited, trained and developed a staff of 15 employees to high performance levels.

TOYOTA, Del Rey, CA   1992–1994
Sales / Client Relations
CONSISTENTLY RANKED #1 IN SALES
RECIPIENT OF MONTHLY ACKNOWLEDGMENT AWARDS

- Initiated new sales tactics to achieve maximum productivity and profit.
- Successfully and professionally exceeded all established sales objectives.
- Personally sold vehicles at an average of 25 per month.

GOLD EAGLE LIQUORS, Libertyville, IL   1989–1992
Wine and Cheese Chalet Department Manager
Delivered sales and customer service; maintained excellent relations with a diverse clientele.

EDUCATION: LOYOLA MARYMOUNT UNIVERSITY, Los Angeles, CA,
    Business/Communications
    WESTBURY COLLEGE, Long Island, NY, **Associate of Arts**

Strategy: *Emphasized specific sales, customer-service, and staff-training activities to support current goal of sales and management; downplayed his business ownership.*

JOHN LANSING

215 Carnation Street
Laguna Beach, CA 92651

lansingj@aol.com

(949) 894-8744

SALES MANAGER
New Business Development / Sales Training / Customer Service

Experienced, hands-on store manager and former retail store owner. More than 20 years of experience building market presence, leading winning sales teams, and driving revenue growth. Seriously committed to improving market share through the establishment of strong working relationships with clients, the use of effective sales and marketing strategies, and superior customer service.

Well versed in all administrative functions, including payroll, human resources, labor laws, accounts payable and receivable, P&L management, and inventory.

Unique ability to relate to and establish rapport at all levels. Entrepreneurial. Natural leader and team builder. Articulate communicator with well-refined interpersonal skills.

Key Strengths

▪ Customer Service	▪ Employee Training & Motivation	▪ Print Advertising
▪ New Business Development	▪ Customer Relations	▪ Vendor Relations
▪ Leadership & Team Building	▪ Inventory & Loss Control	▪ Displays & Merchandising

LANSING CAMERA SHOP, San Diego, CA   1972–2006
President / General Manager
Family-owned retail camera sales and service store where successful management skills were learned
- Consistently increased revenue through after-sale follow-up, winning referrals and repeat business.
- Hired, trained, and supervised all sales staff.
- Developed and conducted training courses in basic selling skills, merchandising, and the importance and residual value of customer service.
- Performed all administrative and management functions.

ELLIOTT'S RV REPAIR, Mira Loma, CA   1967–1972
Store Manager
- Increased sales of accessories and aftermarket items by more than 40% in less than a year by increasing in-stock inventory, creating attractive merchandise displays, strategically placing key items, and providing high-quality customer service.

OUTDOOR WORLD, Mira Loma, CA   1965–1967
Sales Associate
- Assisted clients in the selection and purchase of proper equipment.
- Maintained and categorized store inventory.
- Scheduled service appointments and collected follow-up data through customer satisfaction surveys.

Education

Long Beach State College, Long Beach, CA—32 units toward B.A. degree

Computer Skills

Basic keyboarding
Proprietary and industry-specific programs

Volunteer Activities

Active Member of Rotary International for more than 20 years

Strategy: *Showed how this individual could be a valuable addition to any small business, enabling him to find a less-stressful job than running his own business.*

RESUME 43: BY SALOME FARRARO, CPRW

JAYNE GRIFFIN

606 Frost Ridge • Canandaigua, NY 14424
585/294-4144 • cell: 585/204-7643 • jaynegriffin@aol.com

Highly talented and creative professional who contributes to organizational success by identifying individuals' strengths and fostering self-confidence and personal initiative. Use excellent communication skills and sense of humor to promote a win-win philosophy.

QUALIFICATIONS SUMMARY

Business Management
- Human resources administration
- Recognition & reward systems
- Policy & procedure development
- Accounting & payroll
- Facilities management
- Client management

- Vendor sourcing/management
- Computer systems management
- Marketing
- Staff supervision
- Advisor to business owners

Non-Profit Leadership
- Board member, board president, volunteer
- Strategic planning
- Grant writing
- Program & exhibition development

- Marketing & public relations
- Volunteer recruiting/management
- Professional development of key leaders/managers

Computer
- Mac: ClarisWorks, PhotoShop, Adobe Elements
- Windows: Microsoft Word & Excel

HIGHLIGHTS OF EXPERIENCE

STRAWBRIDGE ANIMAL HOSPITAL—Canandaigua, NY   1995-present
This busy veterinary practice, with a reputation for high-quality, compassionate care, generates one-half million dollars in annual revenue; ownership changed in 1999. Staff currently totals seven.
Veterinary Practice Manager
- Administer all aspects of human resources: recruiting, hiring recommendations, training, staff development, implementation/reinforcement of practice policies, and recognition systems.
- Oversee business operations, facilities care, and resolution of internal and client problems.
- Manage AR and reminder services.
- Advise owner on all business issues, with a proactive, creative mindset.

Accomplishments:
▸ Stabilized the business during ownership transfer, allowing ease of transition for staff and clients.
▸ Averted a staffing shortfall in a typically high-volume month; allowed the practice to generate its highest-ever monthly income.

SHORTSVILLE VETERINARY HOSPITAL—Shortsville, NY   1991-1995
Joined this practice upon its purchase from the original owner. During tenure, staff grew to 15 and annual revenues reached $300K.
Veterinary Practice Manager
- Hired to develop and implement an organizational foundation for the new practice spanning human resources practices, computer systems, and business operations policies.
- Managed payroll record keeping; utilized two payroll services.
- Handled AR and produced monthly income analyses.
- Served as general business advisor to owners.

Strategy: *Emphasized business management activities and related accomplishments to facilitate the transition to part-time work in a similar function for a nonprofit organization.*

SHORTSVILLE VETERINARY HOSPITAL—continued:
Accomplishments:
▸ Recruited new staff and provided training for all, improving productivity and morale.
▸ Led the conversion from paper records to computerized systems; mapped and organized existing practices and documents in advance of the conversion, allowing for a problem-free changeover completed in six months.
▸ Sourced, championed, and managed the implementation of an industry quality system, resulting in credentialing by the American Animal Hospital Association (passed audit on first attempt).
▸ Advocated for staff and clients, resulting in consistency of both groups.

LITTLE LAKE HISTORICAL SOCIETY & MUSEUM—Canandaigua, NY   1997-present
This not-for-profit organization received its charter in 1936. The museum's collections reflect local history; it is a valued community resource.
President, Board of Trustees
▪ Joined the Board in 1996, at the invitation of the then-President; was elected President in 1997
Accomplishments:
▸ Initiated and directed the revitalization of the group, focusing on strategic planning and organizational development.
▸ Brought in and collaborated with a consultant to redesign the organization's mission and vision.
▸ Authored grant applications on behalf of the museum and earned $50,000 in awards from various funding sources.
▸ Marketed the updated mission to the community; volunteer ranks swelled from 12 to 50 and visitors have exceeded 1,000 annually.
▸ Identified talented local individual and successfully recruited as curator.
▸ Implemented professional development for the group's key leaders.
▸ Designed and coordinated cultural as well as educational programming and exhibits.
▸ Focused on current practices in collection care and management and improved visual displays.
▸ Documented and archivally re-housed photographs in the museum's collection.

OTHER EXPERIENCE

Artist / Photographer
Use camera as a tool to collect images that create personal histories. Assemble and integrate photographic and non-photographic materials as a means of exploring memory and emotion and to evoke thought.
Exhibitions:
▸ Ontario County Arts Council Annual Members' Exhibit; 2003, 2004
▸ Private show: Little Lake Museum—Canandaigua, NY; 2003
▸ Private show: Finger Lakes Community College—Canandaigua, NY; 1998
Grants & Recognition:
▸ Arts Leadership Award for Artistic Excellence; 2004
▸ Individual Artist Grant; 2003
▸ Special Opportunities Award; 1998

EDUCATION

Bachelor of Science, Textile Design: The Art Institute of Philadelphia—Philadelphia, PA

Extensive **professional development** in the arts as well as museum/non-profit management topics

RESUME 44: BY CAROL ALTOMARE, CPRW

LAURA MILLER

10 Olden Drive
Bridgewater, NJ 08807
908-725-0001 ◆ lmiller23@optonline.net

ASPIRING PARALEGAL
*Motivated individual with outstanding investigative and administrative skills and a
proven job record that reflects an enduring determination to succeed*

SUMMARY OF QUALIFICATIONS

- Recently certified paralegal with a diverse background that includes six months as an intern with the Superior Court of New Jersey.
- Highly effective communicator with excellent interpersonal skills. Able to establish rapport with people at all levels. Polished and professional in all dealings. Effective intermediary skilled in facilitator role.
- Strong track record in meeting deadlines. Organized in approach and thorough in follow-through. Flexible in the face of changing circumstances. Resourceful in finding alternative solutions.
- Demonstrated commitment to life-long learning. Inquisitive by nature. Passionate about law.

EDUCATION

FAIRLEIGH DICKINSON UNIVERSITY, Madison, NJ
Certificate of Completion, Paralegal Studies Program, 2005 (Graduated with honors from ABA-approved program.)

STEVENS INSTITUTE OF TECHNOLOGY, Hoboken, NJ   BLOOMFIELD COLLEGE, Bloomfield, NJ
MS in Management, 1992   BS in Business Administration, 1982

SELECT ACCOMPLISHMENTS

➤ **Paralegal Internship:** Gained familiarity with Complimentary Dispute Resolution Program. Assisted with checking in litigants and assigning cases to arbitrators. Completed administrative project for presiding judge that included surveying attorneys to review case awards. Developed color-coded spreadsheet to help court officers track attorney compliance with training requirements. Worked with pleadings, entering complaints and name changes into Automated Case Management System to generate docket numbers. Participated in broad range of other activities to gain exposure to the legal process.

➤ **Paralegal Training:** Built knowledge of complaints, motions, and application of court rulebook through paralegal coursework. Highly motivated to learn; frequently went beyond scope of class requirements, reading cases on own to integrate lessons.

➤ **Project Management:** In earlier career as certified project manager, developed and implemented challenging project plans and schedules while consistently meeting all project timelines. Managed administrative aspects of key projects, serving as intermediary between units to facilitate implementation.

➤ **Administrative Support:** Established reputation for exemplary service while holding various administrative positions in support of key projects. Coordinated departmental communications, serving as liaison between management and staff. Planned, scheduled, and coordinated meetings and business functions.

➤ **Supervision:** Hired, trained, supervised, and mentored administrative support staff consisting of bargaining employees. Distributed assignments and monitored performance. Instituted cross-training program that allowed for greater flexibility in making assignments, ensuring coverage, and minimizing workflow disruptions.

PROFESSIONAL EXPERIENCE

Intern, SUPERIOR COURT OF NEW JERSEY, SALEM CIVIL DIVISION, Jul 2005 to Dec 2005
Licensed Sales Associate, PRUDENTIAL RESIDENTIAL BROKERAGE, 2003 to 2005
Project Manager (and various other administrative positions), BELLCOM CORPORATION, 1980 to 2002

COMPUTER SKILLS

Microsoft Word, Excel, PowerPoint, Project; TitleExpress, Internet and e-mail applications.

Strategy: *Emphasized recent paralegal training as well as strong administrative experience gained in prior career.*

RESUME 45: BY JANE ROQUEPLOT, CPBA, CWDP, CECC

Carol Pearce

1888 Goosedown Road, Mentor, OH 44060
PH: 440-357-1234   E-MAIL: cpearce@comcast.com

NEW GRADUATE

Medical Billing Coding Specialist

At-Home Professionals
Ft. Collins, Colorado

Diploma—June 2006

Final Score—96%

SELECTED COURSEWORK

- Medical Terminology
- Diagnostic Coding
- Procedural Coding
- Anatomy and Physiology
- Medical Claims Procedures
- Medical Ethics
- Legal Issues of Profession

"Congratulations on completing your course! …Your hard work and determination…will help you be successful in your new career."

–Executive Director, At-Home Professionals

" Carol has exceptional medical-billing skills… she has demonstrated her qualification for handling your medical claims and billing needs… an asset in any medical office."

–Graduate Counselor, At-Home Professionals

… bringing 14 years of medical experience, recent training, and a high level of commitment and dedication to the position of

MEDICAL BILLING SPECIALIST

PROFESSIONAL STRENGTHS

➤ Seek and thoroughly analyze information to make tough decisions.

➤ Use balanced judgment while displaying empathy and sensitivity to others experiencing difficulties.

➤ Bring stability to the entire team.

➤ Display persistence and perseverance in approach to achieving goals.

ACHIEVEMENTS

➤ Evaluated abnormal behavior of patient and determined the presence of heart attack symptoms. The accurate conclusion and immediate reaction to her condition resulted in timely, life-saving treatment.

➤ Recommended appropriate treatment to hospital patients as a result of accurate monitoring of vital signs: blood pressure, temperature, and urinalysis.

➤ Effectively trained new nursing assistants while on the job in addition to regular responsibilities to assist new staff in accurately learning new position.

➤ Utilized proper sterilization techniques to clean wounds, reducing patient's risk of infection.

➤ Conducted inspections of patients' beds and living areas to confirm acceptable sanitation standards, eliminating local and cross contamination.

EMPLOYMENT EXPERIENCE

Nursing Assistant   *1993–2003*
Hershey Medical Center—Hershey, Pennsylvania

✓ Entered labs in computer.
✓ Ordered supplies for patients.
✓ Operated a Hoyer lift machine.

Nursing Assistant   *1989–1993*
Patterson Nursing Home—Wheeling, West Virginia

✓ Operated a Hoyer Lift machine.
✓ Monitored and cared for patients.
✓ Maintained reports and records of facility conditions.

Strategy: *Used a distinctive format to call attention to both recent medical billing education and past experience in the health-care field.*

RESUME 46: BY CAMILLE CARBONEAU ROBERTS, CFRW/C, CPRW, CEIP, CARW

KIM C. KOPLIN, PHARM.D.

765 Skyline ▪ Idaho Falls, Idaho 83401 ▪ 208.200.7642 Cell ▪ KimKoplin@cableone.net

—PHARMACIST—

EDUCATION

Pharm.D., Idaho State University, Pocatello, Idaho. May 2006. Dean's List, 2004 and 2005.
Licensed Practical Nurse, Idaho State University, Pocatello, Idaho. May 1995.
Bachelor of Arts Degree, Idaho State University, Pocatello, Idaho. May 1988.

CLERKSHIPS

Completed seven clerkships in primary pharmaceutical rotations. Worked in cooperation with professional pharmacists and staff to compound and dispense medications, prepare IVs, monitor inventory, and provide one-on-one patient training. Rotations included

PHARMACY: **Kmart,** Idaho Falls, Idaho.
GERIATRICS: **State Veterans' Home,** Pocatello, Idaho.
ADULT MEDICINE: **ISU Family Medicine Clinic,** Pocatello, Idaho.
AMBULATORY CARE: **Family Practice Group,** Osgood, Idaho.
COMMUNITY: **Ed's Pharmacy Shop,** Iona, Idaho.
HOSPITAL PHARMACY: **Medical Center West,** Pocatello, Idaho.
MENTAL HEALTH: **State Hospital South,** Rexburg, Idaho.

RELEVANT EMPLOYMENT

PHARMACY INTERN. EASTERN MEDICAL CENTER, Idaho Falls, Idaho. June 2004–May 2006.
- Processed and dispensed prescription orders for high-volume pharmacy.
- Prepared IVs, packaged medications, ordered and stocked medications.
- Input medication information into computer system for robot to pull the medication.
- Communicated with staff and management relative to drug-related issues and concerns, including drug interactions, order clarifications, and therapeutic recommendations.

LICENSED PRACTICAL NURSE. EASTERN MEDICAL CENTER, Idaho Falls, Idaho. May 1995–June 2000.
- Provided IV therapy and medical administration along with total patient care.

ADDITIONAL EMPLOYMENT

INSTRUCTOR. EASTERN TECHNICAL COLLEGE, Idaho Falls, Idaho. June 1994–October 1995.
GRANT WRITER/ADMINISTRATOR. PROSPERITY PARTNERS, Idaho Falls, Idaho. June 1988–June 1994.
COMPUTER SPECIALIST. CC COMPUTER SERVICES, Idaho Falls, Idaho. May 1982–May 1988.

PROFESSIONAL AFFILIATIONS

Member, American Society of Health-System Pharmacists.
Member, Idaho Society of Health-System Pharmacists.

Strategy: *Stressed pharmacy-related qualifications (education, clerkships, and employment) to support this individual's career transition; provide only an abbreviated listing of other work experience.*

HOWARD B. TOWNSEND, M.D.
FACOG
Diplomate, American Board of Obstetrics and Gynecology

665 Center Street
Boston, MA 02116
(617) 524-5000
townsend21@hotmail.com

CAREER PROFILE

Career Target: ⇒ **Program development / implementation in international reproductive health**

Area of Specialty: ⇒ **Obstetrician / gynecologist with board certification in maternal-fetal medicine**

Extensive medical experience that includes working in two private practices, serving on the staff of numerous hospitals, teaching at several universities, and advancing the state of professional knowledge in the field of perinatal medicine. Master of Public Health degree from Harvard University. Conversational Spanish. U.S. citizen.

Field experience in Kosovo as a clinician and consultant working for an American NGO and two UN agencies. Experience coordinating a healthcare survey initiative, analyzing data, and making recommendations about project design and implementation. Knowledgeable about the international donor community. Excellent communication skills and experience making large presentations to both medical and non-medical audiences. Well-developed abilities in negotiation, conflict analysis/management, and maintenance of staff security. Experience working with UN-supported police force.

EDUCATION

Master of Public Health, HARVARD SCHOOL OF PUBLIC HEALTH, Boston, MA (June 2005)
Doctor of Medicine, COLLEGE OF OSTEOPATHIC MEDICINE AND SURGERY, San Diego, CA (1981)
Bachelor of Science, CORNELL UNIVERSITY, Ithaca, NY (1978)

PROFESSIONAL EXPERIENCE

CLINICAL AND CONSULTING EXPERIENCE—INTERNATIONAL REPRODUCTIVE HEALTH

UNITED NATIONS POPULATION FUND, Mission to Kosovo, Pristina, Kosovo (April 2001 to June 2001)
Perinatal Technical Consultant
- Organized, managed, and conducted a comprehensive, Kosovo-wide survey of the maternity services and equipment needs in 20 regional hospitals and health houses.
- Ensured appropriate allocation of $600,000 in medical equipment.
- Analyzed and interpreted Kosovo-wide perinatal health data collected by WHO, Pristina office, to identify problems and make recommendations.
- Convened a Kosovo-wide meeting for representatives of aid agencies to discuss findings and make recommendations for modified or new reproductive and perinatal health strategies and policies.

WORLD HEALTH ORGANIZATION, Mother and Child Health Unit, Pristina, Kosovo (October 2000 to April 2001)
Perinatal Technical Advisor/Medical Officer
- Contributed to the monitoring, analysis, and interpretation of Kosovo-wide perinatal data for WHO.
- Participated in adapting and implementing Kosovo-wide training-of-trainers interventions specifically directed at improving obstetric care practices using WHO's Essential Obstetric Care (EOC) educational intervention.
- Made connections within the NGO reproductive health community in the interest of ensuring efficient deployment of resources.

Strategy: *Led with high-powered, relevant degree from Harvard, followed by a summary of international program experience and other valuable qualifications. Relevant experience is listed first, even though it's not the most recent.*

HOWARD B. TOWNSEND, M.D.   PAGE 2

DOCTORS OF THE WORLD/MEDECINS DU MONDE USA, Pristina, Kosovo (July 2000 to October 2000)
Clinician—USAID-Funded Maternal and Infant Health Project

- Provided perinatal technical assistance to the Maternal and Infant Health Project at tertiary and regional hospitals.
- Provided medical monitoring of pregnancy-related health outcomes of a minority Roma population in Kosovo.
- Contributed to the reformulation of project goals, objectives, and priorities after assessing the clinical services and perinatal and neonatal health indicators.
- Acquired knowledge of and experience with the policies and procedures of a wide range of international humanitarian assistance and reproductive health programs, including USAID.
- Analyzed and interpreted Kosovo maternal and neonatal data. Wrote two abstracts of findings and presented them at an international perinatal meeting in Bosnia.

CLINICAL EXPERIENCE—PERINATAL MEDICINE

SAINT JOSEPH'S HOSPITAL, Boston, MA (2002 to Present)
Medical Director, Maternal-Fetal Medicine
- Developed and launched a Maternal-Fetal Medicine component of Boston Critical Care Transport and provided physician expertise in the training and supervision of the maternal transport nursing team.

PERINATAL & PEDIATRIC SPECIALISTS MEDICAL GROUP, INC., Sacramento, CA (1999 to 2002)
Associate—Private practice in maternal-fetal medicine and perinatal genetics

CALIFORNIA DIABETES & PREGNANCY PROGRAM, NE Region, Sacramento, CA (1996 to 1999)
Regional Medical Director
- Ensured attainment of objectives through regional implementation of statewide plans.

SUTTER PRENATAL DIAGNOSIS CENTER, Sacramento, CA (1995 to 1996)
Co-Director
- Ensured compliance with state requirements for quality performance of obstetrical ultrasound and amniocenteses.

SUTTER MEMORIAL HOSPITAL, Sacramento, CA (1994 to 1995)
Medical Director, Sweet Success Pregnancy Program—Provided managed care for obstetric diabetic patients.

Hospital Appointments

Via Christi Regional Medical Center, St. Francis and St. Joseph Hospitals, Sacramento, CA (1996 to 1999)
Professional Staff (Transitioned from provisional to active status in February 1998)

Sutter Community Hospitals of Sacramento, Sacramento, CA (1994 to 1996)
Professional Staff

Medical College of Virginia Hospitals, Department of Obstetrics and Gynecology, Richmond, VA (1992 to 1993)
Attending Physician

The Jack D. Weiler Hospital of The Albert Einstein College of Medicine Division, Montefiore Medical Center, and Jacobi Hospital, Bronx Municipal Hospital Center, New York, NY (1988 to 1992)
Assistant Attending Physician

BOARD CERTIFICATION AND LICENSURE

Diplomate, American Board of Obstetrics and Gynecology (1990)
Certified by American Board of Obstetrics and Gynecology in Maternal-Fetal Medicine
American Board of Obstetrics and Gynecology
Certification of Special Competence in Maternal-Fetal Medicine (1991)
DEA Physician Registration (1988)

PROFESSIONAL AFFILIATIONS, AWARDS, AND ADDITIONAL QUALIFICATIONS AVAILABLE ON REQUEST

Marilyn Alicia Jacks

15017 South Star Road
Pikesville, MD 21208

Phone: (410) 484-9957
Email: majacks@bcps.com

HIGHLIGHTS OF QUALIFICATIONS

Accomplished educator with Emergency Medical Services (EMS) volunteer experience seeking a position as an Emergency Medical Services Associate Regional Administrator. Qualifications include

Leadership and Personal Interaction
- Diverse experience in a variety of executive and leadership positions within community, liaising with individuals, parents, and public officials.
- Personable, dependable, visionary leadership; track record of community activity and recognition for contributions in the field of education.
- Effective project leadership skills and ability to facilitate cooperation among administrators, faculty, students, and the community.
- Supervisory and leadership experience, overseeing and developing employees and volunteers.
- Excellent team-building and interpersonal abilities; talent for working well with individuals on all levels.
- Recognition as a resource person, problem solver, and creative leader.

Administration
- Special knowledge in administering and evaluating assessments, performing research, and interpreting standards and policies.
- Ability to manage multiple tasks, work under deadlines, and adapt to changing situations.

Community Support and Outreach
- Reputation for "going the extra mile" and displaying a naturally caring and supportive demeanor.
- Extensive EMS volunteer experience in the northern Maryland region.

Planning/Program Development
- Proficiency working independently and as a team member to develop programs from inception to implementation.

RELEVANT EXPERIENCE

- **Co-developer of the Emergency Response Team Guide**—a guide used by first responders when responding to crises in Baltimore County schools. The guide won the first EMS for Children Award given by the Maryland Institute for Emergency Medical Services Systems (MIEMSS).
- **Active member of Reisterstown Volunteer Fire Department and Rescue Squad;** alternate to the Baltimore County EMS Executive Committee and the Baltimore County Association of EMS.
- **Presenter or co-presenter on 38 occasions** of topics including planning disaster drills, involving schools in drills, and drill critiques to a variety of audiences, including the Maryland State Firemen's Association, the Maryland State Department of Education, and the Directors of the Maryland Emergency Management Association (MEMA).

Strategy: *Emphasized extensive volunteer experience because it is this person's primary qualification for her new career.*

Marilyn Alicia Jacks
Page 2

- **Co-developer of the Maryland Virtual Response System (MVERS)**—a collaborative effort of MIEMMS, the Maryland State Police, and MEMA. MVERS organizes vital information, floor plans, and pictures concerning facilities suitable for use by first responders in emergencies.
- **Evaluator for 15 drills throughout the State of Maryland** and member of the planning committee for 10 of them.
- **Practicing Emergency Medical Technician**—Basic (EMT-B) with more than 3 years of experience.

RELEVANT TRAINING

More than 172 continuing education units (CEUs) granted by MIEMMS.
More than 15 certificates from the Emergency Management Institute, including Emergency Response to Terrorism, Multi-Hazard Emergency Planning for Schools, and Emergency Program Manager.

PROFESSIONAL HISTORY

Baltimore County Public Schools, Baltimore, MD
Supervising Pupil Personnel Worker   1997–Present
- Supervise the work of 40 pupil personnel workers in a school system with more than 100,000 students.
- Co-developed the Emergency Response Team Guide. This guide is used by first responders when responding to crises in Baltimore County schools.

Pupil Personnel Worker   1988–1997
- Resource and consultant to school personnel in matters of child safety, laws, local policies and procedures, alternative programming, school climate, and dysfunctional families.

Baltimore County Public Schools, Baltimore, MD   1970–1988
Held positions as Elementary Teacher, Special Education Resource Teacher, and Admission Review & Dismissal Facilitator and Chairperson.

EDUCATION

M.S., George Washington University, Washington, DC—Special Education
B.S., Towson State University, Towson, MD—Early Childhood Education

PROFESSIONAL PROFILE
Honors & Awards
2002 Educator Award from the Baltimore County Chamber of Commerce for Public Safety
2000 Maryland Star of Life Award for Children from MIEMSS–Region II for the Emergency Response Team Manual

Special Accomplishments
    Member, Emergency Education Council, Region II, MIEMMS
    Member, Maryland Critical Incident Stress Management Team

William Mroz

811 66th Avenue North, Apt. C-2
Poughkeepsie, NY 12603

845.555.1212
mroz@aol.com

QUALIFICATIONS PROFILE

Ecology-minded individual with an interest in the restoration of natural areas and the conservation of open space. Ready to find ways to balance the needs of the environment with economic factors and social issues.

Profile

- Experience includes field studies, streambed research, site assessments & preparing environmental impact statements
- Special talent for conducting in-depth research, analyzing and interpreting data, and preparing professional documentation
- Ability to classify and map soils, interpret wetland hydrology, identify regional flora, and conduct species assessments
- Knowledge of environmental laws as well as the structure and operations of state and federal regulatory agencies

Qualifications

- Proven ability to work in variable weather conditions and in remote locations—both independently and with a team
- Proficiency in Microsoft Word and Excel, SPSS; skill at using taxonomy keys and reading topographical maps
- Advanced communication skills combined with strong writing skills and well-developed presentation and debating abilities
- Analytical proficiency; ability to translate survey and research findings into recommendations, reports, and presentations

EDUCATION

Cornell University (May 2005)
Candidate: M.A. in Environmental Ecology (GPA: 3.4)

Thesis: Physical, Chemical, and Biological Processes of a Restored Wetland versus a Natural Wetland

Cornell University (2002)
B.A. in Land Planning & Resource Management (GPA: 3.1)

Herkimer Community College, Herkimer, NY
A.A.S. in Liberal Arts

INTERNSHIPS / INDEPENDENT STUDY

Wetland Monitoring—Hudson Bay / Lake Ontario (3-year study)   2000 to 2003
Initially assigned to this study as a senior project requirement. Volunteered to continue with study when the semester ended. Performed field surveys, wetland and upland evaluations, species surveys, plant identification, and wetland delineation. Utilized quantitative and qualitative monitoring methods and statistical analysis to evaluate data. Presented findings to the Lake Ontario Research Consortium and to a DEC Biologist. Also invited to present study to Herkimer Community College students.

Bio-Diversity Study, *Mohawk, NY* **(2-year study)**   2002 to 2003
Selected by professor to assist with this study to investigate the effects of logging on the biodiversity of a transitional zone. Extensively read forestry reports and current literature. Assessed stream and wildlife habitats, prepared environmental impact statements, collected and analyzed field data, mapped wetland boundaries, and prepared scientific reports.

Mist Netting Project (10-week project)   Spring 2003
Volunteered to assist professor in the capture and tagging of migratory birds.

EMPLOYMENT EXPERIENCE

ABC Plumbing, *Mohawk, NY*	Plumber / Foreman (Residential Projects)	**1989 to 1996**
Enea Heating & Plumbing, *Mohawk, NY*	Plumber (Water & Sewer Main Installation)	**1984 to 1989**
Fulmer Plumbing, *Mohawk, NY*	Plumber Apprentice	**1981 to 1984**

Performed all aspects of plumbing work for residential, commercial, and municipal projects throughout Herkimer County. Consistently promoted based on specialized expertise in project planning, costing, and scheduling as well as verifiable contributions regarding procedural redesign and cost avoidance. Directed field efforts and led crews to maintain cost and schedule guidelines. Met regularly with owners, contractors, and municipalities to ensure compliance to specifications.

Strategy: *Prepared this former plumber for a total job shift by emphasizing his lifelong interests, recent training, and relevant activities. Employment experience is downplayed.*

RESUME 50: BY LOUISE GARVER, MCDP, CEIP, CMP, CPRW, JCTC

JAMES SOMERS

432 Gillette Street • Torrington, CT 09987 • (860) 634-5775 • james_somers@aol.com

TOWN MANAGER

Offering 13 years of leadership experience in town government as an elected chief administrative and fiscal officer. Key contributor impacting operational, budgetary, staffing, and resource needs throughout the municipality.

Extensive human resources and public speaking background. Effective communicator and team builder with planning, organizational, and negotiation strengths as well as the ability to lead, reach consensus, establish goals, and attain results. Additional business management experience in the private sector. Competencies include

- **Management/Administration**
- **Fiscal Management/Budgeting**
- **Project/Program Management**
- **Public/Private Sector Alliances**
- **Economic Development**
- **Staff Development/Empowerment**

PROFESSIONAL QUALIFICATIONS

TOWN OF NORTH GRANBY, North Granby, CT   1993 to Present
SELECTMAN

Administration/Management—Proactive executive providing strategic planning and leadership direction to diverse municipal departments as one of three elected board members governing the Town of North Granby. As board member, direct multiple open town meetings, develop and oversee $10 million budget, and administer various projects. Experience includes chairing Board of Selectmen for 6 years.

Human Resources—Oversee recruitment, promotion, and supervision of town administrator, 10 department heads with up to 214 full- and part-time staff, as well as Department of Public Works and Police Department. Personnel functions also encompass recruitment, contract negotiations, benefits administration, employee relations, and policy development and implementation.

Economic Development—Support strong public/private partnership toward diversified growth and prosperity. Source and negotiate with businesses as well as secure agreements to retain and attract new businesses. Develop financial vehicles for public improvements.

Regulatory Affairs—Develop and manage relationships, as well as advocate for municipal affairs, with federal and state regulatory agencies, local business executives, congressional members, and other legislators.

Public/Community Relations—Instrumental in enhancing Town's image and building consensus with all boards. Active participant in numerous annual community events; act as spokesperson with the media.

Achievements

- **Turned around employee morale and productivity,** instituted training and employee recognition programs, and fostered interdepartmental cooperation, creating a positive work environment while restoring accountability and confidence in the administration. North Granby is recognized by the state municipal association for having the "most responsive and best managed administration statewide."

- **Orchestrated multiple town revitalization projects,** following failed attempts by prior boards:
  - $2.9 million renovations to Town Hall and $5 million public safety complex.
  - $1.3 million public library project with state library grant offsets of $200,000.
  - $15 million sewer project with more than $5 million secured in federal grant funding.

- **Effectively negotiated with company CEOs to relocate their businesses back to North Granby.** Results led to construction of new plants for 4 companies employing 2,550 people combined and an agreement to expand employee base.

- **Instrumental in attracting and retaining businesses** in the community by personally negotiating Tax Incentive Financing Agreements.

- **Spearheaded search for new providers and negotiated improved employee benefits program** while avoiding any rate increase.

Strategy: Focused page 1 of the resume on municipal leadership experience—although unpaid, this was his strongest qualification for his new job target. Business experience is included on page 2 as added value.

JAMES SOMERS—Page 2

BUSINESS MANAGEMENT EXPERIENCE

MONROE & COMPANY, New York, NY   1980 to present
(Global multibillion-dollar manufacturer)

Regional Manager	2002 to present
District Manager	1990 to 2002
Account Manager	1980 to 1990

Promoted to manage $23 million region that extends from the Northeast to Florida at a multibillion-dollar food processing manufacturer. Lead and motivate the direct sales team of 35 plus 5 broker organizations. Develop and execute sales and marketing programs. Manage $2.5 million annual marketing/advertising budget.

Achievements

- **Created sales and marketing initiatives that turned around the region's ranking from #6 to #1** out of 8 regions nationwide. Consistently exceeded annual sales plan despite a declining industry.

- **Led the region's successful transition from a direct sales force to a productive food-broker network;** efforts charted an entirely new direction in the company and the new business model was adopted in all regions.

- **Drove expansion of existing account base while capturing 5 key accounts that generated $10.5 million** in annual business volume for the district.

- **Elected to the Leadership Club in 1997, 1996, 1995, and 1994** for consistently ranking among the top 10% of account managers in overall sales performance throughout company.

- **Renegotiated marketing programs with major customers that increased sales and profits** while achieving acceptable dollar spends.

EDUCATION / PROFESSIONAL DEVELOPMENT

BENTLEY COLLEGE, Bentley, VT
M.B.A., Finance, 1999
B.S., Business Administration, 1995

Additional: Several seminars on municipal administration sponsored by the Connecticut Municipal Association and the Selectmen's Association

COMMUNITY AFFILIATIONS / LEADERSHIP

Selectmen's Association
Vice President, North Granby Rotary Club
Chairman, Conservation Commission

EDWARD G. PAYNE

18 Queens Place
Seaford, New York 11783
(516) 589-3818
E-mail: edpaynemunicpalgov@aol.com

PROFILE

Extensive experience in Municipal Government focusing on managing the police, fire, and buildings and grounds departments. Demonstrated capabilities include contract negotiations, budget preparation, administration, and procurement. Additional expertise includes directing and training various levels of management personnel. Background is supplemented by a successful career in defense industry management. A self-directed and resourceful leader—people-oriented, with excellent problem-solving and communication abilities.

SIGNIFICANT ACCOMPLISHMENTS

- Negotiated and obtained agreements on 3 police contracts ranging in duration from 2–4 years, valued at $2.6 million–$3.0 million.

- Achieved lower salary contract increases than the 2 immediate surrounding police departments.

- Successfully negotiated police contract covering early payouts of accrued vacation and sick pay, which resulted in savings of $20,000–$30,000 per person at retirement.

- Negotiated and modified contractual rate of overtime, achieving annual savings ranging from $50,000–$60,000 per year.

- Attained savings ranging from $30,000–$40,000 per contract by reducing the minimal hours of recall with the Civil Service Employees Association (representing building and grounds personnel).

- Reviewed, evaluated, and adjusted proposed budgets valued at over $6 million, adhering to overall village budget plan and achieving a consistent tax base for residents.

- Interfaced with Village Board and residents at meetings in which the proposed budget was approved for ten continuous years.

- Pioneered and established a monthly budgetary cash-flow system that monitored the income and expenditures and led to achieving budgetary compliance 98% of the time.

- Initiated and established Requirement Contracts (roads, curbs, signs) covering 2-year period and achieving an average of 25% cost savings.

- Developed and instituted a new procurement procedure, establishing purchasing approval levels that enhanced operational efficiency and reduced turnaround time averaging 30 days.

- Researched, developed, and standardized administrative procedures that increased overall productivity of all departments.

Strategy: *Established capabilities and accomplishments from a secondary career, much of it volunteer, to position this individual for a role in municipal government.*

EDWARD G. PAYNE   (516) 589-3818   Page 2

SIGNIFICANT ACCOMPLISHMENTS (Continued)

- Conducted training seminars for groups of 5 to 25 participants covering all aspects of municipal government.

- Planned, organized, and executed as Program Manager a $50 million program, achieving completion 3 months ahead of schedule while enhancing profit margin from the expected 5.5% to 11%.

- Directed the management of 5 sites encompassing business development, engineering, and production and financial controls. Met all schedule milestones for 5-year program.

- Achieved corporate and customer recognition for program management effort in establishing a precedent-setting production parts contract that reduced ordering cycle time from 60 days to 10 days.

PROFESSIONAL EXPERIENCE

TELEPHONICS CORPORATION, Melville, NY

Advanced career from **Group Head of Electronic Technical Writers** through 4 promotions to **Program Manager/Consultant**   1980–2005

Directed and performed program-management functions from proposal stage to delivery of final project.

INCORPORATED VILLAGE OF LINDENHURST, Lindenhurst, N.Y.

Mayor   1992–2002
Trustee   1988–1992

Managed 11 Department Heads directly, and indirectly a support staff of 100 employees in conducting daily operations of village government.

GOVERNMENT ASSOCIATIONS

Elected to a 12-member Executive Committee of New York State Conference of Mayors
President, Suffolk County Village Officials Association
President, Tri-County Village Officials Association
Voting Member, Suffolk County Criminal Justice Coordinating Committee

EDUCATION

ADELPHI UNIVERSITY, Brookville, NY
Bachelor of Science Degree

LAURA HUNTINGTON

17 North Front Street • Buffalo, NY 14202
716/542-6510 • huntington@myemail.com

Elementary Educator

Dedicated, energetic professional offering a strong background in social work and both academic and practical experience. Desire to impart to children a love of learning along with necessary skills for success in life and to contribute meaningfully to society. Recognized for excellent organizational, communication, follow-through, and teaming abilities. Ethical, responsible, and creative.

EDUCATION & RELATED CREDENTIALS

B.A., Elementary & Early Childhood Education: Alfred University—Alfred, NY; 2006
   GPA in major: 3.7; *Overall GPA*: 3.3
   Dean's List
   Concentration: Social Science

A.S., Human Services/Social Work: Alfred State College of Technology—Alfred, NY; 2001
   GPA: 3.5
   Dean's List
   Internship: Erie County Council on Alcohol & Substance Abuse

New York State Provisional Teaching Certification: *Elementary & Early Childhood Education;* pending
   (successfully completed all required exams October 2005)

HIGHLIGHTS OF STUDENT TEACHING & PRACTICUM EXPERIENCE

Olean City School District—Olean, NY   *Fall 2004*
4th grade (inclusion room with 12:1:1 special education population) **& 6th grade** (two 7-week placements)
 ‣ Collaborated with 6th-grade teacher to design and implement a comprehensive behavior-management program; encompassed expectations for behavior and achievement, limit setting, consequences, positive reinforcement, and reward system, helping to create an organized and constructive environment.
 ‣ Worked with same teacher to improve students' organizational, note-taking, and study skills by providing students workable systems and methods.
 ‣ Designed and implemented individualized plans to instruct 4th-grade curriculum after assessing the strengths and weaknesses of 5 mainstreamed special-education students.
 ‣ Developed a language arts program to introduce literary concepts using Sherlock Holmes and his investigative techniques; achieved extraordinary results among the special-education students.
 ‣ Daily 1:1 tutoring of a 4th-grade student in language arts skills over the 8-week period; saw improvement from single-word recognition to reading at the 1st-grade level.
 ‣ Gained experience across all facets of classroom instruction and management, including attendance, grading, and parent-teacher conferences.

Dunkirk City School District—Dunkirk, NY   *Spring 2004*
6th grade (intermediate school level) **& 1st grade** (two 8-week placements)
 ‣ Developed and instructed a 3-week unit on feudalism; utilized interactive groups, whole and small group instruction, and computers to explore, understand, and evaluate this topic; final student projects and exam scores reflected improved learning over earlier units.
 ‣ At 1st-grade level, provided instruction in phonics and developed a unit on fractions.
 ‣ Delivered intensive tutoring to at-risk students.
 ‣ Participated in all aspects of daily classroom management.

Strategy: *Helped this individual—who returned to the classroom at age 50 to earn a teaching degree—transfer all of her diverse skills and experience to an elementary teaching role. Most relevant experience appears up front.*

SOCIAL WORK EXPERIENCE

Catholic Charities of Erie County—Buffalo, NY   *1/2001–present*
Volunteer Youth Mentor (1:1)
- Worked with 1 at-risk child (age 5 at outset) for entire period, exposing her to a healthy lifestyle.

Fresh Start Family & Youth Services—Williamsville, NY   *6/2004–present; 2/2002–8/2002*
Sociotherapist, Children's Home (Amherst; current position)
- Provide daily activities supervision of up to 3 children placed in this diagnostic home for seriously abused and mentally ill children ages 5 to 12.
- Create a structured and supportive environment that encourages appropriate behavior and opportunities to acquire/practice life skills.
- Implement clinical treatment team recommendations.

Case Manager, Halfway House (2002)
- Screened clients and managed caseload of adults for substance-abuse recovery residential site.

Erie County Council on Alcohol & Substance Abuse—Buffalo, NY   *8/2001–1/2002*
Case Manager
- Managed a client caseload from screening through program completion, maintaining thorough and up-to-date records.
- Coordinated client treatment through evaluation and treatment plan development/implementation.
- Counseled individual clients and co-led support and educational group meetings.

OTHER EXPERIENCE

Huntington Therapeutic Massage—Buffalo, NY   *2/2001–present*
Owner/Practitioner
- Licensed Massage Therapist (State of New York, February 2001).
- Earned Certificate of Massage from Finger Lakes School of Massage, Ithaca, NY, March 1999.
- Member, American Massage Therapists Association, since 2001.
- Provide therapeutic massage treatment to clients with work-related injuries as well as those pursuing self-care.

RESUME 53: BY **DON ORLANDO, MBA, CPRW, JCTC, CCM, CCMC**

Martin D. Conner, MBA, MS (Engineering)
14 Calle Medio, Valencia, California 91300 ✉martin.conner@alumni.usc.edu ☎661.555.6000

WHAT I CAN OFFER **MID-WEST STATE** AS YOUR NEWEST **BUSINESS INSTRUCTOR**

❑ The passion to model the learning employers reward their best new people for demonstrating (**building your reputation among students and those who employ them**)

❑ The enthusiasm to show students applicability in everything they see, hear, and learn in my classroom (**positioning you as the college of choice for applicants, students, and employers**)

❑ The dedication to make my thought visible to my students so they can make their thought visible to the community (**equipping your students with the critical-thinking skills employers now demand**)

EDUCATION

❑ MBA, with a specialty in **Global Business**, Pepperdine University, Malibu, California   Dec 04

GPA 3.81. Earned this degree while working more than 40 hours a week and carrying a full academic workload at night.

❑ MS, Engineering, University of Southern California, Los Angeles   Dec 88

GPA 3.24. Worked more than 40 hours a week at nights to complete this degree.

❑ BS, Technology, Southern Illinois University, Carbondale, Illinois   Spring 83

Dean's List (five times). Partial scholarship.

❑ AS, Electronic Technology, Southern Illinois University, Carbondale, Illinois   Spring 81

RECENT WORK HISTORY WITH EXAMPLES OF EDUCATIONAL PROBLEMS SOLVED FOR EMPLOYERS LIKE THE ONES WHO HIRE YOUR GRADUATES

❑ *Hired away by the principals to serve as* **General Manager,** S/Effects, Valencia, California

         02–Present

Our company produces special fire and mechanical effects for motion picture companies, theme parks, and museums. Annual sales approach $8.0M from clients nationwide.

Serve as a compliance officer supervising contract union welders, machinists, technicians, and craftsmen.

Asked to build a learning environment that might have stumped others, but was ideal for someone with my passion for teaching! The challenge: **motivate** a **diverse,** free-flowing group of **youngsters,** most with short attention spans, **to study science** and technology. Did a comprehensive needs analysis, even though the client was 2,100

C O N F I D E N T I A L

More indicators of return on investment **Mid-West State** *can use ...*

Strategy: *Provided examples of how this person has educated adult learners to help him land a position as an instructor at a two-year college.*

Martin Conner	**Business Instructor**	661.555.6000

miles away. Complied with tough pyrotechnics laws. *Outcomes:* From a 75-page feasibility study to **proof of educational concept** in just three months. My customer was thrilled. "Your educational project is one of the few we've seen with a real 'wow!' factor."

Stepped into a challenge **your students might easily face:** I inherited two creative entrepreneurs with no sense, passion, nor interest in business. At their request, built… from scratch… the business plan they should have had five years earlier. Brought out the complementary strengths of each partner to motivate them to action. *Outcomes:* My ideas **saved us $200K** in the first year alone. **Revenue started to rise**. New direction visible in only three weeks.

❑ **Manager** of Animation *promoted by our vice president over others with years more experience to serve as* **Manager** *of Sound and Video; then promoted over five tough competitors to be* **Manager,** Engineering; *then promoted again to be* **Director,** Technical Services, Acme Studios, Acme City, California   93–02

Served as a direct reporting official for up to five union technicians and quality assurance professionals.

Guided a busy executive to **internalize the value of risk management.** When I noticed untrained craftsmen working underwater without the right equipment and training, I negotiated exactly the services we needed from an excellent vendor. *Outcomes:* Senior leadership learned the lesson I taught them so well that **my system became a corporate standard** for reducing liability on the set.

Leveraged what I had learned as a **community college adjunct instructor** to boost productivity in a union labor force that fought management for decades. Designed, helped build, and administered a skills assessment suite that taught our team to work efficiently and safely, yet held them accountable. My 2,000-question evaluation instrument just couldn't be gamed. *Outcomes:* Even union members **loved my new system.** They felt so confident in their new skills that morale rose. They **started studying on their days off.**

Rescued a major source of our revenue that was in danger of falling apart: an exciting theme park ride. When contractors cited a cost of $7M, I pitched a better alternative that cost less. Went beyond just "fixing" the attraction. I wrote the documentation that taught our team of maintainers and operators everything **they needed to know**—even if I wasn't there to instruct them. *Outcomes:* **Saved $250K.** One of our employees **leveraged what he learned into a promotion.**

Asked to "fix" a troubled division. Soon found they had **no in-service training program.** Skill levels were so low, they were regularly using up to 90 hours of overtime a week! Worked with development specialists in our HR department and the other divisions we supported. *Outcomes:* **New** training programs and a

| Martin Conner | **Business Instructor** | 661.555.6000 |

peer-based accountability system made all the difference. Our people felt truly needed. **Quality shot up.** Expensive overtime slashed.

❑ **Adjunct Instructor of Business** (IT), Cactus Valley Community College, Desert Springs, California   Jan 83–Jun 83

Cactus Valley CC served a diverse mixture of traditional and nontraditional students.

Asked by a 10-person search committee to **present a five-minute lesson** — with almost **no guidance** and **very little lead time.** Did a quick needs analysis, and then covered a subject that was vital, but completely unfamiliar (and a little frightening), to my audience. *Outcomes:* Saw **learning take place on the spot.** Fielded many tough questions easily from levels up to the Dean. **Offered the job** soon thereafter.

Invited to teach a brand-new class with just two weeks' notice. Given an empty classroom, no curriculum, no lesson plans, and 30 diverse students, traditional and nontraditional. **Produced every training aid,** every **homework assignment,** and every **evaluation instrument** from scratch. *Outcomes:* **Very high performance evaluations from the students.**

Passed a test every instructor dreads: handling an intelligent, bored, opinionated student intent on disrupting our class with unsupported viewpoints. Gently applied every teaching technique to refocus him. *Outcomes:* Once I showed him, privately, that his drive could either help him pass or get him suspended, he **became a top performer.**

❑ **Integration and Test Engineer,** Space Shuttle Orbiter Division, McDonnell Douglas, Inc., Palmdale, California   83–93

McDonnell Douglas was a prime contractor to construct all five NASA space shuttles.

Went beyond developing a revolutionary engineering technique. I **enlightened every level** — from sophisticated, highly educated managers, to scientists, to engineers, to seasoned professional technicians — to trade their system for mine. *Outcomes:* Recognized by the leadership for my contributions to a very high-risk, unforgiving production system. My method became **the corporate standard from then on.**

COMPUTER SKILLS

❑ Comfortable with Windows XP, Word, Excel, PowerPoint, Outlook, QuickBooks, proprietary asset management and maintenance software, energy management software, and advanced Internet search protocols.

❑ Working knowledge of MS Project

CONFIDENTIAL   *Page 3 of 3*

LISA STANSFIELD
25 California Ave, Cleveland, Ohio 44122
Cell: 216-801-4139 • Home: 216-752-8345

Human Resources
Human Resource Generalist/Counselor/EEO Specialist/Labor Relations Leader

Areas of Expertise:

- *Conflict Resolution/Team Building & Mentoring/Organizational Leadership*
- *Employee Assistance/Multicultural Issues/Workplace Diversity*
- *Performance Reviews/Compensation, Incentive & Bonus Programs*
- *General Office Skills/Report Preparation/Computer and Network*

EDUCATION

BS Human Resource • Cleveland State University • Cleveland, OH • May 2006

Relevant Course Experience:

Organizational Leadership: Issues, theories, and methodologies associated with organizational development and the management of change, with a major emphasis on organizational culture and organizational change processes.

Training and Development: Program development and operation management focusing on design and delivery issues. The impact of technology, the global environment, and modern organizational structures is considered.

HUMAN RESOURCES BACKGROUND

Recruiter: Maintained contacts within the community searching for promising job applicants. Experienced screener, interviewer, and tester of applicants. Located qualified candidates for open positions. Presented job opportunities to qualified candidates and negotiated contract terms. Screened potential consultants through in-house interviews. Became thoroughly familiar with the organization and the human resources policies in order to discuss wages, working conditions, and promotional opportunities with prospective employees.

Human Resource Assistant: Managed all contracts for financial staffing agency. Provided clients with job leads electronically, via uploading employment opportunity information to Internet job boards. Interviewed and screened candidates (who usually work in government agencies), maintain working relationships with local employers, and promote the use of public employment programs and services.

RECENT EMPLOYMENT HISTORY

Dollar Bank • Cleveland, Ohio 44122 • Sept. 1994–Present
Teller • 09/94–08/95   **Recruiter** • 08/95–Present

Strategy: *Pulled out relevant experiences from seemingly unrelated work experience; complemented this experience with recent, relevant education to support a shift to a career in human resources.*

MARY ANNE WARNER

7822 Forester Road • Reston, Virginia 20191 • 703.716.3356 • mawarner@aol.com

GOVERNMENT RELATIONS MANAGEMENT

Innovative strategist of governmental/public affairs initiatives that win legislative support, positive media recognition, and favorable public awareness for manufacturing, healthcare, and food-processing corporations.

Dynamic business professional, political and organizational spokesperson with proven strengths in crisis and project management.

Adept in articulate message development and delivery to address complex issues. **Possess a vast network of influential contacts** at the local, state, and federal government levels.

2004 Fellow—Virginia Excellence in Public Service

RELEVANT EXPERIENCE & ACCOMPLISHMENTS

Governmental Relations / Public Affairs Management: Selected to lead a new department to combat negative perception at a global company. Creatively developed and leveraged political initiatives supporting government relations goals.

- Partnered with Government Relations staff at the state level and played key role in devising comprehensive internal communication strategies that defeated all legislative bans introduced against company.

- Turned around public perception in less than 2 years by designing and launching programs that educated all constituents and positioned company as a responsible corporate citizen. Company now recognized as leading corporate citizen in the environmental arena and winner of numerous awards.

- Forged strategic alliances and relationships with key groups, legislators, and business leaders and created grassroots lobbying campaigns that gained substantial legislative support.

- Executed initiatives that improved company's public image and effectively addressed concerns, as a spokesperson for the organization at international conferences/meetings.

- Key contributor on team that innovated a highly recognized public relations coup and designed a new program that now operates as a standalone $1 billion program.

Community Relations Management: Planned, coordinated, and implemented effective community relations and outreach programs that strengthened the image of a governmental bureau.

- Designed and educated community members countywide on vital information on the bureau's mission, services, projects, and key accomplishments.

- Created programs to address fundamental concerns of senior citizens and produced informational brochures and other outreach materials to inform and promote key programs.

- Managed budget for community-relations projects and programs. Directed volunteer staff and provided training to new personnel on departmental procedures, programs, and functions.

- Built relationships and served as primary contact with the media covering publicized events and cases.

Public Relations/ Marketing Communications Management: Conceived, designed, and executed strategic marketing, sales, public relations, and media programs for corporate clients. Managed projects including creative promotions, advertising campaigns, product launches, special events, trade shows, and collateral material development.

- Retained to assist in transitioning company's Canadian base of operations to the U.S. following financial reorganization and provided strategies for managing the U.S. Public Affairs Department.

- Designed new exhibit booth used at industry events nationwide for $100 million manufacturer that drove trade-show revenue growth of $3 million over prior year.

- Instrumental in winning $1 million account for the largest U.S. trade-show producer. Planned and managed entire production of 13 international events, launching major product lines worldwide.

Strategy: *Used a functional format to draw attention to relevant experience and accomplishments from throughout her career. Led with a strong introduction that is a perfect positioning piece for her current job target of government relations.*

MARY ANNE WARNER — PAGE 2

CAREER HISTORY

MAW ASSOCIATIONS, RICHMOND, VIRGINIA
Marketing & Public Relations Consultant (2003 to present)

MALLOY CORPORATION, RICHMOND, VIRGINIA
Manager, Marketing Communications & Events (1999 to 2003)

SOUTHLAND CORPORATION, RICHMOND, VIRGINIA
Public Affairs Manager (1996 to 1999)
Product Marketing and Communications Manager (1995 to 1996)

RICHMOND COUNTY STATE'S ATTORNEY'S OFFICE, RICHMOND, VIRGINIA
Community Relations Coordinator (1990 to 1995)

POLITICAL EXPERIENCE

VIRGINIA REPUBLICAN PARTY

Assistant Committee Member, Media Advisor, Caucus Judge, and fund-raiser for candidates in local, state, and national elections.

Active member of Virginia Republican Committeewomen's Roundtable, Virginia Federation of Republican Women's Organization, and Richmond County Republican Women's Organization.

COMMISSION ON THE STATUS OF WOMEN IN VIRGINIA

Appointed in a statewide selection process to serve as a commissioner on the 19-member board.

EDUCATION

UNIVERSITY OF VIRGINIA, CHARLOTTESVILLE, VIRGINIA
Master of Integrated Marketing Communications
Bachelor of Science in Education, with honors

PROFESSIONAL DEVELOPMENT

VIRGINIA EXCELLENCE IN PUBLIC SERVICE SERIES
2004 Graduate and Fellow

Awarded a fellowship for women pursuing political and government leadership roles. One of only 15 selected annually in a statewide, highly competitive process to participate in the 9-month educational program. Met with elected officials locally and in Washington D.C. Attended legislative hearings on the Hill and briefings with top White House officials, developing contacts with leaders of key governmental agencies.

ILEANA MENDOZA

95 Island Drive ◆ Hicksville, NY 11801 ◆ 516-572-7501 ◆ imendoza@aol.com

Skilled English-to-Spanish Translator with excellent organizational skills, strong attention to detail, and a demonstrated commitment to providing top-notch service.

SUMMARY OF QUALIFICATIONS

- Dedicated, conscientious individual with fluency in both English and Spanish.
- Trained in translation skills, earning translator certificate from New York University in 2005.
- Organized and detail-oriented. Easily able to balance competing demands of multiple projects.
- Polished and professional, yet warm and accommodating. Highly responsive to customer needs.
- Born in Chile and schooled in Europe; enjoy broad multicultural perspective.

TRANSLATION HIGHLIGHTS

➢ Hired as proofreader for Linguista, successfully took on translation assignments for contract clients. Translated flyer to encourage participation in a clinical research program and brochure to promote well-childcare clinic.

➢ As volunteer for county helpline, tapped to translate public service information from English to Spanish for the benefit of non-English-speaking community members. Successfully translated pamphlets describing county's shuttle services, senior citizen benefits, and healthcare programs.

➢ As member of healthcare taskforce subcommittee, translated flyers for county health and wellness fair. Also participated onsite at fair to provide link to Spanish-speaking population.

➢ Translated pamphlets and flyers on behalf of the county's diversity council, whose mission is to foster tolerance of and create an inclusive environment for all community members.

EXPERIENCE

LINGUISTA, New York, NY   2005 to present
Proofreader/Translator (Part-time)
Provide translation, proofreading, and administrative assistance in busy translation agency.
- Hired as proofreader; quickly earned respect of managers to merit translation assignments.

MENDOZA PAINTING & CARPENTRY, LLC, Hicksville, NY   1982 to present
Administrative Manager (Part-time)
Manage all administrative functions for small, family-run business.
- Take active role in ensuring the success of business, capably addressing all administrative issues. Provide level of service that has proven effective in building customer loyalty and attracting repeat business.

EDUCATION & PROFESSIONAL CREDENTIALS

New York University, New York, NY
Earned English-to-Spanish Translator Certificate, December 2005.

Nassau County Community College, Garden City, NY
Completed coursework in keyboarding, computer literacy, business law, litigation, paralegal skills, and English.

Member, American Translators Association, 2005 to present.

KEY SKILLS

Computer: Word, Excel, PowerPoint, Access, Internet, E-mail
Language: Bilingual—fluent in both English and Spanish

Strategy: *Highlighted recent education and community volunteer experience that support this individual's goal to find full-time work as a translator.*

Teresa A. Jones

5415 N. Broad Street	tajones@yahoo.com	Home: (773) 555-1212
Chicago, Illinois 60641		Cell: (312) 555-1212

OBJECTIVE: A position in pharmaceutical sales, medical device sales, or a related area.

PROFILE: **Results-driven professional** with a background in nursing (13 years) and sales (12 years).

Strong communicator who knows how to speak to physicians and medical professionals in a way that wins their trust and cooperation.

Versatile team player who has worked in several medical units, managing care, dispensing medication, and educating patients.

NURSING EXPERIENCE:

SOUTHWEST HOSPITAL, Naperville, Illinois   1998–Present

RN: OB-GYN (2003–Present)
Manage postpartum and nursery care for mothers and newborns as well as patients recovering from gynecological surgery (hysterectomies). Educate patients in infant care. Administer medications, including narcotics. Conduct postpartum assessment of mothers.
- Cared for babies delivered by c-section, assisted with intubations, and performed positive-pressure ventilation.
- Completed training in neonatal resuscitation and certification in CPR.

RN: DETOX & PSYCHIATRIC (1998–2003)
Cared for patients recovering from addiction to drugs and alcohol. Educated families regarding medications, lifestyle changes, and referral services. Dispensed medications (anti-seizure, Librium), taking into account contra-indications for other medical conditions. Performed CPR several times. Mentored less-experienced nurses.

MEMORIAL HOSPITAL, Niles, Illinois   1993–1998

RN: TRANSITIONAL CARE & MEDICAL-SURGICAL
Provided care for patients who need extensive care, including heavy use of cardiac and anti-seizure medications. Managed wound care and treated bed sores. Counseled families on home-care issues.

SALES EXPERIENCE:

C. BROWN REALTY, Chicago, Illinois   1980–1992

REAL ESTATE AGENT
Sold residential properties and negotiated contracts. Organized and hosted open houses to emphasize each home's unique selling features. Canvassed neighborhoods to drive new business. Developed trust with clients that led to repeat business and referrals.
- Generated more than $2 million in annual sales (1992).
- Won several awards as Sales Agent of the Month.
- Organized a 4th of July parade as a marketing vehicle.

EDUCATION: **ILLINOIS UNIVERSITY SCHOOL OF NURSING,** Chicago, Illinois
Associate of Science, Nursing (graduated with distinction)   1984

COMPUTER SKILLS: Software for patient charting, word processing, Internet, e-mail

References Available upon Request

Strategy: Selected experience from this person's nursing career that relates to her target goal of pharmaceutical sales; also included direct sales experience, although it was in a different industry.

Suzanne G. Eriksen

33 Farmstead Lane • Guilford, CT 06437
(203) 453-7555 • mobile (203) 301-6832 • sgeriksen@msn.com

Sales • Account Development • Nutrition • Health • Natural Foods / Supplements

- **Accomplished and results-oriented Sales / Account Management Professional** with track record reflecting ability to establish relationships, cultivate and fully develop accounts, consistently produce business, and achieve sales objectives. Expert analytical and strategic-planning abilities. Outstanding customer-service orientation. Background complemented by successful 11-year ownership/management of natural-foods business.

- Consumer-products industry expertise: specializing in grocery, drug, and mass merchandising disciplines.

- Collaborative and highly motivated professional with reputation for consistently exceeding performance expectations. High-energy team player and skilled consensus builder. Methodical follow-through skills.

- PC skills: Microsoft Word, Excel, and PowerPoint.

Professional Sales / Account Management Experience

GILLETTE • Hartford, CT / Boston, MA—**Personal Products Company** (2 years)

BEESON LABS • Boston, MA—**Consumer Products Division** (2 years)

BENJAMIN MOORE COMPANY • Montvale, NJ—**Stain & Paint Division** (2.5 years)

<u>Sales and Marketing Account / Territory Manager</u>   **6.5 years of experience**

Managed accounts, including full territory cultivation and direct account development, throughout successful sales career characterized by consistent track record of achievement. Proven sales expertise in food, drug, and mass merchandise lines. **Significant accomplishments and scope of responsibility:**

- **Exceeded sales goals 3 consecutive quarters** (Gillette) in first year … **Promoted to Territory Manager** (Boston, MA).
- **Earned Regional Achievement Award** (Beeson Labs) **for surpassing sales goals 2 consecutive quarters.**
- **Successfully developed account base** throughout CT, NY, RI, MA, and VT.
- **Effectively launched new products,** achieving maximum distribution within all strategic accounts.
- **Substantially boosted brand through participation in industry tradeshows** (Beeson Labs and Benjamin Moore); set up and managed company booths, attracted new accounts, and secured promotional orders.
- Skillfully delivered **high-impact sales and marketing presentations to highest-level decision makers, strategic and headquarter accounts, distributors, and distributor sales forces.**
- **Ensured sell-through of promotions/support materials** (circular, print, and flyer ads; in-store displays); **successfully negotiated increases in shelf space** (boosting overall sales); proactively managed inventories.

Additional Professional Experience

TWIN PINES HEALTH CENTER • Madison, CT—**SUZANNE'S** • Old Lyme, CT   **1997–Present**

<u>Private Practice Licensed Cosmetologist</u>

Manage and operate 2 independent businesses as a state-licensed professional providing hairstyling services to a clientele of more than 150. **Key achievements:**

- **Cultivated and successfully developed loyal client base** at full-service salon within an affluent community and within a 180-bed healthcare facility providing comprehensive services.
- **For the past 6 years, have consistently grown business in excess of 10% annually.**
- **Designed and deliver customized services for special-needs and home-bound clients.**   *… continued*

Strategy: *To help this individual transition back to the kind of work she had done more than 20 years ago, brought to the forefront all of the early-career experience, omitting dates and simply indicating number of years. More recent experience is then listed chronologically.*

Suzanne G. Eriksen
Page Two

TWIN PINES HEALTH CENTER • SUZANNE'S • ***continued*

- **Market and sell high percentage of add-on services** (conditioning treatments, highlights, colors, etc.).
- **Promote and sell-through high-margin haircare products;** effectively merchandise products.
- **Ensure full compliance** with Connecticut Department of Health regulations.

MAKE'EM & BAKE'EM—All Natural Fresh & Frozen Foods To Go • Milford, CT   **1984–95**

President / Co-Founder

Managed successful retail/wholesale frozen food business with commercial kitchen, 2 retail outlets, and a catering division which served customers in Greater New Haven/throughout Connecticut as well as nationwide (mail-order operations) for 11 years. With partner, developed business model, wrote plan, and conceived/launched complete concept of developing 100% natural and nutritious frozen foods of exceptional quality. **Performance highlights:**

Sales & Marketing Management …

- **Doubled business within first year and achieved annual growth rates in excess of 15% thereafter.**
- **Implemented host of innovative sales and revenue-building programs** featuring high-net-profit services/menu items.
- **Planned and secured key media and promotional tie-ins** (i.e., soup preparation segment in commercial kitchen on local-access TV, in-store food prep and sampling, and participation in Milford Octoberfest and New Haven Days).
- **Initiated and executed comprehensive marketing and advertising program;** utilized multimedia approach to broaden market reach (newspapers, radio, Val-Pak, etc.).
- **Earned reputation for exceptional customer service and keen customer satisfaction;** successfully prospected and established new customer relationships that consistently transitioned to long-term clientele.

Operations Management …

- **Recruited, hired, trained, and managed professional staff** of up to 30 employees.
- **Innovated upscale frozen-food products and boosted sales/cross-selling** through development of low-fat food line, frozen hors d'oeuvres "to go," bulk soup sales for restaurants, packaged soups for grocery store resale, select catering menu, and corporate delivered-lunch programs.
- **Developed menu, hired Registered Dietician, and ensured packaging reflected nutritional values;** gained in-depth industry knowledge of food manufacturing process and product application.
- **Managed business expansion to second upscale retail location** (Milford); secured investment capital, negotiated lease/buildout, oversaw staffing, and implemented Grand Opening program.
- **Consistently earned highest marks from local and state Boards of Health and Consumer Protection.**

Education   WHEATON COLLEGE • Norton, MA
- **Bachelor's Degree in Business Administration—Accounting Major**

    Continuing Education Highlights include
- **Extensive sales and executive selling skills programs throughout professional sales management career**
- **Certification in Cosmetology** (full-time studies, 1995–96; Danbury, CT)

Civic
- **YWCA** Crisis Counselor and **Big Brothers and Big Sisters** Volunteer (New Haven, CT)
- Board Member / Treasurer, not-for-profit **Health Collective** (New Haven, CT)
- **Salvation Army** Volunteer, adolescent girls' recreational program (New Haven, CT)

LORI MORGAN
lmorgan@msn.com

30343 Honeysuckle Hill
Santa Clarita, California 91387

Residence: 661-422-1553
Cellular: 661-422-0967

SALES / KEY ACCOUNT MANAGEMENT

Dynamic, well rounded, results-oriented individual looking to apply energetic sales capabilities in the sales arena where a proven ability to communicate effectively and a determined focus on success and achievement can play a vital role in increasing revenue and market share.

Uncompromising consideration for customer retention and premier service. Excellent analytical skills and quick problem-solving approach when dealing with new concepts, systems, and procedures. Resourceful and versatile, accustomed to handling diverse responsibilities. Highly self-motivated, responsible, tenacious. Professional appearance and demeanor.

- Several years of professional sales and sales management experience.
- Strong presentation, negotiation, and sales closing skills.
- **Sales talent** to cultivate strategic relationships, expand customer base, and maximize account sales.
- **Business savvy** to anticipate contingencies, control expenses, stretch operating dollars, and maximize profitability.
- Management of key account relationships; conscientious attention to detail; continuous follow-up.
- Success in the training and development of other sales professionals.
- Outstanding interpersonal skills; ability to establish positive rapport with professionals, peers, and superiors.

SPECIAL KNOWLEDGE AND SKILLS

Interior Design Industry	Design and construction industry expertise; knowledge of specifications necessary to complete entire project management for both residential and commercial applications and space planning.
Finance/Administration	Preparation of statistical, accountability, and shrink reports; inventory control; ordering; purchasing; accounts payable and reconciliation; correspondence; file organization.

REPRESENTATIVE ACCOMPLISHMENTS—University of Phoenix

Challenge:	Improve customer shopping experience.
Action:	Team member on group project. Redesigned customer flow and added "touch points" to bring customers in contact with service staff.
Result:	In limited test, program increased customer sales 27% and satisfaction scores 10 points.

Challenge:	Align sales activities with growth targets and improve accountability of sales team.
Action:	Worked collaboratively with finance team to install new sales programs that integrated activity reporting with revenue and profit results.
Result:	Pilot program produced 5% revenue growth and 17% profit growth by increasing sales of high-margin goods and services.

Strategy: *Highlighted skills, accomplishments, and proven capabilities on page 1, leaving job details until page 2. Accomplishments from recent MBA studies are also highlighted.*

LORI MORGAN - Page 2

PROFESSIONAL EXPERIENCE

EXPEDITOR ASSOCIATE   1992–Present
Do It Yourself Center - Santa Clarita, CA

Sales / Customer Relationship Management: Sell commercial and residential whole-house packages from the ground up (all building materials, plumbing, electrical). Interact strictly with general contractor or owner/builder. Involved in contract negotiations with vendors, customers, and contractors. Structure merchandise and installations according to clients' needs and budget. Act as mediator between customer and vendor contact. Manage and prioritize issues and conflicts.

Training / Merchandising: Serve as in-store special services trainer. Instruct customers on how to hang wallpaper, install blinds, and apply faux finish. Handle displays and visual merchandising.

ACCOMPLISHMENT / AWARD

Saved more than $10,000 in shrink and loss inventory (paperwork errors).
Operations Employee of the Month

EDUCATION

Master of Business Administration, University of Phoenix, expected 2006.
Bachelor of Arts, Interior Design, American Intercontinental University, 1991.
Diploma, Interior Design, Brooks College, 1988.

RESUME 60: BY MICHELE ANGELLO, CPRW

JON PAUL ANTHONY

9216 S. Yosemite Parkway • Greenwood Village, CO 80237 • Home: (303) 557-8521 • Cell: (303) 556-1145
jonpaul@aol.com

SALES & MARKETING MANAGEMENT PROFESSIONAL

Successful at Securing New Business & Generating Revenues

Results-driven, achievement-oriented Sales & Marketing Management Professional with more than 20 years of experience. Highly motivated self-starter with a unique mix of strong business background combined with sales acumen to effectively solve business problems and propel sales. Excellent time management and organizational capabilities; outstanding interpersonal, negotiation, and sales-closing skills. Proven ability to quickly and effectively direct team efforts as well as perform as integral team member. Exceptional skill as instructor and public speaker. Top-ranking and outstanding personal sales record. Expertise in

Sales Planning	**Product Management**	**Relationship Management**
New Business Development	**Consultative Sales**	**Key Account Management**

BUSINESS MANAGEMENT & SALES EXPERIENCE

CORBEL SHADE & DRAPERY, GREENWOOD VILLAGE, CO   79–PRESENT
Owner & Manager
Directed operations of successful drapery business. Managed six employees. Accountable for ordering and procurement. Oversaw marketing campaigns and conducted sales with internal clients. Demonstrated excellent consultative sales skills. Created sales and operations plans.
- Attained numerous awards from Hunter Douglas for outstanding dealer sales. Awards included cruise and all-expense paid vacation to New York.
- Propelled continuous improvements to sales methods, resulting in successful endurance of small business.

ADDITIONAL EXPERIENCE

STATE OF COLORADO, DENVER, CO   2005–PRESENT
DIVISION OF SAFETY
National Incident Management System (NIMS) Instructor
COLORADO POLICE INSTITUTE
Safety Instructor

CENTER FOR DOMESTIC PREPARATION, LUBBOCK, TX   2005–PRESENT
Weapons of Mass Destruction (WMD) Instructor

UNITED STATES DEPT. OF NATIONAL SECURITY/FEMA   2001–PRESENT
NATIONAL MEDICAL RESPONSE TEAM (NMRT)
PPE Instructor, Logistics Professional, WMD First Responder
- Recognized as Volunteer of the Year, 2002.
- Served on NMRT as only airborne team in the nation for WMD DHS/FEMA.

INTERNATIONAL TRANSPORTATION ASSOCIATION (ITA)   2002–PRESENT
Hazardous Materials Air Transportation Officer

MSU NATIONAL CENTER FOR BIOMEDICAL RESEARCH
INSTITUTE OF COUNTER TERRORIST EDUCATION
Law Enforcement Response to Weapons of Mass Destruction, Certified Field Instructor

Strategy: *Emphasized part-time business ownership to transition this individual from his primary career in counterterrorism and disaster assistance to sales and management in the interior design industry.*

MICHAEL J. THOMPSON

12400 MACON LANE, BOWIE, MD 20718
301-300-6125   301-255-0420
MJTH12@HOTMAIL.NET

AWARDED TOP SECRET CLEARANCE

GOAL: PROJECT MANAGER

Dynamic professional with 20 years of proven ability in process improvements, project leadership, and customer relations.

A SOLID U.S. NAVY TRACK RECORD OF EXPERIENCE AND SUCCESS IN...

OPERATIONAL IMPROVEMENTS AND PROBLEM SOLVING

- Improved efficiency in NAVSEA military detachment division via strategic procedure changes.
- Designed procedures for use in system development and acceptance testing.
- Wrote more than 50% of testing procedures administered for new fleet equipment.
- Created testing procedures for Developmental Engineers to improve functionality and enhance system capability.
- Deciphered mechanical drawings and electrical schematics to determine operational requirements.

COMMUNICATIONS, LEADERSHIP, AND RELATIONSHIP BUILDING

- Developed and maintained performance training requirements for fellow fleet personnel.
- Earned a reputation for excellence and willingness to initiate/successfully deliver quality-improvement projects.
- Enforced and tracked compliance with all organizational policies and procedures.
- Gathered and circulated information from status reports for presentations to management and staff.

ATTRIBUTES AND EDUCATION

Challenge-driven leader and goal setter adept in technical support, staff training, and quality control. Problem solver who can overcome obstacles and deliver results. Natural relationship builder who quickly establishes rapport and motivates teams. Effective project director with excellent communication and organizational skills.

Certificate of Completion, Advanced Leadership Development Program, 2004
Certificate, Electronics Mechanic, United States Navy Apprenticeship Program, 2000
AS with honors, Computer Science, Hawaii Pacific University, 2001
Certificate of Completion, Kings Bay Naval School, 1997

Available for relocation and travel

Strategy: *Emphasized operational and leadership qualities while highlighting skills easily transferable to target role of project manager.*

MICHAEL J. THOMPSON   PAGE 2

NAVAL CAREER HISTORY

Sonar Technician, 2003–Present   *Washington, D.C.*
NAVSEA (*Naval Sea Systems Command*)
- Provide engineering support via Lockheed Martin for various Naval subcontractors.
- Troubleshoot operational functions to ensure productivity and optimize quality.
- Assist engineering contractors to design, develop, test, and manufacture equipment for varied Naval submarines deployed throughout the fleet.

Sonar Technician, 1997–2003   *Pearl Harbor, Hawaii*
SSEP (*submarine surveillance equipment program*), USS *LOS ANGELES*
SSEP, 2000–2003:
- Mechanical Technician for Sea/Shore Command for Submarine Fleet.
- Maintained sonar systems to ensure operation at peak efficiency.
- Supported 27 to 30 submarines annually with a mission-support process of 21 to 30 days.

USS *Los Angeles*, 1997–2000:
- Supported navigation and underwater acoustic technologies as Sonar Technician.
- Responsible for all operational and administrative aspects of the submarine's computer and control mechanisms used for underwater surveillance and scientific data collection.
- Managed shipboard functions and communications for inspections and compliance with Quality Assurance protocol.

Sonar Technician, 1990–1995   *Key West, Florida*
USS *Key West*
- Supported navigation and underwater acoustic technologies.

RESUME 62: BY JANICE SHEPHERD, CPRW, JCTC, CEIP

ANTHONY A. ARBOR
ACCOUNTANT

111 Langley Lane, Apt. 3
Spokane, WA 99201

willing to relocate

(509) 777-3737
aaarbor@aol.com

- Background and education provide a "big picture" understanding of business, encompassing full knowledge of accounting disciplines and business strategies.

- Innate relationship-building qualities and lead-by-example philosophy; recognized for effective use of humor.

- Passion for analysis; thirst for variety and challenge. Very strong problem-solving and communication skills.

- PC proficiency—particular expertise with Pro FX (Tax), GO Systems (Audit), and MYOB (Accounting) software.

"...an impact player without being loud"

"...brings to the table a very nice mix of personality traits, aptitude, and intelligence..."

"...analytical, quick learner, knowledge seeker..."

"...thoughtful comments... refreshingly constructive"

comments from evaluations

EDUCATION

Certificate Program in Accounting, Graduate—Outstanding Student Award, 3.9 GPA
University of Washington, Seattle, WA, August 2004
Accelerated Accounting Course covering Intermediate
Financial Accounting, Cost Accounting, Auditing Standards and Principles, and Tax Effects of Business Decisions.

MBA, Western Washington University, Bellingham, WA, June 2004

Graduate work in Mathematics, University of Seattle, 2000–2001

B.S., Mathematics, Maharishi University of Management, Fairfield, IA, June 1998
Won "Tony Nader Award" in school-wide writing and presentation competition.

MEMBERSHIPS / COMMUNITY SERVICE

Active Member, Western Washington University Accounting Society
Active Member, Beta Alpha Psi—*Honors Accounting and Finance*
Treasurer/Accountant, Hamlet Railway Museum—*new-formed non-profit organization*
Volunteer, Habitat for Humanity

EXPERIENCE SUMMARY

Staff/Tax Intern, Professional Accounting LLP, Spokane, WA   2004–present
Prepared tax forms, trial balance sheets, income statements, and adjusted journal entries for U.S. and Canadian corporations, individuals, and partnerships. Recognized by management for ideas and workable suggestions, and by co-workers for team spirit.

Accounting Consultant, Keller Realty, Spokane   2002–Present
Assist owners with accounting strategies for complex franchise/partnership entity.

Instructor, Math Department, Edmonds Community College, Lynwood, WA   2002

Teacher Assistant, Math Department, University of Washington, Seattle   2001–2002

Instructor, Math Department, Maharishi University of Management, Fairfield, IA   2000

Strategy: *Highlighted recent accounting education and internship while making no mention of prior career as a math teacher. Quotes at the top are powerful endorsements.*

RONALD JACKSON

847-445-4679 (residence)   1044 Seminole Lane
847-224-4552 (fax)   rjackson@aol.com   Mt. Prospect, IL 60056

FINANCIAL PLANNING / ACCOUNTING MANAGER

Dynamic Professional Career in accounting and financial planning. Proven leadership of accounting, budgeting, financial analysis, and reporting issues. Consistent success linking accounting and finance to business operations to drive forward organizational development. Strong project management, team building, and leadership skills. Sound analysis of income statement and balance sheet matters. Equal effectiveness capturing cost reductions through process redesign and performance management.

PROFESSIONAL EXPERIENCE

A&R DESIGNS INC., Peoria, Illinois   2000–Present

Entrepreneur / Controller

As a partner, directed the start-up of a complete corporate accounting function for this newly formed company. Assumed additional accounting, financial, and human resource responsibilities as the company grew rapidly into a thriving, multimillion-dollar enterprise.

- Maintain full responsibility for hiring and training of personnel; held to original headcount levels by creating multi-functional positions.

- Customized computer system to link sales orders, purchase orders, receivables, payables, and general ledger reporting.

- Provided quarterly financial information to bank president, ensuring the attainment of performance goals and covenants.

- Purchased credit insurance on key customer accounts to minimize risk. Established credit limits with customers and negotiated favorable terms with vendors.

RESULTS: Instrumental in increasing sales revenue of $5.5 million in 2000 to $13.3 million in 2006.

DIAMOND AUTOMOTIVE, Streamwood, Illinois   1995–2000

As Manager

Prepared annual operating plan for $1 billion Suspension and Exhaust Manufacturer, including line-item income statement, detailed balance sheet, cash-flow statements, strategic plans, interim forecasts, and quarterly earnings statements. Responsible for month-end-close process and analysis of results. Managed staff of five.

- Established strategy with sales department for realistic revenue targets, including new business, lost business, and sales growth by providing price, volume, and mix analysis.

- Worked with all functional departments to establish budget guidelines, wage increases, headcount, and cost initiatives.

- Interacted closely with controller and senior management on a daily basis.

ACHIEVEMENT: Reduced month-end close process from 8 days to 3.

Strategy: *Highlighted vast accounting experience to support goal of transitioning from business owner-ship to a full-time accounting position.*

Ronald Jackson   Page 2, Résumé

DIAMOND AUTOMOTIVE, continued

As Financial Analyst

As project leader for the implementation of mainframe accounting system (SAP) and the profitability analysis module (PA), worked with functional groups to develop reporting tools and system controls.

- Trained staff accountant.

- Designed new daily net-sales report comparing current month to budget and prior year.

- Designed month-end reporting book for sales force.

- Implemented sales force compensation plan incorporating both sales revenue and expenses.

BRACHS CONFECTIONS, INC., Chicago, Illinois   1990–1995

Manager, Financial Planning

Developed annual operating plan, corporate reporting, forecasts, and strategic plans. Implemented and developed item number detail, plant volumes, and strategies for this national candy manufacturer.

- Worked with all functional departments and plant locations. Created budget templates for all departments, thus minimizing extra re-work and creating consistent formats laying out budget assumptions and goals.

Manager, Deals, Discounts, and Allowances

Analyzed customer deals, including off-invoice promotions, billbacks, volume discounts, and MDF spending. Worked with sales force to track program spending and customer participation. Developed price, volume, and mix analysis; loaded all deals into the order-entry system; reconciled all accrual accounts.

Senior Project Analyst

Project analyst for $250 million restructuring initiative. This included closing two existing plants and expanding three locations. Worked with operations and outside consultants to track spending and manage cash flow. Responsible for cost incurred with plant closings, severance, retention, and asset disposal. Presented monthly financial updates to the project team on spending, current issues, and timelines.

Staff Accountant

General accounting functions. Key contact for MLBPA and MLB owners for baseball royalty statements. Also contact for all brokers.

MEGA NUT, INC., Streamwood, Illinois   1987–1990

Staff Accountant

General accounting responsibilities and daily collateral reports to establish borrowing availability for this $20 million private-label nut manufacturer.

EDUCATION: **B.S. ACCOUNTING,** NORTH PARK UNIVERSITY

OWEN GRAHAM

ADMINISTRATIVE MANAGEMENT PROFESSIONAL

Non-Profit Organizations • Program & Project Management

Strategic and hands-on leader dedicated to achieving the mission and goals of the organization by improving operational effectiveness, programs, productivity, and strategic focus. Able to create consensus and build support for significant organizational changes and improvements, as evidenced by 22-year record of results leading programming, administration, and strategic initiatives for growing, thriving organizations.

Expertise		
Strategic Planning	Team Building & Team Leadership	Problem Solving
Budget Management	Policy & Procedure Development	Consensus Building
Fund-raising	Program Development & Management	Communications Strategies
Project Management	Property Acquisition & Construction	Website & Newsletter Publishing

Experience and Achievements

Associate Pastor, Education: Reedville Baptist Church, Dallas, TX   *2003–2006*

Assumed leadership for vigorous program serving 600+ children (birth–6th grade) each week via 300+ volunteers and 6 paid staff. Scope of responsibility included teacher training, volunteer and staff management, educational and recreational programs, child-care programs, and management of $30K budget. Member of 7-person senior management team for church that averages 2,500 at Sunday services and employs a total of 40 paid staff.

- **Invigorated children's ministry: Resolved problems and removed obstacles that were affecting morale, volunteerism, and ability to serve growing numbers of children.** Initiated regular communication with volunteers and solicited their feedback. Improved planning and preparedness to eliminate major sources of irritation. Created a new website incorporating up-to-date information on children's programming.

  Outcomes:
  - Added 20 new volunteers through positive word of mouth.
  - Increased capacity of most popular children's program from 150 to 250 children.
  - Improved reputation of children's ministry and eradicated complaints.
  - Freed up paid staff time that had been devoted to problem-solving for the children's ministry.

- **Stemmed teacher drain by creating informative, no-pressure means for potential volunteers to learn more about teaching religious education.** Created an orientation program for people considering becoming teachers to let them know what to expect, what training is provided, and the various ways they could get involved.

  Outcomes:
  - Increased knowledge and confidence of potential volunteers.
  - Added 125 new teachers to the faculty.

- **Drove the development and implementation of the first comprehensive policies for safety and security of children participating in church programs.** With 325 adult volunteers serving 600+ children in numerous programs each week, the church was at risk regarding charges of child abuse and related lawsuits. Chaired committee that reviewed policies of other churches, met with legal and policy experts, and developed written policies on all safety and security issues for children's ministry and entire congregation. Created PR plan to cover all eventualities.

  Outcomes:
  - Smoothly processed volunteers through newly required criminal background check, without incident.
  - Reduced risks and raised awareness of potential issues and pitfalls.
  - Improved parents' security and confidence in leaving their children in the care of workers.
  - Enhanced the church's reputation for caring about children within its community.

Minister of Education & Administration, San Marcos Baptist Church, San Marcos, TX   *1987–2003*

Functioned as VP of Administration for $1.2M organization. Performed effectively within a consensus/committee decision-making culture, using leadership and influencing skills to gain support for major initiatives and strategy shifts. Managed operating budget and 10 paid staff. Planned and coordinated multiple committees, team-building events, retreats, staff meetings, educational programming, and mission trips.

749 East Fork Road, Dallas, TX 75206   (H) 214-761-0921 • (M) 214-908-1206 • owengraham@yahoo.com

Strategy: *Emphasized measurable outcomes for a variety of programs to help minister transition to a career in administrative management, preferably for a nonprofit organization.*

OWEN GRAHAM   (H) 214-761-0921 • (M) 214-908-1206 • owengraham@yahoo.com

- **Spearheaded strategic growth of the organization, leading planning, execution, and continuous refinement of the strategy to meet and exceed all goals.** Led multifaceted initiatives to expand and improve programs, volunteers, and facilities. Overcame space limitations through creative solutions and surmounted internal resistance to change through team-building and extensive communication. Helped launch building drive and managed acquisition and construction projects, including $3M construction of multipurpose facility from concept to completion. Investigated and adopted best practices from organizations facing similar challenges.

  Outcomes:
    - Sunday School attendance expanded from 325 to 750.
    - Teaching staff grew 83% (60 to 110) and classes nearly doubled, from 25 to 47 weekly.
    - Offerings increased from $275K to $1.5M annually.
    - Acquired 12 pieces of property and added 30,000 square feet of space (200% growth).
    - Increased capacity to help people and fulfill our mission; improved standing in the community.

- **Built a unified, collaborative, high-performing team.** As manager of 5-person senior staff, improved effectiveness and cohesion of the team through formal team-building programs, recreational activities, and the conscious creation of a culture of trust and openness.

  Outcomes:
    - Achieved extraordinary retention: 60% stayed together for 18 years, and shortest tenure was 12 years.
    - Team functioned as a single unit with streamlined decision-making and instinctive collaboration.

- **Clarified values, mission, and purpose of the church.** Led committee in exploring and defining what was most important to the church to guide organizational decision-making. Communicated regularly with the congregation and invited feedback and input. Held "Town Hall" meetings to gain buy-in for the defined mission. As committee chair, scheduled and ran meetings, set deadlines, and held team-building activities.

  Outcomes:
    - Church approved, accepted, and bought into an overall purpose/mission statement that drove the organization and helped in decision-making.
    - Created list of values that helped guide budgeting, programming, and special events.
    - Reduced complaints and established a sense of unity within fast-growing organization.

- **Established business procedures and operational policies for large, growing organization.** Chaired committee that evaluated and rewrote existing policies, incorporating input from stakeholders and securing buy-in for changes.

  Outcomes:
    - Created one manual with all policies and procedures, job descriptions, constitution, and by-laws.
    - Streamlined committee meetings and overall organizational decision-making.

- **Led the drive to adopt new curriculum choices for all age groups.** Spearheaded a comprehensive review of existing curriculum and gently pushed the adoption of new, more balanced materials that provided a broader world view. Led numerous education and communication initiatives to gain support for what was a significant change.

  Outcomes:
    - New curriculum materials selected and embraced.

Minister of Education & Activities, Dallas Bible Baptist Church, Dallas, TX   *1985–1987*

Selected for new position. Oversaw educational programming for all ages; trained and recruited volunteers; planned special events and social functions; provided resources and support for all workers.

Outcomes:
  - Developed the first policy handbook for volunteers.
  - Created a recreational ministry and established long-term goal of building a Christian Life Center.

Education

Master of Arts in Christian Education	The Southern Baptist Theological Seminary
Master of Divinity	The Southern Baptist Theological Seminary
Bachelor of Arts in Education	University of Texas at Austin

RESUME 65: BY BRUCE BAXTER, CPRW

Paul Marion

3212 Idlewild Lane • Onondaga, New York 13315
(H) 315-412-1234 • (C) 315-218-2392 • pmarion@aol.com

OBJECTIVE

Retail Management

Professional interest in management-in-training program with a "big box" retail chain.

PROFILE

Highly effective goal-oriented manager, leader, and supervisor with more than 20 years of leadership experience—managing an 800-member fitness center and performing extensive personnel, administrative, facility, and operations management in the U.S. Army. History of steady advancement in military career from noncommissioned officer to rank of Major. Versatile management experience ranging from small group supervision supporting objectives to overall management of objectives and supervision of up to 232 individuals. Demonstrated ability to train, mentor, and develop staff to achieve top performance.

Core Competencies

- Facility Management
- Inventory Control
- Business Development

- Strategic Leadership
- Team Building
- Staff Training

- Meeting/Exceeding Goals
- Personnel Management & Development
- Customer Relations/Service

Strengths

Energized personal strengths as a member of the Airborne Ranger Infantry of the U.S. Army. Carry those intensified qualities into all professional interactions—*"can-do" attitude, drive to exceed established goals, leadership by example, dedication to task completion, loyalty to mission and team, commitment to established rules but also providing innovative solutions to problems or new situations.*

PROFESSIONAL EXPERIENCE

EXCELLENCE FITNESS CENTER, DeWitt, NY   *2000–2006*
Manager

Managed 10 employees and entire operation of 24-hour fitness center with more than $250,000 worth of equipment and 800 members. Directed all aspects of club operation, including sales, marketing, advertising, customer service, maintenance, accounts payable/receivable, personnel, payroll, and scheduling.

Selected Achievements
- Grew membership each year while 2 new competitors entered the immediate market.
- Successfully managed business through sale without losing one employee and while increasing membership 10% in the final quarter; transaction concluded May 2006.

UNITED STATES ARMY, Ft. Darcy, NY, and various locations worldwide   *1980–2000*
Major—acquired officer rank at time of discharge.

Served as Non-Commissioned Officer in both mechanized and light infantry units. Supervised, trained, and counseled soldiers. Managed and maintained equipment and materials related to combat readiness.

Served in the following capacities:

Company Commander—**Managed** logistics, supply, equipment, vehicles, arms room, training, discipline, morale, security, and personnel in a 232-soldier unit.

...Continued...

Strategy: *Called immediate attention to career target of retail management and provided extensive description of activities and achievements during army career that relate to this target.*

Paul Marion
(H) 315-412-1234 • (C) 315-218-2392 • pmarion@aol.com

Page 2

Staff Officer—Acted as **Operations Manager** as Assistant Secretary of the General Staff. Supervised all administrative operations of the 10th Mountain Division during its activation. Supervised 8 soldiers and civilian employees. Liaised with other staff sections to ensure complete and accurate flow of information. Handled responsibility for terminal area security.

Company Executive Officer—**Supervised** 45 men and **managed** more than $6 million in equipment. Performed as supply officer, maintenance officer, training officer, and acting commander during the commander's absence. Successfully maintained all company vehicles and supply room to the highest standards of the 4th Infantry Division.

Platoon Leader—**Supervised** 30 men and **managed** more than $1 million worth of equipment.

Selected Achievements

- Successfully managed "Armed Forces Day" event at Ft. Darcy. Event attracted about 15,000 people and drew praise throughout the Southern Tier of New York as the best event to date for what had become the largest and most involved public event in the region.
- Wrote first installation training guidance for units at Ft. Darcy. Its implementation greatly assisted units in preparing their Long Range Training Calendar.
- Organized, trained, and commanded the Airfield Control Group in support of division deployments and redeployments.
- Received numerous Army Commendation Medals and Letters of Commendation from Generals praising performance and results.

EDUCATION / TRAINING

Bachelor of Arts Degree • State University of New York College at Brockport, NY, 1990
Major: Communications Studies—*Magna Cum Laude*

Military Training

Officer Candidate School, 1980
Infantry Officer Basic Course **(Distinguished Leadership Graduate)**, 1982
Infantry Officer Advance Course, 1987
Combined Service Support School, 1990
Command and General Staff Course Correspondence, 1992
U.S. Army Ranger School (Distinguished Leadership Graduate), 1984

Louise M. Ormond

(315) 422-1234 lmormond@aol.com
2886 Friendship Rd., Syracuse, NY 13203

Funeral Director
New York State Licensed / Certified by National Funeral Service Examining Board

—SUMMARY OF QUALIFICATIONS—

Professional Profile

Confident and highly organized Funeral Director with 3 years of experience, including 1 year of residency. Hardworking team player with history of achievement while working concurrent employment and irregular hours. Proven leadership skills developed through prior experience as a Reserve Deputy Sheriff and as an on-site construction supervisor.

Strengths / Awards

- ❑ **Customer Service** — Recognized by superiors for commitment to highest levels of service.
- ❑ **Communication and Interpersonal Skills** — Able to remain poised and focused during stressful situations and tight deadlines. Tactful in handling sensitive situations. Communicate easily with the public and able to comfort people in a time of sorrow.
- ❑ **Program/Project Management** — Detail-oriented manager skilled in analysis, prioritizing, problem solving, and quality assurance. Proven team leader dedicated to superior performance.
- ❑ **Received VIP award** and **numerous recognitions** for job performance.

Education / Credentials

HAFNER INSTITUTE OF FUNERAL SERVICE, North Syracuse, NY
Associate of Occupational Studies — Mortuary Science, *Dean's List,* graduated 2005

CERTIFICATIONS / LICENSES

Licensed Funeral Director — New York State, 2006
Certified Funeral Director — National Funeral Service Examining Board, 2005

Emergency Medical Technician — previous certification/Advanced Emergency Medical Respiratory Technician/First Aid & CPR — Red Cross certified

ADDITIONAL EDUCATION

Medical Assistant Program — Empire University, East Syracuse, NY
Completed 1 year of medical coursework.

Criminal Justice Program — Madison Community College, Oneida, NY
Completed 54 credit hours of coursework.

Sign Language and Spanish — Presently taking self-directed home instructional courses.
Computer Skills — Familiar with various business software packages.

—PROFESSIONAL EXPERIENCE—

DONOVAN FUNERAL HOME, INC. (2 locations), Onondaga and Clay, NY   2004–Present
Acting Funeral Director (part-time on-call basis)

GADDIS-MAURY FUNERAL HOME, Dunkirk, NY   2003–2004
Residency — Apprenticeship

✶ ✶ ✶ ✶ ✶ ✶ ✶

Additional Experience

Overland Inc. — *Assistant to Executive VP/Project Manager,* DeWitt, NY, 1997–2001, 2003–2004

NYSGE — Promoted through series of positions including *Nuclear Armed Guard, Electrician, Maintenance, Nuclear Locksmith,* Nine Mile I & II, Oswego County, NY, 1984–1996

Cortland County Sheriff's Department — *Reserve Deputy (part-time),* Cortland, NY, 1985–1994

NYS Department of Environmental Conservation — *Park Ranger Assistant* (concurrent w/education)

Strategy: *Created a functional resume that calls attention to proven skills as well as recent training for her current goal of Funeral Director.*

JOHN REYNALD

Dedication
Committed to Your Success

Leadership
Develop Leading Teams

Established
Top-Ranked Sales Professional

Marketing
Product Positioning; Relationship Marketer

Research
Market Dynamics & Vertical Futurist

Proven
Extensive Sales Record

Opportunity
Strategy & Tactics Guidance & Direction

Credentialed
Certified Business Professional

100 E. Montana Ave.
Bozeman, Montana 59718
406.265.3430
johnreynald@email.com

Sales and Marketing Consultant

High-performance sales professional with proven history of increasing revenue by the millions. Extensive history of meeting customer needs and exceeding personal and company sales goals. Established leadership skills with aptitude for motivating teams. Accomplished facilitator and negotiator with capacity to relate to company personnel at all levels. Top sales producer at Sales Services International. Previous clients include Applied Materials, Bell & Howell, ConAgra, Delphi Auto, Hewlett Packard, and NGK North America.

Qualifications Overview

Sales
- Generated $1.3 million in sales equaling 50% of company's 2002 revenue and more than $1.3 million in 2000 at gross margin of 26%.
- Produced more than $1 million gross sales at 23% margin in 1999.
- Orchestrated $700,000 sale of new product in the first year of the product line.
- Cultivated $350,000 account, the largest single account in company's history.
- Managed three of five largest accounts in 2001 and 2002.
- Introduced proposal-based selling and trained inside sales staff.

Product Development
- Delivered presentations and conducted thorough on-site interviews with domestic and international clients to determine needs.
- Collaborated with Product Development team to incorporate customer feedback; introduced four new units to product line.
- Organized and created technical support and customer service program.

Research and Marketing
- Studied and developed new vertical market for capital equipment line of products.
- Positioned company as leader in industry by conducting thorough research and market analysis of competition.
- Devised marketing strategy and created all sales materials; oversaw development of company online presence and all promotional copy for product line.
- Developed advertising/sponsorship marketing and sales agenda for ESPN's "On The Fly" national television series.

Professional History

Sales Services International, Billings, Montana   1997–2004
Product Manager, 2004
Oversaw all product and marketing development for company capital equipment line.
Business Development Director, 2003–2004
Delivered worldwide sales presentations marketing new product line.
Western Regional Sales Manager, 2001–2003
Directed all vendor and supplier distributor agreements; negotiated preferred pricing and territorial expansion.
Technical Services Director, 1997–2001
Conducted online and telephone high-tech sales of machine vision hardware and software components to domestic and international clientele.

CompanyWide, Inc., Billings, Montana   1992–1996
Vice President of Production
Wrote, produced, and directed television programming.

Education

Hecht & Associates, Business Professionals Course, Certified Professional, 2000
Montana State University, Bachelor of Science, Film and Television, 1986
San Bernardino Valley College, Associate's Degree in Electronics, 1974

Strategy: *Employed the left column to highlight key distinguishing characteristics that will be attractive to consulting clients. Used functional headings in the summary to highlight areas of expertise.*

ANDREW WESTMORELAND

4357 Dogwood Ave.   Home: 208.474.6349
Aberdeen, ID 83210   awest@isp.com   Mobile: 208.474.3210

BRANDING AND MARKETING CONSULTANT
ROI-FOCUSED ADVERTISING / MEDIA STRATEGIST

Multicultural Marketing Skills • Lateral Marketing Expertise Consumer/Customer Segmentation
Test Marketing & Simulation Modeling • Channel/Distribution Expertise

Bottom-line-oriented integrated marketing leader with a proven record in the creation and development of profitable brands across numerous industries in both domestic and global markets for multinational enterprises. Passionately committed to understanding and leveraging consumer/customer needs and wants that increase share, loyalty, and profits.

~ **Doubled U.S. retail sales in five years to $1.1 billion and secured #1 brand share in U.S.** over perennial competitor while increasing total brand profits by 6 percent.

~ **Revitalized aging product line with industry-first** infomercial linked to comprehensive direct-response effort, resulting in a brand share increase of 300 percent.

~ **Increased Fortune 50 bank share by 5 points** in less than a year through image-enhancement advertising.

PROFESSIONAL EXPERIENCE

EMPOWERED MEDIA MARKETING   1999–Present
SVP/General Manager   Idaho Falls, ID
Managed the creation and staffing of the Western Division office of a $650 million media buying and planning company headquartered in Cincinnati.

Key Clients

- **DIVERSITY MARKETING, Los Angeles, CA—world's leader in multicultural advertising.**
  - Provided strategic leadership in the areas of communication, research, and direct marketing for major Las Vegas hotel chain resulting in a corporate diversity marketing plan that increased visitor levels by 25 percent.
  - Achieved highest level of checking acquisition share among African-American consumers at Pan American Bank based on the development of culturally relevant marketing tools.
  - Designed image-enhancement advertising for Pan American Bank that was directly credited for 5-point jump in share value in 9 months.
- **AIR–TEC CORPORATION, New York, NY**
  - Developed the strategic marketing direction focused on product superiority for Air-Tec Corp. This positioning led to strategic alliances with two complementary technology firms, increasing revenues by 30 percent.
- **EAST ALABAMA COLLEGE, Huntsville, AL**
  - Developed university's first strategic marketing plan, which has resulted in a 13 percent increase in enrollment in its first year of implementation.
- **GENONE CORP., Los Angeles, CA**
  - Developed consumer focused on-line and off-line advertising and promotion programs that led to site leadership based on unique visitors.
  - Initiated product and advertising alliances with home medical equipment, insurance, and pharmaceutical companies, leading directly to 15 percent jump in revenue.
- **MEDIA MARKETERS, Seattle, WA**
  - Revitalized media-delivered radio promotions, leveraging local DJs for Premier Fast Foods, America Video, and AutoOne clients; produced traffic increases of 15–30 percent for stores and dealers.

Strategy: *Quickly made an impact by highlighting select accomplishments at the top of the resume, and then cast corporate experience using terms such as "clients" and "projects" to project the appropriate image for a consultant.*

Andrew Westmoreland • PAGE 2

INTERNATIONAL FOODS, INC.
Pan American Marketing Director

1991–1999
Seal Beach, CA

Led the brand management team, accounting for more than $1.5 billion in sales for pet care brands throughout the Americas.

- Doubled U.S. retail sales in five years to $1.1 billion and secured #1 brand share in U.S. over market leader Doggie Brand while increasing total brand profits by 12 percent.
- Increased profitability by 20 percent and exceeded share targets by launching several new products across canned meat, dry, and snack pet food segments while maximizing the company's retail category management impact and merchandising prominence.
- Revitalized Puppy Lovers Dog Food with infomercial TV advertising linked to comprehensive full-year direct-response effort, resulting in significant category expansion and a 25 percent conversion among competitive users.
- Enhanced Puppy Lovers advertising attribute effectiveness and created unified advertising focus across the Americas.

EARLY EXPERIENCE HIGHLIGHTS

WORLD WIDE LIGHTING COMPANY
Director of Marketing Services

Long Beach, CA

Managed North American Marketing Services Department with a staff of 12 people. Directed worldwide copy development process from Munich, Germany, world headquarters, leading to global advertising consistency. Focused on developing joint merchandising and consumer promotion programs with global consumer electronic firms that increased spending efficiency while leveraging brands at the point of purchase.

TRANSWORLD ADVERTISING
Vice President/Management Supervisor

Syracuse, NY

Directed the American Burger, Photo World, and TelcomPlus multicultural business strategies. Increased brand awareness and agency range of services to public relations, marketing research, and consumer promotions.

PREMIER COLA CORP.
Senior Marketing Manager

Albany, NY

Held six marketing management positions in both the retail and foodservice divisions with increasing levels of supervisory responsibilities and business complexity.

EDUCATION

BA Liberal Arts—Minor: Business, University of California at Long Beach, Long Beach, CA
MBA, Marketing, University of Northern California, Berg School of Management, San Francisco, CA

AFFILIATIONS/RECOGNITION

- Won Clio, Effie, and CEBA awards for advertising excellence at World Wide Lighting, International Foods, and Empowered Media
- Member of the Board of Directors of the Riverside County Children's Museum
- Certificate from the Institute of Premier Leadership
- Member of *Who's Who of African-Americans*
- Member, Future Leaders, a senior executive group developing programs to nurture inner-city youth
- Member of the Association of North American Senior Executives
- Featured in Special Events Publication for achievement in event marketing while at Premier Cola Corp
- Company spokesperson for Puppy Lovers awards broadcast on North American Broadcasting
- Awarded the highest honors from Professional Speaking Association

NORMAN BEACON

555 Valley Glen Ridge • Valley Glen, California 91405
Home (818) 535-1234 • Mobile (818) 209-9876 • normanbeacon@email.com

PUBLIC RELATIONS / COMMUNITY / FUND-RAISING CONSULTANT—NON-PROFIT SECTOR

- Retired Corporate Executive, committed to providing expertise in communications to promote the public good.
- Distinguished career building and leading successful company growth combined with extensive background contributing efforts to charitable causes.
- Proven strengths in the fine art of communication and negotiation with the ability to establish confidence and trust, resolve conflicts, build consensus, and motivate parties with divergent opinions toward common goals.
- Excellent listening skills with focus on a "win/win" philosophy.
- Extensive network of contacts.

Verifiable Record of Raising Significant Amounts of Money for Charitable and Public Causes

PROFESSIONAL BACKGROUND

Personal Sabbatical—Travel, Community Involvement

WEST COAST SPECIALTY CONFECTIONS, Los Angeles, CA
Managing Partner / Chief Operating Officer • 1976 to 2004

Launched and directed activities of confectionery manufacturing company from start-up through 20 years of successful operations.

- Built business from initial capital investment of $10,000 to annual revenues in excess of $40 million.
- Established and nurtured key contacts with retail and wholesale operations (including major chain stores) on local, regional, and national level.
- Sourced vendors and contractors and directed manufacturing operations in U.S. and abroad.
- Negotiated with union and non-union personnel, consistently achieving a win/win outcome.
- Generated widespread goodwill for company though extensive, ongoing involvement with numerous community charitable organizations. Recognized by city for contributions.
- Named "Local Business of the Year" by *Valley Glen Business Journal*.
- Finalized sale of company to international conglomerate in 2004 to devote time to travel and community involvement.

EDUCATION

B.A. in Humanities, UNIVERSITY OF CALIFORNIA, Los Angeles

COMMUNITY ACTIVITIES—Partial List

Fund-raising Chair—Friends of Valley Glen Hospital
Platinum Donor, Chair of Steering Committee—Valley Glen Youth Association
Member, Past Officer—Valley Glen Chamber of Commerce
Member, Board of Directors—Neighborhood Youth Industries, Inc.
President—Valley Arms Homeowners Association
Fund-raising Chair—Friends of the Glen Wilderness Project

ADDITIONAL INFORMATION

Foreign Language—Fluent in Spanish
Computer Skills—PC and Mac proficient on Microsoft Office Suite
Military—United States Army, Honorable Discharge
Activities & Hobbies—Los Angeles Marathon (annually since 1995), Golf, Tennis

Strategy: *Created a concise synopsis of corporate and community leadership to support this individual's goal of consulting to nonprofit organizations.*

SANDY T. LAYNE
123 Sunrise Place, Savannah, GA 31401

Telephone: (912) 123-4567
E-mail: stlayne@email.com

SALES ADMINISTRATION CONSULTANT

CAREER SKILLS

- Marketing/Sales Management
- Sales Promotions
- Staff Development
- Audit Operations
- Profit Maximization
- Revenue/Profit Turnaround

- National Account Programs
- Strategic Planning
- Contract Negotiations
- Business Restructuring
- Sales Territory Planning
- Dealer Recruiting/Relations

RELEVANT EXPERIENCE

TRAY MEDICAL, Inc., Savannah, GA   1995–2005
Director, Sales Administration
Accountable for three separate departments: Corporate Accounts, Individual Vendor Rebates, and Sales Representative Territory Alignments. Performed performance appraisals and Kronos payroll functions for 12 employees.
Corporate Accounts
- Created a processing calendar for corporate account fee calculations processed monthly and quarterly. Requested fee totals in excess of $10 million annually.
- Reduced reporting time by 50% by creating procedure and format manuals that expedited the reporting process.
Individual Vendor Rebates
- Implemented rebate programs for 3 separate sites.
- Increased sales 40% on custom procedure trays containing rebate items.
- Implemented a rebate program offering incentives to sales representatives. Rebate totals doubled within first year, raising annual individual rebates above $2.4 million.
Sales Representative Territory Alignments
- Maintained alignments for more than 500 sales representatives. Performed realignments during region transitions, new employment, and terminations.
- Developed alignment audits to ensure accurate sales and commissions for U.S. and Canadian sales representatives.

SCOTCH MEDICAL, Inc., Charleston, SC   1977–1995
Marketing Manager
- Designed multiple vendor seasonal cough/cold planners, suntan planners, and weekly merchandisers (distributed to 600 stores).
- Implemented and designed a profitable automated scan-down program.
- Established a profitable vendor commission report program.
- Conceived and wrote HBC/GM weekly and monthly "Great Buy" promotional advertisements for the Great Value Group (50 independent stores).
- Conducted presentations with the Great Value group to increase sales. Assisted in motivating vendors to produce additional advertising funds and special promotions for the stores.

EDUCATION

Master of Business Administration, University of Richmond, Richmond, VA
Bachelor of Science in Business, College of Charleston, Charleston, SC

Strategy: *Showed diversity in several areas that relate to marketability as a consultant, including strong accomplishments in directly relevant corporate positions.*

RESUME 71: BY JANICE SHEPHERD, CPRW, JCTC, CEIP

EXTRAORDINARY

STRATEGIC

PLANNING

11 Fountain Court, Woodland, WA 98222
(955) 372-5599

33 3rd Street, Suite B, Hamlet, WA 98888
(955) 249-7709

GRACIELA FINLEY

**Independent Consultant
working with
banks and small businesses**

Highly respected, recognized business leader with more than 30 years of experience in the banking industry—20 years in upper management.

Well-developed business acumen with ability to see the "big picture," pinpoint organizational objectives, and set goals and priorities to achieve results.

Background includes successful personalized management of teams of diverse business professionals within established and start-up businesses.

Track record in driving innovation in process redesign and in creating and implementing organizational solutions that positively affect the bottom line—improved efficiency, communications, and employee morale and reduced employee turnover.

comments from satisfied clients:

"…strongly related to all levels and respected their individual skills…knows what's required for growth…understands people and how they work…asks the right questions to get the right answers needed to make things happen…strong ethics and morals…highly respected…."

- Organizational Restructuring
- Strategic Planning and Recommendations
- Company-wide Action Plans
- Marketing Plan Development
- Salary Administration Program Development and Implementation
- Staff Building, Coaching, and Mentoring
- Mediation / Goal Negotiation
- Career Path Identification
- Cross-Functional Team Development
- Productivity / Efficiency Improvements
- Interdepartmental Workflow Management

EXEMPLARY SUCCESSES

District Manager, National Bank, Hamlet, Washington—Supervised operations of 9–23 branches and up to 900 people—continually negotiated goals and mediated personnel issues. District consistently ranked within top 5 districts of the state for outstanding overall performance.

VP / Regional Operations Manager, Community Bank, Eastern Washington—Established an audit program in the branches that helped all branches receive high scores from independent and in-house auditors.

CFO, Rivers Bank, Tri-Cities, Washington—Developed and implemented operational policies and procedures subsequently adopted by other banks.

Administrative Assistant, West Henderson Bank, Joliet, Illinois—assisted with launch of new bank that was profitable the first year.

Instructor, Columbia Basin Junior College—Taught Personnel Administration and Principles of Banking; created and taught Supervision course; created weekly instructional classes for banking class using American Institute of Banking text.

Strategy: *Used an unusual format to draw attention to broad and specific areas of consulting expertise. Added "comments from satisfied clients" to further support the image of a successful consultant.*

Henry E. Wolcott, Jr.

2432 Emerald Road
Grand Rapids, MI 49501

hew604@earthlink.net

Residence: (616) 791-1099
Mobile: (616) 607-2345

MANAGEMENT CONSULTING ♦ INTERNATIONAL BUSINESS

Seasoned executive with illustrious career encompassing manufacturing, operations, and marketing for the world's leading producer of specialty laboratory materials headquartered in the U.K. Recently opted for early retirement, but desire to share my wealth of knowledge with organizations seeking to develop business in the global marketplace. Outstanding ability to lead, motivate, and achieve new levels of performance, improve margins, and increase product awareness.

SELECTED ACCOMPLISHMENTS

❖ Assumed leadership for a product group in England that had declining sales and a dismal outlook for success. By using a "sense of urgency" approach, modest capital investment, and restructuring the manufacturing and development groups, **achieved 70% sales growth in 4 years with continued growth necessitating new plant construction.**

❖ Flat to declining sales of traditional products required identification of new markets for existing products. Led a project team that developed a new use in diagnostics for a modified standard product. Coordinated the efforts of the Danish patent holder and the Japanese test-kit manufacturer. **First year sales amounted to $1.5 million.**

❖ In the wake of "right-to-know" legislation and "cradle-to-grave" liability in the chemical industry, recognized that the facility was outdated and would not satisfy future customer liability concerns. Successfully convinced the Group Board that relocation was required to remain in that segment of the business. **Plant move resulted in rent savings of $200,000 per year, continuing customer satisfaction, and increased sales.**

❖ Challenged to make a silica-based product cost-competitive with other separation media for a customer in Scotland. Using unique bonding mechanisms, developed a new higher-capacity separation media. **Realized $900,000 in sales for this product, with this application currently being evaluated by several other customers.**

❖ Assumed control of a subsidiary consistently losing money. Changed market focus from research to commercial products and altered operating procedures. **Restored profitability within 2 years and continued to remain profitable.**

❖ Recognized that manufacturing efficiencies were unpredictable and directed the implementation of an efficiency program. Reviewed and modified procedures in purchasing, engineering, quality control, and manufacturing. **In less than a year, improved efficiencies from 78% to 88% and eventually reached levels of 95%, resulting in an annual savings of $400,000.**

❖ Faced with rapidly escalating health insurance premiums, convinced the Group Board and two area presidents of the benefits of self insurance. **Reduced employee contribution by 20%, offered a better medical package, and saved the company $345,000 per year.**

❖ As thin-layer chromatography products had no sales presence in Eastern Europe, organized a joint venture with a Russian company to attempt to correct this condition. Although the original joint venture was not successful, **follow-up efforts resulted in identifying a raw-material supplier for a yearly savings of $3 million.**

Strategy: *Focused on international business experience and accomplishments to facilitate a transition to a full-time consulting career in this specialized area.*

Henry E. Wolcott, Jr.   *Page 2*

PROFESSIONAL EXPERIENCE

Kensington Products, PLC
Surrey, England   *1978–2006*

❖ For the past 19 years, worked for U.S. subsidiaries of this $300 million, 250-year-old manufacturer of filtration, purification, and analytical products used in the medical, chemical, and food-processing industries.

❖ During tenure, progressed from a plant manager's position at a small facility to senior executive in charge of all product research and development in the U.S.

❖ Established a reputation for an honest and ethical management style and for motivating the workforce to achieve higher quality and productivity despite staff reductions.

Positions Held:

Vice President and General Manager, Technology Operations (1998–2006)
   Kensington Products USA, Grand Rapids, MI

Vice President, Marketing (1995–1998)
Vice President, Manufacturing (1990–1995)
   Filtration Products Division, Saginaw, MI

Plant Manager (1987–1990)
   Shelton Grant Technologies Division of Kensington Products, Grand Rapids, MI

Earlier Experience in the U.K.:

Plant Manager (1985–1987)
Production Manager (1983–1985)
Research Technician (1978–1983)

EDUCATION

University of Michigan Executive Program	1990
M.B.A., Nichols College, Derbyshire, England	1983
B.S. Business Administration, Haverford University, London, England	1981
A.S.M.E., Worcester Junior College, London England	1978

Robert Menzies

2876 Rainfall Drive, Ottawa, ON K1V 1L9
Phone: (613) 271-6139
Email: rmenz2000@yahoo.ca

INTERNATIONAL CONSULTANT ♦ ORANIZATIONAL DEVELOPMENT
Specializing in business reform/tax & customs procedures/regulatory institutions

Hands-on, performance-driven professional offering +10 years of international project management in Iraq, Montenegro, and Ukraine that includes work on high-profile national banking projects with IMF and World Bank. Strategic thinker with extensive expertise in designing, developing, and implementing new organizational frameworks to meet challenging business demands. Effective cross-cultural communicator with strong team-building skills.

Relevant professional proficiencies:

✓ **Technical expertise:** With 35 years of senior experience at Revenue Canada, hold vast knowledge of governmental processes and procedures relating to tax and customs procedures, utilized to successfully resolve and report on sensitive issues.

✓ **Project Management:** Expert in analyzing existing resource operations and moving quickly and effectively into reform and implementation of enhanced business practices, while focusing on teamwork, service level, and cost containment.

✓ **Change Management:** Proven change agent, gaining cross-functional collaboration during national-level projects within political environments.

✓ **Communications:** Extensive customer presentation experience reaching professional peers, business partners, senior executives, and politicians worldwide.

Strong competencies in:

Organizational Diagnosis & Design	Taxation Policy & Procedures	Program Design & Evaluation
Corporate Vision & Planning	Formal & Informal Audit	Work, Budget & Resource Planning
Corporate Systems Construction	Taxpayer Service	Training Development & Delivery
Staff Development	Accounting & Collection	Oral & Written Communication

Aligning organizational goals with realistic operational strategies.

NOTABLE STRENGTHS AND CAREER ACHIEVEMENTS

♦ Exceptional organizational, administrative, and time-management skills with ability to set priorities while managing projects in tandem, without compromise to quality. *Illustration: Led and contributed to the establishment of formal tax administration systems in Ukraine, Montenegro, and Iraq, involving organizational structures, policies and procedures, objectives, measurement systems, and training programs.*

♦ Introduced new collection-enforcement and wage-withholding system and taxpayer service centers in Ukraine. Wrote guidelines for computerization of both systems. Obtained hardware, trained staff, and oversaw implementation. *Result: Substantial reduction in accounts receivable, significant increase in the registration of new employers, and subsequent growth in tax dollars being submitted by employers. Tax Centers provided more reliable on-site information, reducing errors and thereby greatly reducing costs.*

♦ As tax administration consultant in Ukraine, reported to employer, to the Head of each Tax Administration, and, on occasion, to the Minister of Finance. *Illustration: Designed, drafted, and communicated a high tech computerized presentation of plan to transform the Tax Administration in Ukraine.*

♦ Designed, developed, and implemented an initial Large Taxpayer organization in Kiev. Designed methodology for forecasting workload and resources. Developed objectives and targets and devised reporting systems that measured results against targets. Wrote job descriptions for all positions, specifying roles and responsibilities of all members of the group. Drafted communication package for the overall information of senior management and staff. *Result: Allowed overall control of all large taxpayers. Established clear lines of accountability. Advanced the implementation of Western-style computer programs for work selection and assignment in both audit and collection.*

Strategy: *Translated technical accomplishments into an easy-to-read story that would hold the attention of international development recruiters or clients needing expertise in this area.*

Robert Menzies

Page 2

RELEVANT CONSULTANCY HIGHLIGHTS

FINTAX GROUP, Ottawa, ON
(Provides tax, audit, and advisory services in 148 countries.)

Tax Advisor on short- and long-term assignments, 2004–2006

➢ Designed and developed new functional headquarters and field organizational structures for the Departments of Revenue of Montenegro and Iraq. Included details of all roles and responsibilities, policies, and procedures.

➢ Designed a new wage-withholding system that set out, in booklet format, employer and employee responsibilities, a computerized accounting and enforcement system, job descriptions, training material, and training guidelines.

➢ Designed new individual and corporate tax returns with filing and processing instructions.

➢ Drafted policies and procedures for Taxpayer Service Centers and developed individual and corporate accounting procedures to allow for the processing of returns and recording of payments. Interviewed, hired, and trained all staff to service call centers for taxpayer service.

ECONO POINT, Ottawa, ON
(Provides financial, economic, and fiscal advisory services to both developed and developing countries.)

Tax Advisor on IMF contract to Ukraine, 2002–2004

➢ Designed and developed new collection enforcement organization in headquarters, regional, and field offices, establishing clear lines of responsibilities and accounting. Instituted training sessions.

➢ Established automated collection workflow and reporting system, which allows overall control of debtor cases and measures collection results against agreed targets.

➢ Developed a framework for collection-enforcement plan and designed a methodology for forecasting collection workload and resources.

➢ Implemented pilot project in a field office to test results of recommended changes. Selected and trained staff and established evaluation process.

➢ Defined clear lines of accountability to include workload selection, organizational flow, and computerized reporting systems. Prepared workflow info packages for all senior officials and collection staff.

➢ Designed, drafted, and implemented job descriptions for all of the positions within the new organizations.

➢ Provided all technical information on new collection computer operation to include generation of computer letters and allocation of workload to field offices.

Selected Achievement. **Challenge:** Upon arriving at Tax Administration Office in Ukraine, I quickly learned that all senior officials, including the Director, had a very jaundiced, prejudicial, and biased view of consultants. They assigned six young and inexperienced individuals to assist me in designing and implementing a new collection-enforcement system. These individuals had no tax knowledge whatsoever. **Action:** As my initial contract was for six months, I knew it was imperative for operational efficiency to take the time and effort to fully explain to these individuals my goals and objectives, convince them of my sincerity in meeting these goals, train them in all aspects of collection enforcement work (a very large undertaking), and get them to understand their roles and responsibilities. **Result:** My training program established a knowledgeable and committed team that was an integral part of the design and implementation of a state-of-the-art computerized collection enforcement system. The team continues to operate under severe restrictions but are great supporters and promoters of the system. I continue to work closely *pro bono* with the modernization team through e-mail.

PRIOR CAREER PROGRESSION

Revenue Canada 1970–2001, retired. Steady progression of career advancement with Canada's federal tax agency, including Internal Auditor, Unit Supervisor and Group Leader in field offices and headquarters, Senior Collection Officer, Head of Large Taxpayer Unit, Assistant Director Revenue Collections Toronto Tax Services Offices, Headquarters Director, and Regional Operations Co-coordinator.

JANICE O'BRIEN, CNM, OB/GYN NP, MPH

111 44th Street N.W. • Washington, D.C. 20007 • 410-562-1234 • janice800@obrien.net

Accomplished Certified Nurse-Midwife possessing broad, in-depth, multicultural knowledge of midwifery, nursing practices, and global health matters. Extensive experience developing, monitoring, and evaluating prevention programs with HIV/AIDS, managing and teaching midwifery protocols, and developing curriculum promoting Safe Motherhood Initiatives. Dedicated to advancing Millennium Development Goals to combat poverty and accelerate human development.

Areas of Expertise

Research & Grant Funding	Women's/Children's Health	Infectious Diseases
Clinical Instruction/Lectures	OB/GYN and Midwifery	USAID and NGOs
Staff Management/Training	HIV/AIDS Treatment/Prevention	Community Education

EDUCATION

Certified Nurse-Midwife and OB/GYN Nurse Practitioner
University of California, San Francisco

Master's in Public Health, Specialty in Maternal/Child and International Health
University of Hawaii, Manoa

Bachelor of Science Nursing
University of San Francisco

PROFESSIONAL EXPERIENCE

NURSING & MIDWIFERY INSTRUCTION

Georgetown University Hospital, Washington, D.C.—Certified Nurse-Midwife/Adjunct Faculty
Johns Hopkins University, Baltimore, MD—Adjunct Faculty, Midwifery Preceptor/International Health
University of Maryland, Baltimore, MD—Guest Lecturer, Reproductive Health and STDs
University of San Francisco, San Francisco, CA—Nursing Instructor in Community/International Health
Dominican College, San Rafael, CA—Nursing Instructor MCH, clinical and didactic

ADMINISTRATIVE/MANAGEMENT

Nurse-Midwife Consultant, Al Ain, U.A.E. (Current Position)

- Advising, developing, and implementing current standards of care utilizing ACNM, ICM, and WHO protocol criteria. Developed and conducted 30+ PowerPoint presentations in less than six months.
- Instruct and supervise 15 nurse midwives, strengthening skills in utilizing Safe Motherhood Initiative protocol and the WHO document entitled *Making pregnancy safer: The critical role of the skilled attendant.*
- Provide instruction and administrative guidance for managing obstetric emergencies, infectious diseases, and patients with HIV/AIDS.

Prenatal/Health Educator, Hawaii Medical Services Association (HMSA)
Supervised 25 employees and assisted in grant proposal writing. Developed educational programs targeted to high-risk populations with regard to Native Hawaiian culture. *Specific Accomplishments include the following:*

- Developed numerous health educational modules that were widely adopted and standardized for use among other trained health educators throughout the Hawaiian Islands. These modules included prenatal education, diabetes, hypertension, drug/alcohol abuse, teen pregnancy/prevention, and HIV/AIDS.
- Implemented training program for health educators for effectively marketing and administering programs to the public and private sectors.

Strategy: *Grouped medical experience into specific categories to highlight teaching experience, clinical practice, work with high-risk populations, and multicultural/international experience—all of which would be of value for the international consulting opportunities she was seeking.*

Janice O'Brien • 410-562-1234 • janice800@obrien.net   page 2 of 2

NURSING/MIDWIFERY
Certified Nurse-Midwife, International Health, in Ghana and Liberia, West Africa
Provided specialized care within orphanages in Accra and Monrovia. Treated high-needs children suffering from malnourishment, HIV/AIDS, and other infectious diseases. *Specific accomplishments include the following:*

- Developed a triage system to quickly assess and prioritize patients' medical needs and isolate high-risk patients from healthy patients.
- Designed protocols for managing daily influx of refugees and displaced people with PTSD in Liberia.
- Lived and interacted with USAID community and assisted with funding and project proposals.

Registered Nurse, U.S. Peace Corps
Trained by Italian OB/GYNs in midwifery care. Worked throughout hospital in med/surgery and operating room. *Specific accomplishments include the following:*

- Delivered more than 800 babies in two years.
- Developed curriculum for traditional birth attendants training program.
- Worked with Expanded Program of Immunizations (EPI) in the rural areas of Pemba Island, Tanzania, East Africa, developing effective cold-chain system for viable vaccines.

Extensive experience practicing nurse-midwifery and providing women's and children's health services in traditional medical settings. Provided medical care for vulnerable populations subject to a high risk of STDs, STIs, HIV/AIDS, drug abuse, and addiction in pregnancy. Managed high volume of patients whose needs included primary, prenatal, and gynecological care. *Specific accomplishments include the following:*

- Developed and administered education modules to high-risk, vulnerable populations.
- Designed educational modules on rape, infanticide, violence, and PTSD as part of a series targeting gender-based violence against women.

PUBLIC HEALTH/COMMUNITY EDUCATION
Nurse-Midwife Internship, USPHS Hospital, Shiprock, NM
Provided midwifery services to the Navajo population in a full-scope, high-volume practice at Indian Health Service Hospital. Conducted and administered counseling services for women with Fetal Alcohol Syndrome (FAS) and other substance abuse issues. *Specific accomplishments include the following:*

- Coordinated and produced a video on traditional Navajo birthing practices.
- Developed a reproductive health education program.
- Implemented and promoted HIV/AIDS education and prevention module.

Nurse-Midwife, St. Petersburg, Russia
Participated in a cross-cultural work exchange program in Russian maternity hospitals.

- Conducted community-based needs assessment with the goal of improving and modernizing existing protocols in Russian maternity hospitals.
- Organized and taught HIV/AIDS prevention with high-risk sex-worker populations in St. Petersburg.

PROFESSIONAL MEMBERSHIPS
American College of Nurse-Midwives • American Public Health Association
International Childbirth Education Association • Transcultural Nursing Society

RESUME 75: BY DR. HERMAN KASSELMAN

Keith P. Wentwood, M.D.

Medical Consultant : Anaesthesiology

Postal Address: 9 King Arthur Drive
Newlands, 7407
South Africa
Telephone: (021) 326 5313(H)
(021) 326 7996(W)
E-mail: wentwoodk@blueyonder.co.za

Languages: English and Afrikaans
Date of birth: 17.2.1948

Profile: A Specialist Anaesthesiologist since 1975 with extensive experience in full-time academic practice at a university-affiliated training hospital, then head of anaesthesia department at a tertiary hospital. Areas of expertise are paediatric anaesthesia, neuro-anaesthesia, and regional blocks. Background includes extensive research and publication. Additional experience as medicines evaluator for the South African medicines regulatory authority—the SA Medicines Control Council.

Areas of Experience and Expertise include

Providing anaesthesia cover for juniors and anaesthetising high-risk or major surgery cases. This includes all surgical specialities, excluding cardiac bypass, major neurosurgery, and major paediatric surgery. Ensure that medical officers and registrars obtain suitable training and examination qualifications and supervise continuing medical education. Foster the smooth running of the anaesthesia department and seamless cooperation with other hospital departments by ensuring that all equipment is functional and maintained.

Providing paediatric anaesthesia and general anaesthetic supervision of trainees in all spheres. Responsible for neuro anaesthesia and regional block techniques; registrar seminars in paediatric anaesthesia, neuro anaesthesia, and regional block anaesthesia. Perform own research and supervise registrar research as well as presenting such at international congresses.

Providing general clinical services to a tertiary teaching hospital. Teach registrars and ensure standards of practice are maintained. Liaise between the registrar and the specialist groups of the anaesthesia department. Developed personal area of interest/expertise in anaesthesia—i.e., paediatric anaesthesia.

Employment Summary:

1999–Present Chief Specialist and Head of Department, Provincial Hospital, Cape Town

1982–1999 Principal Specialist, Victoria Hospital, Cape Town

1980–1981 Senior Specialist, Victoria Hospital, Cape Town

1979 Anaesthetics Tutor Specialist, Auckland Hospital Board, New Zealand

1977–1978 Anaesthetics Registrar, Auckland Hospital Board, New Zealand

1975–1976 Anaesthetics Registrar, Victoria Hospital, Cape Town

1974–1975 Senior Medical Officer, Victoria Hospital, Cape Town

1971–1974 Medical Officer in Outpatients and Casualty, Victoria Hospital, Cape Town

1970 Intern, Groote Schuur Hospital, Cape Town

Strategy: Focused on achievements and experience while retaining much of the traditional CV format that is widely accepted in medical fields. This resume includes personal data, as is customary in South Africa.

2

<u>Career History</u>:

▶ **1999 to date:** **Chief Specialist and Head of Anaesthesia Department, Provincial Hospital, Cape Town, South Africa.**

Achievement Highlights

- Extended clinical services to provide specialist anaesthetists for all ASA 3 or above cases and all major surgery of any ASA grade. Successfully instituted a labour ward epidural service.

- Ensured successful training—90% of all medical officers passed the diploma in anaesthesia examination. Success was achieved with two registrar posts. Incumbents passed their examinations after I was appointed as Head of the Department.

- Updated equipment to acceptable standards of care prescribed in South Africa. Purchased new-generation anaesthetic machines to replace the old mechanical machines. Replaced monitors to prescribed standards of care.

- Developed accurate budget for the anaesthesia department and directed appropriate pre-planning to ensure meeting all budget criteria.

- Provided professional and efficient management of the anaesthesia department.

- Effectively managed medical personnel. The anaesthesia department comprises two external consultants, three registrars, and six medical officers. They are encouraged to further their anaesthetic careers, attend congresses, and maintain standards.

▶ **1982–1999:** **Principal Specialist, Victoria Hospital, Cape Town**

Achievement Highlights:

- Placed clinical services in paediatric anaesthesia on a tertiary footing. Successfully managed all neonatology and paediatric major surgery. I was involved with the separate cardiac surgery section for paediatrics.

- Trained 6–7 candidates for specialist examinations each year. Success rates were high at ±80%. Trained 10–15 supportive training specialists as well each year.

- Conducted research, published 45 papers (averaging 1–3 per year), and delivered annual congress presentations of the publications, including the third chapter on paediatric anaesthesia in the textbook *Introduction to Anaesthesiology* by Hugo and Kroon.

- Earned Doctorate in Medicine from the University of Pretoria. Thesis title: "Midazolam in Paediatric Premedication. The pharmacokinetics, clinical efficacy and ability to moderate behaviour patterns postanaesthesia."

- Promoted 7 successful Master of Medicine theses by registrars.

- Managed administrative duties to achieve a smoothly running department with full staffing of the available posts.

3

▶ **1980–1981:**   **Senior Specialist, Victoria Hospital, Cape Town**

Achievement Highlights:

- Established and managed the paediatric anaesthesia service.

- Trained and supported candidates for specialist examinations each year. Passing rates were high at ±80%.

- Performed research, developing a variety of research interests and commencing publications. Congress presentations of the publications were done annually.

▶ **1979:**   **Anaesthetic Tutor Specialist, Auckland Hospital Board, New Zealand**

Achievement Highlights:

- Developed teaching skills and supervisory skills in a major academic teaching hospital.

- Acquired Fellowship training in paediatric anaesthesia.

<u>Outside Interests:</u>

I am actively involved in nature conservation as the Secretary for CORMM (Care of Rehabilitated Marine Mammals in Cape Town). I love outdoor activities and I am also an avid gardener.

Certificates, references, and information on publications will be provided on request.

CHAPTER 6

Resumes for Return-to-Work Baby Boomers

As detailed in chapter 2, your return-to-work resume will focus on skills, experience, and accomplishments as they relate to your target profession, no matter where, when, or how they were acquired.

The resumes in this chapter will help you create your own return-to-work resume that communicates your capabilities without dwelling on your gap in employment.

Professions included in this chapter:

JOANN D. SMITH
80 Beachcomb Drive, Toms River, NJ 08755
Home (732) 408-5998 • jdsmith@optonline.net

SPECIAL EDUCATION TEACHING ASSISTANT
Special education and mainstream classroom experience, with a particular interest in teaching the arts.
Experience facilitating student assessments from both school and clinician perspective.
Proven ability to organize and implement systems. Effective communicator.

SUMMARY OF QUALIFICATIONS

Early Education Teacher's Assistant—5 Years of Experience
- Classroom work during school year and summer programs with all disciplines of special education students, ranging from learning disabled to children with severe mental retardation.
- Organized busing for more than 60 Chicago special-education students. Conducted periodic bus drills.
- Coordinated art projects for special-education students, mainstream kindergarten classes, and extracurricular groups, including tempera, water, brush, sponge, finger, basic clay techniques (coiling and rolling), puppet making, and skit production, to develop gross- and fine-motor skills and address individual educational goals.

Administration & Coordination
- Exceeded expectations by collecting payment on more than 2,500 Board of Education cases outstanding for more than 3 years.
- Coordinated up to 100 clinicians to conduct assessments and submit timely results to Board of Education.
- Six years of experience facilitating triennial compliance, assessment, and suspensions with School-Based Support Teams. Served as Case Manager for non-public school placement cases and liaised with Board of Education's Central-Based Support Team covering approximately 35 schools district-wide.
- More than 15 years of experience coordinating art events, productions, and fund-raising activities for such groups as the Chicago Board of Education, Glen Oak Public Schools, Cub Scouts, and Girl Scouts.

Computer Skills
- Chosen as an end-user consultant to develop compliance tracking system.
- Maintain, track, and follow through on information housed in a district-wide central database.

PROFESSIONAL WORK HISTORY

Supreme Evaluation, Inc., Chicago, IL—*Office Manager*   1994–1995
- Scheduled clinicians and recruited translators to perform assessments for Chicago Board of Education.

Committee on Special Education, Chicago, IL—*Triennial Coordinator*   1988–1994
- Reported directly to Chairperson to expedite student assessment, compliance, and funding decisions.

Glen Oak Board of Education, Glen Oak, IL—*Special Education Paraprofessional*   1983–1988

COMMUNITY INVOLVEMENT

Cub Scouts, Den 4, Pack 46, Toms River, NJ—*Volunteer*   2003–Present
Girl Scouts Troop #241, Toms River, NJ—*Volunteer*   2001
Parent Teacher Association, Thompson Elementary School, Glen Oak, IL—*Volunteer* 1995–1997

EDUCATION

Chicago Technical College, Chicago, IL   June 1993
Associate's Degree in Graphic Arts with Academic Honors
Honors: Dean's List (1990–'92), Leo Perskie Memorial Award (1990), William Conti Service Award (1991)

Strategy: *Led with a qualifications profile that is right on target for this person's desired position of teaching assistant.*

RESUME 77: BY MJ FELD, CPRW, MS IN COUNSELING

Joan Pomerantz

66 Meade Drive, Melville, NY 11746 • home 631-351-3434 • mobile 516-211-8704 • pom22@go.net

Seeking a position as a
Librarian Trainee / Librarian Assistant

Desired job emphasis to include some of the following:

Circulation / Reference / Children's Programs / Internet Research

Database Information Retrieval / Cataloging

Qualifications:

MLS degree over 50% completed.

Excellent customer service skills developed through prior position dealing directly with the public (Citibank).

Passion for literature as well as locating and using informational resources.

Computer skills include Word, PowerPoint, Internet, e-mail, and various library databases.

Education:

Master of Science, Library & Information Science, *anticipated summer 2006.* Queens College, Flushing, NY
Certificate in Children's & Young Adult Services, *anticipated summer 2006.* Queens College, Flushing, NY

Bachelor of Arts, Sociology, 1982. Hofstra University, Hempstead, NY

Librarian Training:

Public Library Field Work

Children's Room—Harborfields Public Library, Greenlawn, NY
Observed and assisted children's librarian with tasks such as book retrievals, database queries, and children's programming. (Spring 2005)

Program Development

As part of a graduate course, conceptualized, researched, and wrote comprehensive action plans for two public library programs. The early childhood program, "Happy to Be Me," had a self-esteem focus. The young adult program focused on supplying college information and introducing students to the library's resources on this topic. Each program was graded "A."

Business Experience:

Financial Associate (2000–2004). CITIBANK, Melville, NY

- Processed a full range of customer transactions while providing superior customer service.

- Utilized computer system to retrieve account information and troubleshoot/resolve discrepancies.

- Provided information on bank products (e.g., high-yield money market accounts, insurance, 529 plans).

- Recognized by branch manager for one of the best accuracy rates in the bank.

- Trained several new associates.

Marketing & Sales Coordinator (1982–1986). REGO CORPORATION, Lake Success, NY

Strategy: *Positioned new education and training credentials toward the top of the resume as a primary qualifier; relegated prior work experience to a brief mention at the bottom.*

PATRICIA G. WAGNER

177 Carey Coast Road, Rockaway, NJ 07866 ◆ pat_wagner101@gmail.com
(973) 957-5555 HOME ◆ (973) 957-5556 FAX

PROFESSIONAL OBJECTIVE:
Arts Counselor / Arts & Recreation Facilitator with teaching and recreation program coordination experience in community outreach programs (pre-school through adults).

DEDICATED CREATIVE PROFESSIONAL with Bachelor's degree and proven experience in teaching and arts/recreation program instruction as Recreation Activities Instructor, Arts Program Director, and Teacher of Special Arts Programs. Use diverse arts and crafts media, music, dance, and recreation sports to design and deliver socially, physically, and mentally stimulating programs for children and adults, including special-needs students. Demonstrated multitasking abilities with strong relationship building and community outreach skills. Cooperative team player; work well with people on all levels.

AREAS OF EXPERIENCE

Arts & Crafts Instruction	Innovative Instructional Methods	Special Arts Programs
Curriculum Design	Identifying Learner Needs	Project Management
Classroom Management	Student Rapport and Advocacy	Multimedia Art Teaching

PROFESSIONAL EXPERIENCE

Youth & Family Teacher and Arts Counselor for After-School Program   1/05–present
The Union Center YMCA, Union, NJ

- Design and lead fun-filled creative arts and crafts projects, recreation games, and pool activities for Arts, Sports & Splash classes (ages 3–5), and for after-school program funded by United Way.

Substitute Teacher—All grades and subjects   9/03–12/04 and 3/01–6/02
Rockaway Public Schools, Rockaway, NJ

- Instructed children in grades K–12, following prescribed lesson plans in a creative, positive learning environment. Set up day's activities and projects, maintained classroom discipline, administered tests, conducted labs, graded papers, and wrote daily reports for classroom teacher.

Art Director   6/03–8/03
Performing Arts Studio, Rockaway, NJ

- Led Stagecraft class for summer theater camp students (grades 3–6). Guided and instructed students in using their creative potential in staging, sets, and props for theater productions.

Teacher—Special Arts Program / Visiting Artist   6/03–7/03
St. Agnes Summer Camp, Scotch Plains, NJ

- Created multidisciplinary program incorporating language arts, arts media, music, and dance to enhance learning experience for preschool and kindergarten students (ages 3–5).

Recreation Activities Instructor / Art Instructor / Art Director   6/02–6/03
Union Recreation Commission, Union, NJ

- Served in overlapping instruction/program facilitation roles for well-attended arts and recreation programs geared to children, adolescents, and adults. Created and/or revamped educational programs and lesson plans with fresh avenues for expression. The following highlights each role:

Strategy: Incorporated meaningful volunteer experience into the summary and included just the relevant highlights from prior paid positions in different fields.

PATRICIA G. WAGNER ◆ (973) 957-5555 ◆ pat_wagner101@gmail.com   **Page Two**

Recreation Activities Instructor—Toddler to Adult Programs
- Designed, planned, and implemented 16 arts and recreation programs (toddlers to adults). Programs included Youth Soccer, Young Crafts, Young Artists, Drawing, Painting, Multimedia Art, Teens Night Out, Adult/Senior Painting, Mind Challenge (strategy games), and Music and Me.

Art Director—Community Playground Program (Grades 1–8)
- Restructured 8-week art program, infusing innovative lesson plans and methods, to spark artistic interest. Managed daily operations and special theme events, trained and supervised staff, purchased supplies within restricted budget, and troubleshot problems. Established pioneering open forum for children and staff to provide feedback on potential modifications to programs.

Art Instructor—Multimedia Arts Class (Grades 2–6)
- Taught diverse art media techniques, encouraging personal development of children's art skills.

PREVIOUS CAREER HISTORY
Assistant Production Manager, Tommy Hilfiger, New York, NY
Sales Administrator, New Mode Advertising, Scotch Plains, NJ
Advertising Coordinator, Gambier Agency, Edison, NJ
Assistant Manager—Major Accounts, Betsey Furstenberg Designs, Inc., New York, NY

VOLUNTEER COMMUNITY INVOLVEMENT
Art Director/School Volunteer, Cornwall E.S. & Providence M.S., Union, NJ   1995–present
- Guided and supervised school productions at elementary and middle school levels, including set design and creation, theatrical support for acting and staging, and theater arts instruction. Led and/or collaborated in diverse arts, recreation, community outreach, and fund-raising school projects, including Enrichment Day (2003) and St. Patrick's Hospital Project (2002).

Visiting Artist Exhibit, Evangelical Reform Church, Scotch Plains, NJ   2002, 2005
- Chosen to display original patent oil painting for National Prayer Day (2002). Subsequently exhibited two original patent oil paintings for National Prayer Day and Wholeness Service in 2005.

Adult Leader/Chaperone, Susan G. Komen Relay for Life Event, Union, NJ   June 2004 and 2005
- Supervised adolescents in overnight program for fund-raising event.

Den Leader/Camp Advisor, Boy Scouts/Girl Scouts of America, Rockaway, NJ   1995–2004
- Received Outstanding Service Award in 2004 from Boy Scouts for "beyond the call of volunteer service." Activities Leader for young boys and girls in formative years. Coordinated camping, arts & crafts, sports, and community service projects. Archery & BB Gun Certified.

Teacher, Vacation Bible School/Union Chapel, Union, NJ   July 2003
- Prepared lesson plan around theatrical setting for religious education program (grades K–5). Created set design with props, music, games, dance, and food to enhance multimodal learning.

Teacher, St. Hedwig Church, Scotch Plains, NJ   1999–2001
- Wrote and delivered religious education classroom curriculum for grades 3–5, incorporating creative classroom projects. Recognized and encouraged individual talents and participation.

EDUCATION & CERTIFICATION
Bachelor of Arts—Business Administration, Kean University, Union, NJ   2001–present
New Jersey Certification as Substitute Teacher, K–12, All Subjects

Residence: (315) 678-4321
E-mail: anna52@twcny.rr.com

Anna Kocinski

404 North Avenue, Fairmount, New York 13224

Human Services Professional

PROFILE SUMMARY
Knowledgeable and committed human services professional with 10 years of community service in a variety of positions, including rape crisis intervention and working with at-risk children ages 5–12 in an after-school program.

Strengths...
Able to handle high-volume and stressful work situations. Can remain calm and poised in emotionally charged situations and focused on the task at hand. Excel in independent work situations and decision making as well as being a highly regarded team member in group-coordinated teamwork. Highly organized and detail oriented. Strong ability to gain an individual's trust through understanding and by being sensitive to the individual's dignity and needs.

Bilingual...
English/Russian. Extensive work as an interpreter and translator, including ESL Interpreter for Russian-speaking family in the Fairmount School District and translator of educational, medical, and legal documents for Russian families in the Central New York area.

EDUCATION

Bachelor of Arts Degree in Psychology, Ithaca College, Ithaca, NY (2002)
    Honors: Graduated with honors, **Cum Laude**
        Psi Chi—The National Honor Society in Psychology
        Alpha Sigma Lambda—Premier National Honor Society for adult students in higher education

Associate of Science Degree in Human Services, Cayuga Community College, Auburn, NY

COMMUNITY SERVICE EXPERIENCE

INTERNATIONAL CENTER OF CENTRAL NEW YORK, Syracuse, NY (1999–Present)
Board of Directors, *Member*
Russian Interpreter
Homestay Host
- Work with people from all over the world, including direct work with immigrants.
- Assist Executive Director by translating and interpreting.
- Organize fund-raisers and coordinate visitor trips to Niagara Falls.

MORELAND FAMILY CENTERS, Ithaca, NY (1999–2000)
Internship for two semesters while studying at Ithaca College.
- Supervised 15 to 25 inner-city children in after-school program.
- Helped children with their school work.
- Organized and coordinated first-ever fashion show that had the children modeling used clothing that had been donated to the center.

RAPE CRISIS CENTER, Utica, NY (1998–2000)
Crisis Intervention Counselor for phone hot line and Abused Person's Unit.
- Local Hospital Advocate offering support to the victim while at the hospital.
- Participated in 40-hour training program.

AMERICAN RED CROSS, Utica, NY (1994–1997)
Waitress, Kitchen Worker at "Great Chef's Dinners."

ADDITIONAL WORK AND VOLUNTEER EXPERIENCE

Catholic Charities, Auburn, NY—*Volunteer*
Interreligious Council of CNY, Utica, NY—*Volunteer, Translator*
Tompkins Country Club, Fairmount, NY—*Banquet Waitress, 1980–1997*

Strategy: *Emphasized education, internship, and extensive and varied community service to highlight this individual's assets for a human services position.*

NICOLE HANOVER, M.S.W.
23 Newton Avenue
Cambridge, MA 02138
(617) 359-4587
nhanover@aol.com

PROFILE

Clinical Social Worker with demonstrated success in counseling individuals, families, and groups on a wide spectrum of issues in a variety of settings. Strong interpersonal, analytical, and communication skills. Particularly adept in working with children and with traumatic brain-injured clients and their families. Additional background includes advocacy, fund-raising, and program development.

SELECTED ACCOMPLISHMENTS

Individual and Group Counseling

- Conduct detailed intake interviews and psychosocial assessments to diagnose and assess needs, strengths, and coping mechanisms of clients for Cambridge Behavioral Mental Health Clinic. Client population is diverse and encompasses children, adults, and families.
- Develop and implement treatment plans to meet identified goals. Provide one-on-one counseling, with focus on behavioral methods, to deal with issues related to substance abuse, separation and divorce, bereavement, juvenile delinquency, and education.
- Co-lead weekly recovery group for women with history of substance abuse. Group outcomes are positive with fewer incidences of recidivism.
- Provided individual counseling to traumatically brain-injured population at world-renowned Russell Center for Rehabilitation Medicine. Utilized cognitive remediation techniques to help individuals develop strategies to compensate for intellectual deficits.
- Worked with families to facilitate post-traumatic growth process. Issues addressed included those of chronic sorrow and ambiguous loss.
- Handled telephone inquiries and assessed eligibility of individuals requesting services from Northeast Lawyers for the Public Interest, a not-for-profit legal organization. Conducted intake interviews for those meeting eligibility criteria. Referred others to more appropriate service providers.
- Developed and led well-attended social and physical fitness groups for senior centers.

Program Development

- Serve on joint student-faculty curriculum committee for Massachusetts School of Social Work, playing active role in reviewing and instituting changes related to curriculum and course design.
- Initiated and developed mentorship program for teenage parents for Help Parents Save Their Children, providing platform for clients to learn parenting and social skills. Program was very successful and enabled participants to keep their children at home and out of the foster-care system.
- Co-founded Gerontology Association of Massachusetts State College, with mission of promoting awareness of social issues impacting the elderly.
- Played key role in planning and execution of numerous fund-raising events for non-profit organizations, including the Cambridge Board of Family and Children Services.
- Serve on Board of Directors of Boston Independent Group Home Living Foundation. Play active role in reviewing issues and policies related to residential and day treatment programs.

Strategy: *Create a functional format to emphasize strong accomplishments, and then showcase volunteer and educational qualifications on page 2.*

NICOLE HANOVER, M.S.W.
nhanover@aol.com
Page 2

EXPERIENCE

SOCIAL SERVICE STAFF / INTERNSHIP / CONSULTING POSITIONS   1990–present
Assignments include

Cambridge Behavioral Mental Health Clinic, Cambridge, MA (2004–present)
Social Work Intern

Massachusetts School of Social Work, Boston, MA (2003–present)
Curriculum Committee Member

Boston Independent Group Home Living Foundation, Boston, MA (1991–present)
Member—Board of Directors; Advocate/Fund-raiser

Northeast Lawyers for the Public Interest, Boston, MA (2003–2004)
Social Work Intern

Russell Center for Rehabilitation Medicine, Boston, MA (2000–2002)
Rehabilitation Specialist—Brain Injury Day Treatment Program

Help Parents Save Their Children, Cambridge, MA (1999–2004)
Program Manager/Mentor

Gerontology Association of Massachusetts State College, Boston, MA (1998–2002)
Founding Member

Cambridge Board of Family and Children Services, Cambridge, MA (1990–1993)
Fund-raiser

Prior Background:
Marcellus Clothiers Inc., Newton, MA
Co-founded women's division of designer clothing manufacturer. Oversaw production, marketing, and sales functions.

EDUCATION

M.S.W., Boston College School of Social Work, Boston, MA, 2005

B.A., Psychology, University of Massachusetts, Boston, MA, 2002

Professional Development, University of Massachusetts:
Certificate of Gerontology
Certified Fitness Instructor for Older Adults

Awards:
University of Massachusetts:
• Alumni Research Grant
• Women's Forum Education Award

Computer Skills:
Windows 2000; MS Word, Excel; SPSS; Internet

GRACE-ANN COLEMAN, RN, BSN

7655 5th Avenue
New York, NY 13407

(212) 456-8713
graceann@aol.com

EXPERIENCED REGISTERED NURSE

Competent and reliable nurse with solid technical abilities, proven assessment skills, and experience in primary-care nursing. Background includes medical/surgical (general and oncology), critical care, recovery, and outpatient surgery. Offering a great deal of energy and a proven ability to establish productive communications with physicians and other medical professionals.

- As an oncology nurse, acquired experience in multidisciplinary care and highly individualized treatment plans. Maintained a thorough understanding of all body systems as well as the breakdown of each system.

- Exposed to a strong teaching environment and experienced in serving as a resource person for ancillary and professional staff regarding oncology cases, technical equipment operation, and complex procedures.

- Experienced in working all shifts and able to adapt to the varying responsibilities of each shift. Working style reflects excellent time management, confident decision making, meticulous follow-up, and a team-driven focus.

NURSING EXPERIENCE

St. Agnes Medical Center, *White Plains, NY*   1995 to 1996
(A 76-bed acute-care hospital that offers emergency, surgical, and critical-care services.)

Staff RN—Outpatient Department
Provided pre- and post-operative care and teaching to patients with a wide range of complex conditions. Worked independently with direct accountability for admissions, discharge, IV treatments, recovery, and post-procedure follow-up. Served as a liaison/resource for the oncology department to help with difficult procedures or protocols. Consistently worked after hours to maintain continuity of care.

Michael Smith, MD, *New York, NY*   1994 to 1995
Staff RN—General Surgery (Private Practice)
Involved with the start-up of this office, which included hiring, supply purchasing, and examination room set-up. Position required constant coordination of care and a wide range of administrative duties, including staff training and inventory control. Prepped patients and assisted doctor during office procedures.

Lenox Hill Hospital, *New York, NY*   1989 to 1994
(Community teaching hospital that has an educational partnership with Westchester Medical Center, New York Medical College, and Columbia University College of Physicians & Surgeons.)

Staff RN—Oncology Med/Surg (1991 to 1994)   Staff RN—Med/Surg (1989 to 1991)
Administered all aspects of quality patient care in this technologically advanced teaching hospital, acquiring experience with innovative surgical procedures and state-of-the art equipment. Provided clinical and surgical support for oncology-related surgical procedures and tended to some of the most complex of patient-care situations. Oriented new nurses and trained other healthcare professionals on the use of new equipment. Actively involved with the start-up of the Bone Marrow Transplant Unit. Served on the Colostomy Committee, Pain Management Committee, and as IV Team Liaison. Served as charge nurse during shift, which required workload delegation and integration of care across settings.

EDUCATION / CREDENTIALS

New York University, School of Nursing
Bachelor of Science in Nursing

Clinical Experience (Six Months)
Sloan-Kettering Medical Center—Leukemia Floor

Certifications: CPR / First Aid

VOLUNTEER WORK

Overlook & Titusville Elementary Schools
Active PTA Volunteer and Parent Assistant (2000 to present)

Herkimer County Girl Scouts
Troop Leader (2001 to 2004)

Herkimer County Swim Club: Parent Volunteer (2002 to present)

Strategy: *Because this individual's training and prior experience are directly relevant to her goals, they are positioned strongly toward the top of the resume. The volunteer section subtly communicates what she has been doing for the past 10+ years.*

BRENDA CHRISTOPHER

2713 McKenzie Road, Buffalo, New York 14217 • (716) 555–0320 • bchrphr@adelphia.net

MEDICAL OFFICE
Medical Billing and Coding / Ward Clerk / Medical Secretary

Professional Profile

- Demonstrated skills in keyboarding at 60 WPM, word processing in Microsoft Word, and spreadsheet development in Microsoft Excel.
- Gained knowledge in medical insurance and medical billing using ICD-9-CM, CPT-4, and HCFA coding.
- Received training in processing and completing claims for Medicare, Medicaid, Blue Cross, HMOs, and Workers' Compensation.
- Assembled, maintained, and updated thorough and confidential medical records, and ensured that they were kept in an accurate, meticulous, and complete manner.
- Interviewed patients and gathered data to assess patients' needs and problems; developed and implemented individualized care plans.
- Provided care and support to adolescent and adult patients with a wide range of medical conditions.
- Monitored patients' health, including disease progress, wound status, vital signs, and effectiveness of treatment, and reported changes in status.
- Educated/trained patients and family members on maintaining wellness/health and techniques for disease and infection prevention.
- Collaborated with interdisciplinary team members to provide comprehensive treatment planning and consistent patient care.
- Coordinated, trained, and directed the activities of RNs, LPNs, and CNAs; assigned duties, supervised staff, and prepared charge reports.
- Operated and monitored dialysis and telemetry equipment.

Education

Williamsville Community Education, Williamsville, New York
Medical Billing Clerk Certificate, 5/05
Curriculum included

Personal Computers	*Medical Terminology for the Office*
Medical Insurance and Billing	*Keyboarding*
Microsoft Word	*Microsoft Excel*

Medaille College, Buffalo, New York
A.A.S. Nursing, 5/03

Bryant & Stratton Business Institute, Syracuse, New York
Medical Secretarial Course

Experience

Registered Nurse—BUFFALO MEDICAL CENTER, Buffalo, New York (6/03–10/03)
Medical-Surgical, Hemodialysis, Psychiatric, Cardiac Step-Down, and Quality Improvement Units

Senior Clerk / Typist—SYRACUSE GENERAL HOSPITAL, Syracuse, New York (9/82–8/85)
Medical Records and Emergency Departments

Strategy: *Included strong qualifications in the profile, followed by recent educational credentials and prior work experience that adds value to her skills as a medical office professional.*

JESSIE C. DAMON

33 Tumbleweed Lane   Evanston Park, IL 60202
773.823.5555 Cell   jcdamon@xls.net   773.914.4578 Home

Focus: Medical Aesthetician

CREDENTIALS

- Currently completing professional training program to become a Licensed Aesthetician with enthusiasm and excitement for developing a career in this field. Areas of concentration:
  - microdermabrasion   - skin care
  - body care   - Tresartes® product knowledge
- Passionate about the field of aesthetics; perfect attendance record; fast-learner.
- Knowledgeable, customer-driven, and committed to providing outstanding service.
- Team player who works equally well independently or in a team-oriented environment.
- Dedicated; willing to give much more than is expected; energetic; confident; competent; friendly.

EDUCATION

Licensed Aesthetician Candidate, *SKIN-MED* INSTITUTE, INC.   **7/05–Present**
Division of Aesthetics, Chicago, IL—Graduation Date: 9/06
- Cumulative GPA: 3.92/4.0; perfect attendance
- Top-ranked student in class of '06
- One of three *Skin-Med* scholarship recipients for academic achievement

KEY SKILL AREAS

Field of Aesthetics:
- Completed 800+ hours of study in subject areas of anatomy, chemistry, and business.
- Extensive hands-on, practical experience with broad client base of males and females.
- Studied all facets of skin care and body care, both internal and external care and treatment.
- Knowledgeable of various types of acids, enzymes, formulas, trends, and product lines.

Administration / Organization:
- Strong organizational, planning, and administrative skills to maximize workplace productivity.
- Motivated individual with quality work ethic; counted on to get things done quickly and accurately.
- Pay attention to small details to ensure project success; excellent follow-through abilities.
- Computer skills with Microsoft Word, Internet, and e-mail applications.

Customer Relations & Service:
- Effective communication skills with all types of people; good conversationalist who puts others at ease. Helpful, caring attitude; cooperative and outgoing demeanor; fun to work with.

EXPERIENCE

- Actively involved in rearing family while contributing to school / civic activities, 1995–present
- Evanston Business Partners, Evanston, IL—Business Administrator, 1990–1995
- Greenbelt Auto Dealers, Naperville, IL—Auction Secretary, 1985–1990
- Brody Shoe Retailers, McHenry, IL—Sales Associate, 1980–1985
- Brokers Business Exchange, Chicago, IL—Administrative Assistant, 1980–1985

INTERESTS

Family, horses, snow-skiing, and gardening

"Jessie is an outstanding student at *Skin-Med*. She's intelligent, confident, and deeply immersed in launching herself in a new career. She will excel in any endeavor."
—Andrea Miller, M.S.Ed., Enrollment Advisor, Skin-Med Institute, Inc.

Strategy: *Highlighted strongest "selling points" that relate to this person's new field, for which she is about to complete her training and certification. Closed on a strong note, using a testimonial from a respected source.*

ANGELA P. WARREN

4389 Main Street, Apt. 2 • Syracuse, New York 13206 • apwarren@aol.com • 315-555-5269

RESEARCH ASSISTANT / DATABASE MANAGER

Talented and highly educated professional with training and hands-on experience in statistical analysis, research design, and teaching. Superior computer knowledge and ability to bring keen observation and attention to detail for any project.

STRENGTHS & KNOWLEDGE

- Conducted follow-up study using national longitudinal sample of more than 10,000 subjects with data from National Center for Educational Statistics.

- Employed factor and variance analysis to build statistical model to explain complex factors contributing to academic success.

- Assisted in teaching and mentoring university students, providing academic support and personal guidance.

- Contributed skills and expertise in numerous unpaid tutoring and research positions, as well as a research fellow at Cambridge University.

- Participated in research activities for Syracuse University.

TECHNICAL PROFICIENCIES

Platforms: Windows 98/ME/XP, VAX, and CYBER

Applications: Longitudinal Databases, SPSS, LISREL, Minitab, Paradox Relational Database, and Microsoft Word, Excel, Outlook, and PowerPoint

PROFESSIONAL EXPERIENCE

SYRACUSE UNIVERSITY—Syracuse, New York
Teaching Assistant—Counseling and Educational Psychology Department
Research Assistant—Counseling Center

EDUCATION

SYRACUSE UNIVERSITY, Syracuse, New York
Ph.D.—Educational Psychology
Concentration: Statistical Data Analysis and Research Methodology
M.A.—Educational Psychology

STATE UNIVERSITY OF NEW YORK COLLEGE AT BUFFALO, Buffalo, New York
B.A.—Philosophy

Professional Development: SPSS Base Module and Advanced Statistics Seminars, Eric Gardiner National Conference on Statistics (nine years of participation); Visiting Scholar at Cambridge University

Honors: Who's Who in Science and Technology; MENSA Membership

Professional Affiliation: American Association for the Advancement of Science

Strategy: *Highlighted skills, knowledge, training, and accomplishments without drawing attention to this person's total lack of paid work experience.*

JOHN BARNHAM

Telephone: (08) 8225 9000

30 McGregor Avenue
GLENELG SA 5045

BROAD EMPLOYMENT OBJECTIVE

Process Worker
- Light engineering • Timber shop

QUALIFIED BY

Background in practical farm work with more than ten years of additional experience in quality-controlled precision engineering process work and in timber assembly. Contributed six years to process-line production of car components, working in a team environment. Subsequently worked for five years on an assembly line for wooden door frames and windows, using a range of hand-held power tools.

AREAS OF EFFECTIVENESS

- Experienced in working on engineering and timber assembly production lines
- Competent in using a wide range of hand and mechanical tools and jigs
- Familiar with workshop health and safety processes
- Able to understand and apply technical instructions
- Experienced in teaching practical skills to juniors
- Demonstrated ability to learn new skills quickly
- Quality-controlled process work including spot welding
- Work well without supervision
- Good forward-planning skills

EXPERIENCE

Process Worker	Jupiter Doors and Windows	1985–1990
Assembly Welder	Austral Auto Supplies	1979–1985
Farm Hand/Contractor	Barnham Echunga Cattle Stud	1972–1979
Truck Driver	Western Motors	1970–1972
Car detailer	Western Motors	1968–1970

VOLUNTARY COMMUNITY WORK

Youth Leader	Glenelg Adventist Church	1995–present

Strategy: *Stressed previous practical employment in farm work, light engineering, and timber assembly as well as community work that reinforces his work ethic while providing some information for the years he has been out of the work force.*

RESUME 86: BY DEBORAH FERNANDEZ, LPC, NCC

Maria Martinez

985 Six Forks Road
Raleigh, NC 27615
(919) 763-3287
mmz@carolina.net

Qualifications

- 12 years of experience in customer service and bank operations
- Excellent communication and presentation skills; Competent Toastmaster (CTM)
- Proficient in Microsoft Word, PowerPoint, and Excel
- Extensive travel and international experience
- Bilingual; fluent in English and Spanish

Education

Bachelor of Arts, University of North Carolina, Chapel Hill, NC

Experience

Senior Teller
United Carolina Bank
Supervised 17 employees and bank operations for a branch with $25 million in assets. Expanded portfolio of products and services available to customers. Trained tellers in computations, transactions, and other banking procedures. Developed loyal banking relationships through attentive service and effective communications. Received 9.8 (out of 10) on customer-satisfaction survey.

Teller/Customer Service Representative
United Carolina Bank
Tailored bank services to fit customers' requirements and recommended appropriate banking products. Cross-trained to perform customer-service functions. Provided responsive assistance, consistently ensuring that customers received a superior level of service. Resolved complaints according to guidelines established by the bank and to the customer's satisfaction. Awarded four outstanding customer-service certificates. Selected for Teller Advancement training.

PTA President
Raleigh High School
Elected to direct the affairs of the association in cooperation with other members of the executive board. Served as liaison between parents and school personnel. Conducted monthly meetings attended by more than 200 parents. Served two consecutive terms.

Banking ♦ *Customer Service* ♦ *Retail Operations*

Strategy: Removed dates to deemphasize gaps in employment while highlighting qualifications obtained on the job, as a volunteer, and through other life experiences.

TRISH MARTIN

339 Voorhees Road • Easton, PA 18040 • (610) 250-0125 • tmtm@go.net

Conscientious individual with proven bookkeeping and accounting skills.

SUMMARY OF QUALIFICATIONS

- Recent college graduate with B.S. in Accounting and background in banking.
- Strong knowledge of bookkeeping, accounts payable, accounts receivable, bank reconciliations, and other general accounting functions.
- Organized and detail-oriented with strong computational skills.
- Team player who is always willing to help as needed to achieve business goals.
- Motivated professional driven by challenge and recognized for diligence, thoroughness, and autonomy.

EDUCATION

B.S. Degree in Accounting, May 2005
East Stroudsburg University, East Stroudsburg, PA

KEY SKILLS & ACCOMPLISHMENTS

- **Bookkeeping/Accounting:** Competently maintained books for small-business owner, organizing records and setting up filing systems to facilitate accounting. Successfully managed household finances.

- **Banking:** As teller, accurately handled diverse array of banking transactions, consistently closing out drawer with zero balance at day's end.

- **Organizational Skills:** Organized and oversaw annual cookie drive fund-raiser. Capably managed process, effectively tracking orders and payments.

- **Strategic Management:** As part of coursework, analyzed business performance of assigned company and identified ways to simplify and streamline operations. Authored paper summarizing recommendations and presented findings to class.

PROFESSIONAL EXPERIENCE

FIRST NATIONAL TRUST, Somerset, NJ   1984 to 1992
Bank Teller/Head Teller
Handled broad range of duties, including cashing checks, processing deposits, and issuing savings bonds. Addressed customer inquiries, conducting research as necessary to resolve problems and ensure satisfaction.

SELF-EMPLOYMENT   1984 to 1990
Bookkeeper (Part-Time)
Kept books and handled filing for gas-station owner.

COMPUTER SKILLS

Windows • Word • Excel • PowerPoint • Internet • E-mail

VOLUNTEER SERVICE

Brownie Leader—Troop 2051, Easton, PA
Conducted meetings, developed newsletter, scheduled work for badges/service projects, and ran annual cookie drive.

Strategy: *Highlighted key skills and accomplishments along with recent, highly relevant education.*

SUZANNE JONSEN
879 North Street • Teaneck, NJ 07666

(201) 530-9089   sjonsen789@aol.com

INSURANCE PROFESSIONAL

Ten years of experience in insurance underwriting, customer service, and management combined with a background in community relations, event planning/coordination, fund-raising, and administration. Recognized as a well-organized, efficient professional with a strong work ethic and leadership qualities. Proven ability to meet deadlines, achieve goals, and accomplish results. Excellent customer-relations skills. Computer literate.

Earned Charter Property Casualty Underwriter designation.

INSURANCE EXPERIENCE

NORTHEAST INSURANCE, Teaneck, NJ

Assistant Manager (1988–1995)
Senior Account Analyst / Account Analyst (1985–1988)

Promoted to supervisory role with increasing responsibilities in Commercial Lines Unit for marketing, profitability, customer service, agency relations, and underwriting. Assisted District Manager in new program development and decision-making activities in the unit. Supervised, trained, motivated, and evaluated team of 7 underwriters. Recruited, appointed, and maintained positive relationships with up to 30 agents. Implemented new product programs and trained agents. **Accomplishments**:

- Assumed supervisor's role during leave of absence and ensured smoothly running unit operations.
- Consistently achieved/exceeded goals for production, new business development, and profitability.
- Assisted in implementing District Assistant Program and trained new staff in essential job functions.
- Reorganized District Assistant Program, resulting in earlier renewal processing and issuance.
- Supervisor's evaluation: *"Suzanne continually distinguishes herself with hard work and dedicated effort. She is an extremely important part of the operation."*

COMMUNITY RELATIONS EXPERIENCE

TEANECK HIGH SCHOOL, Teaneck, NJ (1995–Present)

Board of Directors Member/Fund-raising—Sports Club (5 years)
- Contributed to event planning and organizational and administrative activities to benefit school programs. Created display posters to promote events; coordinated raffles and direct-mail campaigns. Established sponsorships and led fund-raising efforts that generated more than $100,000.

Teaneck Parent Teacher Association (10 years)
Various leadership roles in the organization:

- **Co-Chair/Committee Member—Cultural Enrichment** (4 years)—Researched, planned, and coordinated cultural/educational programs presented to audiences of 600 students at the elementary and middle schools. Managed program budget. Presented "Person of Character" Governor's Award in 1999.

- **Chair, Membership** (5 years)—Coordinated efforts that increased new membership by 10–15%.

- **Chair, Safe Homes** (5 years)—Compiled and distributed directories to parents.

- **Fund-raising Chair, Cub Scouts Award** (3 years)—Honored for service and dedication.

EDUCATION

Bachelor of Arts (English), Columbia University, New York, NY

Strategy: *Created a concise resume summarizing relevant skills, strengths, and experience, even though it was dated; account for the employment gap with a strong section of community-relations experience showcasing leadership skills.*

RESUME 89: BY KRISTIN COLEMAN

KENDALL ROSE

76 Columbia Street
Malibu, CA 90263

kendallrose@verizon.com

Home (209) 555-3243
Cell (209) 123-8372

PROJECT MANAGEMENT PROFESSIONAL
Offering progressively responsible IT project experience and an advanced understanding of best practices and methodologies.

Multidisciplined manager with a broad understanding of applications development and management, delivery management, and software engineering. Highly skilled at building constructive business relationships and consistently successful in ensuring business partner satisfaction. Equally skilled at identifying critical issues and leveraging internal competencies to turn around troubled projects. Comfortable dealing with ambiguity and delivering articulate and effective presentations to different audiences. Proven ability to anticipate, mitigate, and resolve conflicts across project workgroups.

AREAS OF STRENGTH & EXPERIENCE

- Commercial Account Management / Critical Account Management
- Vendor Relations / Performance Measurement / Capacity Planning
- Quality Assurance / Resource Planning / Critical-Path Scheduling
- Customer Fulfillment / Contract Analysis / Contract Negotiations

- Benchmarking / Status Reporting
- Budget Controls / Program Management
- System Testing / Software Engineering
- Applications Management / Software Development

PROFESSIONAL EXPERIENCE

GXT COMPUTER ASSOCIATES   1978 to 2005
(Promoted through a series of progressively responsible positions involving technical, people management, consulting, project management, program management, client relationship management, and account management.)

Delivery Project Executive *(8/99 to 5/05)*

Served in a leadership role to manage the delivery of IT services to several internal customers. Challenged to manage key accounts and commercial account IT project applications portfolio. Provided guidance to customers in establishing, tracking, and reporting their annual IT budget. Maintained direct accountability for client satisfaction, quality support, contract negotiations/administration, and end-to-end project management. Established capacity models, strategies, and plans with full responsibility for making certain that skill demands were met.

Collaborated extensively with cross-functional business groups to coordinate project prioritization, scope, business requirements, design, and deliverables. Accountable for ensuring that project milestones were delivered on time and within targeted budgets—meeting or exceeding customer expectations. Championed best practices, standards, consistency, and process improvements to ensure that requested work was matched to qualified and available project management resources.

Selected Highlights

- Managed several projects that focused on integrating business partner IT Services into global services, which required educating business partner staff on managing $8 million annual budget.

- Managed multiple applications development projects representing $11 million for an internal customer, which required well-coordinated negotiations with external vendors in order to meet requirements of leading-edge technology.

- Key member of the corporate performance council, customer advisory council, and workload strategy team.

- Drove the development of an application design guide for cooperative processing, integrating customers', vendors', and developers' requirements.

EDUCATION

Pepperdine University, *Malibu, CA*
B.S. in Computer Information Systems

Project Management Institute
Project Management Certification

Strategy: *Avoided the candidate appearing overqualified by including only the experience that is relevant to her goal of a position as a project manager. The gap in employment is not explained because it is relatively short.*

Mary Scott

88 Woodward
Irvine, CA 92604

Home: (949) 555-9960
mscott@verizon.net

TELECOMMUNICATIONS ANALYST

Highly motivated, goal- and detail-oriented Telecommunications Analyst with excellent organizational and time-management skills. Possess extensive experience in the telecom industry with expertise in PBX maintenance, telecom invoice management, and customer service. Recognized as a productive team member with integrity and a high level of commitment. Apply experience, knowledge, and analytical expertise to successfully fulfill telecom requirements. Identify challenges and find solutions that increase customer satisfaction.

AREAS OF EXPERTISE

Telecommunications Voice:	Programming/Installation	Control Inventory
Configure / Test ACD	Telecom Systems Design	Provision Telecom Services
ARS, CMS, & SMDR		Schedule Telecom Services
Cabling Standards	Administrative:	Train Staff
Call-Center Technology	Audit Phone Bills	
Cellular Equipment	Create Telecom Procedures	Customer Service:
Interactive Voice Response	Design Management Reports	Effective Communications
Moves, Adds, & Changes	Evaluate Usage	Follow-Up & Support
PBX Equipment	Interact with Vendors	Interpersonal Skills

PROFESSIONAL EXPERIENCE

Full-Time Parent   2003–Present

FINANCIAL FEDERAL CREDIT UNION, Seal Beach, CA   1995–2002
Telecommunications Analyst
Supported all telecommunication services for headquarters and four branches of a multi-site credit union.

- Reviewed and analyzed voice/data communications invoices to ensure accuracy and contract adherence.
- Provisioned all local, long distance, toll-free, data, pager, and cellular services, maintained current inventory of all active services, and coordinated all telecom services and repairs.
- Coordinated on-demand programming and installation of telephones, modems, and fax lines at all branch locations.
- Analyzed monthly usage to determine that correct rates were being applied.
- Developed detailed procedures for all telecommunications equipment.
- Audited monthly telephone bills for accuracy, fraud, and trends; managed and resolved disputes.
- Designed detailed management reports on call-center activities.
- Performed configuration, scripting, testing, and implementation of Automatic Call Distribution (ACD) and Automated Attendant.
- Developed and maintained positive working relationships with vendors and suppliers.
- Provided formal classroom telephone and etiquette training for new hires.

Achievements:
- Performed all moves, additions, and changes that saved the company considerable expenses.
- Recommended and implemented PBX features that substantially lowered costs.
- Negotiated new long-distance contract resulting in a 40% savings.
- Researched and recommended a telecom upgrade that saved approximately $15,000 per year.
- Implemented an ACD application to the voice-response system, which increased productivity by 100% and reduced customer failures by 89%.

Strategy: *Created a profile and keyword summary that provide a strong introduction to relevant work experience that ended only a few years ago.*

Mary Scott—mscott@verizon.net   Resume—Page 2

PROFESSIONAL EXPERIENCE (continued)

BUSINESS COMMUNICATIONS SYSTEMS, Orange, CA   1993–1995
Customer Service Representative
Coordinated customer requests for equipment modifications and moves, additions, and changes, including price quotations.

- Provided customer and technical support.
- Coordinated telecom orders and vendor meetings for customers.
- Provided formal end-user training and post-cut-over support.

FUJICON, INC., Brea, CA   1987–1993
Database Project Coordinator
Managed, collected, and designed customer databases for sites ranging from 40 to 7,000 lines, including voice mail, least-cost routing, system commands, special applications, and user features.

- Developed special databases and reports for cable records and call accounting systems.
- Led technical training programs and coordinated post-cut-over support for end-users.
- Created database collection forms and customer contact book that streamlined the database collection process.

TECHNICAL SKILLS

Fujitsu F9600 PBX	Baypoint (Centigram): VoiceMemo II
Fujitsu Intelli-Center	Captaris (AVT) Call Express
Ericsson MD110 PBX	Syntellect Vista 3.5 (IVR)
MDR Call Accounting System	eCAS Call Accounting System

SOFTWARE

Proficient with Windows XP, Microsoft Office Suite, and Visio.

EDUCATION

Certification in Data Communications Engineering (in progress)
University of Fullerton, Fullerton, CA

Bachelor of Science Degree
University of California, Fresno, CA

Margo Weiss

25 Gina Drive, Centerport, NY 11721 • margoweiss@hotmail.com
residence 631-754-6876 • cellular 631-827-7809

Investigative Research

Desired job emphasis to include the following:

Background Checks / Fraud Investigations / Insurance Claims / Evidence Collection
Fact-Finding / Investigative Report Writing / Court Decision & Legal Research

QUALIFICATIONS

Certificate in Legal Investigation. Year-long program, 280 hours, encompassing numerous mock investigative projects involving medical insurance fraud, immigration status discovery, missing person search (skip tracing), personal injury/traffic accident investigations, and financial forensics.

Excellent research and writing skills honed through prior work as a journalist.

Strong computer skills including Westlaw, Lexis, Shepard's Citations, Excel, Word, PageMaker, and Internet research.

PROFESSIONAL EXPERIENCE

Corporate Communications Coordinator (1997–1998) SEGAT INTERNATIONAL, Woodbury, NY

- Handled public relations and technical-writing projects for this international manufacturer and distributor of audio equipment.
- Conducted industry research, compiled competitive market intelligence, and wrote articles for trade publications.
- Contacted and established relationships with editors; decision-making authority for article selection and placement.
- Authored sales brochures and marketing materials; contributed to internal communications newsletter.
- Reviewed and ensured the correctness of technical information for equipment manuals.

Public Relations Manager (1995–1997) BUNGIE STUDIOS, Glen Cove, NY

- Developed and executed public relations campaigns to promote company's interactive video games.
- Wrote and disseminated press releases. Credited with securing print publicity in the *Wall Street Journal*, the *New York Times*, and *Newsday*.
- Overhauled the company's internal monthly newsletter and directed its content and production.
- Pursued, cultivated, and maintained beneficial relationships with editorial staff at trade magazines.
- Supervised two employees—public relations assistant and public relations coordinator.

Staff Journalist (1980–1995) BUCKINGHAMSHIRE FREE PRESS, High Wycombe, England

- Generated story ideas, researched content, conducted interviews, and produced weekly articles for this news periodical.
- Delved into court records, legal documents, and public information to investigate/corroborate facts.
- Compiled crime statistics for the "crime report" section.
- Edited the writing of other journalists; coordinated workflow between 15 writers and 2 editors.

EDUCATION

Certificate in Legal Investigation, 2005. BRIARCLIFFE COLLEGE, Bethpage, NY
Master of Arts, Public Relations, 1995. NEW YORK UNIVERSITY, New York, NY
Bachelor of Journalism, 1980. UNIVERSITY OF MANCHESTER, Manchester, England

Strategy: *Used an introductory Qualifications section to showcase recently acquired certification, and then showed the transferable skills and relevant accomplishments from prior professional experience. Dates are included but are visually downplayed.*

KATHY HUDNALL

2500 Lake Sammamish Blvd.
Seattle, Washington 98911
(425) 655.1440
hud@msn.com

PRE-SALES AND PROJECT MANAGER

Consensus Building and Executive Collaboration ~ Strategic Planning ~ Team Selling
Fortune 100 Medical and Defense Environments ~ Proposal Development and Presentation
Client Training ~ Leadership ~ System / Operations Analysis

SYNOPSIS

Ten years of Project and Team Leadership with accolades for selling skills, managing complex decision-making processes, and advising Fortune 100 executives. Specific skill sets for sales include

Account Identification	Needs / Requirements Analysis	Presentations
Demonstrations	Negotiations	Closings
Time / Material Management	Relationship Management	Documentation

PROFESSIONAL HIGHLIGHTS

Parker Medical—Seattle, Washington   1990 to 1995
Project Manager (1992 to 1995)

Selected to co-manage the $30 million, 3-year conversion and consolidation of all nationwide sales reporting systems into a cohesive Oracle-based platform. Orchestrated enterprise-wide implementation effort with corporate headquarters and directed diverse efforts of cross-functional teams installing custom-developed software on multiple technical platforms.

o   Guided ongoing conversation among sales, IT, finance, and other senior managers with regard to project status, financial considerations, and timetables. Determined hardware provisioning levels including memory, bandwidth, and storage.
o   Led efforts of software engineers in resolving database reporting structures for sales and finance; acted as subject matter expert for senior corporate executives and managers.
o   Received three Silver Awards for outstanding effort during analysis and project rollout/completion.

Senior Database Administrator—New Technology Analyst (1990 to 1992)
Recruited to evaluate emerging technologies and prepare company for eventual conversion from Computer Associates Datacom database to Oracle. Considered integration interconnectivity capabilities across multiple technologies and platforms.

o   Acted as Project Lead in the design, installation, and testing of new systems.

The Computer Consortium—Washington, D.C. / Dallas, Texas   1987 to 1990
Pre- and Post-Sales Engineer

Guided sales process for company's graphics products as one of two quota-based, pre-sales engineers in the Commercial Graphics segment. Called on CIOs, CTOs, and Project Managers to specify software in bundled financial packages or as freestanding sales.

o   Outpaced quotas two years in a row as a Commercial Pre-sales Engineer, guiding decision-making process for major financial institutions and Fortune 100 accounts. Received Sales Award for meeting regional quota.

Strategy: *Played up sales aspects of past jobs along with key sales skills of collaboration and consensus-building. Led off with a strong profile that is an ideal "positioning statement."*

Kathy Hudnall—hud@msn.com—(425) 655.1440   page two of two

o   Consulted with senior officials in development of bid specifications for RFPs from both commercial and federal accounts. Advised multiple departmental managers in development of requirements and built consensus for both functionality and costs. Managed a two- to six-month sales cycle.
o   Provided on-site, client-side staff training, a well as product demonstrations in a variety of environments, including Parker Medical (above) and Redstone Arsenal.

TRINITY SYSTEMS—Dallas, Texas   1985 to 1987
Software Engineer / Team Lead

Part of development team that designed and implemented Executive Information System (EIS) for Headquarters Air Force Systems Command, used to track contractor progress on development of the Air Force's major weapon systems. Top Secret Clearance—not active.

o   Appointed Acting Manager responsible for daily activities of seven other software engineers.
o   Conducted strategic meetings with high-level Air Force and TRW management teams to clarify system requirements, baselines, and deadlines.
o   Participated in all phases of development: requirements definition, detailed design, design reviews, database design, coding, testing, and documentation.

EDUCATION

Bachelor of Science—Computer Science
Washington State University, Pullman, Washington
Significant coursework in both Physics and Chemistry

LINDA KRAMER

719 BEACH DUNE LANE
SPRING PALMS, CA 94111   LINDAKRAM92@AOL.COM

HOME: (650) 925-8547
CELL: (650) 925-8966

SUMMARY OF QUALIFICATIONS

Sales Professional with proven skills in recruiting and business-to-business sales. Possess strong communication, presentation, and negotiation skills applicable to all aspects of the sales process. Creative problem-solver with strong organizational and multitasking skills. Self-directed and highly driven; capable of managing projects/accounts with minimal supervision. Exceptional cold-calling and account-management skills. Proven business-development skills, including networking, negotiations, and multi-level communications. Expert in initiating, building, and supporting client relationships.

PROFESSIONAL EXPERTISE

BUSINESS-TO-BUSINESS SALES

- ◇ Top-notch sales performer noted for consistently achieving above quota.
- ◇ Extensive experience in coordinating and/or exhibiting in trade shows/vendor shows.
- ◇ Consistently fully engaged in account development, resulting in accelerated revenue growth.

RECRUITING SALES

- ◇ Expert ability to develop and manage business relationships with Fortune 500 accounts and drive accelerated revenue growth.
- ◇ Demonstrated ability to serve as liaison between employer and candidates through an extroverted, consultative approach during job fairs, college days, and client meetings.
- ◇ Originated sales incentives and special promotions in support of sales initiatives.

CAREER EXPERIENCE

BioBay Technologies   Sasparilla Bay, CA
Account Manager   2000–2002
Biotech media company specializing in supplying laboratory media for use in biotech companies. Captured sales and profitably managed accounts due to vigilant attention to detail and superior customer service. Utilized relationship-building skills to secure additional accounts. Strategized, managed, and up-sold while ensuring technological needs were met and core business was enhanced. Coordinated 4 vendor shows and participated in 15–25 trade shows per year. Completed sales analyses, proposals, and progress documentation. Developed system of follow-ups, stock checks, and communication to determine product orderliness/availability and ensure continued customer satisfaction.

- ◇ Held sole accountability for 25% of company sales.
- ◇ Built initial account base of 4 companies to 10 accounts due to exceptional customer-service and business-development skills.
- ◇ Initiated sales training sessions, resulting in improved individual sales abilities.
- ◇ Promoted from Account Representative to Account Manager within 6 months of hire due to proven customer-service and relationship-building skills. Earned additional promotion to larger territory within 9 months of hire.

Strategy: *Created a traditional chronological resume, preceded by effective summary sections; the gap in employment is explained in this job seeker's cover letter.*

Worldwide Staffing   Culver City, CA
Account Manager   1999–2000
Temporary staffing company with more than 2,000 employees. Provided marketing and executive administrative staff for Fortune 500 companies. Accountable for operations of 3 offices in San Francisco, San Mateo, and Culver City. Performed sales and public relations responsibilities, including participating in job fairs, college days, customer visits, and lunches in order to develop company contacts and capture staffing contracts. Developed exceptional customer-relationship skills, including ability to interact effectively with line managers up to C-level executives. Collaborated with on-site staffing to determine staffing needs. Prospected, established, and sustained accounts in new markets through excellent customer service and follow-up.

◇ Gained promotion from Staffing Specialist to Account Manager within 3 months. Top producer.

◇ Selected as manager for 3 locations, a unique responsibility in company.

◇ Utilized relationship-building skills to increase sales, resulting in more than 80 placements in one year with a consistent record of 10 placements per week.

◇ Attained 4 direct-hire placements, an unusual accomplishment in a temporary-staffing environment.

◇ Displayed excellent business-development skills; closed 11 new corporate accounts.

◇ Developed and initiated performance contest among 5 locations under single manager, resulting in improvement in teamwork and increased sales performance.

Mega Rent-A-Car   Culver City, CA
Management Trainee   1999
Gained business-operations skills, including managing staff, customer service, and car rental agreements/service. Accountable for new business and revenue acquisition through business/relationship development. Designed creative and innovative proposals that presented custom strategies for specific communication needs. Coordinated corporate events with key prospects and customers.

◇ Recognized as Top Sales Producer by Regional Vice President. Attained 40+ sales of corporate accounts in one quarter.

◇ Gained large corporate/on-site account with major hotel corporation.

◇ Selected to coordinate local fund-raiser for United Way. Personally raised $2,000 in 1 week in addition to organizing a silent auction to raise additional funds.

PROFESSIONAL EDUCATION

College of Notre Dame   Belmont, CA
Bachelor of Arts Degree, Sociology & Behavioral Science, Graduated with honors with 3.87 GPA
Human Resources Certificate

◇ Originated, coordinated, and established College of Notre Dame's chapter of Delta Epsilon Sigma, an honor society for sociology students.

◇ Co-organized, conducted fund-raising, and launched nonprofit organization for troubled adolescents.

◇ Completed 1-year internship at Belmont Volunteer Center. Interviewed and coordinated placement of volunteers into community. Displayed excellent communication and multitasking skills.

◇ Volunteered for Center for Domestic Violence, including conducting awareness and educational programs. Currently serve as advocate for this organization.

College of San Mateo   San Mateo, CA
Associate Degree

California Academy of Art & Design   Sacramento, CA
Associate Degree, Merchandising, Marketing, & Advertising

ELISE KEARNS

6 Oleander Lane • Dix Hills, New York 11746 • (631) 423-5442 • eke@msn.com

PHARMACEUTICAL SALES REPRESENTATIVE

Representative of the Year Award
Top Honors for Sales Call Volume

PFIZER, Inc., New York, NY
Hospital/Institutional Representative
Senior Medical Sales Representative
Medical Sales Representative

Medical Terminology

Rapport with Physicians

Creative Selling

High-Impact Sales Calls

Hospital Formularies

Speaker Programs

Territory Planning

Sales Projections

Competitive Intelligence

With a 14-year track record, cultivated new business and broadened market penetration for company's key products. Delivered long-term sales effectiveness by **consistently meeting or exceeding set quotas on all products.** Managed Long Island and Manhattan territories with **excellent call plans** and cyclic itineraries.

Called on a variety of healthcare industry decision makers. **Chosen for 1-year special assignment** to launch company's premier product across the Long Island district. Delivered enormous results, **capturing 80% of business** in category, despite competitive marketplace.

Cultivated relationships with prominent professionals who became part of a speakers program, and in so doing, promoted the company's products to their peers.

Promoted to tackle key account challenges at some of the region's most prestigious hospitals (Lenox Hill, Memorial Sloan Kettering, New York Hospital, Beth Israel, and North Shore University). Established rapport with influential decision makers, out-distanced competitive field, and gained formulary acceptance.

THE WELCOME WAGON, Northport, NY
Co-Owner

Strengthened company's advertising programs, which involved the distribution of vouchers from local merchants to new area residents. Managed bookkeeping and purchasing. Created voucher coupons using graphic arts software.

Customer Service
Advertising Sales

WORKS IN CLAY, Syosset, NY
Instructor/Event Coordinator

Event Planning
Presentations
Budgeting

Explained class options to interested parents and booked children's parties. Over two years, frequently raised average party revenue by selling additional goods. Managed the business one day each week in owner's absence. Adhered to budgets while purchasing goods needed for pottery classes. Created curriculum and handouts. Provided group instruction.

Bachelor of Arts, English. University of Rochester, Rochester, NY

Strategy: *Designed a unique format to hide the fact that no dates are included on this resume. The creative format also allowed up-front placement of her most relevant experience, even though it is the oldest.*

MARCELLA MILLER
marcella@printedpages.com

188 Racetrack Way • Cincinnati, OH 45222 • Home: (513) 598-9100 • Mobile: (513) 598-9220

SALES • BUSINESS DEVELOPMENT • RELATIONSHIP BUILDING

Diversified background encompassing sales, professional staffing, public relations, promotions, key account management, and customer relationship management. Strengths: communications, presentations, project management, and ability to "think outside the box." Well organized and attentive to detail; efficient in managing multiple simultaneous projects. Persuasive, articulate communicator; group presentation experience. A natural leader with a management style that brings out the best in people. Consistently successful in achieving challenging objectives by focusing on the customer, watching the bottom line, and delivering as promised.

EXPERIENCE PROFILE

Sales & Business Development

➢ More than 10 years of successful experience in outside sales to businesses. Cold-called, prospected, and developed leads while expanding business with established accounts.

➢ Cultivated strategic relationships and maximized sales volume by identifying and seizing market opportunities and aggressively pursuing new business.

➢ Employed an entrepreneurial, customer-focused approach to build sales while ensuring customer retention by providing superior service.

Project Management & Event Planning

➢ Organized annual conventions to educate the public on how to start and operate block clubs in community neighborhoods. Secured locations, speakers, booths, and refreshments. Wrote educational materials and coordinated printing of literature. Managed publicity, convention operations, and post-convention follow-up.

➢ Played a key role in renovating and updating St. John School's library. Researched other libraries to generate ideas. Coordinated renovation plans, participated in fund-raising activities, and helped organize and execute the move.

➢ Volunteered in local and state-level political campaigns for candidates and issues. Helped organize and publicize fund-raisers, delivered literature door-to-door and at community events, made calls to arrange sign locations, wrote letters, and obtained signatures. Assisted with developing television, radio, and print ads. Worked the polls and answered voters' questions.

➢ Collaborated in organizing special events for St. John School, including the Haunted House (largest annual fund-raiser), Spring Fashion Show, Market Day, and Everybody Counts (educates students about disabilities). **Delivered record revenues and profits** through a combination of effective leadership, careful control of expenses, and successful advertising/publicity (obtained radio, TV, and newspaper coverage—all at no cost).

Communications

➢ Chaired Future Funding Committee, charged with soliciting major gifts ($10,000+) for St. John Church. Made presentations to individuals and corporate officers. Surpassed revenue goals by 23%.

➢ Maintained order in high-school classrooms as a substitute teacher.

➢ Developed and taught creative-writing workshops.

➢ Published author of articles on topics ranging from travel and entertainment to issues and events of local interest. Writing samples furnished upon request.

Strategy: *Used a functional format to focus on volunteer and business achievements that relate to her goal of a career in sales.*

MARCELLA MILLER

PAGE 2

**Leadership &
Community Service**

➢ Served as Block Chairperson for a coalition of 53 households and local business owners in East Clifton Hills. Co-founded the group for the purpose of improving quality of life for residents by addressing issues such as safety, crime, and neighborhood beautification. Developed programs, facilitated monthly meetings, and secured guest speakers such as city and state officials, police, and firefighters.

➢ Organized St. John's participation in a drive to collect food, clothing, and money for victims of Hurricane Katrina. Recruited 100 parishioners to assist in sorting and packing donations for shipment to needy families in New Orleans. Filled and shipped 3 full truckloads.

➢ Cooked dinner and hosted meals and activities for St. John's Interfaith Hospitality Committee, a ministry for the homeless.

➢ Worked in many capacities for St. John Parish—PTA officer, religious education teacher, open house tour guide, field trip chaperone, Cub Scout leader, reading tutor, Eucharistic minister, lector, Festival Committee member, etc.

➢ Scheduled and coordinated the activities of hundreds of volunteers for all types of school events.

WORK HISTORY

Parent/Volunteer/Homemaker		Cincinnati, Ohio	1994–Present
Substitute Teacher	Clifton Hills Local Schools	Cincinnati, Ohio	1997–1999
Account Executive	Daysen Staffing Services	Cincinnati, Ohio	1983–1994
Sales Representative	Advanced Business Solutions	Cincinnati, Ohio	1979–1983

Selected Business Achievements

Daysen Staffing Services—Managed a tri-state territory encompassing 30 ZIP codes. Analyzed customers' usage to establish programs, develop pricing, and prepare bids. Worked with customers to find solutions within their allotted budgets; negotiated pricing and terms to ensure profit margins were achieved and maintained.

➢ #1 sales producer in Cincinnati office, 1990–1994. Earned President's Club honors for exceeding sales quotas by at least 25% for 6 consecutive years.

➢ Trained more than a dozen new Account Executives. Wrote sales training manual.

➢ Ranked among top 10 Account Executives for sales production out of 700+ Daysen offices nationwide, 1989–1994.

➢ Landed and managed key accounts with companies such as Procter & Gamble.

Advanced Business Solutions—Successfully earned a living in a straight-commission sales position. Researched prospective customers, analyzed business needs, and recommended appropriate products and services. Made 50–100 cold calls each week.

➢ Successfully won new business by selling on value, despite intense pressure from discount-priced competitors, in a highly price-sensitive market.

EDUCATION

UNIVERSITY OF CINCINNATI, Cincinnati, Ohio
Bachelor of Arts, Communication. Minor in German.   1979
➢ Worked two jobs (30 hours/week) to pay 100% of living expenses while attending school full-time.

RESUME 96: BY GEORGE DUTCH, CMF, CCM, JCTC

TINA TRENTON

4250 SECOND LINE RD
DUNCASTLE, ONTARIO
PHONE: (613) 675-1234 ◆ E-MAIL: tina.trenton@maxwell.ca

PUBLIC RELATIONS ◆ COMMUNICATIONS MARKETING
Skilled at developing new markets and new business in hi-tech space.

Dynamic, results-oriented team player with history of implementing strong communication and marketing strategies that increase corporate brand visibility. Creative thinker with direct hands-on experience to quickly conceive, develop, and execute plans to optimize revenue and exposure. Experience with start-ups, early-stage ventures, high-growth organizations, mature companies, and a Fortune 500 company.

Professional Proficiencies:

✓ Strategic marketing leader able to plan, prioritize, motivate, and steer aggressive marketing and PR plans while retaining focus on big-picture goals.

✓ Strong performance in developing targeted business communications, managing budgets, coordinating goal setting, and directing daily operations to achieve goals.

✓ Write and edit annual reports, case studies, media kits, news releases, and promotional material.

✓ Successfully pitch editorial ideas to editors of leading industry publications and national business media.

✓ Direct website development and content management, coordinate tracking, and evaluate visitor activity/behavior.

✓ Manage all aspects of trade shows, including booth design, public and media relations activities, logistics, and more to generate new leads.

✓ Develop and maintain excellent relationships with key industry and financial analysts.

✓ Negotiate all advertising pricing and placement.

Strong Competencies in:

Special Event Management	New Business Development	Public & Community Relations
Work, Budget, & Resource Planning	Marketing Campaign Design	Staff Training & Mentoring
Corporate & Brand Marketing	Media Training	Media Buying
Marketing Communications	Public Speaking	Advertising Agency Relations

Highlights of Accomplishments:

◆ Renegotiated series of advertising contracts in major trade publication. *Result: Saved $500K in advertising budget while securing editorial support, access to subscription list, guaranteed placement for ads, website link, and placement on its technology board.*

◆ Launched new Y2K product to SMEs in North America and around the world. *Result: Generated more than $1M in sales in first year.*

◆ Over a one-month period, organized the largest corporate event in Goodyear history—the groundbreaking ceremony of its flagship production facility in Balderston, ON. *Result: Attracted 25,000 people to event in a city with population of 5,000.*

◆ Initiated a direct-marketing campaign to invite public-safety organizations to an "open-house" event introducing a new 911 product. *Result: 25 organizations attended, 5 requested needs analysis, 2 shortlisted company for RFPs, and company won contract worth $2M.*

◆ Created and implemented first direct-mail campaign for Humane Society of Ottawa. *Result: Generated more than $500K in new donations in first 6 months.*

◆ Managed "Challenge Capital Campaign" as Director of Major Gifts at King's University. *Result: Delivered 200% of quota ($10M).*

Strategy: *Created a high-impact marketing document, zeroing in on key accomplishments on page 1 while avoiding employment history until page 2.*

TINA TRENTON — tina.trenton@maxwell.ca   PAGE 2

CAREER HIGHLIGHTS

➤ **Horse Farm Manager,** Dunrobin, ON   2001–Present

• Manage 3 staff who train and care for 30+ horses, a busy riding school, client relations, grand prix sponsorships, horse sales, and vet/blacksmith relationships. *Achievements:* Increased riding school revenues by 22% through direct marketing campaign. Reduced feed and hay charges through effective supplier negotiations.

➤ **Director of Marketing,** *MOY Networks,* Ottawa   2000–2001
  (Data storage solutions with 50 employees and offices in Canada, U.S., UAE, and Europe)

• Managed and led a full marketing team for the company. *Achievement: Successfully planned and implemented the launch and media coverage of the company's new storage software less than one month after starting with the firm.*

➤ **Director of Corporate Marketing,** *ZBN Corporation,* Ottawa   1998–2000
  (Software producer with 200 employees and offices in Canada and U.S.)

• Led marketing and public relations initiatives for the corporation's six operating divisions. *Achievement: Designed and implemented an aggressive direct-marketing campaign that increased qualified sales leads by 75%. Tracked sales cycle time and supported the efforts of the sales staff in each division.*

➤ **Chief Operating Officer,** *TopSpin Corporation,* Ottawa   1996–1998
  (Y2K Product for SMEs with 20 employees and offices in Canada and U.S.)

• Led the company during its crucial start-up phase. This included full business and marketing plan development and strategy, product development and manufacturing, all public relations efforts, policies and procedures, and terms and conditions for the sale and distribution of the education product for small business. Responsible for day-to-day operations. Negotiated all $25K+ contracts with the Federal and Provincial governments and worked closely with them to ensure that the Y2K product met their organizational needs.

EARLY EMPLOYMENT PROGRESSION   1985–1990

Advanced through a series of positions as a communications generalist gaining valuable broad knowledge of communications, marketing, and public relations.

• Journalist, *Parisburg Leader,* 1978–80 • Freelance Journalist, *Lawrence Valley Weekly Newspapers* 1980–82 • Family Leave, 1982–88 • PR Consultant, *Best Tire & Rubber Co.* 1988–90 • Director of Major Gifts, *King's University,* 1990–92 • Development Manager, *Boys & Girls Club,* 1992–94 • Development Manager, *Humane Society of Ottawa,* 1994–96

Post-Secondary Education & Professional Development:

Broadcast Journalism, Loyalist College, Belleville, ON 1978
Variety of Marketing, PR, and Communications courses (Algonquin College), 1994–1999

RESUME 97: BY JANICE WORTHINGTON, CPRW, JCTC, CEIP

LaVerne Peterson

350-B Village Pointe Drive ♦ Columbus, OH 43229
Phone: 614/891-3255 ♦ E-mail: peterson4@yahoo.com

MARKETING / COMMUNICATIONS PROFESSIONAL

Communications ♦ Advertising ♦ Promotions/Events Management ♦ Publishing/Print Production

... Developing and Growing Market Share within Competitive Venues ...

Innovative, solution-oriented, entrepreneurial marketing professional with visible success developing new markets, growing market presence, reducing expenses, and driving revenues. Articulate communicator with proven ability to lead, motivate, and inspire teams to develop and introduce pioneering programs that increase productivity, boost infrastructure growth, increase project efficiencies, and surpass strategic objectives. Recognized for exemplary integrity, sense of passion, work ethic, and thorough commitment to professional excellence.

AREAS OF EXPERTISE

♦ Strategic Business Planning	♦ Program Development/Implementation	♦ Vendor Negotiations
♦ Relationship Building	♦ Contract Review/Recommendations	♦ Project Management
♦ Client Needs Analysis	♦ Client Relationship Management	♦ Contract Negotiations
♦ Tracking & Quality Control	♦ Troubleshooting & Problem Solving	♦ Budgeting/Forecasting
♦ Market Analysis & Research	♦ Advertising Development Oversight	♦ Direct-Mail Campaigns
♦ National Shelf Ad Campaigns	♦ Public Relations & Media Relations	♦ Market Penetration

CAREER HIGHLIGHTS

♦ **Authored/managed strategic marketing plan to redesign/produce/track 100+ brochures/applications within 8 months.** Praised by direct competitors for marketing materials that were "of the finest caliber ever seen in the marketplace" (NASFAA conference) and received unanimous standing ovation at National Sales Meeting from bank's internal sales/marketing team (80+ attendees). **Bank of Worthington, N.A.**

♦ **Strengthened company's corporate image and increased profitability** by spearheading joint promotional efforts between Product Management and Success Club. Instituted salon detailing (visitation) program and published 2 editions of "Out and About with Success Club" newsletter giving salon owners/staff the opportunity to provide spontaneous feedback/perceptions of the programs. **Mammoth Industries, Inc.**

♦ **Realized cost savings of $85,000+** by streamlining corrugated boxes, replacing chip grid inserts with polybags, and conducting an internal manhours cost/benefit analysis to compare current practices with direct shipping. Previous deliveries of Success Club Kits encountered lengthy delays due to logistical "red tape." **Mammoth Industries, Inc.**

♦ **Initiated ad placement in *Washington Post* Weekend Section that resulted in largest revenue-producing promotion since gallery opened its doors.** Built media, public, and commercial awareness of world's first touch-screen technology learning lab/gallery. **American Galleries**

♦ **Originated and maintained monitoring guidelines that tracked completion of all marketing activities for 40-person staff.** These fulfilled commitments, along with other vital information mandated by the Public Service Commission, were used as bases for consumer rate cases. **Scioto River Power Company**

♦ **Skyrocketed net profitability from minus $250,000 to plus $250,000** (within first year) by completely restructuring disorganized and unprofitable operation. To ensure program's continued success, crafted comprehensive marketing plan, including an organizational checklist, brochure, client lead file, and detailed advertising campaign. **Forsythe College**

♦ **Successfully orchestrated 100+ on-site conferences and meetings with as many as 200 international attendees.** Supervised up to 15 employees in the areas of logistics (reservations, housing, transportation, space planning), hospitality, support services, security, and contract negotiations. **Forsythe College**

Strategy: *Front-loaded impressive career achievements to create a favorable first impression before reaching employment dates that are now more than seven years old.*

LaVerne Peterson
peterson4@yahoo.com
-2-

CAREER CHRONICLE

BANK OF WORTHINGTON—Worthington OH
One of the nation's largest bank-based financial services firms, providing investment management, retail and commercial banking, consumer finance, and investment banking products and services to individuals and companies throughout the U.S. Employs 25,000 with $78 billion in assets.

Marketing Project Manager (1998–2000)

Accepted challenge to manage production of all national marketing materials (brochures, applications, flyers, invitations, inserts, enrollment supplies, print ads, trade booth illustrations) for undergraduate, graduate, and private K–12 education loans. Tasked to serve as liaison among Corporate Marketing, Agency, and line of business; to perpetuate rapport with sales force and vendor representatives; and to foster open communications, maximize efficiency, contain costs, and consistently provide fulfillment vendor with clear, concise direction to ensure timely execution of multiple projects.

♦ **Created process that ran like "a finely tuned piece of machinery"** by forging and fostering an outstanding relationship with division's fulfillment vendor. Presided over management of national collateral/application inventory of 200+ items.

♦ **Advanced promotion of Ohio's 529 college savings plan** by serving as lead contact for the Education Lending Division's co-sponsorship with the Ohio Tuition Trust Authority. Helped bank project positive corporate image and public sentiment: "We care about helping your children receive a college education."

♦ **Instrumental in saving bank's largest health professions school account and restoring exclusive lender status with Chicago Medical School** by expediting revision of the 1999–2000 medical loan application in 5 business days, and by delivering the 2000/2001 medical loan application two weeks early.

MAMMOTH INDUSTRIES, INC.—Columbus, OH
Nation's leading professional hair care and hair color company, providing salons with comprehensive range of hair care, skin care, and cosmetic products. Maintained 1,700-distributor sales force and employed 1,500. Division of Hair Care International

Marketing Program Manager—Salon Development (1993–1997)

Served as production manager of five dynamic, business building/promotional kits for 26,000+ salon owners. Managed both Synergy Salon Success Club and Co-Op Advertising program budgets totaling $7+ million. Areas of accountability included forecasting, budgeting, cost containment, invoice approvals, creative brainstorming, purchase order requests, competitive research, out-of-the-box initiatives, vendor relations, requests for proposal, traffic oversight, proofreading, foreign-language translations, internal warehouse coordination, external fulfillment execution, quality control, and ongoing reporting to appropriate departments/team members.

♦ **Championed team efforts that saved $2,192** by redesigning kit box using 25% less corrugated material and **$6,725** by replacing packet sample chip grid inserts with polybags.

♦ **Achieved 59% cost savings** by initiating internal/external bidding process for banding product samples and selecting out-of-house vendor.

♦ **Negotiated and administered contracts worth $1.5+ million** with graphic design firms, photographers, color houses, printers, display firms, fulfillment packers, and other allied vendors.

PRIOR EMPLOYMENT

Marketing Project Manager—Scioto River Power Company (1991–1993)
Manager of Marketing—American Galleries (1990–1991)
Director, Summer Housing and Conference Planning—Forsyth College (1987–1990)
Marketing Coordinator—Metropolitan Life Insurance Company (1981–1987)
Marketing Coordinator—Morgan Stanley (1981–1985)

EDUCATION

MIAMI UNIVERSITY—Oxford, OH
BA, Business Communications/Marketing (1981)

MICHAEL K. GRZYNSKY
727 Spruce Forest Lane
Rochester, New York 14626
585-889-3959
mikeg@resumesos.com

HUMAN RESOURCES DIRECTOR / HUMAN RESOURCES MANAGER / HR GENERALIST
Benefits Administration ♦ Employee Development ♦ Employee Satisfaction
Seasoned professional with extensive experience establishing personnel policy and procedures, developing and implementing benefits plans, and interviewing/hiring professionals and hourly staff. Exposure to union and non-union environments, plus experience administering provisions of New York State Civil Service Law.

RELEVANT HUMAN RESOURCES EXPERIENCE

Director of Human Resources (20-Plus Years)
St. Jerome's Hospital; Batavia, New York
Directed HR functions for rural hospital with 350 employees. Accountable for recruitment and hiring, wage/salary policies, pension and benefits administration, and employee training.
- Administered health insurance, pension, 403B, disability insurance, and Workers' Compensation programs.
- Developed selection standards for new hires; interviewed and hired professional staff.
- Established and regularly reviewed personnel policy and wage/salary guidelines.
- Designed and implemented employee orientation and ongoing training programs.
- Instituted uniform performance appraisal process.
- Represented corporation in hearings on unemployment, discrimination, and other labor-related issues.
- Developed recognition programs for employees and retirees.

Major Achievements
- Implemented Kronos automated time, payroll, and ID system. This system, using barcode badge readers, improved labor cost accounting, time keeping, and attendance tracking.

- Effectively managed rapid expansion of staffing needs from 30 to 200 employees. Led transition that ultimately brought total workforce to approximately 350 employees.

- Developed, coordinated, and implemented the employee pension plan. Researched investment firms, participated in selection process, and worked closely with Smith-Barney to implement plan.

- Established comprehensive personnel policies and prepared documentation on employment guidelines, procedures, and benefits. Developed employee policy and procedure handbooks.

Director of Human Resources / Personnel Officer (One-Year Assignment)
Orleans County; Albion, New York
Managed human resource programs under provisions of NYS Civil Service Law and in accordance with County Legislature directives. Administered HR functions for all county, municipal, and school district employees within the county that were covered under Civil Service Law.
- Prepared classifications and job descriptions for all positions, including ensuring ADA compliance.
- Maintained personnel records for all employees subject to Civil Service Law.
- Directed recruitment initiatives and evaluated candidates to determine eligibility for various positions.
- Maintained eligibility lists for all Civil Service job titles.
- Administered all employee benefit programs; certified payroll for all Civil Service positions.
- Addressed disciplinary and/or fair labor issues and ensured compliance with federal and state labor statutes. Responded to grievances under provisions of CSEA bargaining agreement.
- Prepared annual budget and reported regularly to county legislature on personnel matters.

Significant additional experience in human resource and administrative positions with Genesee County, St. Mary's Hospital, City of Batavia, and various federal government agencies.

Strategy: *Indicated number of years rather than specific dates for each position; emphasized solid experience as a human resources executive.*

Michael K. Grzynsky
Résumé - Page Two
585-889-3959
MikeG@resumesos.com

MILITARY SERVICE

Commander, United States Naval Reserve

Instructor, U.S. Naval Reserve Forces School
Trained military officers in Navy management philosophy, leadership, and strategic techniques. These training courses are a prerequisite for officers seeking promotion to senior command positions.

Executive Officer, Civil Affairs Unit
Assisted commanding officer with management and operations of unit charged with public relations and liaison functions in foreign countries where U.S. military operations were taking place. Ultimately responsible for 120 military reserve personnel, including training, evaluation, and human resource issues.

Shore Patrol, Subic Bay, Philippines
Active duty. Performed a variety of administrative and supervisory functions, as well as safety and investigative duties.

COMPUTER SKILLS

Microsoft Office XP; MS Project; PeopleSoft

EDUCATION

Bachelor of Arts, Psychology
University of Toledo; Toledo, Ohio

Diploma—Office Management & Supervision
Cornell University Center for Industrial & Labor Relations; Rochester, New York

United States Naval War College
Three-Year Advanced Educational Program for Career Officers
(Comparable to Master's program at a civilian university)

PROFESSIONAL AFFILIATIONS

Society of Human Resource Management
Past Member, American Society of Hospital Human Resource Directors

References Available upon Request

RESUME 99: BY MARILYN FELDSTEIN, JCTC, MBTI, PHR

PETER M. PREITMAN
4205 Sleepy Hollow Drive, Daytona Beach, FL 32127
(386) 257-1540
pmpreitman@comcast.net

SUMMARY

Detail-oriented management professional with extensive operations, inventory-control, and project management experience. Results-oriented problem solver known for ability to organize, plan, and successfully execute complex programs. Effective leader with demonstrated commitment to excellent customer service, teamwork, and employee development.

Strong track record of accomplishments in quality improvement and cost control.

PROFESSIONAL EXPERIENCE

Sterling Aircraft, Providence, RI
Supervisor of Manufacturing Services 1998–2004
Senior Manufacturing Engineering Assistant 1995–1998
Manufacturing Assistant 1991–1995
Lead Man / Tool Coordinator 1980–1991

Managed a team of 30 employees covering 7 sites; held full responsibility for staff interviewing and selection, scheduling, performance evaluation, mentoring, and development for advanced responsibility. Controlled inventory of fixtures, gauges, templates, molds, and blueprints for designing, developing, and assembling commercial, government, and foreign military aircraft.

- Trained team to use barcoding, batching, and radio frequency equipment to monitor and perform quality control of all inventory. Increased inventory accuracy to 98% for 150,000 tools valued at $255 million.

- Selected as Team Leader, representing all tooling organizations, to manage the project for new SAP system.

- Led several projects to evaluate and coordinate with other departments and external suppliers the overseas outsourcing and relocation of 10,000 tools from inventory. Recognized by senior management for outstanding efforts in team leadership and project results.

- Participated on several teams utilizing Kaizen, Lean Manufacturing, and Total Quality Improvement methodologies that improved performance and increased inventory turnover.

- Developed a standardized ergonomic tooling catalog for all departments by working with manufacturing representatives and ensuring all equipment was ergonomically safe for employees.

- Created a department-specific management training manual for supervisors.

- Received numerous outstanding performance awards and recognition for 4 years of zero OSHA incidents.

EDUCATION

B.A., Business Management, Providence College, Providence RI, 2000
- Cum Laude
- Sigma Beta Delta National Honor Society/International Business Honor Society

Strategy: *Focused on skills and accomplishments that are applicable to just about any industry; minimized dates to avoid overemphasizing recent employment gap.*

Gabe Connor

19 Waverton Circuit
Ultimo NSW 2007

Mobile: 0414 981 062
Home: (02) 9999 9999
E-mail: gabec@bigpond.net.au

CERTIFIED PRACTICING ACCOUNTANT / SENIOR FINANCIAL ANALYST

Project Management ◆ System Improvements ◆ Economic Evaluations ◆ Policy Development

Top-performing, solutions-driven financial expert with 20+ years of experience leading organisations through change, revitalisation, turnaround, and accelerated growth. Recognised for ability to think "outside the square" to improve operations, impact business growth, and maximise profits through achievements in finance management, internal controls, and productivity/efficiency improvements.

Proven team builder who delivers effective senior executive support and serves as a catalyst to create new business opportunities and establish strategic partnerships. Strong qualifications in general management, business planning, project management, and systems implementation, combined with superior presentation and training—Certificate IV Assessment & Workplace Training.

AREAS OF EXPERTISE

◆ Risk Assessment	◆ Negotiation	◆ Communication
◆ Economic Evaluations	◆ Analytical Thinking	◆ Team Leadership
◆ Business Plan Development	◆ Project Management	◆ Profit & Loss Management
◆ Sensitive Issues Management	◆ Policy Development	◆ Technology Implementation
◆ Strategy Development/Execution	◆ Budget Planning & Forecasting	◆ Strategic & Financial Planning
◆ Process Improvements	◆ Client Relationship Management	◆ Judgement/Problem Solving

PROFESSIONAL EXPERIENCE

POWER SAVER—*Sydney, NSW—(4 years)*

Manager, Financial Planning & Performance Reporting

Appointed for expertise in analysing information and evaluating results to choose the best solution and solve problems. Key responsibility was driving the annual budget process and monthly reporting to the Board of Executives. Advocate for delivering quality financial advice while ensuring a high level of strategy development was maintained among team members.

Considerable input into the strategic and planning requirements of the business, with position extending to managing special projects and developing accounting policies, procedures, and processes.

RESULTS / ACCOMPLISHMENTS:

➢ **Restructured systems for greater efficiencies** through the identification, upgrade, and implementation of improved business processes. Key projects included

→ Upgrade of existing SAP and TM1 installations within strict budgetary constraints. Developed business strategy for management approval and led teams in project execution, resulting in significant improvements in business reporting and analysis.

→ Identified and rectified interface discrepancies between the payroll system and SAP. Existing system was relatively complex, with 400 cost centres and more than 1,000 internal order types. By enhancing the interface between SAP and the separate payroll system, it was possible to attach all labour (including office-based staff) costs to internal orders and projects.

➢ **Improved accuracy, efficiency, and overall effectiveness** of month-end accounting journals through the implementation of electronic initiatives, coordinating the timely delivery of data from group members.

➢ **Delivered solutions** to budget cycle process, which had languished under previous leader, through the implementation of timely, transparent budget processes. Involved building an enhanced budget model in TM1, developing strong timetables, improving presentation, and ensuring the timely delivery of data.

GABE CONNOR CONFIDENTIAL 1

Strategy: *Designed a high-impact executive resume that includes extensive accomplishments; eliminated dates and simply listed the number of years in each position.*

PROFESSIONAL EXPERIENCE, CONTINUED...

NSW CABINET—*Sydney, NSW—(4 years)*
Senior Financial Analyst

Recruited for extensive financial knowledge and problem-solving abilities. Widely known across the department for an extraordinary ability to deliver solutions to legal and economic accounting issues.

In recognition of superior performance and operational vision, was selected to act as the Principal Financial Analyst on several occasions, while concurrently managing ongoing duties. Attended a number of Upper House Estimate Committees at the State Parliament as a reference expert on budget detail.

RESULTS / ACCOMPLISHMENTS:

➤ Worked collaboratively with Treasury to **drive system improvements** within the organisation through the implementation of SAP and accrual accounting. The system enabled NSW State Government budget reporting to meet the Australian Bureau of Statistics government outlays and standard accrual accounting requirements by aggregating all financial data from State Government agencies using a common chart of accounts.

➤ **Appointed as Agency Relationship Manager** for several large NSW Government agencies with $2 billion annual budgets in recognition of expertise in stakeholder liaison affairs and sensitive issues management. Enhanced planning and monitoring arrangements, while effectively managing a range of legal, accounting, and economic issues. Identified areas for reducing government expenditure.

➤ **Guided government and industry regulators** on infrastructure matters by providing definitive financial data and recommendations for use in strategic planning and decision making. Measured financial risk associated with making particular decisions on the Port Botany extension proposal, Port Kembla Coal Loader, amusement parks, football stadiums, major road development projects, regional entertainment centres, and conversion of surplus government sites into hotels prior to the 2000 Olympics.

➤ **Provided strong organisational leadership** by contributing to the development of numerous government proposals and projects. Identified areas that represented risk and provided solutions where necessary. Key proposals / projects included

  → Natural Disaster: Improved processes in dealing with major agencies and for natural disasters.
  → Rent Rebates for Pensioners: Reviewed proposal and had it adopted following extensive research on Commonwealth Department of Social Security files.

SYDNEY AREA HEALTH SERVICE (SAHS)—*Sydney, NSW—(2 years)*
Contract Accountant—Projects

Appointed to assist in driving the organisation's financial modelling, business development, and strategic planning processes. Delivered positive financial results while working on cross-finance and cross-company initiatives that impacted the bottom line.

RESULTS / ACCOMPLISHMENTS:

➤ **Delivered business solutions** through the development of a uniform chart of accounts to facilitate comparability of accounting data to assess performance of hospitals under Casemix funding arrangements. The report **provided accurate accounting and reporting solutions,** leading to its acceptance and implementation by the NSW Department of Health.

➤ **Identified increased exposure to risk to State Government finances** through economic evaluation of establishing a private hospital next to Royal North Shore Hospital.

➤ **Implemented infrastructure improvements** through the development of a centralised treasury accounting function at SAHS and the introduction of the ORACLE Financials suite of accounting software. Ensured new system operations were effectively supported and integrated into existing technology systems and applications.

➤ **Led proposal to privatise the Centre for Bone and Joint Disease** at Ryde Hospital. Complete responsibility for economic evaluation, ensuring compliance of parties with reversion agreement and with Department of Health Policies, defining relevant accounting entries for KPMG Peat Marwick, development of reversion agreement, and assisting Finance Chief in related policy matters.

GABE CONNOR   CONFIDENTIAL   2

PROFESSIONAL EXPERIENCE, CONTINUED...

OPTUS—*Sydney, NSW—(6 years+)*
Manager, Asset Accounting
Delivered measurable results through investigative problem solving, implementing corrective actions to turn around financial performance, and providing in-depth analytical, cost, and financial performance data as a baseline for business strategy and operation. Included development of policy, input into system development, and control of fixed assets worth $6 billion.

RESULTS / ACCOMPLISHMENTS:

➢ **Increased clarity and accountability nationally** through the implementation of unitised asset accounting and income taxation accounting for major customer division.

➢ **Led national project** bringing switching, data, and transmission spare parts into compliance with accounting and taxation requirements.

➢ **Improved budgeting process** through the implementation of system upgrades to provide better support and analysis; coordination of seminars with key budgeting personnel state-wide; and educating senior management on alternative solutions, conclusions. and approaches.

EDUCATION & QUALIFICATIONS

MACQUARIE UNIVERSITY	**Master of Economics (Accounting & Finance)**
UNIVERSITY OF NSW	**Bachelor of Commerce (Accounting & Financial Management)**

CPA, AUSTRALIA	**Certified Practising Accountant**
LICENSED TRAINER	**Certificate IV Assessment & Workplace Training**

TECHNOLOGY SKILLSET

Tools:	MS Suite: Word, Excel, PowerPoint, Project, Access, Outlook; Internet, E-mail
Other Tools:	SAP, TM1, Oracle Financials, Minitab, PL/1 (COBOL & Basic)
Platforms/OS:	PC, Windows 2000/XP

References Available upon Request

GABE CONNOR CONFIDENTIAL 3

RESUME 101: BY LOUISE KURSMARK, MRW, CPRW, JCTC, CEIP, CCM

JAY MEREDITH

8 Constitution Street, Charlestown, MA 02129
617-209-3490 • jaymeredith@yahoo.com

SENIOR EXECUTIVE: President • CEO
AUTOMOTIVE INDUSTRY   U.S. • Import & Export • Original & Aftermarket

Industry expert with a track record of success building and leading profitable enterprises in U.S. and global markets. Hands-on strategist able to identify and capture emerging market opportunities. Natural leader and team builder with strong operations experience and a history of cost control, profit enhancement, restructuring, and business turnaround.

- Twice built thriving organizations that grew to quick profitability and market acceptance.
- Transformed stagnant firm to dynamic growth enterprise successful in new markets.
- Created and launched 2 private-label programs, achieving rapid success and attractive profit margins.
- Established impeccable reputation and sound relationships with key players in the industry.

CAREER HISTORY AND ACHIEVEMENTS

AUTO-EXPORTERS, INC., Boston, MA
PRESIDENT

Overview **Built $8MM automotive exporter from the ground up.** Led company from vision through start-up to rapid profitability. Managed all facets of business strategy and operations. Negotiated agreements with numerous aftermarket and genuine parts suppliers, service providers, and banks. Traveled extensively to establish and cement relationships with international clients.

Financial & Operational Performance

- **Achieved $2.8MM first-year sales and 30% annual growth** over the next 3 years.
- **Identified niche opportunities** in multiple international markets with thriving economies and rapidly expanding base of U.S. vehicles.
- **Initiated sales in high-profit aftermarket products,** later adding genuine parts to meet demand and position company as a full-service supplier.
- **Launched OEM brown-box program,** using industry relationships to successfully source multiple products.
- **Secured financing,** including an EWCP loan through the SBA and a direct loan with a banking institution secured by the exim bank.

INTERNATIONAL MOTOR PARTS, INC., Medford, MA
PRESIDENT / OPERATIONS MANAGER

Overview **Transformed stalled $4MM company to thriving $44MM enterprise via strategic growth and subsidiary launch.** Provided executive and operational leadership for both companies; managed sales/marketing, warehouse/inventory, finance/accounting, and technology as business grew from 7 to 50+ employees; drove expansion into new markets; enhanced profitability through continuous improvement of business policies, processes, and operations.

Created and maintained reputation for impeccable service, on-time delivery, and integrity. Built and managed an extensive network of relationships across the industry, both domestically and abroad.

Strategy: *Completely eliminated dates to avoid calling attention to a 10-year gap in employment caused by health issues. Instead, focused on quantifiable achievements in multiple areas that paint this individual as an expert in his field.*

JAY MEREDITH   617-209-3490 • jaymeredith@yahoo.com

Strategic Growth / Market & Product Expansion

- **Conceived, launched, and led export subsidiary.** Identified emerging business opportunity and led new business from start-up to $28MM, representing 65% of total revenue of the combined companies.
- **Captured nearly 12% market share** in a volatile and competitive export niche. Reduced competition to marginal players.
- **Established 2 highly successful private-label programs** that grew to 20% of total business volume at 35% profit margins.
- **Targeted and captured new customer base** of large-volume importers (for export division) and jobber network (for domestic sales). Created "shotgun delivery" program that was key to jobber channel growth to 15% of U.S. revenue.
- **Achieved immediate 25% sales surge** by expanding sales to consolidators requiring same-day delivery; sustained and grew this channel 4% annually.
- **Reinvigorated product line,** continuously testing and adding new products to stimulate sales and meet changing needs.

Finance / Operations / Cost Control

- **Transformed antiquated business operations.** Restructured the company, modernized equipment, added technology, improved communications, and revamped accounting procedures. Reorganized internal departments to promote teamwork and eliminate redundancies.
- **Cut 8% from operating costs** by consolidating facilities and renegotiating union contracts and equipment purchases.
- **Ramped up management talent,** bringing on board key staff in areas of sales, operations, and technology.
- **Secured critical capital,** negotiating all financing (credit lines, letters of credit, and long-term equipment contracts) with banks. Achieved a strong financial position essential for growth in industry.

EDUCATION

BUSINESS ADMINISTRATION   Boston College, Chestnut Hill, MA

APPENDIX

Internet Career Resources

With the emergence of the Internet has come a huge collection of job search resources for diverse individuals, including baby boomers of all ages and at all career levels. Here are some of our favorite sites for finding job information and getting career advice.

Baby Boomer Web Sites

As we wrote this book, the first of the baby boomers turned age 60 and, as a result, there was a great deal of press about baby boomers, their careers, their lifestyles, their plans for retirement, and more. We urge you to do an Internet search on your own to identify recent articles that will be of interest and value to you in your career efforts. Be sure to visit the Web sites of major media outlets, leading retirement and financial-planning firms, and others. Simply type "baby boomer" into your search engine and you'll find literally thousands of listings.

Here are a few of our favorite baby-boomer Web sites as they relate to careers:

Aging Hipsters	www.aginghipsters.com
American Association of Baby Boomers	www.babyboomers.com
Baby Boomer Tips	www.sobabyboomer.com
Best Employers for 50+ Workers	www.aarp.org/research/press-center/ presscurrentnews/ 2005_aarp_best_employers.1.html
Boomer Net	www.boomernet.com
Global Generations Policy	www.genpolicy.com
Mature Market	www.thematuremarket.com
National Council on Aging	www.maturityworks.org

Prime Time	www.myprimetime.com
Third Age	www.thirdage.com

Dictionaries and Glossaries

Outstanding information on keywords and acronyms.

Acronym Finder	www.acronymfinder.com
Babelfish Foreign-Language Translation	http://babelfish.altavista.com/
ComputerUser High-Tech Dictionary	www.computeruser.com/resources/dictionary/
Dave's Truly Canadian Dictionary of Canadian Spelling	www.luther.ca/~dave7cnv/cdnspelling/cdnspelling.html
Duhaime's Legal Dictionary	www.duhaime.org
High-Tech Dictionary Chat Symbols	www.computeruser.com/resources/dictionary/chat.html
InvestorWords.com	www.investorwords.com
Law.com Legal Industry Glossary	www.law.com
Legal Dictionary	www.nolo.com/lawcenter/dictionary/wordindex.cfm
Merriam-Webster Collegiate Dictionary & Thesaurus	www.m-w.com/home.htm
National Restaurant Association Restaurant Industry Glossary	www.nraef.org/pdf_files/IndustryAcronymsDefinitions-edited-2-23.pdf
Refdesk	www.refdesk.com
Technology Terms Dictionary	www.computeruser.com/
TechWeb TechEncyclopedia	www.techweb.com/encyclopedia/
Verizon Glossary of Telecom Terms	http://www22.verizon.com/wholesale/glossary/0,2624,P_Q,00.html
Washington Post Business Glossary	www.washingtonpost.com/wp-srv/business/longterm/glossary/index.htm
Webopedia: Online Dictionary for Computer and Internet Terms	www.webopedia.com
Wordsmyth: The Educational Dictionary/Thesaurus	www.wordsmyth.net

Job Search Sites

You'll find thousands and thousands of current professional employment opportunities on these sites.

GENERAL SITES

6FigureJobs	www.6figurejobs.com
AllStar Jobs	www.allstarjobs.com
America's CareerInfoNet	www.acinet.org/acinet
BlackWorld Careers	www.blackworld.com/careers.htm
BlueCollar.com (Australia)	www.bluecollar.com.au
Canada WorkInfo Net	www.workinfonet.ca
CareerBuilder	www.careerbuilder.com
CareerJournal	www.careerjournal.com
Career.com	www.career.com
Career Exposure	www.careerexposure.com
Careermag.com	www.careermag.com
CareerShop	www.careershop.com
Contract Employment Weekly	www.ceweekly.com
EmploymentGuide.com	www.employmentguide.com
Excite	http://careers.excite.com
Futurestep	www.futurestep.com
GETAJOB!	www.getajob.com
Help Wanted	www.helpwanted.com
The Internet Job Locator	www.joblocator.com
JobBankUSA	www.jobbankusa.com
Job Circle	www.jobcircle.com
Job.com	www.job.com
Job-Hunt.org	www.job-hunt.org
JobHuntersBible.com	www.jobhuntersbible.com
KiwiCareers (New Zealand)	www.kiwicareers.govt.nz
Monster.com	www.monster.com
NationJob Network	www.nationjob.com
Net Temps	www.net-temps.com
NowHiring.com	www.nowhiring.com

Online-Jobs.Com	www.online-jobs.com
The Riley Guide	www.rileyguide.com
Saludos Hispanos	www.saludos.com
Spherion	www.spherion.com
The Ladders	www.theladders.com
TrueCareers	www.careercity.com
Vault	www.vault.com
Yahoo! HotJobs.com	http://hotjobs.yahoo.com
WorkTree	www.worktree.com

CAREER-SPECIFIC SITES

Accounting Careers

American Association of Finance and Accounting	www.aafa.com
Career Bank	www.careerbank.com
CFO.com	www.cfonet.com
CPAnet	www.CPAnet.com
SmartPros Accounting	ww.accountingnet.com

Arts and Media Careers

Airwaves MediaWeb	www.airwaves.com
Auditions.com	www.auditions.com
Fashion Career Center	www.fashioncareercenter.com
Playbill (Theatre Jobs)	www.playbill.com/jobs/find/
TVJobs.com	www.tvjobs.com

Education Careers

Chronicle of Higher Education Career Network	www.chronicle.com/jobs
Council for Advancement and Support of Education	www.case.org
Education Jobs.com	www.educationjobs.com
Education Week's Marketplace Jobs Online	www.agentk-12.org
Teaching Jobs	www.teaching-jobs.org/index.htm
University Job Bank	www.ujobbank.com

Food Service Careers

Chefs Job Network	www.chefsjobnetwork.com
Culinary Jobs	www.pastrywiz.com/talk/job.htm
Escoffier On Line	www.escoffier.com
Foodservice.com	www.foodservice.com

Government Careers

Federal Jobs Net	www.federaljobs.net
FedWorld	www.fedworld.gov
FRS Federal Jobs Central	www.fedjobs.com
GetaGovJob.com	www.getagovjob.com
GovExec.com	www.govexec.com
HRS Federal Job Search	www.hrsjobs.com
PLANETGOV	www.planetgov.com
USAJOBS	www.usajobs.opm.gov

Health Care/Medical/Pharmaceutical Careers

Great Valley Publishing	www.gvpub.com
HealthJobSite.com	www.healthjobsite.com
J. Allen & Associates (physician jobs)	www.NHRphysician.com
MedHunters.com	www.medhunters.com
Medzilla	www.medzilla.com
Monster Healthcare	http://healthcare.monster.com
Nursing Spectrum	www.nursingspectrum.com
Pharmaceutical Company Database	www.coreynahman.com/pharmaceutical_company_database.html
Physicians Employment	www.physemp.com
RehabJobsOnline	www.rehabjobs.com
Rx Career Center	www.rxcareercenter.com

Human Resources Careers

HR Connections	www.hrjobs.com
HR Hub	www.hrhub.com
Human Resources Development Canada	www.hrdc-drhc.gc.ca/common/home.shtml
Jobs4HR	www.jobs4hr.com
Society for Human Resource Management	www.shrm.org/jobs

International Careers

EscapeArtist.com	www.escapeartist.com
International Career Employment Center	www.internationaljobs.org
LatPro	www.latpro.com
OverseasJobs.com	www.overseasjobs.com

Legal Careers

Greedy Associates	www.greedyassociates.com
Legal Career Center	www.attorneyjobs.com

Sales and Marketing Careers

American Marketing Association	www.marketingpower.com
MarketingJobs.com	www.marketingjobs.com
NationJob	www.nationjob.com/marketing
SalesJobs.com	www.salesjobs.com
Sales Ladder	http://sales.theladders.com

Technology/Engineering Careers

American Institute of Architects	www.aia.org
American Society for Quality	www.asq.org
Brainbuzz.com IT Career Network	www.brainbuzz.com
CareerShop	www.careershop.com
Chancellor & Chancellor Resources for Careers	www.chancellor.com/fr_careers.html
ComputerWork.com	www.computerwork.com
Computerworld Careers Knowledge Center	www.computerworld.com/careertopics/careers?from=left
Dice	www.dice.com
IEEE-USA Job Service	www.ieeeusa.org
Jobserve	www.jobserve.com
National Society of Professional Engineers	www.nspe.org
National Technical Employment Services	www.ntes.com
Quality Resources Online	www.quality.org
Resulté Universal	www.psisearch.com

Sites for Miscellaneous Specific Fields

AG Careers/Farms.com	www.agcareers.com
American Public Works Association	www.apwa.net
AutoCareers.com	www.autocareers.com
CEOExpress	www.ceoexpress.com
Environmental Career Opportunities	www.ecojobs.com
Environmentalcareer.com	www.environmental-jobs.com
Find A Pilot	www.findapilot.com
Hire Vets First	www.hirevetsfirst.gov
International Seafarers Exchange	www.jobxchange.com
Logistics Jobs	www.jobsinlogistics.com
MBACareers.com	www.mbacareers.com
Social Work Jobs	www.socialservice.com

Company Information

Outstanding resources for researching specific companies.

555-1212.com	www.555-1212.com
Brint.com	www.brint.com
EDGAR Online	www.edgar-online.com
Experience	www.experiencenetwork.com
Fortune Magazine	www.fortune.com
Hoover's Business Profiles	www.hoovers.com
infoUSA (small business information)	www.infousa.com
Intellifact.com	www.igiweb.com/intellifact/
OneSource CorpTech	www.corptech.com
SuperPages.com	www.bigbook.com
U.S. Chamber of Commerce	www.uschamber.com/
Vault Company Research	www.vault.com/companies/ searchcompanies.jsp
Wetfeet.com Company Research	www.wetfeet.com/asp/ companyresource_home.asp

Interviewing Tips and Techniques

Expert guidance to sharpen and strengthen your interviewing skills.

About.com Interviewing	http://jobsearch.about.com/od/interviewsnetworking/
Bradley CVs Introduction to Job Interviews	www.bradleycvs.demon.co.uk/interview/index.htm
Dress for Success	www.dressforsuccess.org
Job-Interview.net	www.job-interview.net
Northeastern University Career Services	www.dac.neu.edu/coop.careerservices/interview.html
Wendy Enelow	www.wendyenelow.com/articles/?page_id=11

Salary and Compensation Information

Learn from the experts to strengthen your negotiating skills and increase your salary.

Abbott, Langer & Associates	www.abbott-langer.com
America's Career InfoNet	www.acinet.org/acinet/select_occupation.asp?stfips=&next=occ_rep
Bureau of Labor Statistics	www.bls.gov/bls/wages.htm
Clayton Wallis Co.	www.claytonwallis.com
Economic Research Institute	www.erieri.com
Janco Associates MIS Salary Survey	www.psrinc.com/salary.htm
JobStar	www.jobstar.org/tools/salary/index.htm
Monster.com Salary Info	salary.monster.com/
Salary and Crime Calculator	www.homefair.com/homefair/cmr/salcalc.html
Salary.com	www.salary.com
Salary Expert	www.salaryexpert.com
Salarysurvey.com	www.salarysurvey.com
Wageweb	www.wageweb.com
WorldatWork: The Professional Association for Compensation, Benefits, and Total Rewards	www.worldatwork.org

INDEX OF CONTRIBUTORS

The sample resumes in chapters 4 through 6 were written by professional resume and cover letter writers. If you need help with your resume and job search correspondence, you can use the following list to locate a career professional who can help.

You will notice that most of the writers have one or more credentials listed after their names. In fact, some have half a dozen or more! The careers industry offers extensive opportunities for ongoing training, and most career professionals take advantage of these opportunities to build their skills and keep their knowledge current. If you are curious about what any one of these credentials means, we suggest that you contact the resume writer directly. He or she will be glad to discuss certifications and other qualifications as well as information about services that can help you in your career transition.

Carol Altomare, CPRW
World Class Résumés
P.O. Box 483
Three Bridges, NJ 08887
Phone: (908) 237-1883
Fax: (908) 237-2069
E-mail: caa@worldclassresumes.com
www.worldclasresumes.com

Michelle Angello, CPRW
Corbel Communications
19866 E. Dickenson Place
Aurora, CO 80013
Phone: (303) 537-3592
Fax: (303) 537-3542
E-mail: corbelcomm1@aol.com
www.corbelonline.com

Marcia A. Baker, CFRW
MARK of Success, LLC
1282 Smallwood Dr. W., Ste. 123
Waldorf, MD 20603
Phone: (301) 885-2511
Fax: (301) 843-6138
E-mail: resumes@markofsuccess.net
http://markofsuccess.net

Bruce Baxter, CPRW
Baxter Communications
4176 Gemini Path
Liverpool, NY 13090
Phone: (315) 652-7703
Fax: (315) 652-7758
E-mail: baxtercom@juno.com

Laurie Berenson, CPRW
Sterling Career Concepts, LLC
P.O. Box 142
Park Ridge, NJ 07656-0142
Phone: (201) 573-8282
Fax: (201) 255-0137
E-mail:
laurie@sterlingcareerconcepts.com
www.sterlingcareerconcepts.com

Arnold G. Boldt, CPRW, JCTC
Arnold-Smith Associates
625 Panorama Trail, Bldg. 1, Ste. 120
Rochester, NY 14625
Phone: (585) 383-0350
Fax: (585) 387-0516
E-mail: arnie@resumesos.com
www.resumesos.com

Nita Busby, CPRW, CJTC, CTC, CAC
Resumes, Etc.
438 E. Katella, Ste. G
Orange, CA 92867
Phone: (714) 633-2783
Fax: (714) 633-2745
E-mail: nbusby@resumesetc.net
www.resumesetc.net

Eric Caesar, MBA, CC, CCC
ECG Coaching
330 Main St. 203-B
Seal Beach, CA 90740
Phone: (562) 795-5560
Fax: (562) 795-5501
E-mail: info@ecgcoaching.com
www.ecgcoaching.com

Clay Cerny
AAA Targeted Writing & Coaching Services
5415 N. Clark St.
Chicago, IL 60640
Phone: (773) 907-8660
E-mail: claycerny2@msn.com

Lisa Chapman, CPRW
Chapman Services Group, LLC
115 Beason Rd., Ste. 122
Niles, MI 49120
Toll-free: (866) 687-9700
Fax: (309) 401-3390
E-mail: lisa@chapmanservices.com
www.chapmanservices.com

Freddie Cheek, CCM, CARW, CPRW, CWDP
Cheek & Associates
406 Maynard Dr.
Amherst, NY 14226
Phone: (716) 835-6945
Fax: (716) 831-9320
E-mail: fscheek@adelphia.net
www.cheekandassociates.com

Tammy W. Chisholm, CPRW
MBA Resumes
9962 Brook Rd. #610
Glen Allen, VA 23059
Phone: (804) 878-9296
Fax: (320) 306-1752
E-mail: twchisholm@mba-resumes.com
www.mba-resumes.com

Kristin Coleman
Coleman Career Services
Poughkeepsie, NY 12603
Phone: (845) 452-8274
E-mail: Kristin@colemancareerservices.com

Beth Colley, CPRW, CFJST
Chesapeake Résumé Writing Service
P.O. Box 117
Crownsville, MD 21032
Phone: (410) 533-2457
E-mail: resume@chesres.com
www.chesres.com

Jean Cummings, MAT, CPRW, CEIP, CPBS
A Resume For Today
Concord, MA 01742
Toll-free: (800) 324-1699
Fax: (978) 964-0529
E-mail: jc@yesresumes.com
www.aresumefortoday.com

Norine T. Dagliano, CPRW
ekm Inspirations
14 N. Potomac St., Ste. 200A
Hagerstown, MD 21740
Phone: (301) 766-2032
Fax: (301) 745-5700
E-mail: norine@ekminspirations.com
www.ekminspirations.com

Michael S. Davis, CPRW, GCDF
940 Ashcreek Dr.
Centerville, OH 45458
Phone: (937) 438-5037
E-mail: msdavis49@hotmail.com

George Dutch, CMF, CCM, JCTC
George Dutch Career Consulting, Inc.
750-130 Slater St.
Ottawa, ON K1P 6E2
Canada
Phone: (613) 563-0584
Toll-free: (800) 798-2696
E-mail: george@GeorgeDutch.com
www.GeorgeDutch.com

Wendy Enelow, CCM, MRW, JCTC, CPRW
Enelow Enterprises, Inc.
Coleman Falls, VA
Phone: (434) 299-5600
Fax: (434) 299-7150
E-mail: wendy@wendyenelow.com
www.wendyenelow.com

Salome Farraro, CPRW
Careers TOO
3123 Moyer Rd.
Mt. Morris, NY 14510
Phone and fax: (585) 658-2480
E-mail: sfarraro@careers-too.com
www.careers-too.com

Dayna Feist, CPRW, CEIP, JCTC
Gatehouse Business Services
265 Charlotte St.
Asheville, NC 28801
Phone: (828) 254-7893
Fax: (828) 254-7894
E-mail: gatehous@aol.com
www.bestjobever.com

MJ Feld, CPRW, MS
Careers by Choice, Inc.
205 E. Main St., Ste. 2-4
Huntington, NY 11743
Phone: (631) 673-5432
Fax: (631) 673-5824
E-mail: mj@careersbychoice.com
www.careersbychoice.com

Marilyn Feldstein, JCTC, MBTI, PHR
Career Choices Unlimited
P.O. Box 23913
Jacksonville, FL 32241-3913
Phone: (904) 262-9470
E-mail: mfeldstein@careerchoicesunlimited.com
www.careerchoicesunlimited.com

Deborah K. Fernandez, LPC, NCC
dkfernandez career services
P.O. Box 1283
Cary, NC 27512-1283
Phone: (919) 656-0326
E-mail: info@dkfernandez.com
www.dkfernandez.com

Louise Garver, MCDP, CEIP, CMP, CPRW, JCTC
Career Directions, LLC
115 Elm St., Ste. 103
Enfield, CT 06082
Phone: (860) 623-9476
Fax: (860) 623-9473
E-mail: louisegarver@cox.net
www.careerdirectionsllc.com

Jill Grindle, CPRW
Resume Inkstincts
Agawam, MA 01001
Phone (413) 789-6046
Fax: (203) 413-4376
E-mail: j.grindle@resumeinkstincts.com
www.rersumeinkstincts.com

Lee Anne Grundish
Grafix Services/Achieve Success!™
249 Evergreen Rd., Ste. 5
Toledo/Ottawa Hills, OH 43606
Phone and fax: (419) 534-2709
E-mail: GrafixServices@aol.com
www.GrafixServices.com

Susan Guarneri, NCC, NCCC, CPRW, CERW, CPBS, CCMC, CEIP, IJCTC, DCC, MCC
Guarneri Associates
6670 Crystal Lake Rd.
Three Lakes, WI 54562
Phone: (715) 546-4449
Toll-free: (866) 881-4055
Fax: (715) 546-8039
E-mail: susan@resume-magic.com
www.resume-magic.com

Loretta Heck
All Word Services
924 E. Old Willow Rd. #102
Prospect Heights, IL 60070
Phone: (847) 215-7517
Fax: (847) 215-7520
E-mail: siegfried@ameritech.net

Gay Anne Himebaugh
Seaview Résumé Solutions
2855 E. Coast Hwy., Ste. 102
Corona del Mar, CA 92625
Phone: (949) 673-2400
Fax: (949) 673-2428
E-mail: resumes@seaviewsecretarial.com
www.seaviewsecretarialsolutions.com

Maurene J. Hinds, MFA, CPRW
Right-On Resumes
E-mail: rightonresumes@msn.com
www.maurenejhinds.com

Diana Holdsworth, CPRW
Action Communications Résumé Service
P.O. Box 234
Rowayton, CT 06853
Toll-free: (888) 831-0070
Fax: (203) 831-0541
E-mail: hold@optonline.com
www.action-resume-writer.com

Gayle Howard, CCM, CERW, CARW, CPRW, CMRS, CWPP
Top Margin Resumes Online
P.O. Box 74
Chirnside Park 3116
Melbourne, Australia
Phone: +613 9726 6694
Fax: +613 8640 0538
E-mail: getinterviews@topmargin.com
www.topmargin.com

Dr. Herman Kasselman
South African Department of Defence
Private Bag X137, Pretoria 10001
South Africa
Phone: +27 12 392 2499
Fax: +27 12 392 2498
E-mail: hermank@acenet.co.za

Myriam-Rose Kohn, CPRW, CEIP, IJCTC, CCM, CCMC, CPBS
President, JEDA Enterprises
27201 Tourney Rd., Ste. 201M
Valencia, CA 91355
Phone: (661) 253-0801
Fax: (661) 253-0744
E-mail: myriam-rose@jedaenterprises.com
URL: www.jedaenterprises.com

Louise Kursmark, MRW, CPRW, JCTC, CEIP, CCM
President, Best Impression Career Services, Inc.
Reading, MA
Toll-free: (888) 792-0030
Toll-free fax: (877) 791-7127
E-mail: LK@yourbestimpression.com
www.yourbestimpression.com

Brian Leeson, MSc
Vector Consultants Pty Ltd
P.O. Box 553
Echunga, South Australia 5153
Australia
Phone: +61 8 8388 8183
E-mail: vectorconsultants.com.au

Jan Melnik, MRW, CCM, CPRW
Absolute Advantage
P.O. Box 718
Durham, CT 06422
Phone: (860) 349-0256
Fax: (860) 349-1343
E-mail: CompSPJan@aol.com
www.janmelnik.com

William G. Murdock, CPRW
The Employment Coach
7770 Meadow Rd., #109
Dallas, TX 75230
Phone: (214) 750-4781
E-mail: bmurdock@swbell.net
www.resumesinaction.com

Kris Niklawski
A-Professional Résumé Service
3317 144th Ct.
Cumming, IA 50061
Phone: (515) 240-2950
Fax: (515) 981-9329
E-mail: krisnik@L2speed.net

Melanie Noonan, CPS
Peripheral Pro, LLC
560 Lackawanna Ave.
West Paterson, NJ 07424
Phone: (973) 785-3011
Fax: (973) 256-6285
E-mail: PeriPro1@aol.com

Don Orlando, MBA, CPRW, JCTC, CCM, CCMC
The McLean Group
640 S. McDonough St.
Montgomery, AL 36104
Phone: (334) 264-2020
Fax: (334) 264-9227
E-mail: yourcareercoach@charterinternet.com
www.phoenixcareergroup.com

Karen Palevsky, Certificate—Adult Career Planning and Development; MA, Vocational Counseling
Professional Resumes Plus
301 E. 22nd St. #9F
New York, NY 10010
Phone: (212) 387-8223
E-mail: Karen@proresumesplus.com

Richard Porter
CareerWise Communications, LLC
332 Magellan Ct.
Portage, MI 49002
Phone: (269) 321-0123
Fax: (269) 321-0191
E-mail: careerwise_resumes@yahoo.com

Michelle Mastruserio Reitz, CPRW
Printed Pages
3985 Race Rd., Ste. 6
Cincinnati, OH 45211
Phone: (513) 598-9100
Fax: (513) 598-9220
E-mail: michelle@printedpages.com
www.printedpages.com

Camille Carboneau Roberts
CC Computer Services
P.O. Box 50655
Idaho Falls, ID 83405
Phone: (208) 522-4455
E-mail: camille@superiorresumes.com
www.superiorresumes.com

Jane Roqueplot, CPBA, CWDP, CECC
JaneCo's Sensible Solutions
194 N. Oakland Ave.
Sharon, PA 16146
Toll-free: (888) 526-3267
Fax: (724) 346-5263
E-mail: resume@janecos.com
www.janecos.com

Jennifer Rushton, CRW
Keraijen—Cerified Resume Writer
Level 14, 309 Kent St.
Sydney, NSW 2000
Australia
Phone: +61 2 9994 8050
E-mail: info@keraijen.com.au
www.keraijen.com.au

Barbara Safani, MA, CPRW, NCRW, CERW, CCM
Career Solvers
470 Park Ave. S., 10th Floor
New York, NY 10016
Phone: (212) 579-7230
Toll-free: (866) 333-1800
Fax: (212) 580-2388
E-mail: info@careersolvers.com
www.careersolvers.com

Janice M. Shepherd, CPRW, JCTC, CEIP
Write On Career Keys
Top of Alabama Hill
Bellingham, WA 98226-4260
Phone: (360) 738-7958
Fax: (360) 738-1189
E-mail: janice@writeoncareerkeys.com
www.writeoncareerkeys.com

Bob Simmons
Career Transition Associates (CTA)
1670 Old Country Rd., Ste. 117
Plainview, NY 11803
Phone and fax: (516) 501-0717
E-mail: ctasimmons@aol.com
www.ctajobsearch.com

Billie Ruth Sucher, MS, CTMS, CTSB
Billie Sucher & Associates
7177 Hickman Rd., Ste. 10
Urbandale, IA 50322
Phone: (515) 276-0061
Fax: (515) 334-8076
E-mail: billie@billiesucher.com

Brenda Thompson, CCMC
TH and Associates
P.O. Box 1043
Bowie, MD 20718
Phone: (301) 266-1115
Fax: (301) 352-6135
E-mail: thworks@comcast.net
www.thworks.net

Vivian VanLier, CPRC, CPRW, JCTC, CEIP, CCMC
Advantage Career & Life Strategies
6701 Murietta Ave.
Los Angeles (Valley Glen), CA 91405
Phone: (818) 994-6655
Fax: (818) 994-6620
E-mail: vvanlier@aol.com
www.CareerCoach4U.com

Ilona Vanderwoude, CPRW, CEIP, CCMC, CJST
Career Branches
P.O. Box 330
Riverdale, NY 10471
Phone: (718) 884-2213
Fax: (646) 349-2218
E-mail: ilona@careerbranches.com
www.careerbranches.com

Pearl White, CPRW, JCTC, CEIP
A 1st Impression Resume & Career Coaching Services
41 Tangerine
Irvine, CA 92618
Phone: (949) 651-1068
Fax: (949) 651-9415
E-mail: pearlwhite1@cox.net
www.a1stimpression.com

Beth Woodworth, MS in Human Resource Counseling, CPC, CPCC
Senior Career Counselor
Job Training Center of Tehama County
718 Main St.
Red Bluff, CA 96080
Phone: (530) 529-7000
Fax: (530) 529-7015
E-mail: bwoodworth@ncen.org
www.job.trainingcenter.org

Janice Worthington, CPRW, JCTC, CEIP
Worthington Career Services
6636 Belleshire St.
Columbus, OH 43229
Phone: (614) 890-1645
Fax: (614) 523-3400
E-mail: janice@worthingtonresumes.com
www.worthingtonresumes.com

Daisy Wright, CDP
The Wright Career Solution
Brampton, ON L6Z 4V6
Canada
E-mail: daisy@thewrightcareer.com
www.therightcareer.com

INDEX